Justin McCarthy

A Short History of Our Own Times

From the accession of Queen Victoria to the general election of 1880. Vol. 2

Justin McCarthy

A Short History of Our Own Times

From the accession of Queen Victoria to the general election of 1880. Vol. 2

ISBN/EAN: 9783337323578

Printed in Europe, USA, Canada, Australia, Japan

Cover: Foto ©ninafisch / pixelio.de

More available books at **www.hansebooks.com**

A HISTORY

OF

OUR OWN TIMES

FROM THE DIAMOND JUBILEE 1897
TO THE ACCESSION OF EDWARD VII

BY

JUSTIN M^CCARTHY

IN TWO VOLUMES

VOL. II

LONDON
CHATTO & WINDUS
1905

CONTENTS

CHAPTER	PAGE
XIV. EDUCATIONAL AND PHILANTHROPIC MOVEMENTS	1
XV. NEW IRELAND	29
XVI. ANOTHER DEATH-ROLL	62
XVII. THE COMING SOUTH AFRICAN WAR	82
XVIII. THE WAR IN SOUTH AFRICA	110
XIX. THE GENERAL ELECTION OF 1900	142
XX. YET ANOTHER DEATH-ROLL	182
XXI. LAST YEARS OF THE REIGN	224
XXII. THE DEATH OF THE QUEEN	247
XXIII. A RETROSPECT—POLITICAL	280
XXIV. A RETROSPECT—THE ARTS OF PEACE	339
INDEX	377

A HISTORY

OF

OUR OWN TIMES.

CHAPTER XIV.

EDUCATIONAL AND PHILANTHROPIC MOVEMENTS.

THE early spring of 1899 showed some significant events in the progress of great educational and philanthropic movements. Not long after the opening of the Session a measure entitled 'The Education of Children Bill' was introduced by Mr. W. S. Robson, Q.C., which proposed to make a serious change in the relations between the employment and the education of children. The principal object of the measure was to provide that the earliest age at which a child might give up attendance at school in order to enter into employment should be advanced from eleven to twelve years, and should apply to all children, except such as, under peculiar and legally recognised conditions, were wholly or partly exempt from attendance at school. The principle involved in this proposed measure had already been a subject of much public discussion in England and in other European States. A Conference had been held at Berlin in 1890 on the general subject of factory labour, and there the principle of the Bill with regard to children employed in factories had been accepted by the British representatives with, it was generally understood, the express approval of Lord Salisbury. Since that time nothing had been done by any English Government, whether Conservative or Liberal, to put the principle into action by force of statute. In some other States where the principle of limiting the working time for children had been acted upon in the interests of education the results had been found to be entirely satisfactory.

Mr. Robson had a full opportunity, when moving the second reading of the Bill on the first of March, to go into the whole subject. He showed that England thus far occupied a position which compared unfavourably with that of some Continental States, and he strongly condemned the half-time system, as it was then termed, on the ground that it proved prejudicial not only to the interests of education, although that would have been in itself enough to condemn it, but also to the real interests of the manufacturing industries. A strong and very outspoken opposition came from some of the representatives of Lancashire manufacturing districts and from some Conservative representatives of agricultural regions. The most remarkable stand made for the Bill was that of Sir John Gorst, then Vice-

President of the Council, who acted in this instance with the characteristic independence he had shown many times before, and was to show again in later days. Sir John Gorst was well known to have made a close practical study of the whole question, and the House listened to him with deep interest, none the less deep because it was well understood that he was now speaking for himself and not for the Administration. He gave his full support to the principle of the measure so far as it applied to the employment of children in the factories of cities and towns, or in any manner of factory work wherever carried on. England, he contended, was already pledged to such legislation by the part which it had taken in the Berlin Conference. Sir John himself had been a representative of the English Government during the sittings of that Conference. He went into the question with great precision of detail and clearness of argument. He insisted that no real loss, even of a pecuniary kind, would come to the manufacturers in the end from the proposed arrangements which were to secure for the children of the poor a better education before being handed over to the making of money in order to help in the support of their families. He drew, however, a clear distinction between the employment of children in factories and factory districts and their employment in the fields and in agriculture, and pointed out that the employment of children in field work was not one of the subjects which came directly under the consideration of the Berlin Conference. He showed how to growing children a certain amount of light daily employment in the open fields might well be made conducive to the promotion alike of health and education. Sir John Gorst contended that the educational system which it was found necessary more and more to enlarge where children employed in factory towns were concerned might not be necessary or even suitable for children working in the country. He told the House that it was quite possible to reconcile the employment of children in the country with a steady progress in education, and that, according to his judgment, the children employed in the fields might well be obliged to attend school until a comparatively advanced age, and might be saved from any possible disadvantages coming from too much study by the closing of the schools in summer during the time when regular agricultural operations were going on.

Mr. Asquith, on the part of the Liberals, took a decisive view as to the advantages which might be secured by the passing of such a measure as that then under discussion. He declared that there could be no possible doubt as to the course which most members on the Liberal side of the House would take with regard to the question. Indeed he went so far as to assert his emphatic opinion that, even after the enforcement of the policy represented by the measure, the standard of education in England as compared with that of foreign countries would be ridiculously low, and he explained that he accepted Mr. Robson's Bill not as anything like a final measure but only as a welcome step on the way to reform. The second reading was carried by 317 votes to 59. The slight interest which the Government took in the measure was made manifest by the fact that only one of the members of the Administration having seats in the House of Commons voted for the second reading. That one Ministerial supporter of the measure was Mr. Ritchie, who had often shown an independent activity in the help which he rendered to measures of industrial and educational reform, coming from whatever party or section.

At any early subsequent period of the Session Sir John Gorst, having in his Ministerial capacity to deal with the general question of secondary education, referred to the large support given to Mr. Robson's Bill as an evidence that public opinion was making satisfactory progress with regard to the question of education for the poorer classes, and especially as to the necessity for extending the age of compulsory attendance at school. He expressed his conviction that the change proposed by that Bill was the first necessary reform, and that without it all other reforms would be found unavailing. Mr. Robson's Bill came before the House of Commons again on

May 31, a day which might seem singularly ill suited to secure a good attendance for a measure brought forward by a private member and receiving no general support from the statesmen in office. Under the new regulations the House met on Derby Day, and on that day Mr. Robson's Bill came on for discussion in Committee. Fortunately for the progress of the measure, it soon appeared that the opponents of the Bill included a much larger proportion of men for whom the Derby Day had an irresistible charm than of those who were disposed to favour the Bill, or were willing to give it an unprejudiced hearing. On the motion that the Bill go into Committee an amendment, known in the House of Commons as 'dilatory,' was moved, to the effect that the further progress of the measure, or, at least, its operation in law, should be postponed for five years so that the employers might be allowed a proper opportunity to prepare for the new conditions which the measure was destined to introduce. The proposal for delay was made the occasion of some superfluous debate, but when a division came to be taken it was supported by only ten votes in a House that contained the somewhat large attendance for the Derby Day of 173 members. The next proposal was that the age for children entering employments should begin at eleven and a half instead of twelve years, a proposition which was effectively disposed of by Sir John Gorst, who declared that the British Government had pledged themselves with other Governments, not only to the general principle represented by Mr. Robson's Bill, but also to the understanding that the minimum age for children to enter into employment in factories and workshops should be twelve years. Yet even this decisive expression of opinion coming from so high an authority did not succeed in carrying the new regulation without a long discussion and even a division, although only 18 members voted against it while 177 gave their votes in its support. Mr. Robson consented to one slight alteration in his measure, an alteration which had to deal with rural districts only, where the local authority had fixed thirteen years as the minimum age for exemption for children employed in agricultural work. Mr. Robson expressed his willingness to make such an alteration in the terms of his measure as to allow children over eleven years of age and under thirteen, who had passed the local standard exempting them, not to be compelled to attend more than 250 times in a year. Mr. Yoxall, an advanced Radical who was greatly interested in the School Teachers' Union, opposed this proviso on the ground that too much had been yielded already in the vain hope of conciliating the support of the factory interests, and thereupon other alterations were also proposed by opponents of the measure, to which Mr. Robson offered a steady resistance. Finally, the concession he offered to the agriculturists was carried by 245 votes against 26.

Again and again efforts were made to effect other alterations in the Bill, or at least to prevent it from getting any farther forward during the limited time which a private measure could have in the course of so busy a Session. The closure moved in the interest of the Bill was agreed to by 263 to 26 votes, and the clause as it now stood was finally carried. When the Bill was brought on for its third reading on the 14th of June, some new attempts were made to prevent it from completing its progress, but by this time the great majority of the House had become alive to the genuine importance of the measure and to the very moderate nature of the wholesome reforms which it introduced, and all further opposition of a pertinacious kind was allowed to end in mere grumblings. The Bill passed through the House of Commons, and early in the following month went successfully through its ordeal in the House of Lords. The measure was only a step in the progress of a great and beneficial movement, but it was a measure thoroughly characteristic of the spirit of modern improvement.

One of the proposed reforms in our social legislation, about which a great deal was heard during these later years of Queen Victoria's reign, was the scheme for a Government system by which industrious and provident persons in the poorer classes could be enabled to secure a certain amount of pension for their old age. The central idea of the scheme was that an arrangement should be made by which the working-classes might be enabled to deposit certain periodical sums under public security, with the result that when they had reached the period of life after which hard work can no longer be carried on they might reckon on having a small weekly pension which would be enough to keep them out of the workhouse. The principle of the proposed system was thoroughly economic in the best sense of the word. It would at once enable the working-man to make a secure, although small, provision for his old age, and would at the same time help to relieve the community from some of the cost entailed upon the public by the necessity of supporting the ever-increasing mass of pauperism. Mr. Chamberlain at one time identified himself with the scheme, and was indeed entitled to be regarded as its author, so far at least as our modern days are concerned. But though the project was brought forward again and again, and created much discussion both in Parliament and outside it, and seemed for a time as if destined to create an agitation and a party of its own, it began after a while to hang fire. Other subjects of debate and of agitation came up every now and then, and the plan for enabling the industrious poor to provide themselves by the help of the local authorities with some means of living for their old age was put aside. Nothing could have been in the true sense more pressing as a project of social reform on the attention of the whole public. But it had the disadvantage that it did not clamour for immediate settlement, and the leaders of parties and sections appeared to find that something else was always coming up which political interests would not allow them to overlook at the moment. The poor we shall always have with us, and it is the fate of the poor, as of all other classes, to grow old if only they live long enough.

Therefore the provision for that descent into the years when hard work is no longer possible did not present itself as a business which pressed for instant arrangement. The project appeared as if it were likely to take its place among other social reforms which are quietly left to be dealt with by philanthropists and social reformers, but which practical politicians, leaders of Parliamentary sections, and eminent personages who claim to be regarded as statesmen are not bound to encumber themselves with at any given moment. Even the most practical statesmen gave it their approval and encouragement, but apparently they approved and encouraged it as they approved of and encouraged the temperance movement, missionary work in heathen regions, the efforts to promote decent and moral ways of living among the slums and alleys of great cities, and the campaigns of the Salvation Army. Such is the only plausible explanation of the manner in which the statesmanship of the hour allowed this really great project for old-age pensions to pass for the time into the background of legislation. We may be sure, however, that the proposal for a national system of old-age pensions is destined before long to come to the front again and to be carried to its full accomplishment. When some Government made up whether of Liberals or Conservatives, or of a combination of the more moderate members of each political party, comes into power which shall recognise that the first duty of a British Administration is to look after the social improvement and the wellbeing of the people in these islands, we may be sure that the system of old-age pensions will be promptly and satisfactorily established. It may be anticipated that before long there will be a reaction against the sudden modern passion for extension of territory and for rivalry in armaments. When that time of reaction has set in there can be little doubt that Parliament and the country will recognise the immense national importance of that great project with which Mr. Chamberlain's name was so long associated, but which he did not find time or see his way to carry to success during the reign of Queen Victoria.

In the meanwhile it will interest our readers to know the high-water level to which the agitation for old-age pensions reached. A Committee had been appointed by Parliament to consider the whole subject, and of this Committee Mr. Henry Chaplin was chairman, and many men of mark, such as Mr. Lecky, Lord Edmund Fitzmorris, and Sir Walter Foster were members. The Committee were not by any means in unanimity as to their decisions, and some of their most important recommendations were only carried by a not very large majority. The Committee recommended that the receipt of a pension should be open alike to men and women, and that the applicant should be a British subject at least sixty-five years of age who had not within the previous twenty years been convicted of any offence and sentenced to penal servitude, or to imprisonment without the option of a fine, and had not received poor relief except medical relief, unless under special and exceptional conditions, during twenty years before the application for a pension. It was also recommended that each applicant should have lived for not less than twelve months within the district of the local authority granting the pension, should have an income from all sources of not more than ten shillings a week already, and should be able to show that he had done the best by his industry and providence to make a provision for himself and for the family dependent on him. The Committee also offered several recommendations with regard to the creation of an authority in every division of the country to receive and decide on applications for the pensions, and that the authority should be appointed by the guardians from their own number in the first instance, and, with additions made under regulations framed by the Local Government Board, should afterwards be independent of the Board of Guardians. It was recommended that the cost of the pensions should be borne by the common fund of each union; that a contribution from Imperial sources should be made to that fund, and that the amount of the pension should be fixed at not less than five shillings or more than seven shillings a week at the discretion of the Committee; that the pension should be awarded for a period of not less than three years, but could be renewed at the end of each such period, and was liable to be withdrawn at any time if, according to the judgment of the pension-granting authority, any circumstances should demand or justify the withdrawal. Such was, in fact, the internal construction of the scheme prepared and recommended by the Committee, and it will enable our readers to see at once the shape taken by the project when it had reached to its latest and most authoritative form, and will help them the better to understand the justification for the establishment of such a system and the chances it would have of proving a real and substantial benefit to the community.

Among the many projects of social reform which occupied the attention of Parliament in this Session was a measure known as the Money-Lending Bill introduced into the House of Lords by Lord James of Hereford. The preparation of this Bill was the result of the labours of a Select Committee appointed for the purpose of taking into consideration the troubles and evils arising from the spread of the professional money-lending system, and the possibility of devising some legislative protection against its temptations and dangers. The Committee had received much important evidence from various sources, and had very fully considered the whole subject. Lord James of Hereford had drawn up a Bill framed upon the recommendations of the Select Committee, and it appeared to be a measure thoroughly practical in its character, which, while applying itself to repress, by feasible legislation, the worst abuses of the system, did not go in for a moral crusade against the whole principle of lending money on various proportionate terms of interest. It proposed to deal with the abuses and the excesses of usury, and not to fix a precise limit of interest which was never to be overstepped under any conditions. One provision of the Bill was that every person undertaking to carry on the business of a money-lender should be registered under one name only, and that his own name, and should not be allowed to start an imaginary company under names invented for the purpose. Another clause was to the effect that the words 'professional money-lender' should not include the ordinary pawnbroker or banker, or other person carrying on a recognised commercial or financial business, during the operations of which he might have to advance money on the ordinary terms to those with whom he had dealings. This clause required that a copy of every contract with the conditions set forth in it should be given to the borrower. The main purpose of this clause was to give fair protection to those who, in the legitimate way of business, had to make advances to some of their customers. The measure was to have the effect of giving full power to the courts of law to revise and annul any contract with the money-lender, and to relieve the borrower in cases where the contract, which he had been prevailed upon to accept, imposed on him the payment of interest at a rate entirely out of proportion to any benefits that he could receive from it. Where the interest demanded and agreed upon was less than 10 per cent. per annum the court of law was not to interfere. Thus far it was assumed the borrower might be safely left to exercise his own discretion as to the amount which he was willing to pay for a temporary and desirable relief, and the object of the measure was to put down actual usury, and it was not intended to declare that under no conditions might the lender go beyond the ordinary rate of interest even when dealing with a somewhat uncertain borrower. But where the interest exceeded 10 per cent. and became extravagantly usurious, or where unreasonable charges were made for making inquiries and conducting the business arrangements of a loan, the law courts were to be entitled to review the whole contract between lender and borrower, might call for a full statement of accounts, and might, after an examination into all the conditions of the bargain, decide upon the amount which the court should ascertain to be reasonably and justly due by the man who borrowed to the man who lent.

An objection was made to the proposal that the court should be empowered to overrule contracts where the interest charged was more than 10 per cent. This objection was founded on the general principle that any limitation of the rate of interest was an interference with freedom of contract, and that freedom of contract was the very life of trade. But those who pressed this objection did not seem to remember that in all the dealings of civilised society the law of a country claims the right to protect the weak against the strong, and that in many or most of our ordinary business dealings the principle is acknowledged that the rate of interest may be fixed by legal supervision. It became therefore a matter of consideration whether the evils created by the practice of usurious money-lending had or had not reached that height when the law in all civilised countries is called upon to intervene for the protection of the needy and the weak. Lord James, in defending his Bill, told the House of Lords that without this particular clause he feared that not only must the measure fail to be of any use for the prevention of usury, but that the withdrawal of the clause would strengthen the hand of the money-lender by enabling him to say that Parliament itself had compelled his opponents to moderate their opposition to his ways of doing business. The opposition in the House of Lords came to little or nothing, and the Bill passed its second reading without a division.

An attempt in the same direction was made by Lord Russell of Killowen, who brought forward a measure intended to check a system of corrupt and secret dealings between private companies of money-lenders, or individual money-lenders, and the large numbers of persons whose immediate need or love for pecuniary speculation makes them ready to accept any conditions of usurious interest with the hope of escaping from some immediate pressure, or with the hope of doing a good stroke of business in the future. This measure was the result of inquiry made into the whole subject by a special Committee of the London Chambers of Commerce, and of the recommendations which the Committee proposed for bringing the law to bear on the corrupt and corrupting system. The Bill was welcomed by the Lord Chancellor as a much needed reform, although he expressed a fear that the difficulties of dealing with some of the corrupt practices would be found insurmountable. The Bishops of London and Westminster both spoke strongly in favour of the general principle

VII.   B embodied in the measure, and offered advice as to the means of making its application more effective. The Bill went into Committee on the 8th of June, but it made no further practical progress. This Bill was eventually dropped, as was the Money-Lending Bill of Lord James of Hereford, though his Bill had passed all its stages in the Lords and had been sent to the Commons. Mr. Balfour proposed, on July 17, to drop this Bill —with several others—owing to pressure of time and the approaching end of the Session. It came to represent, in fact, one other of the foreshadowed social reforms of that period, and thus has its claim to be recorded as an event of some significance.

On April 21, 1899, a great meeting was held at the Mansion House in London to promote the objects and maintain the funds of the organisation known as the Salvation Army. Lord Aberdeen, Lord Monkswell, and Mr. Cecil Rhodes were present. Mr. Cecil Rhodes bore high personal testimony to the work which the Salvation Army was accomplishing in South Africa and gave in his contribution of £200 to the funds. Lord Aberdeen tendered his high tribute of praise to the labours of the Salvation Army in Western Australia. The Salvation Army had at length come to be recognised by all classes in England as a power of the highest influence and value in the promotion of sobriety, morality, industry, and intelligence among the poor of these countries and of all countries where its work had been carried on. For a long time the Salvation Army had not been taken much into account by the majority of those who belonged to what are conventionally described as the higher classes of society. There was, indeed, a very common inclination among those classes to take account only of the peculiarities in the movement which invited ridicule. There was even at one time an apparent inclination among newspaper critics to regard the Salvation Army as just the sort of professedly religious and really grotesque institution which Charles Dickens would have described in some of his most humorous chapters. But the Salvation Army had been giving every year more and more distinct and practical evidences of its capacity for doing great work, and evidence also of its capacity to judge as to the best manner in which its own especial work could be carried to success. Public opinion, therefore, abroad as well as at home, was now coming to understand and appreciate the success of the Salvation Army. The great meeting we have just told of was only one of many public demonstrations got up in appeal to the country for the support and the spread of the Salvation Army's work.

It was Emerson, if we remember rightly, who said that every great idea, no matter how universal may have been its gradual acceptance, had its origin in the mind of one man. This might be said with marked emphasis of the work accomplished by the Salvation Army. General Booth, as he has always been called since he began his campaign, originated the enterprise of the Salvation Army; gave it a name which it has ever since borne; acted as its leader; led its invasions of every civilised country in the world and of many not yet civilised; and even when he had grown into old age continued to be its Commander-in-Chief. William Booth was in his early days a minister of the Methodist New Connection, and in this capacity came to settle in the East End of London. There he had ample opportunities of observing the misery, the ignorance, the utter lack of education, and the many vices prevailing in all that region of the great city. He found that a large proportion of the poor in the East End had no ideas whatever on the subject of religion and never attended any place of worship. He saw, too, that drunkenness was a vice which seemed to cling to poverty and to ignorance, and that even among the wives and mothers of that poorest class drunkenness was common to a terrible extent.

Mr. Booth, the Rev. Mr. Booth as he then was, started, in the first instance, what he called a Christian Mission, having for its object to bring home to the minds and hearts of the poor some better and higher ideals of life. But he soon found that the evils against which he was striving would have to be encountered by a bolder and more aggressive form of strategy than the quiet work of moral conversion which he had begun to carry on. The idea came into his mind that those evils must be assailed by some form of actual invasion, and from that idea came the scheme of the Salvation Army. He gathered around him a number of earnest and devoted men and women who were willing to be led by him as their Commander-in-Chief into an organised invasion of the realms of ignorance, squalor, and vice. He then assumed that military title which he has ever since retained, and which is now accorded to him with the hearty approval of the civilised world. He arranged his great army according to the ordinary divisions and subdivisions of military organisation, and he sent out an army corps here, there, and everywhere to invade the homes of the enemy. The military titles and divisions of rank were set up in his army after the same model, and his troops went about endeavouring to establish their 'slum posts,' their rescue homes for fallen women, their systems of labour and their offices for the hire of labour, their shelters, food depôts, homes for inebriates, and their centres of religious and moral instruction. The Salvation Army had its habitual marchings and counter-marchings in something like military form, with banners, bands, and uniforms, throughout the poorer quarters of every city. The poor and the suffering were thus not merely invited and encouraged to come and seek help and teaching and the means of making a livelihood, but found their regions actually invaded by the Salvation Army, and were compelled to listen to its appeals.

For a time the general public regarded this idea of starting an imitation army for the conquest of poverty and vice as something approaching very nearly to the burlesque, and did not believe that any really beneficent, substantial, and enduring results were likely to come from this sort of sham army. But General Booth understood thoroughly the nature of the work he had to do and the best means of accomplishing it. He knew that nothing would be so likely to attract followers to such a mission as to prevail upon men and women to enrol themselves as members of his organisation, to give them definite position and title and regular occupation in his work, and thus to stir within them those honourable feelings of professional comradeship which would bring out in aid of the work whatever spirit of generous emulation was in their hearts. A public opinion of its own thus grew up in the ranks of the Salvation Army, and as there was never a system of purchased commission existing in General Booth's force it was open to the very poorest and humblest to make his way by honest and effective service to a position of honour among his comrades. General Booth appears to have known full well also how much of the dramatic or, at all events, of the theatric sentiment there is in the minds of most human beings, and how stimulating it is to feel that one is playing the part of a gallant soldier, even though the enemies he has to encounter are the vice and the poverty of a city's most squalid and most inglorious regions. The General's eldest son became his chief of the staff, another son was put in charge of the Salvation Army corps in Australasia. The General's eldest daughter directed with her husband the work to be done in Holland and Belgium, another daughter, with her husband, had charge of operations in the United States, and so on through the whole family, each one being entrusted with a separate department in the work of conquest. The General's wife was at her husband's right-hand side in all his work until she died of cancer in the autumn of 1890. Her death, a terrible calamity to her husband, was yet a calamity which only seemed to nerve him for more energetic effort in that great cause towards which, as he well knew, her dying wishes would have sped him on.

The Salvation Army established its posts and stations in every country throughout Europe, in the United States and South America, in Australasia, India, South Africa, the West Indies, Japan, and indeed in every region where a foothold could be obtained and where there was any good work to be done. Of course all this enterprise required large funds to support it, and General Booth made appeals again and again to the generosity of the public in every country he invaded, and his appeals seemed everywhere to have met with generous response. In 1890 he announced that £100,000 would be needed in order to begin one of his great schemes of social rescue, and it is understood that he obtained all the money that he wanted. Two years later he announced that £30,000 a year would be necessary to carry out and permanently sustain one especial project of his for the invasion of 'Darkest England.' General Booth's appeal was recommended to the public of England by the Earl of Aberdeen, Lord Compton, Archdeacon Farrar, Mr. Henry Labouchere, and many other public men whose names do not exactly suggest the likelihood of their being taken in by any showy project of professional philanthropy. Later on the working of this particular scheme was submitted to the consideration of a committee of inquiry, and the committee, after a careful study of the subject, gave a favourable report as to the nature of the scheme and the manner in which the funds subscribed for its support were applied to its purposes. The members of this committee of inquiry were the Earl of Onslow, Lord James of Hereford (Sir Henry James as he then was), Mr. Walter Long, Mr. E. Waterhouse, President of the Institute of Chartered Accountants, and Mr. C. E. Hobhouse, M.P.

General Booth thoroughly understands the

use of the printing-press, of the newspaper and the pamphlet, for his projects of world-wide conquest, and he has published many volumes and pamphlets and written many articles in exposition of his views. In 1880 he started a weekly gazette devoted to his regenerating projects, called by the appropriate name of the *War Cry*. A version of the same journal is published at every colonial and foreign centre of the Salvation Army, and the *War Cry* is understood to have in this way a circulation of nearly 700,000 copies. General Booth publishes a French version of his journal entitled *En Avant* in Paris, and issues appropriate versions translated into the language of the people in many great cities and towns throughout Europe, Asia, Africa, America, and Australia. He has personally visited again and again the headquarters of his various organisations; it would seem as if age could not wither nor custom stale the infinite variety of his enterprises. His main plan of action seems to be to keep things going everywhere and never to allow any feeling of languor or sense of monotony to come over those who are acting under his command. No merely philanthropic movement has in our time kept alive and controlled so active and so widespread an organisation.

There are religious and missionary bodies which have even surpassed General Booth in the extent of their work throughout the world, but no lay movement set on foot for the spiritual rescue as well as the promotion of morality, good order, industry, and physical comfort amongst the poorest classes has ever, so far as we know, equalled the amount of work done by the Salvation Army. It is one of the peculiar institutions of our time, and has come of late years to receive the recognition and encouragement of sovereigns as well as of private philanthropists and philanthropic institutions. The inspiring purpose of the Salvation Army's work appears to be the awakening of the poor themselves to some sense of the immediate causes of their poverty and their misery, and to bring to their huts and garrets the means of obtaining a better living by their own exertions and their own powers of self-discipline. The Salvation Army does not merely preach sermons or chant songs to the poorest classes with the view of teaching them that they ought to be sober and steady, moral and industrious, no matter how miserable may be the conditions of their lives and how little opportunity they may have for lifting themselves out of the slough of despond. Every man and woman to whom a direct appeal is made is offered by the Salvation Army the means of entering on a better course of existence. The drunkard is put in the way of obtaining the shelter of an inebriate asylum until his physical and nervous system shall have grown strong enough to enable him to come out into active life and make a decent livelihood for himself, and then the means of making that decent livelihood are brought within his reach. There are homes for fallen women, and they too are helped to earn their daily bread in decency and morality. The agricultural labourer has employment on the land found for him, and the denizen of the slums is not allowed, for sheer want of work, to drift into abject pauperism.

Throughout the whole organisation a direct appeal is made to that spirit of comradeship which is the very life of enterprise. Those who seek the help of the Salvation Army are invited to enrol themselves in its ranks and are taught to feel that they are no longer mere waifs of society, but are members of a powerful organisation and are serving under a common flag. Each man and woman who is enrolled in that Army and serving under that flag becomes a missionary of the order, and feels a natural and a personal pride in proclaiming its doctrine and expanding the field of its work. The Salvation Army is always moving under the full light of public opinion, indeed under the very glare of hostile criticism, and we have already shown that it was for a long time the object of much ridicule from the outer world. As the years of its movement have gone on it has more and more been able to vindicate not only its purposes but its practical results, and to be regarded as one of the great reforming movements of the age. The immense gatherings, exhibitions foreign and domestic, held periodically by the Salvation Army in London and other capitals keep the attention of the world alive to the results of its work. We have heard now and then of dissensions among leaders of the Army, as we have heard of dissensions in other war offices, but in the former case, as in the latter, the temporary disputes do not seem much to affect the movement of the army at the word of command. The Salvation Army has made for itself a place in our history.

CHAPTER XV.

NEW IRELAND.

THE Irish National party had for some time been passing through changes which led to a new and, for Irish National purposes, a very auspicious development. After the death of Charles Stewart Parnell the Nationalists had remained for a while divided into two separate and, it might even be said, antagonistic, parties. The large majority of Irish National members remained under the one leadership while the other party, led by Mr. John Redmond, was very small in numbers, made up, indeed, only of a group of men who had remained attached to Parnell under all conditions. Mr. John Redmond was a man of undoubted Parliamentary capacity. He had a remarkable gift of eloquence, which he could adapt alike to the House of Commons and the public platform. He had an attractive presence and a singularly powerful, resonant, and musical voice which gave expressiveness and effect to every argument and, when occasion needed, to impassioned appeal. He belonged to that class of life which usually represents the landlordism of the country. But he was a convinced and most earnest Nationalist, and his whole style, manner, and bearing were admirably suited to the House of Commons. He had been a member of that House from his early manhood, and no member, even among the official ranks, better understood the rules and could better follow the precedents of the Parliamentary assembly. His absolute sincerity and genial ways had secured for him the respect and regard even of those former colleagues from whom of late years he had been completely separated. It seemed a singular stroke of evil fate which had left such a man to be the leader merely of some half-a-dozen followers acting in habitual opposition to the large majority of the Nationalist members. There was still in the hearts of Irish Home Rulers a vague hope that sometime or other he might be enabled to take his place, and that a leading place, among the Irishmen in the House of Commons who were maintaining the national cause.

Meanwhile the majority of the party was led for some sessions by Mr. John Dillon, himself a typical and commanding figure in Irish political life. Mr. Dillon was the son of a distinguished Irish patriot, John Blake Dillon, who had always been devoted to the cause of Ireland, and was by the side of Smith O'Brien in the unsuccessful effort at rebellion made by the Young

Ireland party in 1848. The elder Dillon, it was well known, had not been in favour of that hasty and unprepared movement, but when it suddenly broke into an actual struggle against the power of England he had preferred to take his stand beside his leader in the open field rather than seem to desert him in the hour of his desperate effort. He had then been for many years an exile in the United States, but when an amnesty was granted to all concerned in the movement of 1848 he returned to Ireland, and accepted a place in the House of Commons. There he made many friends among English Liberals, and gained especially the esteem of John Bright. His son John Dillon had entered public life with a full endowment of his father's national spirit and political capacity, and as leader of the Irish majority he won the esteem of all parties in the House. But John Dillon was not satisfied with the conditions under which he had to lead the majority of the party, and his unselfish and patriotic nature yearned for a complete reconciliation between the two sections of Irish Nationalists. It had become his conviction that a complete reconciliation between these two sections was not easy of attainment while the majority remained under the leadership of one of those who had felt compelled to separate themselves from Parnell and his minority of followers. John Dillon was convinced that a most important step towards reconciliation would be taken if the majority were to invite that reconciliation by the announcement of their wish to choose a leader from the ranks of the Parnellite minority. It seemed also to Dillon that the majority who had won so complete a victory in Ireland at the General Election might well afford to make a generous sacrifice in order to bring the whole body of Irish Home Rulers once again into cordial co-operation.

There had been a General Election throughout Great Britain and Ireland as a result of the famous division on the Cordite question described in a former volume of this History. As the result of that election in Ireland only ten representatives of the Parnellite section had been elected while some seventy Nationalists on the other side found places in the House of Commons. The moment therefore seemed singularly auspicious to Mr. Dillon and to many others of his party for a direct movement in favour of reunion. A suggestion was made about this time by the Catholic Archbishop of Toronto, Canada, and by other colonial sympathisers with the Irish national cause, that a National Convention representative of the Irish race throughout the world should be held in Dublin with the object of bringing about a reconciliation between the separated sections of the Irish Parliamentary party. At a meeting of the party held in Dublin, Mr. Dillon moved a resolution accepting the Archbishop of Toronto's suggestion, and inviting immediate action for the holding of an Irish National Convention. This resolution was cordially agreed to, and not long after Mr. Dillon carried his purpose one stage further by moving a resolution at another meeting of the Parliamentary party, earnestly inviting Mr. John Redmond and his friends to co-operate in the forthcoming National Convention, and to join with them in making such arrangements as would secure to them a full representation in the Convention. Some of Mr. Redmond's leading followers promptly responded to the invitation, and took an active part in carrying out the arrangements.

The Convention assembled in Dublin in the early days of September 1896. More than two thousand representative persons from all parts of Great Britain and Ireland, from the United States, the Canadian and Australasian colonies, and from all parts of the world where Irishmen were settled, took part in the proceedings. The Convention came to a complete agreement as to all the principles and demands of the Irish Nationalists at home, the claims for an Irish Parliament, for political, educational, agrarian, and industrial reform, and for a complete restoration to unity in the Irish Parliamentary party. A deep impression was made on all intelligent and fair-minded observers in Great Britain by the unanimity and the moderation of the claims put forward by what might fairly be described as the representative Convention of the whole Irish race. It seemed clear that the influence of such a meeting must be decisive in bringing about the restoration of harmony and union in the Irish Parliamentary party, and every one concerned in the Irish cause knew well that Mr. Dillon was ready and anxious to resign the position of leadership if by that step an acceptable opportunity could be offered to Mr. Redmond to assume the place of leader of the reunited party.

Other influences soon came up to forward the accomplishment of this result. One of the most conspicuous among Ireland's active political workers at this time was Mr. Michael Davitt, a man who had devoted the whole of his working lifetime to the advocacy of Home Rule for Ireland and of some complete reform in that land tenure system which had so long kept the Irish agricultural tenant a pauper in a country abounding with the means of comfort, and was driving, year after year, hundreds of thousands of Irish men and women to find new homes in the United States, Canada, or Australasia. Mr. Davitt's career has already been told in this History, and we have only to say that the course which he took was in every way consistent with his previous action in public life. He exerted all his great influence over his countrymen in order to bring about that union of the separated parties which John Dillon was endeavouring to accomplish.

In October 1898 John Dillon delivered a speech to a Glasgow meeting, in which he carried his policy of reunion a step farther than it had hitherto been advanced. He strongly recommended that a conference should be held of men chosen from the two sections of the Irish party for the express purpose of considering the desirability and the possibility of a full reconciliation. The leaders of the minority did not signify any public desire to accept this proposition, but it must be borne in mind that these men, representing only a very small minority, naturally hesitated to accept too readily propositions coming from the stronger side. Mr. Redmond and his few followers may very reasonably have felt that until the offers from the majority took a more precise shape and had a more authoritative sanction it would not be well for the small group of Parnellites to commit themselves to any basis of negotiation. The Redmondites might have said to themselves that it would be of little use their being admitted once again to the ranks of the majority unless it were certain that their accepting the position would help to forward, in the most effective manner, the policy on which the whole party had worked in Parnell's conquering days. Certainly there does not seem to have been, among Mr. Redmond's most influential colleagues, any disinclination to accept the policy of reconciliation if only it could be made sure to them that the national struggle was to be carried on with the same policy as that which had governed it before, and that the influence of Parnell's better days was to be its guiding spirit in the future.

In the meantime, many public boards and other bodies in Ireland had given a cordial welcome to Mr. Dillon's suggestion. It was agreed upon that a conference of the Nationalist members should be held in Dublin to decide upon some plan of action by which a complete reconciliation of the parties might be brought about. Fifty-six members were present at this conference. Mr. Redmond himself did not attend, but one of his most prominent colleagues and supporters, Mr. James O'Kelly, took part in the meeting and contributed much towards its success. A series of resolutions was drawn up by Mr. Edward Blake, one of the most distinguished and influential members of the party still led by John Dillon, and these resolutions were unanimously adopted. The resolutions declared in brief that all Irish Nationalists were to be reunited in one party on the principles and constitution of the old Parnellite party as it existed before the break-up; that the reunited party was to be absolutely independent of all British political parties; that its main object was to secure Home Rule for Ireland, and also to strive on the old lines for the redress of all Irish grievances, especially those connected with the land, labour, taxation, and education. Thus far the resolutions proposed to the conference were only such as might have been expected in any case, and merely invited the two sections of the Irish National party to combine together once again, and to fight out the old battles on the old lines.

Then followed something in the nature of a distinct and genuine determination on the part of the majority to show that in their dispute with the minority they gave the members of that minority credit for sincere patriotism, and were willing to make a considerable concession to prove the sincerity of their own purpose. The closing resolution said that 'this meeting, mainly composed of those belonging to the larger party, declares its readiness to support the choice of a member of the Parnellite party as first chairman of the united party.' Thereupon Mr. Dillon announced his intention to resign the chairmanship of the larger party in order to carry out the spirit of this final resolution. This had been Mr. Dillon's resolve for a long time, his sole purpose being to accomplish a lasting reconciliation between the two Nationalist sections which, according to Mr. Dillon's own conviction, could best be secured by the agreement to accept as leader one belonging to the Parnellite minority. This resolve unquestionably required some sacrifice on the part of John Dillon. He had proved himself in every sense a most capable party leader in the House of Commons. He was admired and trusted by all who knew him; his manners were genial and polished; although a most sincere and impassioned Nationalist he always behaved with consideration and courtesy to his opponents of whatever political party, and he had won the esteem and confidence of the House of Commons. It could not have been a welcome task to Mr. Dillon, who had no intention of withdrawing into private life, to renounce that position of leadership to which he had been elected Session after Session by his own party and to come under the leadership of one with whom he had been in public antagonism since the split among the Nationalists. But he persevered in his resolution, and was able to convince most of his friends that the course he had decided upon taking was best for the national cause of Ireland. The two Nationalist sections which had been so long in conflict accomplished, in great measure under his inspiration, a complete reconciliation.

On February 7, 1900, the whole party met once more, and John Redmond was chosen as its leader. The reunited party has gone on since that time with entire Parliamentary cohesion and with remarkable success. Even its strongest political opponents have admitted that as a Parliamentary party it has won respect by its close attention to the work of the House, by its unflinching discipline, and its steady recognition of its leader's authority. Mr. Redmond has undoubtedly shown great tact and skill as well as eloquence during the years that have followed his election to the leadership, and neither of the two great Parliamentary parties can fail now to take careful account of the probable action of Mr. Redmond and his followers.

The position of the new leader was much strengthened by the founding, at this time, of an organisation in Ireland for a thorough combination of the whole Irish Nationalist people into a self-governing league for the promotion of Home Rule and land tenure reform. This new institution was called the United Irish League, and it may be briefly described as differing from former national associations in the fact that it created a more complete and more unified combination of the whole Irish people, and proposed to make the United Irish League, and not the Irish Parliamentary party or the various political institutions, the ruling power in Irish national politics. The United Irish League asserted its right to make the Irish Parliamentary body a part of its machinery for the working of the Irish cause instead of allowing itself to be, as former organisations of the same character had been, a part of the machinery worked by the Irish Nationalist members of Parliament. The United Irish League was called into existence and put into commanding action by one of the most influential men of the Irish Nationalist party. Mr. William O'Brien had won for himself a peculiar position in Irish political life. He was at once an enthusiast and a practical politician. He had a natural gift of thrilling eloquence which told splendidly from a public platform, and his earnestness, his desire to persuade, and his thorough knowledge of every subject with which he dealt, made his speeches effective in the House of Commons. There was a poetic fervour in the tone of his appeals which one might have thought little qualified to win favour in Parliament, but it is quite certain that William O'Brien often succeeded in making a deep impression on the House. Mr. O'Brien was a journalist by profession, and had founded a newspaper of his own. He had devoted his literary talents, which were remarkable, to the promotion of that national cause which always held his devotion, and he had never tried to make a personal profit out of any of his newspaper enterprises. He might be regarded as a typical figure of the Irish Nationalist agitator during Ireland's recent years. A man of honourable character, who won the esteem of every one who knew him, whether political friend or political enemy, his whole life was devoted to purposes which he and all those who worked with him believed to be absolutely rightful; he was incapable of endeavouring to serve any even of these purposes by act or policy inconsistent with the moral laws and the laws of honour. Yet he had been prosecuted time after time for what the exceptional laws prevailing in Ireland just then regarded as political offences, and had spent some two years of his life in prison.

The English reader must understand that during this period Ireland was ruled by a system of exceptional laws which rendered a man liable to trial, conviction, and imprisonment in Ireland for speeches or doings which could have brought on no penal consequences in England, Scotland, or Wales. These laws had of late been made more and more exceptional, until it would have been hardly possible for a prominent Irishman to speak out in public his real opinions of the policy of the Government or the conditions of the land system without making himself liable to prosecution and to probable imprisonment. It will be said that the condition of Ireland itself was then exceptional, and therefore required at the hands of legislators an entirely exceptional policy to deal with it. It is only necessary to say here, in answer to that argument, that the growth of the peaceful condition which has been so remarkable in Ireland during the last few years has been mainly owing to the fact that English Governments, whether Liberal or Conservative, have alike shown themselves more willing to carry out the reforms which agitators like Mr. William O'Brien were imprisoned for recommending. The whole system of exceptional laws has lately been abandoned in Ireland, and an

Irishman in his own country carries on his political work as he might do if he were living in England. Those who introduced and maintained the exceptional system have had to confess that its abandonment had been rendered possible even in their eyes only by the adoption of some of the reforms which the lawless agitators were imprisoned for striving to accomplish. Mr. O'Brien is an essayist and a novelist as well as a writer of leading articles, and he might have made for himself a name in letters alone if he had not found his work cut out for him in the political service of his country.

We have taken Mr. O'Brien as a typical figure of the Irish agitator during his time, a figure somewhat like that of Mr. Davitt and others equally well known, and we have endeavoured to bring home to the mind of the reader the fact that such men as these were day after day the victims of legal prosecution and legalised imprisonment for no other offence than that of endeavouring to make known to the legislature and the public the imperative need of just such reforms as those which the legislature afterwards began to carry out with the full approval of the general public opinion of the British Empire and the civilised world. The United Irish League became a controlling power in Ireland, and was strongly supported by Irishmen in Canada, in Australasia, and all over the American Republic. The League took a very active part in all Irish elections, and it soon became clear that a candidate for an Irish constituency would have little chance of success if he had not secured the confidence and support of the League. We may anticipate the course of history so far as to say that every Session saw some fresh effort made by the Government, up to this time a Conservative Government, to bring in and carry new measures for the improvement of the land tenure system. It appears at last to have become evident to all who were capable of conducting an Administration that the Irish demands for a better system of land tenure could not be reduced to silence by any kind of coercion, and that there were numbers of men in Ireland possessed of high capacity and stainless personal character who were prepared to suffer any legal prosecution and punishment rather than sit still and raise no voice against the maintenance of unjust, oppressive, and exceptional laws.

In the meantime there has been a most distinct and encouraging diminution in all manner of violent agitation in Ireland, and the judges at assizes are constantly proclaiming from the bench the gratification which they feel at the gradual and steady decrease in all cases of violence and outrage throughout the country. The obvious explanation of this is the conviction of the Irish people in general that the protection afforded to them by their Nationalist leaders is becoming more powerful for good, and that

Governments, whether Liberal or Conservative, are recognising that there could be peace in the land only when legislation itself had gone to work in recognition of the national demand and its general justice, and thus made peace possible. We have yet to see how far the same national influences will prevail in bringing the minds of the established authorities to recognise the justice and good sense of Ireland's demand for a Parliament of her own. If we are to judge of the future by the evidences and records of the recent past, we can have little doubt that the national demand, which has been going on and increasing in strength ever since the passing of the Act of Union, will come to be recognised by the British Parliament as the final means for the pacification of Ireland and for Ireland's acceptance of her position as a willing partner in the Imperial system. The colonies have already taught just such a lesson, and it may be Ireland's happy destiny, before long, to give the lesson its final illustration.

A remarkable book has lately been published by Michael Davitt, bearing the name, 'The Fall of Feudalism in Ireland.' We are looking forward somewhat while mentioning this book, for it did not make its appearance until three years or more after the period with which we are now dealing. It is well worth the careful attention of every English and foreign reader who feels any interest in the story of Ireland.

It is written by a man who bore a very prominent and influential part in bringing about the fall of that feudalism which we are glad to say has now become a portion of Ireland's past history. The fact that a man like Michael Davitt has written of Irish feudalism as a thing of the past is in itself an emphatic tribute to the success of that national agitation which no exceptional legislation could suppress, and on which the doors of prison cells were locked in vain.

A new and at the same time a clearly defined and practical agitation had sprung up, and had been for some time carried on in the Irish political world. This agitation had for its object the comparison of the taxable capacity of Ireland with that of Great Britain, and the effort to bring the two systems into equality. The whole question had been raised in a distinct form during the year 1896, and it had the very unusual effect of bringing both or all the Irish political parties into something like confederation. This in itself might have been enough to warn the Government of Lord Salisbury that steps would have to be taken in order to prove that the Conservative Government was not opposed to every measure for the removal of Irish grievances. It must have seemed obvious to any English statesman that if the Irish Nationalists and the Irish Tories, Orangemen included, could find one alleged Irish grievance on which to agree and enter into alliance they would be likely soon to find other such subjects as well, and perhaps to end in a cordial union on the question of Home Rule. The story revealed by this new agitation was of a nature which might well appeal to public feeling in Ireland, and at the same time could easily explain its meaning to the English mind. Even the man in the streets of any English city, who might find it hard to understand why Ireland should want a Parliament of her own when she had already the right to send her representatives into the Imperial Parliament, could have no difficulty in understanding why Irishmen should object to being taxed on a much larger scale in proportion to their means than the taxpayers of England.

When the Irish National Parliament, the Parliament of Grattan's day, was abolished, the Act of Union had provisions specially introduced in order to maintain a separate financial system for Ireland. Time after time, however, the meaning and value of these provisions were removed by succeeding legislation. Before the Union had been twenty years in existence the separate exchequers were made into one system. Two years later the tobacco duties were made the same in both countries, and other changes followed in rapid succession, so that the stamp duties, the income tax, and the spirit duties were made the same, and the taxation of the two countries was rendered equal in the ordinary sense of that term. Nothing could be more misleading than the application of the word equal to the same system of taxation when applied to two countries existing under such different conditions as England and Ireland. England was one of the wealthiest countries in the world, and was, on the evidence of strictly official statistics, growing every year into greater wealth and prosperity. Ireland was one of the poorest countries known to civilisation, and was, according to the same statistics, growing poorer and poorer year after year. Her population was steadily diminishing, and it was quite plain to every observer that there would soon be a much larger, richer, and more populous Ireland on the western side of the Atlantic. Now it is one of the simplest and most obvious principles of financial arrangement that in applying taxation some account must be taken of the relative means of those on whom a tax is to be levied. This principle is arranged and maintained easily and fairly enough in our system of direct taxation. In these countries a man pays income tax according to the amount of his income, and if that income should fall below a certain level the man is regarded as too poor to be visited with any income tax whatever. But when we come to indirect taxation we have to deal with arrangements which ordinarily put a quite disproportionate pressure on the means of the poorer classes. Duties upon ordinary food, for instance, on corn or on tea, are just the same for the poor as for the rich; the millionaire can buy his tea as cheaply as the poorest artisan, while the needs of the poorest artisan, so far as tea-drinking is concerned, are not any less than those of the wealthiest millionaire. These elementary and obvious facts were, all the more because they were elementary and obvious, excellent foundations for the protest which was made by Irish Nationalists and Irish Tories alike against the system of taxation which subjected the wealthy country growing wealthier and the poor country growing poorer to exactly the same rate of impost where indirect taxation was concerned.

The opening of this new agitation has been already described in this History, and we return to the subject now chiefly to show that as the agitation went strenuously on, it gave fresh hopes for the prosperity and pacification of Ireland by the fact that it brought Nationalists from the South and Orangemen from the North to the same public platform. At a still later date it came to be an ordinary feature of a debate on an Irish question in the House of Commons that some of the most influential representatives of the Orange party in the North of Ireland were firmly to support, by speech in the House, and by vote in the division lobby, the position taken up by John Redmond on this question. There was a time within the recollection of many of us when the mere setting up of any claim for Ireland by the Home Rule party would have been enough to arouse an almost instinctive distrust and dislike of it in the minds of the Irish Conservatives and Orangemen. There were thus, in the closing years of Queen Victoria's reign, clear and auspicuous evidences that the long enduring hostility and even hatred between the two sections of Irishmen was growing less bitter, and that a new spirit of intelligent inquiry and of companionship was making its influence felt. The hopefulness of these auguries was much noticed, even at the time, in England as well as in Ireland.

Nor must practical history fail to take account of a struggle carried on between Sir Horace Plunkett and a certain force of Nationalist public opinion in Ireland. Horace Plunkett had held for a long time a distinguished position as a member of the Conservative party in the House of Commons. He was a thorough Irishman in feeling, although strongly opposed to the demand for Home Rule; he was a man of great ability and of some eloquence, and was held in much esteem and friendship by all who knew him well, no matter what their political party. He had given himself up assiduously to the practical study of agriculture, and when an agricultural department for Ireland was instituted by the Government, he was placed at its head. The policy of the Conservative Government, favoured by many Liberals who were not Home Rulers, had been proclaimed as the determination, according to a phrase very popular at the time, 'to kill Home Rule by kindness.' Sir Horace Plunkett, with his winning manners and thorough sincerity of purpose, was the man best qualified to carry such an enterprise to success, if success were possible of attainment. He set himself with heart and soul to the business of proving that Ireland could be made happy by internal reforms and improvements, and could thus be cured of an inconvenient and superfluous passion for an Irish National Parliament. There can be no doubt that Horace Plunkett himself firmly believed in the possibility of making his scheme a practical success, and of banishing for ever from the living world the troublesome spectre of Home Rule. He set himself to devise and to carry out all manner of improvements in the culture of Irish land, to educate the tenant farmers up to what he believed to be the practical level, and to convince them, by such efforts as those he was encouraging them to make, that the agricultural population could become prosperous and happy by their own labours, without any necessity for a change in the constitution of the Imperial Parliament.

On the other hand, the Nationalists devoted themselves, when they had any leisure, to the business of showing that all efforts of the kind must be absolutely futile so long as the intelligent energy of the country was not allowed to work out its own salvation to the best of its capacity by the action of a national legislature. The struggle was conducted, on the whole, with good-humour on both sides, and gave occasion for much amusing and effective speaking and writing. It may briefly be told that Sir Horace Plunkett's scheme, although beyond doubt it encouraged and accomplished some important improvements in Irish agriculture, showed itself unable to soothe into silence the national demand for Home Rule. Sir Horace Plunkett lost his seat as an Irish member, and while the head of a department which ought, in the natural course of things, to have had its official chief in Parliament, he saw no chance of being re-elected for an Irish constituency. It might have been apparent to a man of his capacity and intelligence that so widespread a national political faith as that which believed in and called for Home Rule was not likely to be charmed into submission by any minor compromises tendered even with the best intentions by the Conservative Government. The attempt to kill Home Rule with kindness soon proved itself entirely unsuccessful. The moment the Irish people came to understand the main purpose of the Plunkett policy, even the best intentions on the part of the ruling authorities only lent a new spirit and fervour to the Home Rule agitation. The prevailing weakness of English Governments in our days, with the sole exception of the Administration led by Mr. Gladstone, has been the failure to recognise the sincerity and strength of the Irish Nationalist demand. You cannot placate a whole people as you might a child by gifts of sugar-plums and by pretty declarations of affection. The Home Rule agitation became stronger than ever.

The later years of Queen Victoria's reign were signalised in Ireland by a great movement for the restoration or revival of the Gaelic language and literature. The Gaelic language has been described as the Northern branch of the Celtic tree, and includes Irish Gaelic, Scottish Gaelic, and Manx Gaelic. The native Irish language is always to be called Gaelic. There can be no question that the Irish language contained a very characteristic and very noble literature in prose or verse, and that some of the earliest Gaelic poems would have a high value according to any literary standard. For a long time the Irish language had ceased to be the possession of those who constituted what are called the better classes, or the educated classes, among the Irish people. The use of the Irish tongue had been at different periods prohibited in Ireland under pain of penal consequences, and although no severity of legislation ever prevented the great bulk of the peasantry in most parts of Ireland from speaking in the language of their ancestors, yet among that part of the population who accepted English ways the ancestral language passed utterly out of use. It was considered by the base disgraceful to know Irish.

Stupid schoolmasters beat their pupils for using their native tongue, and strove to kill Irish and to kindle English with the stick. The Irish language that kept alive through the terrors of the seventeenth and eighteenth centuries almost seemed doomed to perish in the nineteenth. But there were at every time eager and devoted scholars among Irish men and women who kept up the study of Irish for the pure love of its literature and its memories, and every now and then some translation of a great Irish poem or some volume of essays on Irish literature was sent forth to remind the world that there had once existed in Ireland a national life not fully depicted in the verses of Samuel Lover or the romances of Charles Lever. Literary and scholarly associations were formed to spread the study of Irish and to give it a systematised direction, but during several generations nothing very important came of these efforts, and the study of the ancient Irish was regarded by most people as a more or less interesting fantasy or whim.

During the later years of Queen Victoria's reign the movement for the restoration of Irish literature began to show the qualities of a practical and distinct organisation. A large number of young and gifted writers, men and women, became captivated by the national purpose, and an enthusiasm was soon generated which caught the heart of the Irish people at large. It was a national movement in the truest sense, but it was not by any means taken up only by those who were in sympathy with the Irish Nationalist cause. Many men and women who had never taken part in political movements which could be regarded as national in Ireland were nevertheless sincerely and actively applied to the revival of Irish national literature. The sentiment prevailed among all who had a real interest in any manner of literary revival, and the fact that a man or woman was devoted to this Gaelic restoration carried with it no assurance as to the position of him or her in society or as to the political opinions which he or she might entertain. In many well-educated Irish families the parents and children now realised for the first time that they belonged to a country having a language and a literature of its own, and it came home to their minds that the tongue they heard spoken and did not understand as they passed through some of the rural districts was not an uncouth dialect which had always been used only by an ignorant peasantry. Many such families thereupon set themselves at once to the study of Gaelic, and even made it their task to obtain a colloquial mastery of the language.

The genuine literature of Ireland seems to breathe the very atmosphere of the Island and to be informed by the spirit of its national traditions and temperament. Amid and around the most beautiful Irish landscapes there is a certain air of melancholy which seems to diffuse itself through the earliest literature of the race and to give to even the most thrilling and passionate descriptions, whether of human emotion or of physical struggle, the idea of a mind unsatisfied with the realities of man's ambition and man's success, and a yearning after higher things than the life of earth has to show. The rescue and restoration of so valuable and so thoroughly national a literature would indeed be a great success for the intellect of modern Ireland to achieve, and there is every hope that so good a result may be accomplished within our day. A general diffusion of the knowledge of Irish as a speaking language among the educated classes would in itself be a great gain to the country, and would secure for its nationality a wider recognition.

As in most organised movements, political, literary, or other, there were some incidents of a humorous kind in the working of this new organisation. Some odd scenes occurred in the House of Commons when one or two members of a somewhat combative nature insisted on addressing the House in Irish. Nothing came of these attempts but an amusing scene or two, and no matter how far the Gaelic restoration enterprise may succeed it is not likely that the House of Commons will soon consent to have its debates intermingled with speeches delivered in a tongue unfamiliar to the great majority of members. It is true that in some Continental and other Parliaments it is found necessary to allow members coming from outlying parts of the State to address the House in their native language, even if it be a tongue with which the majority of the members are not acquainted.

This is only an incidental question, and the real importance of the whole movement must necessarily consist in the rescue of a language and a literature from utter oblivion. In Wales the native language of the country has always held its place and has had to be recognised as a necessary medium of speech in courts of law and at public meetings. Such a result would be of great importance to Ireland now, and the most rigid advocate of existing conditions could hardly suggest a possible disadvantage to come from it to the working of public business and the contentment of the people. Even those who most persistently advocate the maintenance of the Act of Union might be well advised if they were to consider whether a cordial encouragement of the movement by those in authority might not tend to make the Irish people better content with the existing order of things. We do not suggest that Home Rule might be killed with kindness by the encouragement of the Gaelic movement any more than by the teaching of better agricultural systems. The most wholesome lesson that could be impressed on British legislators for

Ireland would be that which taught them to understand the depth and sincerity of the national demand. But apart from all political considerations it may be admitted on all sides that the movement for the restoration of the Gaelic literature and language is one of the important and the hopeful events of the time and should have the cordial support of all who love literature and would fain recover the buried treasures of the past.

A memorable event in the closing years of Queen Victoria's reign was the visit of the Sovereign to Ireland. It was well understood at the time that this visit was projected by the Queen entirely of her own motion, and did not come from the promptings of any among her recognised official advisers. Indeed the general impression prevailing throughout these countries was that her advisers were disposed on the whole to discourage such a project on the Queen's part. They were governed by the idea that considering recent political events the Queen might be received in the Island with anything but a general welcome; that there might even be vehement displays of hostility in some parts of Ireland where the Sovereign was expected to make her appearance. There were many Englishmen who entertained no feelings towards Ireland but those of cordial good-will, and who yet would have been inclined to discourage the proposal for a Royal visit there on the ground that the display of a hostile feeling in Ireland would only tend to create new trouble for both countries. But the Queen appeared to have made up her mind. It may have been—indeed, from some spoken words of her own, it would seem to have been—that the Queen felt at heart a regret for the long estrangement between her and the Irish people. Forty years had passed away since her first visit to Ireland, and there can be no doubt that the general impression prevailing among the Irish was that the Sovereign held them in but slight regard.

We are far from wishing to exaggerate in any way the beneficent effect of the impression which might have been made upon Ireland by more frequent visits from Queen Victoria and a more active interest shown by her in the welfare and even in the sentiments of the Irish people. The national claims, the demand, that is, for an Irish Parliament and for a thoroughly reformed system of land tenure, could not have been charmed away by any personal attentions on the part of the Sovereign. It was not even to be desired that the Sovereign should feel it a part of her duty to make an attempt at charming those demands away. The relations of the Queen to her subjects in Ireland would remain just the same, however frequent her visits, until Ireland had a Parliament sitting in Dublin and until the tenant farmer had been made owner of the soil he cultivated. But it was thought by many that if the Queen had more often visited her Irish subjects, and shown greater personal interest in their welfare, such demonstration of interest might have led the Irish people to believe that their welfare was always a matter of deep consideration to Her Majesty, and might have induced them to wait more patiently and more hopefully for the desired changes which the Imperial legislature could be prevailed upon to bring about on their behalf. The Queen carried out her own resolve, and her visit to Ireland was made in the opening of April 1900.

It should be said that the Queen's visit was preluded on her behalf by the announcement of Her Majesty's desire that on the coming St. Patrick's Day, and on all future returns of that day, the Irish soldiers in her service should wear the emblematic shamrock. This anniversary had, up to that time, been an occasion of dissatisfaction to the Irish soldiers who desired to wear the shamrock, and who were often prevented from doing so by the orders of their commanding officers, who did not believe themselves authorised in allowing the display on parade occasions of that trefoil which had become the recognised symbol of Irish national sentiment. The order now issued by the Queen was therefore welcomed as a graceful act on the part of the Sovereign and as a recognition of the national feeling. The Queen was received in Dublin with every sign of respect, and even with a general expression of popular welcome. The Lord Mayor of Dublin delivered an address to the Queen, in reply to which she declared that she had come 'To this fair country to seek change and rest, and to revisit scenes which recall to my mind, among the thoughts of the losses which years must bring, the happiest recollection of a warm-hearted welcome given to me and my beloved husband and children,' and then followed some words of gratitude to 'the motherland of those brave sons who had borne themselves in defence of my Crown and Empire with a cheerful valour as conspicuous now as ever in their glorious past.'

The Queen's stay in Ireland lasted about three weeks, and it was well known that in order to go to the Island she had given up for that year the annual visit she had for long been in the habit of paying to the South of France for the purpose of recruiting her health in a climate which especially suited her.

No hostile demonstration of any kind interfered with the success of the Queen's visit. Of course the recognised leaders of the Irish party did not take any part in the demonstrations of welcome. These men felt, and not unnaturally, that the Irish National party could not as a whole identify themselves with demonstrations of welcome to a ruler who, whatever her own personal feelings, was the representative of a power which had of late only made itself known in Ireland by the enforcement of exceptional penal laws against the organisations formed to carry out by Constitutional and Parliamentary methods the policy of Ireland's cause. Even the English reader who most thoroughly identifies himself with the legislation maintaining Imperial power over Ireland cannot fail to understand the true meaning of the sentiment which prevented the Irish leaders from taking an official part in the public welcome given under such conditions to the British Sovereign. There was no hostile feeling to the Queen in person among the whole Irish population, nor did the national leaders feel prompted by their sense of duty to take steps or encourage any movement which might have seemed to embody such a feeling. Queen Victoria's visit may, under all the circumstances, be regarded as a success, and there is no doubt that it created throughout the whole country, north and south, a common and sincere desire that the Queen might again come to Ireland. Many a wish was breathed at that time in every part of the Island that the Queen, or some one of her successors, might before long be present at the opening of an Irish National Parliament.

CHAPTER XVI.

ANOTHER DEATH-ROLL.

THE death-list for the year 1899—so far, at least, as it enrolls the names of those who may be regarded as belonging to this History—begins by recording the passing away of the Duke of Northumberland. Algernon George Percy, sixth bearer of the title, was born in 1810, and died on the 2nd January 1899. His career was not one which made a lasting mark on the history of his country, but he was in many ways, apart from his mere ancestral rank, a remarkable man. During the greater part of his long life he was almost incessantly active in a variety of pursuits, and his activity was the more remarkable and honourable because he was so often a victim to that torturing form of nerve disease which at last caused his death. A man of his position had every opportunity from his very earliest days, and the heir to the House of Northumberland was free to choose the path most likely to suit his fancy. The young Lord Lovaine, as he then was, made up his mind, after he had finished his studies at Eton and Cambridge, to look for distinction in the political world. The Northumberland family then, like most other great families in England, were the owners of certain boroughs under the old Parliamentary system, and as soon as Lord Lovaine came of age he was sent into the House of Commons as the representative of one of these. His ambition for a Parliamentary career was subjected to a temporary blight, for in the next year came the first great Reform Act, and there was an end of the family borough. Lord Lovaine then served for a while in the Grenadier Guards, but he retained his predilection for a Parliamentary career, and in 1852 he once again won a seat in the House of Commons as Conservative member for one of the divisions of Northumberland. That constituency he represented until 1865. Lord Derby, when at the head of the Government, offered Lord Lovaine the position of Junior Lord of the Admiralty, and a year later Lovaine passed from the Admiralty Office to become Vice-President of the Board of Trade. It cannot be said that he achieved marked distinction in either of these offices, and although he remained in the House of Commons for several years longer, it was not found that he had left any impression on that House when he succeeded to the Dukedom, and was elevated or removed to the House of Lords. He had the honour of succeeding Lord Beaconsfield in the office of Lord Privy Seal, and there his Parliamentary career came to an end. He was always full of energy, and of an earnest desire to be up and doing, and he probably did not find that the life of the House of Lords would give him occupation enough. During the remainder of his life he gave himself up almost entirely to the local affairs of his county, and he was ready, generous, and unceasing in his contributions by advice, by money, and by help of various kinds to promote all charitable, industrial, educational, and other projects which promised to be of help to the community. He had the curious distinction for the head of a great ducal family in those days of being a member of the Catholic and Apostolic Church, but he was none the less a liberal contributor to the church-building, the schools, and charitable associations of other religious denominations. As a patron of scientific institutions he won for himself a much respected name, and became President of the Royal Institution of London. The Royal Lifeboat Institution received much active support from the Duke of Northumberland, and for a long time he filled the position of president of it. His tenants all were devoted to him because of his interest in their welfare, his liberal ways of dealing with them, and his genial, friendly manners.

On February 25, in his eighty-third year, died the Baron de Reuter, a man of whom it may fairly be said that his career marked, although it did not make, a great era in the world's development of practical science. Julius de Reuter did not create or discover or invent any new force in scientific agencies for the promotion of civilisation, but he certainly called into existence a new and most valuable method for the practical application and the world-wide diffusion of other men's discoveries and inventions. De Reuter accomplished for the overland electric wire something like what Cyrus W. Field accomplished for the submarine cable—he put it into working order, and made it serve the needs of the whole civilised world. De Reuter was born at Hesse Cassel in 1816, and when a small boy was sent to learn business in the office of his uncle. There he had the good fortune to make the acquaintance of a scientific man who was already beginning to acquire distinction by his experiments in telegraphic work. De Reuter seems to have been filled by a kind of inspiration, which taught him to believe that he could turn the new agency to account in a commercial sense. In 1849 the first complete line of telegraph on the European Continent—that between Aix-la-Chapelle and Berlin—was brought into action. Reuter, with what may fairly be called the instinct of genius, seized the opportunity of establishing himself at Aix-la-Chapelle as the transmitter of intelligence through all the Continental newspapers by the electric wire. Some two years after a submarine cable was laid for the first time between Calais and Dover, and it then became evident to de Reuter's mind that he must from that time forth establish his headquarters in London. Accordingly he settled himself in London, and for a time was occupied almost exclusively with the transmission of commercial intelligence to Continental newspapers. Soon, however, he developed his arrangements so far as to make his offices in London the headquarters for the transmission of political news, and, indeed, all manner of information as to current events through the cities of Europe and all over the civilised world. He spared no expense in making such connections by telegraphic wire as would enable him to anticipate the ordinary means of communication between the steamers arriving at various ports and the great central cities to which their freights and passengers were to be conveyed. He entered into arrangements with many companies, and even with many Governments, for the purpose of making his London offices the recognised centre for the reception and transmission of the world's news. He established the Reuter agency exactly as we know it now, and the whole civilised world, and those parts of the as yet uncivilised world into which civilised men made their way, recognised his agency as the authentic and universal news-carrier of modern days. In 1871 he received the title of Baron from the Duke of Saxe-Coburg and Gotha. He seems to have been born for just the very work he accomplished, and there have been during his time far greater men than he who have not made anything like so distinct an imprint on the everyday life of the world.

On the 1st of March the English courts of law and the English Houses of Parliament lost one of their most distinguished figures by the death of Farrer Herschell, who in his later years received the title of Baron Herschell. The death of this distinguished man was the result of an accident which he met with while walking in the streets of Washington, the capital of the United States. Lord Herschell had been made President of the Commission appointed by the Government of England and the United States to consider and decide on an important question which had arisen with regard to boundary lines between the American Republic and the Dominion of Canada. While passing through one of the streets of Washington, on the 15th of February, his foot slipped on the ice which is a familiar feature of the streets of most American cities during the winter, and in the fall he received severe injuries. It was not supposed at first that his injuries were ominous of a serious issue, and his recovery was confidently expected, when suddenly he fell into a state of collapse, probably from heart failure, and within less than twelve hours from that his brilliant and most useful career came to an end.

Lord Herschell was born in December 1837, received his early education at the University of Bonn and afterwards at University College, London. He studied for the legal profession, was called to the Bar in 1860, and gave himself up for the most part to commercial law, in which he won distinction so rapidly that he was made Q.C. within twelve years after his entering into practice. He had always taken an interest in politics, and seemed from the first to be one of those members of the legal profession who are marked out for success in Parliamentary debate. In 1864 he stood for Durham as a Liberal candidate, was elected, and represented the same constituency for many successive years. He soon acquired a high reputation in the House as a clear and convincing speaker who never, like some of his profession, allowed the mere technicalities of a subject to perplex his faculty for comprehending it and expounding it from an outer point of view. He was at once fluent and impressive as a speaker, was effective in voice and in phrase, and was always listened to with the deepest attention by the House. In 1880 he was appointed Solicitor-General, an appointment which was received with great satisfaction on both sides of the House and by the profession and the public out-of-doors. At this time he had for his leader as Attorney-General Sir Henry James, afterwards Lord James of Hereford, and as Sir Henry was constant in his attendance at the House of Commons, and was one of the most brilliant debaters it possessed, Farrer Herschell was not called upon to be incessant in his attention to the work of the Administration in Parliament, and was enabled to give by far the greater part of his time to his own profession.

In that field he continued to rise, and before very long a great opportunity offered itself to him. When Mr. Gladstone came back to office in 1886, with his mind made up to a new and great stroke of policy, he offered to Farrer Herschell the position of Lord Chancellor. It was a surprising success for one who was still comparatively young to hold the highest rank which the legal profession can offer. It appeared, however, that neither Lord Selborne nor Sir Henry James, each of whom might be considered to have had a more immediate claim to the office, could accept Mr. Gladstone's views as to the next step to be taken for dealing with the Irish question, and neither could be expected to take an office, even one so neutral in its political tone as that of the Lord Chancellor, in a Government which was about to bring in a measure for the concession of Home Rule to Ireland. Mr. Gladstone at once offered the position to Farrer Herschell, by whom it was accepted. The new Administration, we need hardly remind our readers, did not last long. The House of Commons rejected Mr. Gladstone's measure, the Bill for his first Home Rule scheme, and the Liberal Government went out of office when Lord Herschell had occupied the Woolsack for only six months. A Conservative Government under Lord Salisbury came into power, and Lord Herschell became one of the most conspicuous and important figures on the Opposition side of the House. He opposed altogether the appointment of the Special Commission which the Conservative statesmen were demanding for the arraignment and the trial of Charles Stewart Parnell and his leading colleages on the charge of having incited to rebellion, assassination, and various other crimes against civil and moral law. Lord Herschell was not able to prevail upon the House of Lords to resist the demand of the Government, but he succeeded, by his cool judgment and lawyer-like skill, in obtaining some modifications in the terms of reference.

The work done by the House of Lords does not make much exaction on the time even of its most active members, and Lord Herschell was able to give himself up for the most part to his duties as a Law Lord of the Supreme Court of Appeal. Many of the judgments which he delivered were of great importance to the general community. The Liberal party again came into power in 1892, and Lord Herschell became Lord Chancellor for the second time. Mr. Gladstone brought in his second Home Rule measure, which was in many of its qualities a distinct advance on its predecessor, and it was carried through the House of Commons, but, as might have been expected, was thrown out by the House of Lords. This did not affect the existence of the Government, and Lord Herschell retained his position until 1895. Later on he was appointed President of the Anglo-American Commission, and then came the accident already mentioned which suddenly brought to a close a career that was still full of promise.

On the 12th of March 1899 Mary Keeley, who had been in her time one of the most successful and popular actresses in London, died at Brompton in her ninety-third year. Mrs. Keeley was the wife of Robert Keeley, who for many years was in his own peculiar line of comedy without a rival on the English stage. This happily associated pair might indeed have won for the period during which they held so high a place in comedy the distinctive title of the Keeley age. Their admirers used to compare them occasionally, and it was found that some maintained the superior qualities of the husband, and others proclaimed their partisanship for the wife. Mrs. Keeley won her great early celebrity as 'Jack Sheppard,' which was brought out in 1839; but the ruling authorities of that day appear to have been rather more strict in their notions as to feminine propriety than is the way of our more recent times, and the performance of the play was prohibited by the Lord Chamberlain. Mrs. Keeley was a singer as well as an actress, and no small part of her attractiveness was due to the admirable manner in which she sang the occasional ballads, mostly humorous, sometimes humorous with a dash of pathos in them, which belonged to many of the parts she performed. Her style as a comic actress had nothing of exaggeration in it, although she could keep her audience in peals of laughter from the opening to the close of the piece. It was broad comedy indeed, but it was the broad comedy of nature, and each character that she was rendering seemed to be merely moving and talking on the stage as such a person must have lived and moved and talked in the ordinary life of the world. Mrs. Keeley made her first appearance in London at the Lyceum in 1825, and she had the good sense and the dramatic instinct not to continue her theatrical performances after the time when she first began to feel that she was no longer qualified to play the old familiar parts in her early captivating way. She retired from the stage in 1859. She outlived her gifted husband by many years. The two daughters of the pair went on the stage, and one of them married Albert Smith, who was in his time one of the most popular authors in the lighter vein of comic fiction, and made a fortune for himself by his entertaining lecture delivered for season after season at the Egyptian Hall in Piccadilly on the ascent of Mont Blanc. The name of Keeley will always have a distinguished place in the history of the English stage.

William Baliol Brett, Viscount Esher, who died on the 24th of May in his eighty-fourth year, was an eminent lawyer who, although he entered the House of Commons, took a prominent place among the members of the Conservative party, and became one of the law officers to the Crown in a Conservative Administration, never made a great impression as a Parliamentary figure on the public mind, and is best remembered by his skill and success in his own profession. He was called to the bar in 1846 and soon came into large practice on the northern circuit, especially at Liverpool. On the death of Richard Cobden, Brett offered himself as a candidate for the vacant constituency of Rochdale in the interests of the Conservative party. This was thought at the time somewhat venturesome on the part of one who had previously been known only as a practising advocate, and it was believed that, if the Conservatives really hoped to defeat a Free Trade candidate in Cobden's own constituency, they ought to have brought forward some one who could offer a name better known to the electors in general. The result was what might have been foreseen — Brett was defeated by Cobden's old friend, T. B. Potter. In the year following this first failure Brett made another attempt to obtain a seat in the House of Commons, and this time with success. In 1868 he was appointed Solicitor-General in a Conservative Administration, and in that capacity he conducted for the Crown the prosecution of the Fenians, who were charged with having planned and accomplished the Clerkenwell explosion. While in the House of Commons he distinguished himself mainly by the promotion of measures which sought to improve the administration of law and justice. He was not destined to a long career in Parliament, for after a few years he was appointed to be a Justice of the Court of Common Pleas, and was afterwards elevated to the position of a Lord Justice. Seven years later he became Master of the Rolls in succession to Sir George Jessel, and at the close of 1897 he withdrew altogether from public life. The Queen then created him a Viscount, an unusual distinction conferred on any judge who has not been Lord Chancellor, and he took the title of Lord Esher.

On the 5th of July 1899 Richard Congreve, who had become famous as the leader of the Positivists in this country, and had borne the designation of Director of the Church of Humanity in England, died at Hampstead. Richard Congreve was educated at Rugby under Dr. Arnold, and at Wadham College, Oxford, of which he became Fellow. He afterwards entered as a student at King's College Hospital, London, and was admitted to the College of Physicians. He did not devote himself to the medical profession, for he had become in the meantime a disciple of Auguste Comte, the great French philosopher of Positivism, and he may be said to have founded the school of positive philosophy in this country. That school had for a time a deep influence over a certain class of intellectual men and women in England, and indeed it was not possible to go into intellectual society anywhere without finding some of Congreve's followers eager to advocate his doctrines. The number of these disciples made up but a small proportion of our

educated population, and could hardly be said to
have found any representation among other sections,
but they were all of them devoted to their principles, and were for the most part well qualified
to maintain them by ingenious and even philosophical argument. Richard Congreve was, as might
be imagined, a profound student and he was a
translator of Aristotle.

Thomas Henry Farrer—Lord Farrer—who died
on October 11, at the age of eighty, was a man
who had exercised a very strong, although a quiet,
influence over the public opinion of his time.
Farrer was the son of a solicitor, was educated at
Eton and Oxford, and was called to the Bar in
1844. He soon discovered that he had no taste
for the legal profession, and gave up all effort to
acquire distinction in it. In 1857 he received an
appointment as Assistant Secretary to the Marine
Department of the Board of Trade, and in 1862
he became Permanent Secretary. In 1883 he was
created a baronet, and ten years after was raised
to the peerage as Lord Farrer. He had retired
from office some years before he was made a
member of the House of Lords, and had given up
much of his time to the work of the London County
Council, of which he was elected an alderman. He
withdrew before long from his membership of the
County Council, chiefly for the reason that his
somewhat rigid principles of political economy did
not always harmonise with the views of his colleagues belonging to the Progressive party, who

were inclined to take a bold and expansive responsibility in shaping and carrying out plans of improvement which might cope with the growth of poverty, and the lack of continuous employment for those of the poor who would work if they could. Lord Farrer, although he withdrew from official life of every kind, did not give himself up to mere rest and recreation. He was a leading and active member of the Cobden Club and of the Political Economy Club. He published many valuable letters maintaining the principles of Free Trade against the sort of reactionary movement which had set in, a movement commending Protection to the public under the plausible title of Fair Trade. Lord Farrer was an uncompromising champion of the genuine doctrines of Free Trade, and there was a calm, unsparing force in his logic, the effect of which is not exhausted or unneeded at the present hour.

Lord Penzance, an eminent, although not a brilliant, advocate, a thoughtful and sagacious judge, died on the 9th of December. James Plaister Wilde, whom later days knew as Lord Penzance, was the son of a solicitor, and a nephew of the first Lord Truro, who became Lord Chief Justice and afterwards Lord Chancellor. Young Wilde therefore had good influence to support him when, after his education at Winchester and Cambridge, he was called to the Bar in 1839. The fact that he came of a distinguished legal family may have had something to do with his early advance in his profession, but it soon became evident that he had capacity of his own which must have secured for him a large practice and the ear of the courts under whatever conditions. Like many other young and rising lawyers, he was taken at one time with an ambition to enter the House of Commons. He offered himself as a Liberal candidate for Lancaster in 1852, but was defeated at the poll, and when he made another attempt at Peterborough some five years later he was equally unsuccessful. Then he seems to have given up the idea, and settled down to his career in the courts of law. He established a high reputation for steady work, for keen insight into complicated details and perplexed questions. In 1860 he was raised to the judicial bench as a Baron of the Exchequer. Three years afterwards he succeeded Sir C. Cresswell as Judge-in-Ordinary of the Probate and Divorce Court. The strain imposed upon him by the incessant work of this much frequented court proved too great for his health, which had never been robust, and in 1872 he retired altogether from the judicial bench. He had before this time received the recognition of the Crown for his services, by being made a peer, and after his withdrawal from regular judicial work he sometimes sat in the Court of Appeal in the House of Lords. Lord Penzance did not withdraw from the service of the public when he resigned his regular official functions as a judge of the Probate and Divorce Court. His mind was too energetic and his interest in judicial questions was too great to make a life of repose congenial with his temperament, and under the Public Worship Regulation Act he became Official Principal of the Court of Arches, Canterbury, and of the Chancery Court of York. Lord Penzance was, in his time, an active and influential member of many Royal Commissions. He took part in courts of inquiry instituted by the Government into the system of judicature, the laws relating to marriage, the regulations of public worship, the purchase of army commissions, the practices of the Stock Exchange, and many other subjects of pressing public interest. He was one of the fortunate men who seem to have found a career exactly suited to their temperament and their best capacities, and to have been fairly rewarded for their willing services.

The death of the Duke of Westminster, on December 22, is an event which might call for historical record from more than one point of view. To begin with, Hugh Lupus Grosvenor, Earl Grosvenor, was the first Duke of Westminster known to the peerage of England. In the second place, during his Parliamentary career he succeeded in throwing out a great measure of reform introduced by Earl Russell, and he helped in forming that secession from the Liberal party which was described by John Bright as sheltering itself in the Cave of Adullam. Furthermore, he was one of the most active and liberal patrons of the turf during his time. He might have been entitled, if he were so inclined, to claim at a later date the approval of the advanced Liberals themselves by pointing out that the defeat of Lord Russell's reform measure had enabled the Conservative party to come into power, and to carry a much larger measure of reform than that which they had unseated the Liberals for endeavouring to introduce. The future Duke of Westminster was much too straightforward a man to find any inclination for such ingenious devices, and he left his action in that and other political struggles to speak for itself. His separation from the Liberal party was not final. When on the death of his father he passed into the House of Lords, he gave a general support to the Liberals, and it was on Mr. Gladstone's recommendation that he obtained from the Queen the title of Duke of Westminster. Later on, when Mr. Gladstone introduced his first measure of Home Rule, the Duke of Westminster once again seceded from the Liberal party, and joined that political section who have since been known as Liberal Unionists. If the Liberal Unionists had been described as retiring to another Cave of Adullam, the Duke of Westminster would have had the satisfaction of knowing that the man who applied that epithet to the former secession was now himself seeking shelter in the new cavern. The Duke of Westminster's political pursuits were only incidents in his career, and he will probably be best remembered as the hereditary owner of immense estates who did much to help his tenantry in the improvement of their condition, as an indefatigable sportsman, and an enthusiastic supporter of the racecourse.

Sir James Paget, who died on the 30th of December, was one of the most distinguished members of the medical profession during the greater part of Queen Victoria's reign. He was born in 1814, and, like his elder brother, showed from his boyish days a distinct inclination and aptitude for the study of medical and surgical subjects. James Paget soon distinguished himself in his career, and became widely known as an instructor by lectures and writings in surgical pathology. Indeed, he may be said to have been, during his time, unrivalled among his English brethren in pathology. Although he did not devote himself to efforts after original discovery, either in physiology or in surgery, he was always able by his luminous expositions and his keen insight to turn to the best possible account, for the benefit of medical and surgical science and of the world in general, every addition newly made to human skill and knowledge in the treatment of disease. Distinctions and honours of all kinds were showered upon him from abroad as well as at home. He was appointed Sergeant-Surgeon to the Queen and Surgeon to the Prince of Wales, was a member of the Institute of France, and in 1871 was made a baronet. He lived to a good old age, even for days like ours when to pass the eightieth birthday is regarded as but an ordinary achievement, and he was during most of his life an unsparing worker. Some few years before his death he found his health somewhat impaired by his long labours, and withdrew into a well-earned retirement, during which he quietly passed away from life.

CHAPTER XVII.

THE COMING SOUTH AFRICAN WAR.

MEANWHILE events of much significance were casting shadows before on the condition of the States in South Africa. Paul Kruger had been elected once again President of the Republic. He was elected by an immense majority. On the 12th of May 1898 the President took the oath of office at Pretoria. On the same day he addressed a large gathering composed of members of the Assembly and others, and in the course of his speech he declared that the Outlanders were very welcome in the Transvaal State, and that so long as they obeyed the laws of the State there could be no wish whatever to urge their departure from it. Shortly after this event President Steyn, of the Orange Free State, was entertained at a banquet by President Kruger, and in replying to the toast of his health he gave it as his opinion that the proposal for the formation of the South African States into one union or federation was not practical for the reason that the Republican States could only join in such a confederacy if it were worked on republican principles, while he assumed that the British colonists would only accept a place in it if it were worked on the lines of the Imperial system.

These words illustrated fairly enough the main difficulties with which South Africa had to contend. It was quite certain that the British colonist would never agree to any terms of union which might make him liable to become or even to be regarded as dependent on the policy of President Kruger and his allies. It was equally certain that the Dutch inhabitants of the Transvaal had only accepted the suzerainty of Great Britain on compulsion. From the beginning, the settlement agreed upon after Majuba Hill had been accepted in a very limited sense, and after open declarations from President Kruger that the suzerainty was understood to apply only to the dealings of the Transvaal Republic with foreign States and not to their relations with the Sovereign of Great Britain. The Orange Free State had already come to be regarded as a close ally of the Transvaal, and any one now looking back at the story of the later events can see that this alliance would have to be faced if any effort were to be made to establish, in fact, the sovereignty of the British Empire. It might have been quite clear also to any observer, even at the time, that the states or communities which may be described as British would never remain content with an arrangement bringing them and their interests to any degree into a position of subserviency to the policy of the two Republics. President Kruger on more than one occasion expressed his willingness to do all in his power for the maintenance and promotion of the interests represented by the mining companies, but the most ordinary observer might well have seen that the mining companies had purposes which could hardly be made consistent with the policy of the two Republics. There was indeed an obvious antagonism between the objects of the British companies and those of the two Republics from the very beginning of the controversy. The existence of the gold mines was the main source of this antagonism. The Transvaal Republic had been founded by men who made their home in that part of South Africa chiefly for the reason that they desired and hoped to be free from all European complications.

The discovery of the gold mines had brought into South Africa a positive rush of adventurous immigrants from various parts of the world, more especially from England and from British territories, whose principal object was to make themselves the absolute owners of all that vast tract of country which was found to be teeming with limitless sources of wealth. As to the moral principle governing either side of the controversy, it is not now necessary to enter into much discussion. The Transvaal immigrants had, unquestionably, a perfect right to seek out a home for themselves in a territory they believed at the time would be left to their undisputed occupation. On the other hand, it is always regarded as the clear right of adventurous treasure-seekers to pour into any new country where gold has suddenly been discovered and to make a settlement there if they have the means to maintain it. At the time when the discovery of gold in California was made, the world saw a rush of treasure-seekers from all countries who settled on the land with the purpose of making fortunes for themselves. If the American Republic had not been powerful and united, it would be hard to say what troubles might not have been brought on that part of the Western world, or what changes might not have been forced upon its governing system, by this flood of bold and capable immigrants who would naturally desire to find an abiding home in that wealthy region and to rule it according to their own interests. But the United States were too strong and too firm of purpose to allow of any innovations dangerous to their own internal supremacy, and the discovery of the Californian gold mines involved nothing more than the irruption of an immense number of foreign settlers. In South Africa the condition of things was very different. The established Republics were by no means strong enough to secure themselves against the internal disturbances to be expected from such an invasion. The invaders may not have had in the beginning any intention or even desire to make themselves the rulers of the whole region, yet it soon became evident, as was to be foreseen, that they would endeavour to sweep away from their path any obstacles the existing systems might set up against the accomplishment of the policy which they believed it was their interest to demand. A distinct antagonism was therefore foreshadowed from the opening of this chapter of history. The rulers and people of the Transvaal Republic were determined, so far as they could, to hold their own and to manage their State according to their own ideas. The newcomers were equally determined to obtain for themselves full opportunities of securing a free way for the promotion of the principal objects which they had in view when they sought for a settlement in South Africa.

The question immediately at issue was that which arose between the Government of the Transvaal and the foreign settlers who were making a home in that region. The settlers may be described as the Outlanders, the Anglicised version of the Dutch name of Uitlanders given to them by the population who had elected Paul Kruger to be their President. The Outlanders claimed the right to be admitted at once as citizens of the Republic and to have a voice and vote in the direction of its affairs. These demands were resisted by the Government of the Republic. Now it is certain that if the foreign settlers in California to whom we have already referred had made such demands upon the Government of the American Republic, their appeal could only have been granted on the regular conditions precedent to the admission of foreign settlers to the full rights of citizenship in any one of the United States. Among these qualifications the foremost was a term of so many years' residence in the State, and that condition would have to be accepted, no matter how blameless might have been the character and the demeanour of those who thus sought to become regular citizens. There again comes in the difference we have already pointed out between the situation of the foreign settlers in California and that of the foreign settlers in the South African Republic. Every foreign Government knew well enough that there would be no chance of forcing on the United States an immediate admission of those strangers to the privileges of citizenship, but so far as the South African Republic was concerned it seemed probable enough that a vigorous demand, supported by the authority and influence of the British Government, might prevail upon or coerce President Kruger into a prompt recognition of the foreign claim. There were many men of great ability and influence among the Outlanders who were well qualified to conduct an effective agitation for that purpose, and a very formidable movement was promptly organised for its accomplishment. This agitation was somewhat disturbed, for the time, by Dr. Jameson's invasion, the story of which has been told in a preceding volume. The invasion having proved a failure, a new chapter in the history was opened and fresh negotiations were begun, but the Transvaal Republic did not seem in the least degree moved towards any prompt concessions in favour of the strangers who had settled within its boundaries.

Meanwhile the Transvaal and the other South African States had much trouble with the native tribes here and there, and were distracted by the frequent necessity of taking arms to suppress the attempts of their enemies. During all this time the various civilised States had been making rapid and surprising advances in the opening up of the surrounding region, and in the application to this very new world of all the recognised scientific instruments of modern civilisation. Railways had been opened in every direction, and lines of telegraph connecting the rising cities with each other had passed over vast spaces previously given up wholly to the desert and to the natural man. There was a sort of rivalry among all the South African States in the civilising of the regions lying around and between them and the conversion of the African waste into something like European or American civilisation. It is impossible not to feel both wonder and regret that the rulers of peoples thus energetic and so far successful in the development of the country could not have come to any common agreement as to the best means of bringing out its resources, and maintaining a good understanding among themselves respecting the forms of Government which each colony regarded as best suited to its own interests and its own form of life. Here it is plain there were faults on both sides, and faults which might naturally have been expected to display themselves under such conditions. Lord Rosmead had done his best before leaving South Africa to bring about mutual conciliation and agreement, but he had not been able during his term of office to carry out his wishes to any practical or even promising extent.

Sir Alfred Milner was appointed to succeed Lord Rosmead as Governor of Cape Colony and High Commissioner for South Africa, and the appointment was welcomed with much gratification by all the British settlers in that region and by English public opinion at home. Sir Alfred Milner was undoubtedly a man of great ability and energy, who had proved his possession of these qualities during the appointments he had held in Egypt under the British Government. Whatever differences of opinion may then have existed or may even still exist as to the effects of his forward policy in South Africa, it cannot be doubted that he was emphatically one of the men who are destined to become makers of history. His ambition, and from his point of view it was a patriotic ambition, was to make the influence of his Government and his country supreme in South Africa. The Outlanders regarded him from the first as the man to whose leadership they could safely confide their demand to be allowed a free and effective share in the government of the State to the development of which they were devoting their energies. But it is beyond dispute that even at home in England there were statesmen and large sections of the public who considered the Outlanders as, for the most part, a body of enterprising capitalists who desired to become owners of gold and diamond mines and thus to 'run' that part of South Africa for their own advantage. Here, then, we have the main source of the antagonism which was set up, and we see before us the two sides of the dispute. Sir Alfred Milner was looked upon by the Dutch populations of the Transvaal as their natural enemy sent over by the Government of England to maintain the cause and enforce the claims of the Outlanders.

The question of franchise in the Transvaal became a primary object of negotiation. President Kruger had succeeded in passing a law requiring a seven years' prospective and retrospective residence as the condition necessary for the admission of Outlanders to the privilege of voting as citizens of the Republic, and these conditions were regarded as altogether unsatisfactory by Sir Alfred Milner, by Mr. Chamberlain, the Colonial Secretary, and by the Government at home. It is not necessary to say that in every State there are conditions for the admission of foreign settlers to the rights of citizenship, one of which is a certain term of residence in the State where they desire to make a settlement. We have some such conditions here in England, and it is hardly possible to see how any civilised State could hope to get on satisfactorily if every foreign immigrant were at once allowed to become a citizen with the full right of voting. In the United States the ordinary conditions are a six years' term of residence preliminary to obtaining the right to vote, unless in the rare instances where some distinguished foreigner, who has already rendered actual service to the Republic, may be endowed by the President with the privilege of citizenship and the right at once to exercise the franchise. President Kruger's terms were unquestionably severe and exclusive, and it is not to be wondered at if Sir Alfred Milner and his Government regarded them as excessive and even as offensive. At one period of the negotiations Kruger showed his willingness to make some reductions in his terms, and a meeting took place between him and Sir Alfred Milner at Bloemfontein at the close of May 1899. There were, indeed, other grievances alleged by the Outlanders as well as that represented by the voting system, but the voting system was the most important question which the President and Sir Alfred Milner had to discuss, and it was soon found that President Kruger was not inclined to make any satisfactory or abiding concessions on that point.

The Peace Congress established at the Hague

was then holding a session, and many observers in Europe and in South Africa were beginning to entertain a hope that such a time might be auspicious for a peaceful and enduring settlement between the Transvaal Government and the Outlanders. These hopes, however, were doomed to disappointment. President Kruger did not seem disposed to make any concession as to the right of voting which Sir Alfred Milner would have been likely to accept, and there were also serious difficulties on other points of the controversy. There was, for instance, the question which may be said to have come up with the formation of the Peace Congress—the proposal that all disputes between the British Government and the Transvaal should be settled by arbitration. Here, again, an irreconcilable difference of opinion arose. President Kruger took it as his position that all differences between England and the Transvaal must be submitted for settlement to the arbitration of some foreign State and not to Great Britain. Sir Alfred Milner refused to accept any principle of arbitration between an independent and a dependent State. In other words, he refused to admit that the Transvaal could claim the right of arbitration when a difference of opinion arose between it and the Government of Great Britain. We may assume that, according to his theory, the Transvaal had no more right to appeal to arbitration for the settlement of any controversy between her and England than an English county would have to invite arbitration if some Act of Parliament were about to be passed which that particular county regarded as prejudicial to its local interests. The position of Sir Alfred Milner was one which brought him into sharp antagonism with Kruger, who had always insisted that the suzerainty of England could be exercised over the Transvaal only with regard to the dealings of the Transvaal with foreign States. Sir Alfred Milner told President Kruger that the British Government would never consent to submit any question between England and the Transvaal to the arbitration of a foreign power.

The whole controversy was beginning to arouse much attention in England, and while the negotiations were still going on, some questions were put to the Colonial Secretary in the House of Commons as to the probability of a satisfactory settlement. Nothing definite could be stated at that time, but in a day or two afterwards Mr. Chamberlain was able to announce that the conference at Bloemfontein had broken up without hope of agreement, and that the Government had therefore an entirely new state of things to take into consideration. Mr. Chamberlain's announcement referred almost exclusively to the negotiations on the subject of the franchise, and the possibility of mediation between the British Government and the Transvaal. There were listeners in the House of Commons who could not help thinking at the time that the difference as to the terms of franchise was hardly great enough to justify a serious rupture between England and the South African Republic. Mr. Chamberlain laid especial emphasis on the contrast between the conditions of naturalisation offered to foreigners by England and the conditions which President Kruger still insisted on for the right of foreigners to vote in the Transvaal. Yet the very emphasis put upon this contrast seemed to many minds only to invite attention to the comparative insignificance of the difference between the terms of naturalisation which we ourselves put in practice and the terms which enlightened human beings could not possibly accept. Mr. Chamberlain explained that a foreigner coming to settle in the British Islands could be naturalised after a residence of five years, and could actually exercise the franchise in six months from that time. This seems a very reasonable arrangement, but President Kruger's proposal with regard to the Transvaal was that immigrants who had arrived in that region before 1899 should have to wait for two years and a half from the passing of the Act and later immigrants for five years, and that for all settlers in the future a settlement of seven years should be necessary to qualify them for a vote. Undoubtedly this was a hard condition to impose on the foreigner, but still the difference between a period of five years and a period of seven is hardly a difference impossible to deal with by some manner of compromise, and it does not seem worth a war and a conquest to secure an earlier voting right for the settler from abroad.

There were many other questions to be settled, involving, among other things, the working and interests of the mining companies, but into these it is not necessary now to enter more fully. The whole dispute was involved in the desire of the Outlanders to obtain a controlling power over the working of the Transvaal Republic, and the desire of the Dutch population to keep them as far as possible from obtaining any such control. Each of the conflicting purposes may be easily understood and is capable of obtaining ingenious and effective argument from its own point of view. The Dutch settlers who had sought out that particular region for themselves, and had created the Transvaal Republic for their own purposes, naturally wished to hold in their own hands the supreme management of the State which they had founded. On their side the foreign settlers who had come into the country to develop its mining resources for their own interests were just as naturally anxious that as their numbers increased their power of controlling the affairs of the State should increase in due proportion. The Outlanders might count with certainty that before long their numbers would far exceed those of the Dutch residents, and it cannot be denied that this foreign population would include a large number of men well qualified by intelligence and experience to manage the affairs of a State.

It may be taken for granted that there never was a civilised community long settled in some region which they had themselves selected as most suitable for their interests who would willingly consent to the admission of an overwhelming number of foreign immigrants to the full rights of immediate citizenship. As the question was put before the public of England by the advocates of the immigrants, it appeared merely to be an occasion in which British patriotism was called upon to sustain the claims of free and enlightened British immigrants against the selfish and exclusive policy of a small Dutch oligarchy. An overwhelming enthusiasm was easily aroused in England on the side of the Britons who were anxious to extend the influence and the power of England over a State already declared to be under British suzerainty. It soon became in the minds of the majority at home a question of the extension of the British Empire over the whole of South Africa.

At this time the great Imperialistic doctrine had already come to be a controlling power in our political life. There were two parties, of whom the Imperialists formed by far the more numerous and influential division. The other party was described by its opponents by the contemptuous nickname of 'Little Englanders.'

The Little Englander was characterised as a narrow-minded and unpatriotic personage, who had no soul for the extension of the British Empire, who would have been content that England should remain one of the smallest Powers amongst civilised States if only the Little Englander could thereby be enabled to eat his meals in peace, and to carry on his own business without having to pay increased taxes for the sake of spreading the Empire. A sort of reaction had set in against the doctrine once preached with so much effect by Cobden and Bright, and the true test of patriotism was regarded by a large proportion of our voters as the heroic passion for an extension of the Empire here, there, and everywhere. It may freely be admitted that some of the Little Englanders, on the other hand, persisted in arguing that the enthusiasm for British supremacy in South Africa was merely the desire of the mining capitalists to obtain an uncontrolled possession of the territory where gold and diamond mines had lately been discovered and were abundant. Some of the most sincere, most gifted, and most distinguished among English public men were branded openly by their opponents as Little Englanders, while some men on the other side who were undoubtedly filled with what seemed to them a purely patriotic emotion, and who never sought extension of Empire only for the sake of making money, were denounced by their antagonists as selfish adventurers who sought to extend the Empire for the getting of gold and diamonds.

By the general public the ethical bearings of the whole controversy were soon put out of sight in the growing fervour of the dispute. President Kruger would unquestionably have behaved with greater wisdom if he had shown any real wish to accept a fair compromise in a dispute through which he could not possibly hold the position he had taken up on his re-election to the highest office in the Transvaal State. It cannot be denied that he followed an undecided and a wavering course, sometimes appearing to hold out concessions from which he afterwards suddenly drew back, and thus giving to his opponents a plausible justification when they insisted that he was a man with whom it was not possible to come to any definite understanding. Sir Alfred Milner, in one of his despatches home, described the case for intervention on the part of the British Government as absolutely overwhelming. He denied that there was any foundation for the happy-go-lucky belief that things would come out all right in time if left to settle themselves. 'The spectacle,' he said, 'of thousands of British subjects kept permanently in the position of helots, constantly chafing under undoubted grievances, and calling vainly on Her Majesty's Government for redress, does steadily undermine the influence and reputation of Great Britain and the respect for the British Government within the Queen's dominions.'

The Outlanders addressed a petition to the Queen on the subject of their grievances, and Mr. Chamberlain wrote a despatch in reference to that petition in which he said that Her Majesty's Ministers, while most unwilling to depart from their attitude of reserve and expectancy, yet, 'Having regard to the position of Great Britain as the paramount Power and the duty incumbent upon them to protect all British subjects residing in a foreign country, they cannot permanently ignore the exceptional and arbitrary treatment to which their fellow-countrymen and others are exposed, and the absolute indifference of the Government of the Republic to the friendly representations which have been made to them on the subject.' In his despatch Mr. Chamberlain seems to have felt it incumbent upon him to protest against any unsatisfactory inferences which might have been drawn from his emphatic assertion of Great Britain's paramount power. He declared that the Government were most anxious to avoid actual intervention if possible, and were sincerely desirous to maintain the independence of the Transvaal Republic, adding the suggestive words that if the English Government had wished for the overthrow of the Republic they would certainly not have advised and urged the authorities of the Republic to satisfy the legitimate demands of the Outlanders, a course which, if taken, could have had no other result than that of greatly increasing the stability of the Transvaal State.

It may be assumed as an established fact in the history of the whole dispute that there were some hardships inflicted on British subjects in the Transvaal, either by the direct power of the Dutch executive or by the undue partiality shown on the part of that executive when dealing with questions under dispute. In an ordinary controversy between two States with regard to the treatment of foreign immigrants some such incidents would always be likely to arise, but there ought not to be, and in most cases would not be, any serious difficulty in arriving at an understanding and a satisfactory settlement. In the case of the disputes between the English Government standing up for the Outlanders and President Kruger maintaining what he declared to be the rights of the Transvaal, the difficulties in the way of a peaceful arrangement were immensely aggravated by the fact that each disputant fully believed the other to have a thoroughly hostile purpose in his mind. The British Government evidently acted to a great extent on the assumption that the Transvaal authorities were determined to treat English settlers as inferiors having no rights of citizenship, and to reduce them, if possible, to a condition of serfdom. On their side, Kruger and his supporters were firmly convinced that the one great and settled object of the British Government was to put an end to the independence of the Transvaal, and to make it the subject and the serf of the British Empire. A dispute between two States beginning under such conditions as these is not likely to be brought to anything like a satisfactory arrangement. Any part of the controversy studied now by an unconcerned observer might seem easily capable of a practical and peaceful arrangement. But the feelings we have described soon began to render this particular dispute insoluble by any arbitration save that of military force.

Early in September the Transvaal Government finally withdrew its somewhat qualified proposal for a five years' term of franchise as a condition precedent to the naturalisation of the Outlanders, and returned to President Kruger's former stipulation for a residence of seven years. Then the Colonial Office issued a formal despatch demanding a five years' franchise, a proportion of representation for the gold fields, and the full equality of English and Dutch in the Transvaal Parliament. At last the Transvaal Government sent in an ultimatum announcing its definite terms, offering to submit to arbitration under the conditions suggested in former despatches, calling for the withdrawal of British troops from all places on the borders of the Republic, the withdrawal to be accomplished within a certain defined limit of time, and giving only a few days for England's reply. This was an ultimatum concerning the acceptance of which President Kruger could have had no possible hope. It was evident that the President regarded the negotiations as being at an end, and had indeed no serious wish that the dispute should come to a peaceful settlement. Boer troops had already been massed along the frontier in considerable numbers. The Outlanders had begun to quit the Transvaal territory; the Boer Government had gone so far as to stop some of the trains leaving the State and to send their passengers back to the place whence they had come, in one instance confiscating to the State a large quantity of gold belonging to Outlander mining capitalists. There was clearly an end to all negotiation, and the reply of the British Government to the Boer ultimatum, a reply declaring that the terms of President Kruger were such as could not possibly be discussed, was merely a matter of form. On the 12th of October 1899 war was declared.

The proclamation of war created no surprise anywhere. At home and abroad it had been thoroughly understood for some time that there could be no peaceful issue to the formal negotiations, and the general impression among most Englishmen was that war had already begun. The result of the futile attempts to secure a pacific settlement was hailed with almost unmingled enthusiasm by the Imperialists in England. The general impression amongst these was that the war would be very short, not very sharp, and promptly decisive. Here, as the events soon began to prove, the general opinion of the Imperialists was formed without a close study of the facts which gave the Boers a good chance of holding out for a length of time, and, with a want of appreciation of the history and the character of the Dutch people. An English writer suggested, in satirical terms but with much reason on his side, that before the English Government decided absolutely on war each member of the Cabinet should be required to prove that he had thoroughly mastered the contents of Schiller's 'Revolt of the Netherlands' and Motley's 'History of the Dutch Republic.' Certainly if the British Cabinet had studied carefully the story told in these two great books they must have seen that the citizens of the Transvaal Republic were not men who could be readily brought to submission by any foreign power, no matter how vastly superior in strength, in resources, and in military organisation. The Dutch Boers were descended from the race who held out so long against Spain, and had also an admixture of French Huguenot ancestry — an admixture not suggestive of ready submission to superior force. At a time when Spain was probably the greatest military Power in the world, the Dutch of the Netherlands had held out for more than seventy years against her determined efforts to crush them into submission, and it is one of the certain facts of history that the Dutch had then made up their minds, if there should be no other way of bringing the war to an end, to break down the barriers they had raised to keep out the waves from flooding their land, and thus surrender their whole territory to the sea rather than to Spanish rule. Nothing that had been done in recent days had given evidence to make men believe that the Dutch of the Transvaal had degenerated from the characteristic qualities of their ancestors.

It is easy to understand that most Englishmen felt sure the war must end in victory for England if only England resolved to carry it on with unceasing vigour for a time long enough to exhaust all remaining possibilities of Dutch resistance. But if the English Government had studied historical facts carefully they must have come to the conclusion that the war would involve a severe and prolonged struggle; that the preparations for carrying it on must be made upon a large scale, and that the greatest display of military power the British Empire could afford must be brought into operation from the beginning of the campaign. There could be no possible comparison between the military resources of the Dutch Republic and those of the British Empire, but England had to contend against a foe who would not give in until all its means of resistance had been exhausted, and in the dearest interests of ultimate peace and of humanity, the first duty of British statesmanship was, in these conditions, to put its best foot foremost at the very opening of the war. This was exactly what the British statesmanship of the time did not exert itself to accomplish. Most of the men in power seemed to be under the impression that they had only to show themselves resolved to carry on the war in order to make the Transvaal population feel that its wisest course would be immediate submission. Apart from all resolve and courage, even rash and reckless courage, on the part of the Dutch Boers, it is clear that England was placed at great disadvantage for the carrying on of the struggle under whatever conditions. A vast extent of land and sea, of mountain and waste, lay between England and the scene of the warlike operations in South Africa. The Dutch fighting force amounted only to some thirty thousand men, which would have seemed a small resisting power to put in the way of a British army, but at the time when war began to be inevitable the British Government had only a very small body of soldiers in the neighbourhood of the Transvaal, and every reinforcement had to come from some distant part of the Empire.

These facts should have been obvious to every English statesman, and if they had been considered in their relation to the condition and character of the Dutch Boers, the necessary result would have been to impress British statesmanship with the urgent need for making the promptest and fullest preparations to encounter a desperate resistance. But the English statesmen then in office seemed to have taken no account of the enemy with whom they had to fight. We might go farther than this, and say that where they took any account of their opponents it was an entirely mistaken and wrong account. English statesmanship—that is, official statesmanship—appears to have made up its mind that the Dutch Boers were not capable of offering a prolonged resistance, and that the first appearance of an armed and disciplined force on the Transvaal frontier would be enough to bring President Kruger and his colleagues to a proper sense of their situation and the necessity of making peace at any price. The fact that such an impression did prevail among English statesmen is all the more strange and the more difficult to understand when we remember that only a very short time before the Boers had shown at Majuba Hill that in fighting capacity they were not unworthy of their heroic Dutch ancestors. Yet no possible explanation can be found for the easy-going and careless way in which the preparations were made for carrying on this new Dutch war other than the assumption that the English statesmen in office undervalued their enemy and believed they could take their own time and their own way for bringing him to submission.

We can all well remember the confident

feeling which then prevailed among the majority of Englishmen at home as to the absurdity of the Boers in attempting resistance to the British invasion, the comfortable assurance that we need not trouble our minds much about the difficulties of the hour, and the still more comforting conviction that the Boers would find out the folly of their conduct, and would make humble submission when they saw that England was determined to go to war. During all this time there was a considerable minority of Englishmen who took an entirely different view, not only of the resistance England must have to encounter and of the resources which she must require in order to obtain an early and complete success, but as to the whole character and principles of the policy which had led England into such a war. There were many eminent Englishmen, in the political world and outside it, who believed and maintained that England's policy of war in this particular instance was founded on no just principle; that the grievances alleged by the Outlanders were no greater than the ordinary disadvantages and disqualifications which come in the way of a mass of foreign immigrants who endeavour for their own purposes and their own advantages to make a settlement in a country where nobody wants them, and where the general inclination of the settled inhabitants is that the country should be kept as free as possible from any foreign incursion. The Englishmen who held these views, and who expressed them in Parliament, on the public platform, and in letters and articles for the Press, were not able to offer much resistance to the flowing tide of public opinion.

The general feeling of the nation was undoubtedly in favour of the war, and the statesmen in office were little inclined to think seriously of anything but the fact that the war was popular, and that those who had to conduct it were therefore certain of at least a present popularity. There was no time to waste in considering the case of the Boers or even pausing to inquire whether the Boer Government could have any case against an English Administration. No doubt there is always some feeling of this kind at the opening of every war, and, when the war has a just and righteous principle to support it, the leaders of the Administration may be excused if they think of little but the advantage to be gained by seizing the opportunity and constituting themselves the heads of a national and an Imperial movement. But in the case of the Boer War there was a more general enthusiasm than usual in support of the promptest measures to put an end to the interval of negotiations and to seek the arbitrament of the battle-field. The very name of Boer became for the time at many an English public meeting, and in many an English newspaper, the synonym for all that was base and cruel, mean and dirty, and even cowardly.

In a recent number of *The Nineteenth Century and After*, an article by Sir Henry Drummond Wolff appeared, entitled 'Some Maxims of the late Lord Dalling and Bulwer.' One of these maxims might now well be regarded as having an especial bearing on the mood of the English public at the opening of the South African War, although no such application could have been in the mind of Lord Dalling, who died many years before the war began. The maxim is—'We have never won a complete victory when we have not gained the good-will of those we have subdued.' Assuredly in all the fervour of British enthusiasm at the opening of this war there was very little hope or thought of our gaining the good-will of those whom we felt sure we were about to subdue. There was just as little thought in the minds at least of our official leaders concerning the most effective means of putting forth our full strength in the most effective way in order to entail the least amount of loss and of suffering on our own side as well as on the side of those whom we had constituted our enemies and whom we were pledging ourselves to subdue. Under these conditions the war began, and the era of negotiations, which were never seriously meant to come to anything, had drawn to its close.

CHAPTER XVIII.

THE WAR IN SOUTH AFRICA.

ONCE again England was entering on what must be described as a thoroughly popular war. A long time had passed since that description could be given to any war at its opening which English statesmanship had voluntarily undertaken to carry on. An Empire like Great Britain, with territory in all parts of the world, is not likely to have prolonged intervals of peace throughout the whole of her various and widely-spread dominions. But it seldom happens that the British public feel any enthusiasm about a remote war in its opening chapters. It may be said with confidence that to the British public at home little or nothing is known about one of those far-off wars until the struggle has gone on for some time and forced itself on the notice of London and the provinces. In some of these instances the English people in general suddenly wake up to the knowledge that a war is going on in some far-off Asiatic or African region where British troops are fighting against heavy odds and displaying splendid courage and discipline. Then a national sympathy is instantly aroused, and the Englishman at home rushes for his newspaper every morning and every evening in the hope of hearing that the soldiers of his country have succeeded in driving back some new attack of their opponents. In the mood aroused by such events it is natural that the Englishman should not, in the first instance, stop to consider the merits of the question at issue between the combatants, and that when he does consider them he should approach the whole subject with every desire and hope to find that his countrymen were thoroughly in the right. Thus it has often happened during late years that some enterprise is undertaken, or perhaps has to be undertaken, by British forces in Asia or Africa, about the purpose of which and the preparations for which the general public in England knew little until the conflict had begun. Some of these warlike enterprises thus suddenly started had afterwards become thoroughly popular with Englishmen at home, merely because of the gallantry with which they had been carried on and the courage and perseverance which had been shown by England's soldiers in the presence of tremendous difficulties caused by the climate as well as by the enemy. Under such conditions it becomes easy enough for the English public to persuade itself that the policy of the British statesmen who undertook the war was in every sense patriotic and just. Along the frontiers of British

India and in far outlying territories there is almost always some warlike expedition going on of which the British public at large knows nothing whatever at the beginning.

But the conditions were entirely different in the case of the South African War. The attention of the public had long been fixed on the conflict of opposing interests in the neighbourhood of Cape Colony. There had been already a fierce struggle between the British forces and the Transvaal Republic, and the story of Majuba Hill had filled a large number of Englishmen with a longing for a national revenge on the audacious Boers. Even many serious-minded and deeply thinking Englishmen were convinced that no satisfactory settlement ever could be brought about in South Africa until the English public should have satisfied its desire to efface the memory of Majuba Hill. Indeed this would not be too much to say of the great majority of Englishmen. Many amongst those who most earnestly wished for peace and believed that peace with honour could still be maintained between Great Britain and the Dutch Republic, if only there were on both sides a sincere desire for peace, were of the opinion that under all the circumstances war was inevitable. Some among those most strongly opposed to a renewal of hostilities were willing to admit that as a war must take place the sooner it began the sooner it could be brought to an end. But there were not many who did not feel assured that the whole struggle would be short, sharp, and decisive. The war therefore began with the full approval of the great majority in England, and no one who was not in the secret counsels of the War Office could have known how ineffective and insufficient were the preparations made by the Administration to carry it on to a quick success.

We shall describe as rapidly and briefly as possible the events of the war as they were known to Englishmen at home. A general advance of the Boers was made shortly after the final rejection of the conditions offered by President Kruger. The Boer forces invaded Natal. From that time we began to hear of many skirmishes, more or less serious, in which fortune showed now on the one side and now on the other, but in none of which any really serious advantage was obtained by either side. It very soon became apparent that the Boers, however limited their numbers, were well prepared for the war, and that they were animated by a spirit of desperate resistance. General Sir Redvers Buller arrived in Natal on November 25, 1899. In December Lord Roberts, who had rendered brilliant services on many a hard-fought field, was appointed Commander-in-Chief in South Africa, with Lord Kitchener as his Chief of the Staff; Sir Redvers Buller remained in command of the Natal Army, Sir Charles Warren leading the Fifth Division under him. It had now become well known to the English public that the struggle was to be serious and prolonged. The enthusiasm of the British public, it must be said, only rose higher and higher as actual events began to prove that the final success was not to be accomplished without heavy losses, daring ventures, and tremendous sacrifice. The national spirit was thoroughly aroused, and even those who entirely disapproved of the policy which led to the war must have been willing to admit that the general feeling at home, now that the war had actually begun, was inspired by patriotic sentiment.

Never in recent times had public feeling in England been more keen and ardent in its sympathy with the efforts of the British troops, against whom the difficulties opposed by the vast extent of the battle-ground were often such as to render the most virile bravery of little account at many a critical moment. There were some observers who had first thought it almost a pity that men like Lord Roberts, Lord Kitchener, and Sir Redvers Buller should have to be employed in what seemed the unworthy service of subjugating on the battle-field the very small population of Dutch farmers from whom President Kruger had to create his army. But the obstacles interposed by rivers and mountain ranges, and the apparently limitless stretches of country to be traversed in the warlike operations, were such as only commanders of the most varied experience and the highest gifts of judgment, foresight, patience, and mental resources could have enabled the British forces to overcome. The Boers and their allies were familiar with the ground and familiar also with the kind of fighting which was suited to it, while the English commanders and the English troops had to pick up their experience from day to day in each new battle.

As week after week passed on it became more and more apparent that the British Administration had made no adequate provision for so peculiar a struggle, and the time lost in the despatch of necessary reinforcements, the seas and the land to be traversed by each fresh body of troops sent out to the help of those already engaged in battle, were enough to give an enormous advantage to Kruger and his allies of the Orange Free State. We were often hearing of prolonged resistance offered by some body of Boer troops encamped or settled down in a mere village—prolonged resistance offered to a large body of English soldiers under thoroughly capable officers, and we found it hard to understand why the English forces could not make quicker work of the enemy. There was, to begin with, the fact that Dutch Boers were thoroughly familiar with the region covered by their fight, knew where to retreat promptly and safely whenever a sudden retreat became advisable, and how to emerge again in the rapidest manner from some wholly unsuspected vantage-ground, and thus to keep on puzzling the British troops as much by their retreats as by their attacks. Moreover, the Boers were men trained from their early boyhood to just that kind of work which came to be of the highest advantage to them in their encounters with the English troops. The Boers had to make their living in great measure by the pursuit of game, and every one was trained to the use of the rifle and to the most effective manner of making it do its work with deadly certainty under whatever conditions of sudden surprise. The training of every Boer made the life of a guerilla combatant come easy and natural to him.

The English force, on the other hand, was made up to a great extent of new levies, young men to whom the business of soldiering, even on British soil, was a novelty, and who had to put themselves, or to be put through, an entirely new sort of training when they were to encounter the Dutch Boers in South Africa. As a matter of necessity a great part of the time during which the war lasted had to be occupied by English officers in acquiring and imparting the best method of adapting British soldiers to carry on war under such entirely unfamiliar conditions. The privations and sufferings which had to be borne by the English soldiers—privations and sufferings quite outside those inflicted by the actual war—were such as might well have broken the strength of any military force, but they were endured with marvellous patience, courage, and even cheerfulness. Even those in England who utterly condemned the policy of the war were filled with admiration for the manner in which the British troops bore themselves during the whole of that long and fitful war. It was, above all things, a fitful struggle, because on many occasions the English forces despatched to some particular scene of warlike operations got the worst in this or that encounter, and Englishmen had to read every now and then an account of some defeat which, considered without reference to the actual scene and surroundings, might have seemed full of evil omen for the success of the British army. That large proportion of home readers who had not made careful study of the map of South Africa, and who received from public official sources the account of a British failure or actual British defeat, were naturally led for the moment into the belief that all the efforts of the British army there were destined to end in disaster. The war was carried on over or through an extent of country nearly equal to the area of Continental Europe, and it inevitably happened that some British force sent out merely to guard a line of frontier was suddenly and unexpectedly attacked by a little army of fighting Boers and driven from the place with a loss large in proportion to its numbers. For the credit of our own troops it had to be acknowledged in England that the Dutch Boers were behaving with remarkable courage, skill, foresight, and discipline. The proportion of the Boer troops when compared with the numerical strength of the English forces sent out for their conquest was almost infinitesimally small, but when a body of English troops sent to the relief of some English encampment had to journey over hundreds of miles of mountainous and waste country, and to cross rivers and swamps and wide, noxious regions to reach the place to be relieved, it is not surprising that many disasters and, for the time, many failures had to be recorded. The Boers were often the invaders as well as the invaded, and our generals had to look after the safety of Cape Colony as well as to see to the occupation of Boer territory.

All these bewildering events had the effect of arousing the mind of the English people into greater anger against the obstinate and clever defenders of the Transvaal, who seemed to be determined to prolong the war to an indefinite period at any risk and suffering to themselves. One result of this feeling was to create a positive fury against any Englishman at home who still ventured to say a word of censure on the policy of the war, or even to criticise the manner in which the Government were endeavouring to carry it on. The nickname of pro-Boer came to be applied to any one who showed the slightest inclination for criticism of this kind, and it was not easy for an Englishman to get a hearing at an English public meeting, or even sometimes in the House of Commons, if an offensive voice suddenly raised against him the insulting outcry which stigmatised him as a pro-Boer. During many other great wars in which English armies have been engaged it has happened that there were long stretches of time during which no great military event of importance aroused the emotions of the British public. But in the South African War some striking event was always coming to pass, and the attention of the English people was kept in a state of constant watchfulness. There were some battles and sieges which would have been regarded as important in any campaign, but the majority of the reports reaching us day after day told of occurrences incidental to every prolonged struggle. It seemed to the readers at home as if each day brought the news of another battle, some fresh siege, some relief of a beleaguered place, or some failure to achieve the desired relief. Thus no relaxation was given to the intensity of the anxious emotion which the daily story of the war brought up amongst those who were following its fortunes from so far a distance.

England had often been engaged in wars involving far more momentous issues than could possibly come even from the complete failure of the English military operations in South Africa.

The worst that could happen for the British Empire then would have been the total loss of England's sovereignty over the Dutch Republics, a sovereignty which, as we have seen, was, even before the outbreak of this war, little more than nominal. There had been wars like that against the great Napoleon; like that which was created by the policy of Russia leading to the Crimean War; or by the Indian Mutiny, in which a failure on the part of the English armies might have led to overwhelming national disaster. Nothing of this kind could have come from the South African War, and yet, for the reasons which have been given, the feeling of the people at home was aroused to a state of impatience and passionate emotion of every kind such as had never been exhibited during these far more important struggles. A feeling of hatred began to be shown among a large proportion of Englishmen towards the Boers who, whether they were right or wrong in the policy which led to the opening of the war, were now, after all, only defending their own homesteads and their own land against the martial force of a Sovereign whose suzerainty they had at one time been allowed to regard as merely titular and technical.

All manner of accusations began to be levelled by English speakers and English writers against President Kruger and his compatriots. The Dutch were accused of treachery, of falsehood, and even of cowardice. Many stories were told and believed of their habitually using the white flag which precedes some momentary suspension of hostilities as a treacherous device to give them an opportunity of approaching safely and closely to some outlying post of their enemies, and then beginning an unexpected slaughter. Some of these stories were undoubtedly true, but the Transvaal forces were made up to a great extent of irregular fighters coming from various races and little used to the honourable principles of civilised warfare. It would be wholly unfair to charge the Boer commanders and troops generally with any share in such ignoble conduct. It was asserted that after a fight the Boers used to bury the still living bodies of English soldiers in order to get rid of their wounded enemies in the promptest and least troublesome fashion. Among the less grave accusations made against them was the charge of being singularly dirty in their persons and habitually indifferent to the use of soap, water, or towels—a somewhat remarkable charge to make against a people of Dutch origin, the Dutch being one of the cleanliest populations in the world. Such charges as these were not originated in any manner by the leading British officers who encountered the Dutch in the open field, and did not receive any support from such men; but the stories were told nevertheless, found circulation in English newspapers, and came to be accepted as gospel truth by large masses of the English public. More than one distinguished foreign writer has asked in much wonder how it comes to pass that the English, whose national courage and spirit of fair-play cannot be questioned, are nevertheless so much given to suspecting and accusing their opponents in war of cowardice and treachery. But it will probably be found that this tendency to accuse our enemies in war of everything we most dislike is not peculiar to the British race, but is common to all peoples, and is the outcome of war's foul atmosphere, just as noxious insects are the outcome of certain climates and seasons. The habit did, however, show itself in England more markedly during the period of the South African War than during any other war in modern English history. There seemed all the less reason for English people to lose their temper over the prolonged resistance of the Boers when we call to mind the marvellous endurance, elasticity, readiness, and resource displayed by the British troops during the whole of this exhausting and not very glorious war. Even the war poets were not able to make much of the subject. The disparity of numbers and resources between the army the Boers could keep in the field, and the almost limitless amount of force which the British Government, if time enough were given, could bring for the extinction of the Dutch Republic, was too great to inspire a Tyrtæus or a Körner with the passionate emotion that comes from the struggle between powers almost equally matched, where the ultimate issue must depend on the superiority of skill, courage, and devotion. While doing the fullest justice to the marvellous fighting qualities of the Dutch Boers, we can never help seeing, never could help seeing, that the only end to such a contest must be England's victory. Had the English Administration taken proper account of the serious resistance the Dutch were likely to give, and made due and prompt preparations accordingly, the war might have been brought to an end much sooner, and with far less sacrifice of the invading English troops.

Though the conditions of the war did not seem qualified to quicken the patriotic ardour of an English poet, yet there were some poems produced by the occasion, or, perhaps it should be said, for the occasion, which at the time were hailed with wild popular enthusiasm. Mr. Rudyard Kipling sent forth some verses which were sung at every music-hall in the country, and aroused raptures of applause wherever they were heard, but the more judicious of Mr. Kipling's admirers wished that he had not gone quite so far out of his way in the endeavour to sound such a trumpet. Mr. Henry John Newbolt contributed some really spirited verses to the development of the war spirit, but one cannot help feeling regret that his verses should have been wasted on a war in which the success of the heroes glorified in them could only be a matter of time and transports and the votes of an immense Parliamentary majority in the House of Commons. A writer in *Public Opinion* has lately explained after his own fashion the success attained by Mr. Newbolt in his songs. 'The truth is,' according to that writer, 'that for some years a patriotic wave has been sweeping over the country, and the feeling has been intensified by the Boer War. In that war Mr. Newbolt's poems ("Admirals All," 1897, and "The Island Race," 1898) were read aloud to over 8000 men, amid scenes of extraordinary enthusiasm and excitement. It is their magnetic and obvious sincerity, and the convinced belief displayed in the great destiny of "The Island Race" that carried away even the roughest of soldiers with pride of the glorious Empire which they have inherited.

These words might apply fittingly to poems intended to arouse the patriotic enthusiasm of British soldiers struggling against an equal foe, when that pride of the glorious Empire which they inherited would have been a needed stimulant to the most heroic and patriotic effort. But it must have been hard for any English poet to arouse in himself or others such an exalted spirit when the struggle was one between the greatest Empire in the world and a small Dutch Republic, the number of whose entire population—men, women, and children—would have counted for little in London or New York. During the course of the war the English Government sent into the Dutch territory a number of armed men greater than the whole Dutch population of the Boer Republic. What England had to fight against was, in truth, the vast extent of the irregular country over which she had to scatter her soldiers and her supplies, and this is not a difficulty to inspire the muse of battle to her most passionate strains. Many readers now feel that there was something artificial in the verse dedicated to the glorification of the South African War, and that patriotic fervour was rather thrown away on such a struggle. We must not attribute to any sudden decay in English poetic or patriotic feeling the fact that the war with the Boer Republic will not go down to history consecrated by a war-song of the highest order. The verses of Mr. Kipling and of Mr. Newbolt sound as if they had been composed, not by the genuine inspiration of their authors, but rather in obedience to that traditional impulse of the author's pen, the request of friends—the request in this instance taking something like the form, 'You really must give us a poem about this war, the public are looking for it, the music-halls want it, and you will be thought unpatriotic if you do not rise to the occasion.'

It must not be supposed that we are in any sense disparaging or making light of the courage displayed and the sufferings endured by the British officers and men who were sent out to conduct the

South African War. Our position is that, where immense and overwhelming superiority of numbers and resources is found on one side of a campaign, and where the end of the struggle, sooner or later, is therefore certain and clearly discerned from the beginning, there is nothing to inspire the martial muse on the side of the great power who has only to put forth her strength in order to win. England sent to South Africa during the whole of the war nearly 450,000 men. Of these nearly 340,000 came from home, the remaining numbers were sent from India, and from the Colonies, and raised in South Africa itself. The total of the Boer force brought into the field was rather less than 75,000 men. Thus it will be seen how overwhelming was the superiority of the invading forces in numbers and in supplies, and how the whole question at issue was merely how soon the Boers could be taught to feel that further resistance was useless. One curious fact about the campaign was the impatience of the British public at the persevering manner in which the Boers maintained their resistance long after the ultimate issue of the war must have been evident to every thinking man on either side. If it had been a contest between any two foreign States in which the invading power possessed so immense a superiority of military strength over the other, it is quite certain that the sympathy of the English people in general would have gone out to the weaker combatant who persisted, in spite of every defeat, in prolonging the struggle to the very last. Most of us can well remember what a large proportion of Englishmen during the Civil War in the American Republic gave their admiration and sympathy to the Southern belligerents, not so much because of any feeling in favour of the Southern States as because the Southerners held out to the last against the greater numbers and greater strength of the Northern forces. But one of the worst evils of war is found in the fact that those who are engaged in it lose sight for the time of all principles and all questions of right and wrong, and are wholly absorbed in longing for the triumph of their own arms and in impatient hatred for the resistance, however brave and self-sacrificing, which stops the way of immediate success.

On the other hand, the sympathy of foreign States and populations even in Europe went strongly with the efforts of the Dutch Boers, chiefly because of the enormous superiority of the strength they were striving to resist. The whole campaign was conducted on the side of the Dutch very much after the fashion of guerilla warfare, in which their knowledge of the country gave them necessarily a great temporary advantage. Many of the events of the campaign were full of brilliant and picturesque interest. In England it was often difficult to form a correct idea as to the importance of each event that was described at great length in the newspapers.

When some comparatively small English force, put into difficulty by the nature of the ground and by some sudden and unexpected attack on the part of the Boers, had been compelled to retreat, a burst of disappointment broke out in this country as if all, not even except honour, had been lost, because the British commander in that particular place had not been able to achieve impossibilities and had thought it better to retire in good time and in good order rather than make a sacrifice of himself and his troops to no real strategic purpose. When the relief of Ladysmith or that of Mafeking was successfully and brilliantly accomplished by the British forces, there was an outburst of national enthusiasm which could not have been exceeded if the success on the British side had been that of another Waterloo.

The author of this History has no desire and no intention to go through in detail the whole record of this three years' war. It is a story, on both sides, of brilliant attack and brilliant defence, of battles and sieges, all belonging to the same struggle, but some as far removed from others as if they were taking place at the two extremes of the European Continent. The Dutch under all conditions were compelled to make it a sort of guerilla warfare, with sudden surprises here and sudden retreats there, and the English on their part were compelled to give themselves up to that same manner of campaigning and to train themselves in the art of outdoing the Boer fighters in guerilla warfare. There were no great battles in the meaning which we give to the words when we think of the wars between England and France, between England and Russia, between the Northern and Southern States of America, between France and Prussia. For three long years the English people had to read the reports of encounters in the open field, of places besieged and places relieved, of camps broken up and strongholds taken by storm, most of which would have been but ordinary events in the progress of a great European war. One of the British successes which created the highest enthusiasm in England was the relief of Mafeking —the very name of Mafeking supplied a new slang phrase in our vocabulary to characterise popular and patriotic enthusiasm, and the word was not always used in a laudatory and sympathetic sense.

The first definite event indicating that the close of the struggle might soon be counted on, was the annexation of the Orange Free State. This annexation was proclaimed on the 28th of May 1900, and the conquered region was described under the name of Orange River Colony. At the end of the same month President Kruger accomplished his flight from Pretoria, and Lord Roberts entered Pretoria and hoisted the British flag there on the 5th of June. When the news of British successes was announced in England a very general impression prevailed, not unnaturally, that the whole struggle was substantially at an end. Position after position held by the Boers had been captured, some of the Boer leaders had been completely defeated and made prisoners of war, and the President of the Transvaal Republic had for the time disappeared from the field altogether. Yet the war was by no means at an end. It was for the most part a guerilla warfare on the side of the Dutch and of the Orange Free State, and such a war might be carried on for an almost indefinite time even after all the strongholds of the invaded States had been occupied by the enemy. In the meantime negotiations were now and then going on for a final settlement of the whole dispute. The Dutch offered terms more than once, but they were not terms which the British with their increasing successes would be likely to accept, and there was a strong feeling among the English Commanders that these negotiations were only started by the Boers with the object of making a delay while they considered what their next move ought to be and how it could be made most promptly effective.

The English Commanders were now becoming better and better acquainted with the Boer tactics, and could see more distinctly that by continually inviting the Boers to collisions here, there, and everywhere with English troops the superior numbers must soon begin to prove their superiority by their ability to destroy every Dutch force in detail, and thus to leave the Transvaal and the Orange Free State without any supply of fighting men worth counting on for the continuance of the war. The truth was forced upon the minds of the Transvaal and Orange Free State Commanders, and even if President Kruger had been inclined to keep on the resistance until the fighting power of the Transvaal had been utterly exhausted, he was now out of the way, and his authority had lost its control. It was therefore made known to the British Commanders that their enemies were willing to consider any proposals for a settlement which did not involve utter ruin and disgrace to the South African leaders and people. A peace conference was held on the 15th and 16th of May 1902, in which some of the Transvaal Commanders, including Louis Botha and De Wet, each of them among the most distinguished fighters and tacticians on the Transvaal side, came into consultation with Lord Milner and Lord Kitchener in Pretoria. The terms were made known by telegraphic communication to the British Government, and the final answer was received just before the end of the month.

Little apology will be needed on the part of the author for the fact that he has thought it well· to anticipate the course of history in dealing with this final settlement. This concluding volume of 'The History of Our Own Times' only professes to bring the narrative down to the close of Queen Victoria's reign, and that close had been reached and a new Sovereign, King Edward VII., had come to the British throne before the first serious attempts were made to bring the long struggle to an end. But as the war began, and was for a long time carried on during the reign of Queen Victoria, the author has thought it well to anticipate events in order that the readers of this volume might have the whole story before them. The British terms were unconditional surrender and absorption of the Transvaal and the Orange Free State into the British Empire. There were some very liberal conditions of surrender offered by the conquerors. There was to be no death penalty inflicted on any of the Boers who had been fighting for their country, the Dutch language was to be used in law courts whenever necessary, and there was to be a liberal Imperial grant and some loans in order to enable the Boers to settle once again in the land which they had made their home. These terms were accepted and signed by the representatives of the Boer cause in the presence of Lord Milner and Lord Kitchener at Pretoria. King Edward sent a cordial message of thanks to Lord Kitchener, and Lord Kitchener himself congratulated the Boers on the stout and gallant struggle they had made, and offered them his welcome in their position as citizens of the great British Empire.

It is gratifying to know that a cordial feeling seems to have prevailed on both sides, and that, while the terms of surrender were still going on, many of the Boer leaders made speeches in which they expressed their loyal willingness to accept terms of peace and to recognise the supremacy of the British Sovereign. One interesting testimonial to this feeling of cordial acceptance of the new order of things is to be found in the dedication of the volume called 'Three Years' War,' written by General De Wet, which he dedicates 'To my fellow-subjects of the British Empire.' De Wet was one of the most distinguished and in every sense one of the most remarkable among those who fought for the South African Republics. His name had become familiar to every English reader. He had a positive genius for sudden surprises, unexpected attacks, and instantaneous disappearances, and had given immeasurable trouble to the British Commanders by the mere fact that they never knew where to have him, could never anticipate his movements of attack, and could never alight on him when it became part of his instantaneous policy to withdraw himself and his band from the presence of the enemy. It is impossible not to believe that when a man of such prominence in war, and who held so high a place in the estimation of the South African populations, thus publicly pledged himself to a willing allegiance towards the conquering Empire, he must have written the words in full sincerity and with good hopes for the future.

The thanks of the King in Parliament were voted to the army and navy, to the Indian and Colonial forces, to the volunteers who had maintained the war on behalf of England's supremacy, and to Lord Kitchener, who had dealt with ninety mobile Boer columns over an area nearly as large as the European Continent. Finally Lord Kitchener sailed for England on the 23rd of June 1902, and the three years' war was at an end. The thanks of the Sovereign and Parliament were indeed due to the Indian and Colonial troops who had taken part in the campaign. The Canadian and Australian Colonies rendered splendid service to England during the whole of the war, and nothing was more remarkable throughout that entire chapter of history than the effect which it wrought by bringing the Colonies into closer and more cordial relations with the mother country. That was one good result at least brought about for England by a war whose policy, and many of whose conditions, had so much concerning which not only colonists but Englishmen as well might be allowed to have serious doubts and misgivings. It is too soon as yet to venture on a confident anticipation as to the ultimate results of the whole struggle, but we may congratulate ourselves on any manifest advantages which came to the Empire from such a contest. Among these advantages must assuredly be classed the strengthening of the feeling between the Empire and the Colonies. The war was especially unpopular in Ireland—that is to say, among that great majority of the Irish people who are national in their sentiments—and it was equally unpopular among Irishmen in the United States and the British Colonies. Yet many or most of the British regiments which fought in South Africa had a large proportion of Irish soldiers in them, and Irish soldiers never fought more boldly and brilliantly than in this campaign. Queen Victoria sent her special thanks to her Irish soldiers for their conduct in the field.

An event in the war to be remembered with grateful feeling on both sides was the noble expedition made by a committee of ladies, under the guidance of Mrs. Henry Fawcett, to visit the refuge camps in South Africa, and lend the best help they could for the reduction of the fearful mortality among Boer women and children. During all modern wars in which the British Empire has been engaged, British women have thus shown themselves ready to perform those works of corporal mercy, which are associated with the Christian faith and are ever finding new and increased development. Such work was done on a large scale during the Crimean War, and in later wars, but the services rendered by the committee of ladies in South Africa was especially difficult and troublesome, because of the distances to be traversed and the unusual discomforts to be endured. This mission of charity may be justly regarded as bequeathing to English history one of the most touching and gratifying memories associated with the story of the war against the Boers. Another honourable characteristic of the war, or at least of the war's conclusion, was the fact that when the war came to an end no death penalties were inflicted on the so-called rebels—an honourable display of mercy, which rarely crowns a conquest of enemies regarded as rebels, and which in our own times was probably first shown by the Government of the United States, when they brought the great Southern rebellion to an end, and allowed its living leaders to return to their homes without the infliction of any punishment.

The limits of this narrative do not admit anything like a record of all the distinguished men who fell in the war. We shall only mention a few whose names give them an especial claim on the memory of the Empire. Major-General Andrew Gilbert Wauchope was killed on December 11, 1899, while leading the Highland Brigade in the engagement on the Modder River. He had seen service in Ashanti; in the Egyptian campaign of 1882; in the Soudan campaign of 1884, where, at the battle of El Teb, he was severely wounded; in the Nile campaign of the following year, and in the Soudan expedition of 1898. He was regarded as one of the bravest, most skilful, and most popular officers in the service. Lieutenant F. Roberts, only surviving son of Lord Roberts, was mortally wounded on December 15, 1899, while trying to save the guns during the attempt to cross the Tugela Falls at Colenso, Natal. Lord Ava, Lord Dufferin's son, was killed on January 6, 1900, during the 'soldiers' battle' at Ladysmith, when the Boer attack was repulsed. On October 29, 1900, Prince Victor of Schleswig-Holstein fell a victim, not indeed of wounds on the battle-field, but no less a victim to the war. He died at Pretoria of enteric fever caught during active service in the field. He was known to the whole army of South Africa as a gallant, an able, and an untiring soldier. Prince Victor was the son of the Princess Helena, daughter of Queen Victoria, who became Princess Christian of Schleswig-Holstein. The Royal family in this war, as in all others, had taken its share in the risks and in the sacrifices of the country. Another death during the war calling for our notice was that of George Warrington Steevens, the brilliant war correspondent of the *Daily Mail*, who died at Ladysmith in January 1900.

There are several interesting and valuable histories of the war. Sir Arthur Conan Doyle is the author of two works; 'The Great Boer

War,' and 'Cause and Conduct of the War.' The *Times'* 'History of the War,' and 'Three Years' War,' by De Wet, are probably the books on the subject which have had the largest circulation. De Wet's work would have been especially attractive to readers, if only because of the singularly active part taken by its author during the whole of the long campaign. A passage from this volume may find an appropriate place here. The author is describing the final meeting at which Lord Kitchener and Lord Milner met the delegates of the Government of the two Republics, at Lord Kitchener's house in Pretoria, and agreed upon the terms of peace. De Wet says:—

'It was a never-to-be-forgotten evening. In the space of a few short minutes that was done which could never be undone. A decision arrived at in a meeting could always be taken into reconsideration, but a document solemnly signed as on that night by two parties bound them both for ever. Every one of us who put his name to that document knew that he was in honour bound to act in accordance with it. It was a bitter moment, but not so bitter as when, earlier on the same day, the National Representatives had come to the decision that the fatal step must be taken. On the 2nd June 1902, the Representatives returned every man to his own commando. It was now their sad duty to tell their brave and patient burghers that the independence which they cherished so dearly was gone, and to prepare them to surrender their arms at the appointed places. I left Pretoria on the 3rd of June with General Elliott, who had to accompany me to the various centres to receive the burghers' arms. On the 5th June the first commando laid down their weapons near Vredefort. To every man there, as to myself, the surrender was no more and no less than the sacrifice of our independence. I have often been present at the deathbed and at the burial of those who have been nearest to my heart—father, mother, brother, and friend—but the grief which I felt on those occasions was not to be compared with what I now underwent at the burial of my Nation. There was nothing left for us now but to hope that the Power which conquered us, the Power to which we were compelled to submit, though it cut us to the heart to do so, and which by the surrender of our arms we had accepted as our ruler, would draw us nearer and ever nearer by the strong cords of love.

'To my Nation I address one last word.

'Be loyal to the new Government! Loyalty pays best in the end. Loyalty alone is worthy of a Nation which has shed its blood for freedom!'

These closing words, written by one of the most active and the most skilled among those who opposed the dominion of England as long as there seemed any chance of holding out with good effect, may well be regarded as full of hopeful augury for the result of England's conquest. That result must mainly depend on Britain's policy and the action of England's representatives in the conquered regions. It is too early yet to venture on a sure anticipation as to the continuance of peace in South Africa, and the endurance of that loyalty to the new rulers which De Wet called upon his countrymen to acknowledge and to maintain. As to the policy of the war, there must always be a large number of educated Englishmen who firmly and conscientiously believe that England made a mistake when she set deliberately to work for the crushing of the two South African Republics; that no merely political or Imperial triumphs could have justified such a course, and that, if another and more generous policy had been adopted, there might have grown up in due time a peaceful and contented South African confederation, which would have done more honour to Great Britain as one of its members than any manner of conquest achieved on the fields of battle. Even if we put aside altogether the theory maintained by so many Englishmen of the highest intellect and of the truest patriotic feeling, that the war was forced upon this country by the supporters of the capitalist and mining interest, and by the advocates of that inflated Imperialism who hailed any extension of British territory, no matter how acquired, as a new glory to England. Even if we put those views entirely out of our consideration and accept the cheerful and balmy doctrine, that those who advocated and urged on the conquest of the South African Republics were one and all inspired purely by patriotic and unselfish motives, it must nevertheless always be held by men whose opinions ought to claim respect that England, in undertaking the South African War, had renewed an evil example to the rulers of great empires. The best that can now be hoped for is that, after all, the results may yet be acclaimed which some of us are more and more inclined to believe could have been accomplished without the terrible risks and sacrifices of war.

CHAPTER XIX.

THE GENERAL ELECTION OF 1900.

Soon after the close of the Parliamentary Session of 1900, the constituencies everywhere began to feel deeply interested in the probability of an early dissolution. There was indeed no imperative or absolute necessity for the dissolution of Parliament during that year. So far as the mere question of time was concerned, the Parliament then sitting might still have had a year or more of life before it became necessary to end its existence. But it was thoroughly understood throughout the whole country that the Government had many critical questions to deal with at home and abroad, and that the statesmen in office might feel themselves called upon to consider whether the interests of the Empire would not be best consulted by inviting the constituencies to give, at the earliest possible moment, a decisive expression of opinion on certain of the most pressing subjects. Here, at home, the one question of greatest urgency was brought up by Mr. Chamberlain's recent announcements of his financial policy. That policy had unquestionably taken the public by surprise, and among many clearheaded persons the great matter for surprise was that such an exposition of financial policy should have been received with anything but either unmingled contempt or absolute indifference. Yet it was certain that a considerable proportion of the public had been attracted by Mr. Chamberlain's proposal for a national attempt to call back into life the long-buried corpse of protectionism. The official leaders of the Government, moreover, did not seem thus far to have made up their own minds clearly as to the position they ought to take with regard to Mr. Chamberlain's recent movements. Many observers were inclined to believe that this delay in speaking out precisely one way or the other, only indicated that the Government were anxious to know what the views of the majority of the constituencies might be before committing themselves to a definite policy.

There was also a very common impression that Mr. Chamberlain, who was regarded as the author of the South African War, was especially anxious to take the opinion of the country on that subject while the war was still going on, and while any hesitation in giving full support to those who had the responsibility of carrying on the war might seem to be an unpatriotic course of conduct, amounting to the withdrawal of support from the British army while that army was yet engaged in its struggle on South African battle-fields. It has long been one of the theories of British policy that a change of Government ought never, unless under the most extraordinary conditions, to be made while a war is still going on. This is, under all ordinary conditions, a healthy and manly principle, and even those who did not in the beginning approve of the policy which led to the war, would naturally feel reluctant to pass a national vote of censure on the Government in power, and thus proclaim them in the eyes of the world as engaged in a war not holding the national approval. Therefore, it was argued, it is the obvious interest of Mr. Chamberlain and his colleagues to bring about a General Election at a crisis when the voter might feel that he is committing an unpatriotic act if he refuses his support to the statesmen who, whether wise or unwise in bringing about such a crisis, are at the very time of the General Election maintaining what they believe to be the cause of the whole Empire against a revolted dependency in arms.

Just then the passions of the country were excited almost to fever pitch. The war had not so far proved to be the easy march to victory that was commonly anticipated. The enemy had held his own and had even succeeded in subjecting British troops to occasional reverses, and now and then to actual defeat, in South Africa. 'Is this a time,' it might be asked, 'when an Englishman at home would be justified, because of any differences of opinion on other subjects between Liberals and Conservatives, in withdrawing his support from the men who had undertaken the whole responsibility of the war in what they believe to be the cause of England, and in thus creating an interval between the overthrow of one Government and the formation of another, during which it might be difficult to carry on the war with full national force?' The Imperial spirit had already been excited to the utmost pitch, and to be called a pro-Boer was enough to make a man seem like a deserter from the national flag and a traitor to the interests of the Empire. On the other hand, the strength and unity of the Liberal party had undergone much damaging change since the days when Mr. Gladstone held office for the last time. There was no leader to the front in whom the whole party placed full confidence and to whom it looked up with unqualified devotion. It was not certain whether Lord Rosebery and those who acted with him were genuine andı whole-hearted Liberals, and it was certain that there were sections of the Parliamentary Opposition who did not accept, and did not even profess to accept, the full creed of Gladstonian Liberalism. Men who were still inclined to argue out the question were asking themselves, 'Who is there to carry on the work' of Government with any prospect of success if we turn out of office Lord Salisbury and his colleagues?'

All these considerations led the public to the belief that the Government would see a distinct and alluring advantage in giving the general election an opportunity of being decided on the one question, 'Imperialist or pro-Boer?' The result fully justified this anticipation. On the 18th of September 1900 the *London Gazette* contained the formal announcement of the dissolution. The existing Parliament was to be dissolved on the 25th of the month, and the general election was to set in immediately after. The same number of the *London Gazette* contained the Queen's Proclamation, announcing the formation of the Commonwealth of Australia, and the fact that the Parliament of that Commonwealth was to be opened by their Royal Highnesses the Duke and Duchess of York. There was something significant and suggestive of curious reflection in the simultaneous appearance of these two announcements. The first made it known that the British Parliament was about to be dissolved in order that a general election might take place, and every one knew that the one main question which that general election would put to the constituencies was, 'Are you, or are you not, in favour of extinguishing by force the self-government of the South African Republic and ruling it as a conquered and vassal dependency of the British Empire?' The second announcement told the world that a new and self-governing Commonwealth of Australia had been called into existence. It is not likely, however, that the spirit of Imperialism was perplexed to any disconcerting extent during the general election by the endeavour to draw a moral lesson from the inconsistency of the two announcements.

The suddenness of the Ministerial resolve to bring on a general election appears to have given much dissatisfaction to the Liberal party. Many of the Liberal leaders criticised the Government severely for the course of action just announced, and argued that it was without precedent to dissolve a Parliament that had not exhausted its mandate, and in which the Ministers of the Crown held a large majority in the House of Commons as well as in the House of Lords. It was not to be expected that the statesmen in power would take much account of this protest if there seemed any decided object to be gained by appointing the earliest possible date for the dissolution. Such a course had undoubtedly been taken on more than one occasion by a Liberal Ministry when it seemed that an earlier rather than a later date would have the result of bringing in a new Parliament more favourable to some line of policy which they had in their minds. It is only fair to say that the temptation then offered to Lord Salisbury's Ministry would have proved too great to be put aside by any Government under similar conditions. The Conservative Ministry would naturally take into consideration the possibility that, if the general election were to be put off for a year or even for six months, something might happen on South African fields in the meantime which would bring discredit on the whole military organisation of the Empire and thus suddenly damage the popularity of the Government. Some of the leading Ministerial speakers, in their public addresses delivered during the general election, made use of arguments which, whether they were quite fair or not, had a powerful effect on the minds of vast masses of voters. Mr. Balfour issued his address as a candidate to the electors of East Manchester, and in it he put this part of the Ministerial case with his habitual clearness and effectiveness. He told the electors that 'The lesson which has been indelibly pressed on the South African mind by that portion of our dealings with the Transvaal which so ingloriously ended at Majuba is that, from a Radical Administration neither firmness of purpose nor consistency of policy need be anticipated in the face of Boer persistence.'

It cannot be denied that for electioneering purposes there could be no more telling hit directed against the Liberals than this allusion to Majuba Hill and to the terms which were afterwards made with the Transvaal Republic under the leadership of Mr. Gladstone. If the whole subject were under discussion at some meeting of impartial men the effect of Mr. Balfour's thrust might have been easily put aside. The British force was defeated at Majuba Hill, and yet after that defeat the Liberal Government came to terms with the Boers which allowed the Transvaal to retain its independence. That was the head and front of the Liberal Government's offending. But in the impartial and intelligent assembly which we have supposed to be gathered together for the discussion of the subject it would have been promptly pointed out that the course taken by the Liberal Government was not taken as a yielding to the persistence of the Boer opponents, but as yielding to the cause of justice and of right. Mr. Gladstone did not believe in the wisdom or the justice of a policy which would convert the Transvaal Republic into a conquered dependency on the British Empire, and even if at Majuba the British troops had won the day and the Boers had no forces left with which to carry on the struggle, Mr. Gladstone would not any the more have believed that England was justified in annexing to her sway that which had been an independent Republic. But the addresses just then issued on both sides of the great electoral controversy were not intended for the discussion of cool-headed and impartial men seated in a quiet study, and it cannot be doubted that Mr. Balfour's allusion to Majuba, an allusion which was again and again repeated by Conservative orators all over the country, had an immense effect in arousing the Imperialism of the electors into passionate fervour.

Mr. Balfour's address went on to amplify his charge against the leaders of opposition, and in one passage it must be owned that he described with accuracy some of the defects which just then greatly weakened the Liberal party. Among the leaders of the Opposition Mr. Balfour went on to say, 'There is no symptom of that unity which can alone give strength in council; and among its followers every shade of doctrine seems represented, from an ardent and resolute patriotism to something not very easy to distinguish from treasonable sympathy with the enemy.' Of course we are all to understand that by 'ardent and resolute patriotism' Mr. Balfour meant the desire to carry on the war to the complete subjugation of the Boers, and by the 'something not very easy to distinguish from treasonable sympathy with the enemy,' the sincere desire of many Liberals holding high position in their party, that the war should be brought to an end on reasonable and even generous terms, and that the subjugation of the Boer Republic should not be a part of England's national policy. But while thus qualifying Mr. Balfour's actual words we cannot pretend to say that there did not exist in the Liberal party differences of opinion on the subject of the war as widely divided as even his words gave out. There were at the time men of influence in the Liberal party who went quite as far as Mr. Balfour himself could go in the desire that the war should be carried on to the very end, and that the end should be the complete annexation of the Transvaal. There were also leading men in the same party who were entirely opposed to the policy of the war from the first and had no desire whatever for the extinction of the Boer Republic. In another sentence Mr. Balfour skilfully pointed the moral of his address: 'Every citizen, therefore, who desires that the blood which men of our race from every quarter of the world have so freely shed in defence of the Empire, shall not have been shed in vain, is bound to dismiss all smaller issues and resolve that, so far as in him lies, there shall be no break in the continuity of our national policy, no diminution in the strength of the Parliamentary forces by which that policy can alone be successfully maintained.'

No appeal could have been more skilfully directed to its purpose than such a presentation of the main issue then before the country. The object of the party in power naturally was to describe the question in dispute as one between those who were patriotically determined to carry on the South African War until its due end should be accomplished by the conquest of the enemy, and the unpatriotic and inglorious Little Englanders who were the friends of every other country rather than of their own. If we regard the Parliamentary crisis brought about by the dissolution merely as a trial of tactical skill between the Ministerialists and the Opposition, it must be admitted that the former could not possibly have discovered a better plan of campaign than that which consisted in representing the entire struggle as one between Imperialists and Little Englanders. The Liberal leaders, while utterly repudiating the construction put upon their policy and their purposes, did not fail to understand from the very first that they were placed at a great disadvantage by the suddenness of the dissolution. Mr. Herbert Gladstone, the chief Whip of the Opposition, delivered a speech at Leeds on the 18th of September, in which he made no concealment of his full belief that, under all the conditions, it was impossible for the Liberals to expect anything but defeat at the general election. He went so far as to say that the Liberals were not then in a position to form a Government capable of retaining power, even if by some strange and wholly unexpected chance they were to come out of the elections with a majority over the Conservatives. His argument was, that unless the Liberals could win 160 seats from the Conservatives in the coming trial of strength, no really responsible Liberal statesman would undertake to carry on a Government, and that it was utterly out of the question to expect that the Liberals could win anything like such a majority at the polling booths.

Nothing could be more frank and honourable, and at the same time more reasonable, than this declaration made by a man whose position gave it full authority. Mr. Gladstone thoroughly understood the whole conditions of the Liberal party, its strength and its weakness, its different shades of opinion on some important and even fundamental principles of that Liberalism which his father had done so much to establish as the recognised policy of the party. He knew that there had been a certain cooling down among some influential Liberals of the ardour which had once supported the cause of Irish Home Rule, and that such Liberals were to be found even among those who did not accept the title of Liberal Unionists. Mr. Herbert Gladstone was an earnest and a chivalrous advocate of the true Liberal cause, and he was too straightforward a man to seek for an immediate advantage by any suppression or even qualification of what he knew to be the realities of the crisis. He did not see how it could be possible for the Liberal party just then to form a strong Government; he had no desire that the Liberals should come into power for a time under such conditions; and it was not in his nature to suppress or to qualify the real facts of the situation with the mere hope of encouraging the Liberal electors to put more ardour and more zeal into their efforts for an unattainable success. But it must be said, that while thus boldly speaking out his judgments as to the results of the general election, Mr. Gladstone did all that he could to urge the Liberals throughout the country to make the best fight possible for the honour of their cause, and that the battle was fought by the Liberals in almost all the constituencies with a vigour and spirit which could not have been greater even if they had been conducting the struggle with some hope of an ultimate victory.

On the other side of the contest a certain discouraging effect was brought about by a letter from Lord Salisbury, which appeared to be addressed, if not exactly *urbi et orbi*, yet at least to the Conservatives all over the United Kingdom. The purpose of this letter was to urge the electors on the Conservative side not to abstain from recording their votes, either because of the preconceived idea that the triumph of the Conservative party was so well assured that the absence of the few votes here and there could make no difference in the final result, or because of any want of unity or dissatisfaction on some questions of lesser importance than the great main issues presented to the country. The main issues to which Lord Salisbury urged the attention of Conservative voters were — the settlement of South Africa, the reform of our whole system of military organisation, and the policy of England with regard to China. On the latter subject Lord Salisbury's letter expressed itself in language of extreme caution. 'The fact,' he said, 'that we are acting with other Powers forbids me from entering without reserve upon questions of Chinese policy.' This was only to be expected, but Lord Salisbury went on to deal with the Chinese question in language which, though absolutely reasonable and truthful, none the less appears to have cast something like a chill of discouragement on some of his self-satisfied Imperialist followers. 'In maintaining our own rights and joining in the efforts of our allies to restore and secure tranquillity, we shall be approaching a task of which it is difficult to overrate the complexity.' Then came the words, 'I earnestly trust that the electors, in confiding the solution of this and the other problems which I have mentioned to the party which is victorious at the polls, will remember that unless that party is armed with a strong majority in the House of Commons, it will lack the authority at home and abroad which is essential to the performance of its task.'

The reader will hardly fail to notice the curious resemblance prevailing between the tone and purport of Lord Salisbury's letter to the Conservative constituencies, and the speech of Mr. Herbert Gladstone to his Liberal electors. Neither appeal, it will be seen, was of a very encouraging nature, and each was thoroughly outspoken in its description of the difficulties and dangers which must lie in the way. The explanation of this curious resemblance is no doubt to be found in the fact, that neither Lord Salisbury nor Mr. Herbert Gladstone regarded the coming struggle from the point of view of the political partisan or of the electioneering agent. Each man was alike inspired by a conscientious desire to put the whole difficulties of the crisis fairly and fully before his own party, and was entirely above the temptation to cheer them on by the assurance that they had nothing to do but to go boldly in and win. The spirit of each address was the same, although the point of view from which each statesman surveyed the field of action was entirely different. Lord Salisbury knew well that the Conservatives might be regarded as sure of success. Mr. Herbert Gladstone knew full well that the Liberals were certain to be defeated at the polls. Lord Salisbury thought it his duty to impress upon his supporters that there must be some difficult tasks before them, although they should be able to carry the general election. Mr. Gladstone thought it his duty to remind the Liberal electors that they must fight to the last, even if it were all but certain that they could not carry the day.

The appeals issued by the Conservative Prime Minister, and by the son of a late Liberal Prime Minister, have seemed to us so unlike in their terms to the address usually issued by leading politicians on the eve of a general election, that we have thought it well worth while to take some account of them in these pages. Each appeal was thoroughly characteristic of the man whose name it bore. But Lord Salisbury's letter did produce for the time a sort of chilling effect on Conservative feeling here and there. There were many ardent Tory politicians, eager candidates, and busy electioneering agents, who thought that the Prime Minister might have abstained from publicly reminding his followers that Toryism in power, and even Toryism in power with a large majority, would find that it had yet many national and international troubles to encounter. To the reader who in later days studies these two manifestoes the most interesting evidence which they give will probably be the proof contained in them that Lord Salisbury and Mr. Herbert Gladstone were statesmen made for something better than electioneering addresses on the occasion of a Parliamentary dissolution.

The Liberal candidates who were not out and out supporters of the more advanced Liberal policy had two especial difficulties to deal with when they addressed public meetings during the general election. The first of these was the question of England's policy with regard to South Africa. Lord Rosebery had helped them as far as possible to get smoothly and safely over this difficulty. In recommending the candidature of a Liberal who had done signal service as an officer of the naval brigade in the South African campaign, Lord Rosebery had declared that if the Liberals were returned to office and to power by the votes of the constituencies at the general election, the results of the sacrifices made in the South African campaign 'should in no jot or tittle be prejudiced.' Many Liberal candidates naturally acted on this hint, and gave it to be understood that while they had not been thoroughly in favour of the South African War at its opening, they were yet not so pedantically and perversely Radical as to prevent the Empire from completing the conquest for which it had squandered so much money and so much life. The more stalwart Liberals, as we may call them, utterly repudiated this way of dealing with the subject, and condemned the war from beginning to end in words as outspoken as John Bright himself could have used had he still been living. There the Conservative candidates had an immense advantage over their rivals. The Conservatives could speak out fairly and squarely on the one question which most occupied the public mind. They could tell the electors that the glory of England, the safety of the Empire, the veneration due to our illustrious ancestors, and our gratitude to the brave British soldiers who had fallen on the Boer battle-field, could only be maintained and proclaimed at such a crisis by the return of the Conservative party to power.

We are not now considering the merits or the demerits of the case for the war, and the case against the war. In this chapter we are merely reviewing the story of the general election, and describing the advantages enjoyed by the Conservatives, and the disadvantages imposed upon the Liberals by the conditions under which the appeal to the country was made. The Conservatives went before the electors as a thoroughly united party maintaining that the honour and the security of the British Empire were involved in the success of the British arms in South Africa.

The Liberals, on the other hand, were not united in their opposition to the policy of the war, or in the desire that it should be brought to an end without the subjugation of the Transvaal Republic. The question of Home Rule illustrated an advantage of a like kind on the Conservative side. Even among the actual leaders of the Liberal party there were some who had fallen away from the Home Rule policy of Mr. Gladstone. Lord Rosebery was now understood not to be an advocate of Home Rule, and other leading Liberals had openly expressed their belief that Home Rule was no longer a subject belonging to practical politics. A considerable proportion of the Liberal representatives throughout the country were happy in the belief that they need not further concern themselves about Ireland's claims for a separate Irish Parliament.

The effect of all this upon the rank and file of the Liberal electors could not but be seriously damaging to the Liberal cause. When a Conservative candidate told the electors that Home Rule meant the dismemberment of the Empire and could do nothing but harm to Ireland herself, and the trimming Liberal candidate could only say that he hoped the Home Rule cause was dead and buried, it is easy to see that the Liberal elector of that constituency who was in favour of Home Rule might fail to discover any great political advantage to be gained by putting himself to trouble and inconvenience for the sake of being represented by a supporter of the Opposition. It cannot be denied, too, that the Home Rule cause was made all the less popular among the Liberal constituencies of Great Britain by the fact that the Irish National members always openly proclaimed that they would give their votes to any Government, Conservative or Liberal, according as it encouraged or discouraged the claim for an Irish domestic Parliament. This policy was but natural and reasonable on the part of the Irish Nationalists. To them the Home Rule question was the most important in legislation, and should have precedence of all others. They were willing for the time to put aside every other question, and to support any Ministry which could be induced by persuasion or by pressure to give a hearing to their demand. But the Liberal elector who had been quite willing to support Home Rule while Mr. Gladstone was still at the head of affairs, was sometimes inclined to regard the Home Rulers as men who might at any moment become his political enemies instead of being his political friends, and was all the less likely to exert himself on their behalf when he found that some of his own most influential Parliamentary leaders had ceased to advocate the Irish National cause. On these two great questions therefore, the South African policy and the Irish Home Rule cause, the Conservatives showed a thoroughly united front at the general election while the Liberals were weakened by uncertainty and disunion.

There were other questions which agitated the country to a certain extent, although not to anything like the same degree as that involved in the South African policy or even that which was raised by the Home Rule agitation. There were some subjects of domestic policy in which a keen interest was felt throughout many constituencies. One of these had to do with the government and the discipline of the English State Church. We have already told how a powerful organisation was growing up throughout the country, having for its object the passing of some laws for the prohibition or the restriction of Ritualistic practices in that Church. The disputants on both sides of this question were forming important organisations in many of the constituencies, and were doing their best to make the whole subject a test question at the general election. The one organisation was ready to oppose almost any candidate who was inclined to tolerate Ritualistic practices, while their opponents seemed equally prepared to combine against any candidate who professed himself willing to subject the Church of England to the control of a severe and sweeping legislative discipline. There were many subjects which had to do with the condition of the working-classes in these countries, with the promises which had been made by Liberal and Conservative Governments to introduce some legislation for their benefit, with, for instance, the proposals to establish by legislation a system of old-age pensions; proposals again and again brought forward, but carried to no definite result.

There was also what is called the temperance question—the question whether legislation could not accomplish some great practical work for the promotion of the cause of temperance, and whether any candidate ought to be supported who did not promise to lend a hand in such an effort. This controversy brought up the whole and long-standing constitutional debate as to how far Parliamentary legislation can be safely pushed in its efforts to check and control the traffic in drink, and, it need hardly be added, that it also brought up a very fierce antagonism between the advocates of temperance legislation and the holders of vested interests in the sale of the liquors which create intemperance. With regard to such subjects as those which we have just mentioned, there was no political creed marked out for either of the great opposing parties. There was no word of order issued by the leaders of either host dictating to their followers how they were to act on the temperance question, the subject of old-age pensions, and the disputes going on among the members of the State Church. In Ireland there were, as before, but the two contending parties. The question was 'For or against Home Rule?' The end of that struggle could be easily foreseen. If any change were to take place there it might be assumed beforehand that the change would be for the benefit of the Home Rulers.

The electoral battle went on without any peculiarities of especial interest. The leaders on both sides were active in their services, and prompt and outspoken in their addresses at various public meetings throughout the constituencies, but it was becoming more evident, as the contest went on, that the Liberals were placed at a serious disadvantage by the fact that the one great issue pressed on the country was the policy of the South African War, and because also on that and some other subjects the Liberals could not present to their opponents a thoroughly united front. There was less of excitement, and less even of intense interest, than there had been during the conduct of many preceding general elections, for the reason that on neither side of the field was there the least expectation that the Liberals could win. When the electoral rivalries had been finally settled at the polling booths, the results were substantially just such as the country had already anticipated. There were 334 Conservatives and 68 Liberal Unionists elected, making, together, a Ministerial party of 402 members. The Liberal and the Labour members, who would naturally be included among the Liberals, numbered 186. The Irish Nationalists were to be represented by 82 members in the new Parliament. Some of the records of the time seem to have included the Irish representatives with the Opposition, giving to the Liberals and the Labour members a total of 268, and leaving to the Conservatives a majority of 134. This result, however, is only to be obtained by dividing the two parties into Unionist and anti-Unionists, if we may thus for a moment attempt to classify those Liberals who were not prepared to insist on keeping up the legislative union with Ireland. This distinction is inaccurate in more qualities than one. As has already been shown, a not inconsiderate number of Liberals had now become opponents of the Home Rule principle, and could therefore not be reckoned on as pledged supporters of the Liberal Opposition under all conditions. It was known to every one that the Irish Nationalists could not be counted as pledged adherents to the Liberal Opposition, except on the single question of Home Rule, and only on that so long as the Liberal Opposition held to the Home Rule principle. It was known, too, that the Irish Nationalists were ready to give their support on momentous Irish questions to any Government, Liberal or Conservative, which could satisfy them in legislation dealing with Irish affairs. The general result of the elections was to give the Conservative party a very substantial majority, larger indeed and more cohesive than the party had to sustain it in the recent Parliament.

As regards the Irish vote, it has also to be said that the new Nationalist party came into Parliament more closely united than it had been for some years before. A conspicuous, single-minded, and eloquent member of the Irish party, Mr. William O'Brien, had started a new agitation throughout his country for two great objects —the exclusion from the party of all wavering or unpledged members, and the creation of a political system in Ireland which would put the representation more directly under the control of the Irish people. These objects Mr. O'Brien proposed to attain by establishing an organisation to bear the name of the Irish National League, into whose hands should be given the central direction of Irish political affairs, in the choice of representatives, and the policy of the Irish Parliamentary party. Mr. O'Brien's agitation met with a thorough success in Ireland, and carried with it the full support of all Irish constituencies represented, or likely to be represented, by Home Rule members. There had been of late, and almost ever since the fall and the death of Parnell, a certain small proportion of Irish Nationalists in the House of Commons who could not be reckoned on as thorough supporters of the political action decided upon by the leader and the majority of the party. These seceders, if they may be called by that name, were some of them very sincere men whom nature had endowed with a certain disinclination to follow any appointed leadership, the kind of men who in American political life would probably have been described as 'cranks.' The immediate effect of Mr. O'Brien's organisation was to leave some of these men out of the party when the general election came to be accomplished. A very small number of them, probably not half-a-dozen altogether, were able to hold their seats, and these were for the most part men whose integrity of character and whose past services entitled them to a certain consideration on the part of their constituents. But the general effect of the elections in Ireland was to send into the House of Commons an Irish National party which, with these few exceptions, might be regarded as thoroughly united in principle and policy, and quite determined to follow the guidance of the new national organisation.

So far as Irish politics were concerned there was practically no change made in the condition of the two great English parties. It was absolutely certain that the Irish Nationalists would give their full support to the first Government, Conservative or Liberal, which showed a resolve to accept the principle of Home Rule, or to introduce legislation calculated to promote the welfare of the Irish tenant classes, or, better still, to carry out the one policy and the other. The conviction of the Irish Nationalists was then, as it has been ever since, that before long some Government, whether Liberal or Tory, would find itself compelled to adopt the principle of Home Rule, and to introduce further reforms into the Irish land tenure system, and any such Government would have the support of the Irish representatives. It was not forgotten in Ireland that in former days the Conservative Opposition, led by

Mr. Disraeli and supported by a Liberal secession, had rejected a measure for the extension of the suffrage among the people of these countries on the ground that it was too democratic and too revolutionary, had turned the Liberals out of office, come into power themselves, and thereupon immediately brought in and carried a measure for the extension of the suffrage still more democratic, and in that sense more revolutionary in its effects. The Irish National party felt quite confident that it might before very long become a question not whether either Government would ever bring in a Home Rule measure, but as to which of the great political parties would be the first to establish a Government pledged to such a purpose. For these reasons the course of the general election created less excitement and less disturbance in Ireland than in England.

The Conservatives may be said to have gained all they wanted by the results of the general election. Lord Salisbury returned to power as Prime Minister, holding also the office of Lord Privy Seal. The Duke of Devonshire was Lord President of the Council. Sir Michael Hicks Beach became Chancellor of the Exchequer. Mr. Chamberlain, it need hardly be said, returned to his old position as Colonial Secretary; and, as a matter of course, Mr. Balfour became First Lord of the Treasury and leader of the House of Commons. Mr. Ritchie was appointed Home Secretary; the Marquis of Lansdowne accepted for the first time the onerous and, just then, peculiarly exacting office of Foreign Secretary. There were some comparatively untried men in the new Administration, the Earl of Selborne became First Lord of the Admiralty, and there were many other appointments to office for which the qualification of the new occupant had yet to be tested. Mr. Gerald Balfour, brother of Mr. Arthur Balfour, became President of the Board of Trade; but it must be said that Mr. Gerald Balfour had already had considerable experience in Administrative office. The only fault found with this and some other appointments by hostile critics was, that the tendency of the new Administration seemed to be for the introduction of too many members of the same family into the one Ministerial group.

There was also a more serious objection made to the number of those who were brought together in the formation of the new Cabinet. Lord Salisbury's Cabinet, as reconstructed after the general election, consisted of no less than twenty members, the names of most of whom we have already given. This was an unusually and even unprecedentedly large number of members constituting a Cabinet, and even on the Conservative side of political life there was some disparaging criticism of the policy which set up this innovation. It was contended, and with much reason, that the Cabinet, which is supposed and intended to discuss from the outset and to prearrange the whole policy of the Government in every question of great importance, and to act on terms of the most intimate confidence with the Sovereign, ought to be but a small body of men with whom the most momentous secret would be absolutely safe until the time should come for making it known to the outer world in the form of a Ministerial proposition. Many subjects, it was urged, have to be discussed by that body of men on some of which the decision to be adopted may be that no action is to be taken or even proposed. Many other subjects may come from time to time before the Cabinet, concerning which it is in the highest degree necessary that nothing shall be known to the general public until the definite decision of the Ministry is ready for announcement and for practical effect. No matter how great the discretion, the caution, and the self-control of the men who form a Cabinet, it must be taken for granted that the larger the number of those to whom an important secret is confided the greater is the likelihood that some hint as to its nature may prematurely break the bounds of the Ministerial enclosure. The new arrangement is worth noticing, partly because it created so much criticism at the time and partly because it is a subject which is certain to come up again for discussion on the formation of other Cabinets under new conditions.

Four conspicuous members of Lord Salisbury's Cabinet, as it existed at the time of the dissolution, were not to be found in the new Ministry. The first of these whom we shall mention was Viscount Cross, who had held some of the highest Ministerial offices under the Crown, and was indeed one of the most hard-working and influential statesmen on the Conservative side of the political field. He had been Secretary for India, and had more than once been Home Secretary. Lord Cross was one of the men whom it had been part of Lord Randolph Churchill's humour, when he was leading the once famous Fourth Party, to describe as 'the old gang.' Lord Cross, although never regarded as a statesman possessed of any originality of mind or as a commanding orator, and who indeed seemed always fully aware of the fact that nature had not intended him for brilliant feats of eloquence, was thoroughly trustworthy and respected, and in his way a capable member of an Administration. It was understood at the time of the reconstruction that Lord Cross, who had recently been holding the office of Lord Privy Seal, had of his own motion retired from office, or at least declined to hold office again. He had reached the age of seventy-seven, and it was made known that he had given his advanced years as a reason why he should not any longer be expected to undertake the fatigue of office.

Mr. Goschen, First Lord of the Admiralty at the time of the dissolution, had also made it known to Lord Salisbury that he did not intend to resume his place in the Government. Mr. Goschen had, in fact, when the dissolution came, announced to his former constituents of St. George's, Hanover Square, that he did not intend to seek re-election to the House of Commons. Every one felt sure that Mr. Goschen's long and valuable services to Parliament and to the public would be rewarded by a peerage, and the general expectation was that entering the House of Lords he would continue to hold a place in the Conservative Administration. But Lord Goschen, as he was to be, contemplated retirement from official life as well as from the House of Commons, and he held to his resolution that he would not again take office. He has often taken distinct and influential part in the debates of the House of Lords on questions of importance, and he is emphatically one of the peers, very few in number it must be owned, to whose declaration of opinions the outer world turns with interest and respect.

Sir Matthew White Ridley, another retiring Minister, was a comparatively young man, considering the positions he had occupied in Administration and the years he had spent in the House of Commons. He was only fifty-eight at the time of the general election, and it was therefore naturally expected that his name would be announced as that of one holding office in the new Government. But his name did not appear there, and no authentic explanation of his absence from the Ministry was ever given. The general impression was that Lord Salisbury had found it necessary to make room for accessions to the strength of the Government, and was therefore willing to rely on the good-fellowship of some among his former colleagues to help him in the task of making vacancies by withdrawing all claims of their own. Sir Matthew Ridley did not disappear from Parliamentary life altogether. A peerage was given to him, and he entered the House of Lords as Viscount Ridley. Another member of the former Cabinet who did not return to office when the new arrangements came to be made was Mr. Henry Chaplin, who had been President of the Local Government Board. Mr. Chaplin seems to have been not absolutely reticent as to the reasons which led to the omission of his name from the new Ministerial roll. Advancing age certainly could not be held as a sufficient explanation, for Mr. Chaplin's years had not then quite run up to sixty, and in our era of long-living public men we have not come to regard such a time of life as any reason for seeking retirement and absolute repose. The explanation which came to be accepted by the political world was that here again Lord Salisbury, feeling called upon to make openings for rising men of the party, had suggested to Mr. Chaplin that one who had seen so much of Administrative life might be self-sacrificing enough to make way for some one who had not hitherto been thus favoured, and that Mr. Chaplin took the hint and consented to become once more a private member of the House of Commons. The new Parliament had lost for the time some figures which were conspicuous in the House of Commons in the former Parliament.

Most conspicuous of these was Sir George Otto Trevelyan, whose retirement from Parliament and public life early in 1897 had created a feeling of regret among all parties. Sir George Trevelyan entered Parliament as a Liberal in 1865, and had since that time held important offices in Liberal Administrations. He was appointed Civil Lord of the Admiralty in Mr. Gladstone's Government of 1868, but resigned office after less than two years, because he could not entirely agree with his leader and colleagues in regard to the Education Bill introduced by them. He was induced afterwards to become Parliamentary Secretary to the Admiralty. After the murder of Lord Frederick Cavendish in the Phœnix Park, Dublin, he was offered and accepted the very onerous position of Chief Secretary to the Lord-Lieutenant. During the most trying times which followed in the next few years he had been successful, and, on the whole, popular in carrying on the business of his office. Successful in the full sense of the word he could not be, for no man, whatever his political capacity, could have reconciled the Irish people to the system which then prevailed for the government of their country. No Chief Secretary could have been welcome in Ireland who did not offer himself as the precursor of a system of Irish local self-government, and Sir George Trevelyan had no authority and no personal inclination to present himself as the promoter of that policy. He had to administer a number of strictly exceptional laws, utterly different from those prevailing in Great Britain, for the management of political affairs. Under this system every Nationalist mounting a public platform in Ireland was liable to immediate trial under special laws, and to immediate committal to prison for an outspoken censure of the Government and its action, which any man might have delivered at Charing Cross without the slightest interference on the part of the authorities.

Trevelyan made himself as popular as any Chief Secretary for Ireland then could be by his genial manners, his genuine sympathy with trouble or distress for which he was able to offer a remedy, and by the unselfish integrity which always characterised him. In 1884 he entered the Cabinet as Chancellor of the Duchy of Lancaster, and in 1885 became Secretary for Scotland. He resigned this position because he could not agree with some of the legislative principles contained in the Home Rule measure that Mr. Gladstone was preparing for Ireland. He again became a member of an Administration under Mr. Gladstone, and once more held the position of Secretary for Scotland. Trevelyan never was an opponent of the policy which would give to Ireland a local Parliament for the management of her own affairs, and only

took exception to some of the arrangements in
the first measure of Home Rule that seemed to
him unsuited to the working of an Imperial Parliament. Trevelyan carried his conscientious
principles so far as to be unwilling to assist
any measure with the full details of which his
own judgment and sympathies could not entirely
agree. Sir George Trevelyan was endowed with
too sensitive a conscience for that policy of
compromise and mutual concession often found
necessary in the details of political administration.
To him it was nothing to resign a Parliamentary
office, and to give up his chances of rising higher
in Administrative life, but it was everything to
keep himself always in the strictest accordance
with his conscientious principles, and even his
conscientious scruples. The general impression
produced on most of those who had been close
and continuous observers of Parliamentary life
was that Trevelyan's political career had not, on
the whole, been equal to its early promise, or to
the intellectual power he had displayed in literature. Trevelyan was indeed a literary man rather
than a politician. His inspiration was literary;
his interest in passing history and public affairs
had brought him into politics. It was said of
another member of Parliament during Trevelyan's
time that he wrote political novels and made
literary speeches. Trevelyan had not written
political novels, but his speeches in the House
of Commons usually had the flavour of literature

in them. Not that Trevelyan's speeches seemed like carefully prepared literary compositions committed to memory and delivered like literary readings. No such fault was to be observed in his style as a Parliamentary speaker. He could speak readily, was an effective debater, and often rose during some sudden and unexpected debate and delivered a most telling argument, which was obviously extemporaneous. But the general tenor of his thoughts and his utterances seemed to be more akin to the world of letters than to the world of politics.

In his earlier Parliamentary career Trevelyan had rendered great service to the promotion of a much needed reform in our military system, the abolition of the sale of commissions. Trevelyan opened a new era in the Parliamentary movement for the abolition of army purchase. For some time a motion had been brought forward every year in the House of Commons advocating that reform, but it was not until Trevelyan made the subject his own that the annual motion became something more vivid and impressive than is the usual fortune of such annual motions. Trevelyan took up the question with so much vivacity and telling argument that he always secured a deeply interested House, and aroused the attention of the public out-of-doors to the whole subject. Still, Sir George Trevelyan will be remembered as an author of books rather than as a Parliamentary orator or a political administrator. His style as a writer sometimes resembles that of his famous uncle, but does not in any sense suggest imitation of Lord Macaulay. This resemblance is nothing more than the natural result of early association and admiration. George Trevelyan, indeed, developed a variety of styles, each one artistically, although perhaps unconsciously, adapted to the peculiar form of literary work in which his mood engaged him at the time.

A sensation of mingled surprise and regret passed through the world when Trevelyan's retirement from public life was announced. It had long been taken for granted that Trevelyan even then was only approaching to the higher level of his political career, and that he was destined to hold an influential and memorable place in the Parliamentary history of his country. His admirers and his friends could console themselves with the thought that the public man has already accomplished a success when his sudden withdrawal creates no feeling but disappointment and regret at his early renunciation of a career which seems to have bright promise before it. The public are still at a loss to understand why he withdrew from the field so soon, and that is as high a tribute as could be paid to his capacity for greater success, and will be regarded as in itself an honourable epitaph.

There could hardly have been in the new House of Commons any member, no matter to what political party or group he belonged, who did not regard the absence of Mr. Leonard Courtney as a distinct loss to the representative chamber. Mr. Courtney's public career is described in preceding volumes of this History. A scholar, an author, a journalist, he had almost immediately on his entering the House of Commons won for himself a high reputation as a Parliamentary debater. He was keen and quick in argument; he could strike into a debate at some critical point and illumine the discussion by the light of his intellect and his knowledge, by the ready aptness of his language and his illustrations, and whenever he rose to make a speech he was sure to command the intense interest of his audience. He could hardly be described as an orator, and indeed never made any effort at the clothing of his statements and his arguments in eloquence of style or phrase, but no intelligent listener could withdraw his attention for a moment while Mr. Courtney was arguing out his case. He had held many high offices in Liberal Administrations, but he was not in any sense a thorough party man, and would stand up for the Conservatives whenever he believed them to be in the right, or would withdraw his support from Liberals and Conservatives alike when, as often happened, he had formed thoroughly independent opinions. He was an original thinker as well as a strong politician, and was a devoted adherent of the principle of proportionate representation for political opinions

—a cause which he championed with unfailing earnestness, but which never won much success among those who are regarded as practical politicians. He had held with unquestioned success the important position of Chairman of Committees, and he would have been Speaker of the House of Commons but that the Liberal Government found that he could not be elected without a division, and it has generally been thought that where such a contest can be avoided it is better not to have the Speaker elected by a mere majority, however large.

Mr. Courtney had come to hold that place in the estimation of the House which is only given to a genuine statesman. His success was all the more remarkable because there has always been a common opinion, a sort of superstition, prevailing in the House of Commons, that a literary man, especially, perhaps, a philosophical writer and thinker, is not likely ever to acquire a commanding position in Parliamentary life. When it was first made known that the writer of leading articles for the *Times*, the profound scholar and teacher, the devoted advocate of some political doctrines which were then regarded by most as mere intellectual crotchets, was about to enter Parliament, it was assumed by many that he would prove a failure in the peculiar arena of the House. None the less ready was the common recognition of the House, after Mr. Courtney had had some opportunities of proving his capacity, that he had won a genuine Parliamentary success which would have made him an eminent man if his name had never been heard of before. There was a feeling of profound disappointment in all parts of the House, and throughout the public at home and abroad, when it was found that Mr. Courtney's adherence to his political principles, and his opposition to the policy pursued with regard to South Africa, had ended in his temporary withdrawal from Parliament. Mr. Courtney, however, has, in the ordinary course of things, ample time yet before him to recover his place in the House of Commons, and we may safely venture to assert that, whenever the opportunity arises and he is inclined to avail himself of it, his return to his old place will be greeted with a welcome from all parts of the representative chamber.

Two of the most brilliant among the members of the former Parliament not re-elected to the new Parliament were Mr. Philip Stanhope and Mr. Augustine Birrell. Both men had made a distinct mark in Parliamentary debate, and Mr. Birrell had won a high position at the bar and in literature. It was understood that Mr. Stanhope and Mr. Birrell lost their seats because they had steadily opposed the war policy of the Government in South Africa. Both men, however, had only come to the age when they might safely count on having a Parliamentary career still before them, and nothing seemed less likely than that two such distinguished debaters and sincere political champions could be long without finding opportunities and constituencies to secure their re-election to the House of Commons.

We may close this chapter of our History with a record of the fact that the new Parliament opened its short session on the 3rd December 1900, and that Mr. Gully was once again elected Speaker of the House of Commons.

CHAPTER XX.

YET ANOTHER DEATH-ROLL.

On the 13th of January 1900 the long and honoured life of Dr. James Martineau, the eminent Unitarian minister, came to an end at his home in Gordon Square, London. He was born in 1805, and was the brother of Harriet Martineau, one of the most celebrated women of her time. James Martineau received his education at Norwich, at Bristol, and at York University. In 1828 he was ordained one of the Unitarian ministers at the Unitarian meeting-house in Eustace Street, Dublin. The Irish capital did not hold any considerable proportion of the Unitarian denomination among its inhabitants, but those who attended the ministrations at the Eustace Street meeting-house soon appreciated the remarkable qualities of the young minister, and his name began to make itself well known in all the cultivated and intellectual sections of society in Dublin. After a few years' work in Dublin Martineau was removed to the pastorship of the Unitarian meeting-house in Paradise Street,

Liverpool, and there for a quarter of a century he continued to preach, to instruct, and to write. He won for himself a reputation, and indeed a fame, which made his name celebrated throughout the whole of the civilised world. As a preacher his style was eloquent, thoughtful, persuasive, with a suffusion of the imaginative and the poetic which gave to all his discourses a positive fascination even for listeners who did not share his views on religious subjects. It was distinctly an ornate style, but the ornaments always seemed to belong fittingly and becomingly to the sentiments and arguments they illustrated, and never were mere purple patches put on to attract attention.

Dr. Martineau was not given much to theological controversy, and never delighted in aggressive onslaughts on any forms of faith which differed from his own. It was his pervading belief that sincere religious faith was its own justification, and that converts were better won by sympathetic appreciation and by an earnest striving for the good of all than by aggressive argument to prove that some article of an opponent's creed was in itself absurd or immoral or absurd and immoral at the same time. He was so willing to recognise and admire all that he believed to be religious in its motive, even where he could not accept its doctrine, that some among his own followers held that he went rather too far in the respect which he showed for the ceremonials of the Church of Rome. He was not an agnostic, even in that higher and better sense of the word which in our days describes a man who has made up his mind that there is no possibility in this life of forming any conclusions as to the existence of a world to come, who resolves to waste no more time or thought in trying to know the unknowable, and devotes himself while on earth to the service of our common humanity. James Martineau was not in any sense a man of such mood. He firmly believed that faith in religion was the highest quality of the human being, and that the world we live in must ever seek for illumination from the world to come. One of his fine utterances was that prayer is not a means but an end; in other words, that the highest mission of prayer is attained for him who prays by the uplifting of his soul into communion with the Higher Power.

Throughout his ministerial career James Martineau devoted himself to the task of spreading education among all classes with whom he came into contact, without any limitation as to sect. While he ministered to his Unitarian congregation in Liverpool he gathered together numbers of young men and boys who held, under his presidency, frequent meetings in one of the rooms of his chapel for the reading of essays on all manner of historical, literary, and philosophical subjects, and for debate on the subjects presented for consideration. No condition as to religious creed was allowed to interfere with the free admission to these meetings, and youths who belonged to the

Church of England were there brought into companionship with youths who belonged to the Church of Rome or to any other of the religious sects, or even with those, if there were any such, who professed no religious faith whatever. Many young men who in after years rose to eminence in literature, in science, and in the learned professions had their earliest intellectual training in these meetings guided and presided over by James Martineau.

When he removed to London he made himself active, as he had ever been, in his efforts to fill the minds of boys and young men with a genuine love for intellectual culture. He received degrees and honours from many great scholastic institutions. He wrote much in reviews of the higher order and published many books, for the most part studies in religion and morals. His ninetieth birthday, in 1895, was celebrated by the presentation to him of a congratulatory address from a very large and distinguished circle of friends and admirers, many of whom did not belong to the Unitarian denomination. His life extended for some five years yet of work after his own heart, and therefore, it may be assumed, of happiness to him. He was a deep and even a profound thinker on the subjects he had striven to make his own, but he never sought after original discovery, nor was he under the spell or the charm which is found for so many in the quest for novelty of enterprise. His life was simple, pure, consistent, and his name will live.

The death of John Ruskin is an event belonging not only to the history of England but to the history of the world's art and literature. Ruskin died on January 20, 1900, at his residence in Brantwood, near Coniston, which he had made the home of his later years. Ruskin was born in Hunter Street, Brunswick Square, London, in February 1819, and while he was still a child his father removed with all his family to Herne Hill, then looked upon by Londoners as a region quite in the country. The father was a wine merchant in a large way of business, who travelled about the country to seek for orders, and often took his son John on long excursions with him, and thus gave the boy ample opportunities of seeing many places in England and Wales. The boy seems to have been filled from the first with that love of external nature, of the hills and the woods and the streams, which had so subtle and so strong an influence on the whole of his career. Ruskin was evidently born with that truly artistic soul which looks through nature into art, and by the inspiration of art learns all the better to appreciate the teaching of nature. Ruskin's mother was of a deeply religious temperament, and from his early childhood she inspired her son with a love for studying the pages of the Bible, and with that religious fervour which suffused all the writings of his manhood. Mrs. Ruskin earnestly desired that her son should become a clergyman, but the boy very soon found himself irresistibly drawn to artistic studies. His father was much given to collecting pictures and drawings, and had become the owner of a set of Turner drawings, the study of which had much to do with the final determination of the son's career.

John Ruskin studied for a time at Christ Church, Oxford, but his health was not strong or sustained enough to admit of his devoting himself to close study, and he had to spend much of his time in health-resorts on the European Continent. During these intervals of leisure he made it part of his recreation to take frequent lessons in painting, and it soon became clear to his mind that the realm of art was the realm in which he was destined to live. So early in his life as the year 1843 he gave to the world the first volume of 'Modern Painters,' which was announced as the work of 'a graduate of Oxford.' In this volume the author tells us that he has 'come forward to declare and demonstrate, wherever they exist, the essence and the authority of the beautiful and the true.' This first volume came out at a time when art culture in the highest sense was not much thought of in these countries. The spirit of art was but little recognised as an influence even among those who made collections of paintings, or among those who painted pictures for galleries and collectors. A beautiful or striking picture was indeed admired and obtained its price, and rich men made it a part of their pleasure and their social duty to adorn their dwellings with collections of paintings. But these rich men and their friends did not concern themselves much with theories as to the teachings of art or the association of art with the highest and most ennobling influences of man's life. Ruskin's book sent a thrill through the whole intellectual world of his time, and startled even commonplace minds with the idea that there was something in the painter's art more divine in its purpose than the production of good portraits or picturesque landscapes to ornament the walls of a respectable residence.

Much of the impression made by Ruskin's first volume was undoubtedly due to the fascination of its style as well as to the bold originality of its theories. Ruskin had been endowed by nature with a gift of rich and peculiar eloquence. His pages abounded in happy and original phrases, in vividly illustrative sentences, and they carried the reader, by a sudden flight, into a rarefied and exalted atmosphere which made him feel almost dizzy with his sudden elevation. Ruskin had come to teach what he believed to be a gospel of the unity of truth and beauty, and that doctrine filled him throughout his whole life with an inspiring faith. He never could believe that there was nothing more in the culture of true art than the production of faithful portraits, picturesque landscapes, symmetrical statues, or largely read books. He believed that the true study of art literature and science meant something more than all this, and was of kindred with, or a part of, religion itself. The manner in which this doctrine was preached by him from his beginning as an author drew a crowd of listeners at once around him, and fascinated many who not only did not accept his doctrines, but were inclined at first, and even continued all through, to regard him as a brilliant inventor of audacious artistic paradoxes. The first volume passed through two large editions before the second volume was published—a success which, in those now distant days, was hardly to be predicted for any book engaging itself with nothing more, so far as its name indicated, than an account of the work of modern painters. The second volume appeared in 1846, and two further volumes after an interval of some ten years; the fifth and sixth volumes, which closed the series, were published in 1860.

By this time an entirely new school of art had grown into existence—a school earnestly avowing the principles which Ruskin had illustrated in his 'Modern Painters,' although many of the school did not profess to be in complete conformity with some of the practical instances set forth by him as embodying his creed. Ruskin might have been regarded as if he had come into this life of artistic teaching for the very purpose of advocating the cause put into movement by the pre-Raphaelites. He became the close friend of Dante Gabriel

Rossetti, Ford Madox Brown, Edward Burne-Jones, and the other leaders of the great new school—the æsthetic school, as it used to be called. That æsthetic school had preachers and teachers of its own in the sister art of poetry, and the loving admirers of Ruskin and the pre-Raphaelite painters were sure to be loving admirers also of the æsthetic poets, Swinburne, Morris, and Rossetti.

Ruskin also gave deep attention to the study of architecture as an art, and therefore as a development in human progress and in the practical illustration of the union between beauty and truth. His 'Seven Lamps of Architecture,' 'The Stones of Venice,' and other works of the same order, opened a new chapter in the story of artistic criticism. Ruskin's whole nature was suffused with religious feeling, and his religious impulses derived much influence from his frequent association with the Rev. F. D. Maurice, and his unceasing efforts to assist Maurice in the promotion of the movement for the maintenance and spread of teaching organisations to instruct working-men. He was also a friend of Thomas Carlyle, and it was probably owing to Carlyle's influence that he became imbued with some theories as to the highest principles of social order which occasionally astonished the outer world. Ruskin had an unresting activity in his pursuit of all theories having to do with human development, and had a complete faith in his own capacity to become a teacher on every subject which concerned man's work in this world and his preparation for the world to come. On many occasions he diverged suddenly from the paths of artistic culture he had traversed so long, and understood so well, into some unfamiliar roads, which he trod as confidently and as rapidly as if he knew thoroughly whither they were leading his steps. It happened, therefore, that some of those who had looked up to Ruskin with unmingled confidence when he instructed them in art found themselves forced into sudden and amazed hostility to his teaching when he undertook to instruct them in the principles of political government, and to expound his theories on the rights of the rulers and the duties of the ruled.

But whatever differences of opinion may have existed concerning Ruskin's teachings when he went out of his own sphere, there could be only one common feeling of admiration for the eloquence of his style and the earnestness with which he devoted himself to the purpose he had in view. There are many of Ruskin's admirers who could wish that he had kept more strictly to his own subjects, the subjects in which he was best qualified to instruct the world, and had not entered into the discussion of questions concerning which he had either to take his opinions at second-hand, or to evolve them out of his own moral consciousness without much reference to the realities of the present or the past. Still, there are some of us who are glad to read what

Ruskin had to say on any subject, whether he quite understood it or not, and who can enjoy his eloquent pages even when unable to agree with the doctrines they so confidently expound. During the later years of his life Ruskin spent most of his time at the house he had bought for himself in the Lake country; that country whose outlines, colours, and atmosphere must have been so congenial with his love and appreciation of the beauty of landscape. His later days were passed in almost absolute seclusion there.

On the 17th of February Joseph Cowen, who had been for many years a prominent figure in Parliament and in public life, a democrat of the truest and the best order, a popular orator, not surpassed in his day, died at his home at Newcastle-on-Tyne. Joseph Cowen was the son of Sir Joseph Cowen, who represented Newcastle in the House of Commons for many years, and to whose Parliamentary seat the younger Cowen was elected on his father's death. Joseph Cowen belonged to a family of extensive coal-owners and manufacturers of firebricks and clay retorts. He was brought up with ample means at his disposal, and spent, during his lifetime, large sums of money in all manner of beneficent and patriotic undertakings. He was educated at Edinburgh University, and from his earliest days took an intense interest in political questions. He soon proved himself to be an advanced Radical of the most genuine order, and a sympathiser with every struggle for liberty going on throughout the world. He became the friend of Kossuth, Mazzini, Garibaldi, and Alexander Herzen, the Russian exile who spent many years in England. Joseph Cowen was not, however, in any sense what is commonly called an anarchist, nor was he a mere political leveller. He was a sincere and even impassioned lover of liberty, but he never associated himself with any movement which encouraged licence, or which was not based on the doctrines of public and private morality. He was a sincere advocate of Home Rule for Ireland, and felt much sympathy with the Parliamentary organisation for that purpose, which was led by Charles Stewart Parnell. When the Special Commission was appointed to inquire into the charges made against Parnell at the time of the Pigott forgeries, Cowen warmly advocated the cause of the Irish Nationalist party and their leader. Cowen was under the impression, at the time, that the expense of maintaining their cause might overtax the resources of the party, and it is said that he privately offered to a friend of Parnell and of himself a contribution of £10,000 towards the cost of the defence. The offer, it appears, was not accepted, because it was certain that the Nationalists of Ireland could not fail to receive from Irishmen the means of meeting the expense, but Cowen's offer was none the less remembered with gratitude.

Joseph Cowen was the proprietor of the *Newcastle Daily Chronicle* and *Weekly Chronicle*, and wrote many articles in these as well as in other publications. He was so eloquent a speaker, indeed so genuine an orator, that he might have won for himself a place amongst the greatest public speakers in our Parliamentary history if only he had devoted himself to oratorical display. In a former volume of this History some account is given of a really memorable speech delivered by Joseph Cowen during a debate in the House of Commons in 1876 on Mr. Disraeli's proposal to confer on Queen Victoria the title of Empress of India. Mr. Gathorne Hardy, a leading member of the Conservative Government, described Mr. Cowen's speech as having positively 'electrified' the House. Mr. Cowen had then been some sessions in Parliament, but had seldom taken any conspicuous part in debate. There can hardly be any question that if he had had the ambition to shine as a Parliamentary orator, Mr. Cowen could have gratified that ambition to the full, and won for himself a distinct renown. But he seems to have had no aspiration of that kind, and he only took part in debate when a subject was under discussion on which he felt strongly, and concerning which his special knowledge enabled him to contribute to the debate some facts and arguments which the House was not likely otherwise to hear. Mr. Cowen devoted himself almost altogether to the work of forwarding, by quiet and practical influence, the interests of every cause he had at heart, and when such results could be accomplished without public speaking, he was only too glad not to mount the platform or to catch the Speaker's eye. Joseph Cowen was emphatically an independent member of the House of Commons, and would have opposed a Liberal Ministry as readily as a Tory Ministry if his own convictions thus inspired him.

A great war correspondent passed out of life on the 29th of March when Archibald Forbes died at his home in Regent's Park, London. The career of Archibald Forbes illustrates an era in the development of war correspondence which has become so remarkable a constituent part of our modern history. So far as the English press is concerned, William Howard Russell represents the period before the telegraph wire became the medium for the transmission of the correspondent's messages, and Archibald Forbes represents the order of correspondents who could send their descriptions of a battle from the battle-ground itself, and with a speed of flight much swifter than that of any arrow from the Tartar bow. Russell was the most brilliant representative of the days when the war correspondent had to take his time in the despatch of his letters, whether he liked it or not, and might, after the close of some great battle, have had hours to plan and write, to revise and improve his letter, for the simple reason that there was no possible means of sending it off any earlier. Forbes came to the front during the more recent conditions when much of the correspondent's letter had to be dashed off on the field of battle itself, and when the battle was over the first thing the correspondent had to do was to make for the nearest point where telegraphic communication could be had, and to send his despatch along the wires. The letters of Forbes are thrilling with movement, and carry a breathless interest in their every word. Each correspondent was at the very head of his own order, and each illustrates admirably the conditions of the period at which he did his work.

Archibald Forbes was the son of a Scottish minister of religion, and a native of Morayshire, Scotland, where he was born in 1838. He studied for a while at the University of Aberdeen, and developed early a passion for military life. His parents did not much encourage his wish for soldiering, but the young Forbes followed his own inclinations and enlisted in a dragoon regiment, where he served for several years. The knowledge he thus acquired of soldiering proved of immense advantage to him in his career as a war correspondent. Archibald Forbes had also from the first an inclination for a literary career, and he would seem to have been destined especially for the life of a war correspondent. He left the army, and sought to make a living by journalism. Among his earliest contributions to newspaper work in London were some articles which he wrote for the *Morning Star*, the newspaper representing the political opinions of Cobden and Bright, articles describing the conditions of military life in barracks and camps, and intended to draw attention to the need of much improvement in some parts of the British military system. Soon after these earliest experiments of his in the work of a journalist, he obtained an engagement as special correspondent for the *Daily News* during the war between France and Prussia, which ended in the German occupation of Paris and the election of King William of Prussia as Emperor of the newly created German Empire. From that time forth Forbes bore his part with ever-increasing celebrity in all the great campaigns that had to be described in the columns of the *Daily News*. He acted as correspondent also in many foreign countries where public ceremonials were going on, having nothing to do with war. He accompanied the Prince of Wales in his tour through India. Later still he delivered lectures describing his battlefield experiences to enthusiastic audiences in England, the United States, Canada, and Australia. During the later period of his life his health broke down so much, in consequence of the unsparing manner in which he had overtasked it during his adventurous career, that he was compelled to give up the work of a war correspondent, and to be content with quiet journalism and literature. He became a voluminous author, published many books describing his various campaigns, several biographies of military men, and a novel called 'Drawn from Life,' which derived its incidents, its characters, and its story from that life which he knew so well and could draw with such realistic effect. He became well known in the social world of London and other great cities, where he found a welcome not only because of his fame as a war correspondent, but also because of his genial unassuming manners, his conversational powers, and his absolute sincerity of character. His name must always hold a distinct and an honoured place in the history of English journalism.

On the 24th of April George Douglas Campbell, Duke of Argyll, died at Inverary Castle, Scotland. The Duke of Argyll was, during his active life, a conspicuous figure in Parliament, in political and religious controversy, in literature, and even in science. He tried many fields of distinction, and he must be allowed to have won some success in each of them. At one time it looked as if he were to become identified with the business of politics; at another time his ambition seemed to be mainly for success as an author of books; then he aroused attention by his writings on scientific questions; and then again he became a prominent and most active disputant in theological controversy. In none of these fields could he be regarded as a failure, but it must be owned that in none of them did he achieve what could be counted as success of the highest order. He was born on the 30th of April 1823, and in 1847 he succeeded to his father's peerage and took his place in the House of Lords. He began his Parliamentary career as a supporter of the policy of Sir Robert Peel, but after a while he became an advocate of the more advanced policy then represented by Lord John Russell, and maintained from that time what we should now call the principles of moderate Liberalism.

The Duke of Argyll was unquestionably one of the most brilliant speakers in the House of Lords; indeed, he ranked fairly among the Parliamentary orators of his day. He held office in many Administrations as a Cabinet Minister, and during the American Civil War he made himself remarkable by his support of the Northern side at a time when most public men of conspicuous position in England were disposed to give their sympathies to the cause of the South. He was the only member of the Cabinet who declared himself in favour of the proposal to detain the *Alabama* at the first British port she entered, a proposal which, if acted upon, might have saved England much trouble, some pecuniary loss, and no small amount of humiliation. He was a supporter of Mr. Gladstone on many important questions, but he fell away from the great Liberal leader in the first instance because of Gladstone's policy with regard to the Irish Land question, and the breach became still wider and deeper when Gladstone pledged himself to the principle of Home Rule for Ireland. In 1888 the Duke of Argyll actually moved a vote of no confidence in the Irish policy of the Liberal leader, and the vote was carried without a division in the House of Lords, an achievement which had, however, no very great effect on Mr. Gladstone's followers in the House of Commons. The Duke opposed Mr. Gladstone's second Home Rule Bill, that of 1893, with as much earnestness and emotion as he had displayed towards the measure of 1886, but Mr. Gladstone nevertheless carried his Bill through the House of Commons. The House of Lords and the Duke of Argyll had their turn then, and by rejecting the measure, left the question of Home Rule to be a subject of strife for some future Parliament.

The health of the Duke of Argyll began to break down in 1895, and his active political life concluded soon after. His name will always hold a distinguished place in the history of Queen Victoria's reign. Those who followed his career with close and living observation may sometimes feel disposed to ask whether it ought to be regarded rather as a success or as a failure. The doubt only arises from the fact that, in each kind of work which he attempted, the Duke at first gave promise of a success which must bring him among the very foremost, and that in no instance did he actually fulfil the expectation he had created. In each particular competition the Duke of Argyll did not shoot his arrow as high as some other competitors had done, and therefore had to be classed among those who failed to carry off the prize. As an orator in Parliament and on platforms he never, for all his splendid promise and his fine performance, rose to the level of Gladstone, Bright, or Disraeli. His literary productions are often admirable in themselves, and, are always interesting, but they do not seem likely to secure an abiding fame for their author. So, too, of his efforts in scientific controversy, and his contributions to theological debate. But if we estimate the career of the Duke of Argyll by what he actually accomplished rather than by what most of us at one time believed him able to accomplish, we must readily admit that he holds a high place in politics and letters among the men of the Victorian era.

On the 30th of July Prince Alfred Ernest Albert, second son and fourth child of Queen Victoria and the Prince Consort, died at Coburg from cancer of the throat. The English Prince was then reigning Prince of Saxe-Coburg and Gotha, having succeeded to that position on the death of his uncle, the Prince of Wales having renounced his right to the succession. Prince Alfred was born at Windsor Castle on the 6th of August 1844. He received his earliest education under private tutors, and then studied at the Universities of Bonn and Edinburgh, and in 1857 he entered the British Navy. An English Royal family without a Prince in the Navy would, in our modern times, be something of an anomaly or even an anachronism, and Prince Alfred soon gave evidence that he had genuine qualifications for the life of a sailor. He served through many voyages as a midshipman, and was the first member of the Royal family who ever visited South Africa. In 1863 he became a Lieutenant, and in 1866 was raised to the rank of Captain in the *Galatea*. In command of this ship he visited India, China, Japan, and Australia, and was received everywhere in the colonies with much enthusiasm, and seems indeed to have made himself welcome everywhere by his frank and genial manners and by the spirit of camaraderie which was part of his nature.

During Prince Alfred's visit to Port Jackson, New South Wales, in the March of 1868, he encountered an experience which seems to be common to every Royal personage even in our civilised days—he became the object of an assassin's attack, and actually received a bullet wound. Prince Alfred's assailant was a man named O'Farrell. The attempt was made while the Prince was taking part in some festivities organised for the benefit of the funds of a sailors' home. A man was seen to approach his Royal Highness suddenly, and to take deliberate aim at him with a revolver, of which he fired one barrel before any one had time to prevent him. The Prince fell to the ground on his face and hands. The assassin was immediately seized, but before he could be disarmed he fired two other shots at his captors, neither having any harmful effect. His Royal Highness was at once conveyed to his tent, and it was found that the bullet had pierced his back, but that no vital part had been injured. The Prince never lost consciousness, and as he was being carried from the place he murmured to those around him, 'I am not much hurt—I shall be better soon.' A crowd gathered round the man who had fired the shots, and it was with much difficulty that the people could be prevented from killing him on the spot. He received some serious injuries, and when rescued from immediate death he was conveyed at once to a prison. There he declared that his intention was to kill the Royal Prince. He stated that he had no companions whatever in his attempt, and 'that there was not a human being in existence who had the slightest idea of the object I had in view.' O'Farrell was tried, found guilty, and sentenced to death, and his execution took place on the 21st of April. Prince Alfred, it should be said, expressed several times his strong desire that the wretched man should have a fair trial, and gave it also as his firm conviction that the attempt at assassination had not been, as was first believed by most persons in the colony, the result of a Fenian plot got up by an organisation in New South Wales. Prince Alfred went so far as to offer his personal intercession on behalf of the convict during his imprisonment, in order that he might be treated as a maniac and not subjected to the death penalty. The Royal Prince soon recovered from his wounds, but as it was feared that the climate of the colony might not help his restoration to health, he was ordered home in the *Galatea*.

Before this event had occurred, Prince Alfred had attained his majority, and had been created Duke of Edinburgh, Earl of Ulster and Kent. We must not omit to mention one very interesting and picturesque event in the earlier career of the Duke of Edinburgh. In 1862, when a vacancy took place in the succession to the throne of Greece, Prince Alfred was not only offered the crown of that kingdom, but was actually proclaimed King of Greece by the National Assembly, and the proclamation was received with demonstrations of enthusiastic welcome by the whole Greek population. Prince Alfred declined to accept any such responsibility, and the crown was then offered to the second son of the King of Denmark, and he became King George I. of Greece. The remainder of the Duke of Edinburgh's life was devoted to the duties of his position in the Navy. In 1874 he married the Russian Grand Duchess Marie Alexandrovna. In February 1899 there came a severe calamity upon him by the death of his only son, Prince Alfred of Saxe-Coburg and Gotha, and from the effect of that terrible shock he seems never to have recovered. His whole career was one of honour to himself, to his family, and to his country.

The 10th of August saw the close of a noble life and a great public career. Charles Russell, Lord Russell of Killowen, died on that day. He had had but a short illness, which at first was not believed to be serious, but soon proved itself beyond the art of physician or surgeon. Lord Russell of Killowen was born at Newry, County Down, Ireland, in 1832. He was educated at Trinity College, Dublin, and there it is said that he distinguished himself more especially in athletics and in riding than in purely scholastic exercises. Those who knew Lord Russell in his years of distinction will find no difficulty in believing this description of his college days, for he was always a splendid rider, and took a great interest in hunting and in racing, although he was never given to gambling on the turf. But those who followed his career must feel assured that he had not wholly neglected his studies at Trinity College, for there was always evident in him the influence of genuine education from the beginning. He was soon found to have a gift for legal work. In 1854 he became a solicitor at Belfast, practised there for a time, and afterwards in Liverpool, but he rose rapidly to the higher walk of the profession, and in 1859 was called to the Bar at Lincoln's Inn. During his early life in London he devoted himself a good deal to journalism, as many young barristers have done in modern days, and he obtained a seat in the Reporters' Gallery of the House of Commons, and made notes of speeches delivered in that assembly, of which he was destined to be one of the leading figures in his maturer years. His abilities as a barrister soon began to show themselves; he distinguished himself on the Northern Circuit, and made a great reputation in the Liverpool Law Courts. In 1872 he became Queen's Counsel, and by that time had come to be regarded as one of the most powerful pleaders at the Common Law Bar. In every great case it might now be taken for granted that Charles Russell would be engaged if only his services could be obtained. He was a master of the common law, a most eloquent pleader, and a skilful cross-examiner. He had a great gift of forensic eloquence, and there was a fervour in his nature which compelled him to throw his whole power into every cause it became his duty to advocate.

Such a man was sure before long to have an opportunity thrust upon him, even if he did not seek it, of entering the House of Commons. Charles Russell received, in 1880, an invitation to become the Liberal candidate for Dundalk, in his native county. He accepted the invitation, and entered the House of Commons. He was a Catholic in religion; a thorough Liberal, and even a Radical in his political principles; a sincere lover of his country, and a champion of her claims on Parliament for just dealing, and might indeed have been described as a Nationalist, except for the fact that he did not go so far in his assertion of those claims as Mr. Parnell and the body of Irish members who bore the distinctive title of Nationalists would have desired him to go. When Mr. Gladstone formed his first Home Rule Administration, Russell, who was by that time member for South Hackney, was made Attorney-General. In the House of Commons he had made for himself, from the very first, a distinguished position, not merely as a lawyer speaking on questions of law, but as a Parliamentary debater on all subjects of public interest, in the discussion of which he felt called upon to take a part. He never spoke but when he had something appropriate and important to say; his arguments were always telling; and where the occasion was great he could move the House by an eloquence really thrilling. He was engaged for the defence in the famous Parnell Commission of 1888, and won for himself there a renown destined to pass into history, destined to be remembered among the greatest triumphs of the English Bar. Russell's cross-examination of Pigott the forger will ever be remembered by all who were present during that remarkable struggle between the dexterous, unscrupulous criminal and the incomparable advocate of the accused Irish Nationalists. The speech which Russell delivered then was undoubtedly one of the most splendid displays of an advocate's eloquence to be recorded to the honour of the legal profession at any time. The presiding judge, Lord Hannen, was seen, when Russell had concluded the last sentence of his speech, to write some words on a slip of paper. The slip of paper was immediately passed on to the great advocate who had just resumed his seat, and it was afterwards known that the paper contained these words written by Lord Hannen, 'A great speech, worthy of a great occasion.'

When Mr. Gladstone came back to office in 1892 Sir Charles Russell once again became Attorney-General, and he acted as counsel in several important arbitration cases where the British Government had to sustain or to resist international claims. In 1894 he was appointed a Lord of Appeal, and received a life peerage, taking the title of Lord Russell of Killowen. Not many months later he reached his highest position, and was appointed Lord Chief Justice of England, the first Roman Catholic raised to that great office since the days of the Reformation. There is a general belief, perhaps not without its general warrant, that a great pleader hardly ever makes a great judge, but this belief was certainly not borne out in the case of Lord Russell's elevation to the judicial bench. The unanimous judgment of the Bar, as well as of the public, declared that Lord Russell proved himself as great a judge as he had already proved himself a lawyer and pleader. Lord Russell was a man of the most genial manners, and had friends in all sections of society. Nature had given him a certain quickness of temper which was in harmony with the rapidity of his intellectual perceptions and the fervour which seemed to identify his whole energies and heart with any great cause which he advocated, whether as pleader or as politician. But there was in him no quality whatever of personal or capricious animosity, and his generous heart could never have harboured any unworthy feeling. He had an Irish love of hospitality, and in his London home rivals at the Bar and rivals in the House of Commons met on terms of friendship. No success of our time was ever more fairly and honourably won than that of Charles Russell, and his was one of those fine natures which are never spoiled by success. The friends whom he had known in his early days of struggle, when fortune and fame still must have seemed to him but vague possibilities, were held in his friendship to the last. His promotion at the Bar and in Parliamentary life was due solely to his personal merits, and not to any favour from patron or party. He won a distinct and independent success at the Bar, in Parliament, and on the judicial Bench.

On the 25th of October, John Sims Reeves, the greatest English tenor singer of his time, died at the age of eighty-two. He was the son of a corporal in the Royal Artillery, and was born at Woolwich. He received most of his early education from the teaching of his father, who appears to have been a man of remarkable intelligence. An enthralling love for music soon made itself evident in the young Sims Reeves, and he taught himself as well as he could the use of many instruments. He obtained an appointment as organist of a church in 1832, and in 1839 he made his first appearance on the stage at Newcastle-on-Tyne. This first appearance of Sims Reeves in opera was a decided success, but he did not long continue to be a baritone singer, and he very soon developed that magnificent tenor voice which never had its equal in the English opera of his time. Two years after his appearance at Newcastle-on-Tyne he was engaged by Macready as second tenor at Drury Lane Theatre. Sims Reeves did not satisfy himself with the assumption that he had now completed his musical education. He went to the Continent, set himself down to musical studies and practice at Paris and Milan, and did not return to England until 1847.

Then began Sims Reeves' career of unbroken success as tenor singer and as actor on the operatic stage, and his equal popularity in oratorio. His voice was an organ of marvellous range and sweetness, capable of expressing every variety of emotion — the strongest passion, the tenderest pathos, the brightest humour—and he did not rely upon these vocal gifts alone. Sims Reeves, if he had never been qualified to appear on the stage as a singer, might have made a reputation and fortune for himself as an actor. Many admirers 'while enjoying the great tenor's performance of such a part as Edgardo in 'Lucia di Lammermoor,' must have felt inclined to doubt whether the singer or the actor was showing the greater power, was coming nearer to absolute perfection in the accomplishment of his part. Sims Reeves left the operatic stage at an early period in his life, feeling, probably, that the success of an opera singer and actor is one which rarely long outlasts the prime of life, and feeling, too, that this is perhaps a fact which singers and actors do not always recognise. After 1860 he may be said to have given up his work on the stage, and from that time forth his voice was only heard in oratorio and at concerts. His farewell appearance was made at the Albert Hall in 1891, and from that time forth he was but a delightful memory to the great public which had so thoroughly appreciated his art.

The name of Max-Müller, for all its German nationality, must ever be associated with the history of Oxford University, and with the philological and other scientific literature of England. He was the son of Wilhelm Max-Müller, a poet of some distinction, and an accomplished philologist, and was born at Dessau in 1823. He received his education, for the most part, from his father, in a home where the literature of all nations was a subject of constant and loving study. He was afterwards a student at the universities of Leipzig and Berlin, where he studied philosophy and philology under some famous teachers, and he obtained very early distinction by his translations from the Sanskrit. Afterwards he went to Paris, where he became a disciple of Eugene Burnouf. In 1848, feeling anxious to expand his studies by recourse to the great English libraries, he came to England, which was destined to be his home for the rest of his life. In London he made the acquaintance of Baron Bunsen, the Prussian Ambassador, and was brought by Bunsen to the notice of the directors of the East India Company, who engaged him to translate the Rig-Veda, the sacred hymns of the Brahmans. Under the advice and influence of Baron Bunsen, Max-Müller made up his mind to settle in England, and in 1848 he took up his abode at Oxford. His capacity as a philologist was at once appreciated by the authorities of Oxford, who appointed him Deputy-Professor of Modern Languages, and afterwards raised him to the rank of Professor, having practically established that rank for his especial benefit. In 1858 he was elected a Fellow of All Souls. He became one of the candidates for the professorship of Sanskrit, and a keen controversy was aroused by this contest. Sir Monier Williams carried the election, and it was commonly believed at the time that theological as well as merely philological considerations had a good deal to do with the result of the contest. Max-Müller felt much disappointed by the result, and had for a while a strong inclination to leave

Oxford altogether and return to Germany. His friends, however, prevailed upon him to relinquish this idea, and, much to the advantage of Oxford, he was induced to remain in the country which had given him such a welcome, and where his influence was so readily acknowledged.

Max-Müller was one of the scientific men of that time who held it an honourable as well as a most useful part of their work to deliver lectures to the general public. At the Royal Institution and in other places he gave courses of lectures on the Science of Language, the Science of Religion, and the Science of Thought. All these discourses appear to have been deeply interesting, and the lecturer's style was brilliant and fascinating. As might have been expected, these lectures created a large amount of scientific controversy, and when they were published in authorised and permanent form the controversy kept on broadening and intensifying for some time. Max-Müller was endowed by nature with a passion for the devolution of great cohesive and comprehensive theories on every subject he expounded, and he was sure to bring up antagonism from all sides with regard to some principle or other which he laid down. But there can be no doubt that his own reputation continued to grow, and that his influence tended to expand and exalt the scholarship of the University. At the invitation of Dean Stanley he delivered a lecture on 'The Religions of the World' in

Westminster Abbey, a lecture which is stated to have been the only address ever delivered by a layman within the precincts of the Abbey. The remainder of his life was devoted to the pursuits in which he had won his fame and had done so much for the spread of the studies congenial with his intellect. He received honours from all the Sovereigns and States of the civilised world, and in England received the distinction, rarely conferred on a teacher of science, of being created a Privy Councillor, and thus entitled to be described as the Right Honourable. His later days were darkened by much physical suffering, but he continued his work almost to the very end. He died on October 28.

'Passed in music out of sight' are words that might appropriately describe the death of Sir Arthur Sullivan, which took place on November 22, 1900. Sir Arthur Sullivan had for many years held the world—a large part of the world which loves music—in thrall by his powers as a musical composer. He may be said to have created a musical school of his own by the method which he introduced of uniting the genius of the musician with that of the literary composer in the creation of dramatic work. For many years the names of Arthur Sullivan and W. S. Gilbert were as closely associated in the public mind with the dramatic art as those of Beaumont and Fletcher. Sullivan and Gilbert worked together in the production of such pieces as

'Trial by Jury,' 'H.M.S. Pinafore,' 'The Pirates of Penzance,' 'Patience,' 'Iolanthe,' 'The Mikado,' 'Ruddigore,' and 'The Yeomen of the Guard.' The two artists seemed as if they had been born to work together. Mr. Gilbert's delightful humours, fancies, fantasies, and even eccentricities, found their perfect expression in the exhaustless variety of Sir Arthur Sullivan's music. But his share in these successes was only a part of his artistic triumphs. He composed the music for many other dramatic pieces, and he would have made a fame for himself if he had done nothing but produce the great oratorios and cantatas which bear his name. He also composed incidental music for 'The Merchant of Venice,' 'The Merry Wives of Windsor,' 'Macbeth,' and other plays. He created hymn tunes and anthems, and gave music to many songs. He conducted great musical festivals, and added compositions of his own to their attraction.

Sir Arthur Sullivan's career, although so rich in production, was not one of great length if measured by the average of men's lives. He was born on 13th May 1842, and was the son of Thomas Sullivan, bandmaster of Sandhurst Military College. The young Arthur Sullivan entered the Chapel Royal as chorister when only twelve years old, and during that time he studied at the Royal Academy of Music, and afterwards spent three years of musical study in Leipzig. In 1862 he composed music for Shakespeare's 'Tempest,' which at once won him a reputation, and in 1867 he came out for the first time as a dramatic composer in a musical farce entitled 'Cox and Box,' a sort of artistic paraphrase of the long-familiar farce. His career from that period was but one succession of musical triumphs, the triumphs of music grave, gay, lively, and severe. In 1872 he composed the 'Festival Te Deum,' to celebrate the recovery of the Prince of Wales from a most dangerous illness. In 1883 Queen Victoria paid her tribute to his genius, which she had appreciated from the first, by giving him his knighthood. During his later years he had been in weak health, and his death came from sudden failure of the heart's action. Queen Victoria made it a special request that the mortal remains of the great composer should be buried in St. Paul's Cathedral, and a representative from Her Majesty was present at the funeral service. The German Emperor sent his representative also, and indeed Arthur Sullivan must fittingly have been attended to his grave by some representative of such a home of song and poetry as the German's Fatherland. Other Sovereigns also paid tribute to his fame. Throughout the whole of his musical career the genius of Arthur Sullivan was thoroughly appreciated abroad as well as at home.

The name of Lord Armstrong is sure of a place in history so long as war employs the aid of artillery, and would even have its record if a time were to come when war and its weapons had ceased to belong to the business of human life. William George Armstrong died on December 27, after a short illness. He was born at Newcastle-on-Tyne in 1810, and was the son of a corn merchant in that town. During his early years his health was delicate, and he spent most of his time indoors. Perhaps the fact that he was thus debarred from the habitual pastimes of boyhood directed his attention to the study of mechanism and mechanical contrivances. He got his early education at the grammar school, spent most of his leisure hours in the engineering factory of a neighbour, and was much absorbed in the study of engineering. His parents, however, were anxious that he should enter the legal profession, and he was articled to a local solicitor, and studied law for some time in London. He actually became a solicitor, and was received as a junior partner in a Newcastle solicitor's office. But the law did not take much hold of him, and he kept on studying mechanics, being especially absorbed in the development of hydraulic power, and in the generation of electricity. He is said to have been the inventor of a hydro-electrical machine which came for the time into general use. He began to win a distinct reputation in this department of practical science, and before long he abandoned all interest in the law, and started on a career destined to be famous in the history of applied science. A new turn was given to his inventive genius by the breaking out of the Crimean War after a long period of peace, so far as the British Empire was concerned. He became inspired with designs for the production of guns having a lighter weight and a longer range than those previously known in the grim business of war.

Towards the close of the year 1854 Armstrong submitted to the War Office the model of an improved gun which the Secretary for War accepted. Before long his continuous experiments enabled him to design and construct a piece of artillery which was submitted to the consideration of a Parliamentary Committee. The Committee made out a report in favour of the gun, which it described as 'a combination of construction, breech-loading and rifling, and the coating of projectiles with a soft metal.' Armstrong refused to protect his inventions by patent because he wished to devote them altogether to the service of his country, and also because of his strong conviction that the patent system interferes with the public usefulness of man's inventive faculties. He then gave himself altogether to the construction of rifle or ordnance guns, the guns which ever since have borne his name. In 1858 the Armstrong gun was adopted by the War Office for special service in the field, and Mr. Armstrong received the honour of knighthood, and was appointed Engineer of Rifled Ordnance. The gun which bears Sir William

Armstrong's name has been adopted as a model by almost all foreign governments. The Committee of Ordnance appointed by the House of Commons stated in their report of July 1863 that they have had 'no practical evidence before them that even at this moment any other system of constructing rifled ordnance exists which can be compared with that of Sir William Armstrong.'

Sir William Armstrong did not long retain his appointment under the Government as Engineer of Rifled Ordnance, and in 1863 he returned to his occupation in the Elswick Manufacturing Company which he and some friends of his had founded near Newcastle, a company which under his guidance became one of the most important and the most successful of its kind in any part of the world. Sir William Armstrong once created a widespread sensation of alarm when, as President of the British Association meeting at Newcastle-on-Tyne in 1863, he dwelt with great emphasis on the gradual diminution of our coal supply and the probability or even the certainty of the exhaustion of the national supply at some not very distant time. This threatened danger brought about the appointment of a Royal Commission to inquire into the conditions of our coal supply, and Sir William was appointed a member of the Commission. Sir William Armstrong came forward as a Liberal-Unionist candidate for Newcastle in opposition to Mr. John Morley at the General Election of 1886. Mr. Morley proved the victor in the contest, and perhaps the warmest admirers of Sir William Armstrong were not much distressed at his failure to enter the Parliamentary arena. In the year of the Queen's Jubilee, 1887, the creator of the Armstrong gun was raised to the peerage as Lord Armstrong.

The early days of the year 1901 saw the close of a most distinguished and valuable career when Mandell Creighton, [Bishop of London, passed out of existence. Dr. Creighton died at Fulham Palace on the 14th of January, from the effects of a severe attack of appendicitis, which the most skilful surgical operations had failed to subdue, and his remains were buried with well-merited honours in St. Paul's Cathedral. Dr. Creighton was born in 1843, and was the son of a man of very limited means. He had his early education at the Carlisle Grammar School, afterwards obtained a scholarship at Durham Grammar School, and in 1862 entered Merton College, Oxford. There he won many distinctions, and in 1873 he entered the Church. His rise in the clerical order was at once rapid and steady, and he was appointed Dixie Professor of Ecclesiastical History at the University of Cambridge. He was nominated Bishop of Peterborough, and was consecrated in Westminster Abbey in 1891. When, in 1896, the Bishopric of London became vacant by the elevation of Dr. Temple to the Primacy, Dr. Creighton was appointed to the vacant bishopric.

In the meanwhile Dr. Creighton was almost constantly engaged in historical work. No man could have been more closely and faithfully attentive to his ecclesiastical and parochial duties, and yet Dr. Creighton succeeded in producing a number of historical volumes and essays which might have seemed in every sense a very satisfactory result of a whole life given up to literary labour alone. His 'History of the Papacy' met with a great success, and appears to have had the remarkable effect of giving, on the whole, satisfaction to impartial readers among Catholics as well as among Protestants. He prepared and published 'Primers of History,' and he was the author of 'The Age of Elizabeth,' 'The Life of Simon de Montfort,' 'Cardinal Wolsey,' and other historical works. In the year 1886 he was sent to the United States as the representative of Emmanuel College, Cambridge, at the celebration of the 250th anniversary of the foundation of Harvard College, Boston, Massachusetts. In 1896 he was present at the consecration in the Kremlin, Moscow, of the Emperor and Empress of Russia. Dr. Creighton was present there as the representative of the Anglican Church, and he was received with great honour by the Emperor and Empress, and, indeed, by the Russian public in general. Dr. Creighton was an active organiser of all works of improvement which came within his range, and he did much to promote the restoration of the Cathedral at Peterborough. He always strove to make his influence productive of good relations among all sections of Protestantism, and it will readily be understood that during his later years he had many opportunities of exerting that influence for the settlement of disputations among the clergy and laity of the Established Church. He was always ready to make liberal allowance for differences of opinion among the clergy of the Church itself; but on the other hand, it was well known that he regarded certain doctrines and forms of ceremonial as essential to the Church, and that he was prepared, if necessary, to exert his power for the maintenance of what he believed to be the genuine character and meaning of Protestantism. It may not be unworthy of mention, that the well-known Mr. Kensit on one occasion endeavoured to enter his public protest against Dr. Creighton's elevation to the Bishopric of London, and that Dr. Creighton's only notice of this protest was a polite and good-humoured invitation to his challenger to talk the matter quietly over with him at Fulham Palace. His own position has been defined in what appears to be an impartial record as: 'That of a Broad Churchman in doctrine, in sympathy, however, with many views of High Churchmen, and recognising their zeal and devotion to their work under the most unpromising conditions.' Dr. Creighton showed, in the exercise of his patronage, a constant desire to promote hard-working clergymen from obscure parishes, and thus to give them a wider field and a more substantial reward for their labours. He lived a life of zealous and conscientious work modelled on the genuine principles of the Christian's faith.

CHAPTER XXI.

LAST YEARS OF THE REIGN.

THE later years of Queen Victoria's reign saw an extraordinary outbreak of a regicidal passion which accomplished some ghastly tragedies. There did not appear to be anything especial in the political conditions of Europe and the world in general to inspire those crimes. Kings and Queens were not becoming more tyrannical or even more self-assertive than they had been before, nor was there any sudden tempest of anarchical enthusiasm sweeping over the world. Yet during the last two or three years of the reign the European Continent was startled by three successive attempts —attempts having, in the majority of instances, a fatal issue; and the reign had not long come to a close when the European crimes of regicide were followed in the United States by the assassination of President M'Kinley. We begin our brief narrative by telling of the event which had the most direct association with the interests of the British Empire.

This was the extraordinary attempt made on

the 4th of April 1900, at the Nord Station in Brussels, to kill the Prince of Wales. The Prince had left England for a visit to Copenhagen. When he was passing through Brussels, and just when the train was leaving the station, a youth named Sipido, aged fifteen, jumped on to the footboard of the carriage in which the Prince sat, and fired from a revolver four times. The revolver twice failed to send forth any bullet, but in a moment after it sent out two bullets, each of which passed very close to the Prince, who retained his composure perfectly all the time, and when a crowd on the platform gathered round Sipido and seized him, the Prince called aloud to them and ordered them not to do any harm to the boy. Then the train moved on, and Sipido was made a prisoner. The would-be regicide was found to be the son of respectable parents, and had up to that time been earning his living in a reputable way. But it was found that he had lately joined a secret political club which was especially hostile to British influence, and there was evidence given to show that Sipido had got it into his head that it was his duty to put to death the Prince of Wales, because the Prince had been an accomplice of Mr. Chamberlain 'in promoting the slaughter of the South African Boers.' Sipido was proved to have been, during his later days, irresponsible for his actions. If the maniacal attempt could be regarded as in any sense worthy of historical investigation, it might well be questioned whether Sipido had not been guilty of a blunder as well as of a crime, for the political reader might find good reason to doubt whether the policy which promoted, and indeed forced on, the South African War had ever been favoured or encouraged by the Prince of Wales.

Sipido, after his arrest by the police, made, at the instance of his father and mother, a full confession of his share in the plot—for it appeared that he had associates—and of the motives which had induced him to enter into it. He was put on trial at Brussels, along with three other boys, on the 2nd of July, and the trial came to an end on the 5th of the month. The jury found that Sipido was guilty of the attempt, adding a qualification with regard to his mental condition, and the court finally acquitted him on the ground of his irresponsibility, but ordered his detention in prison until the age of twenty-one. The other prisoners were acquitted. It should be said that Sipido's parents had in the meantime sent a very humble petition to Queen Victoria, imploring her beneficent intercession on behalf of the boy, whom they described as absolutely incapable of any evil purpose until his imperfect understanding had been practised upon by dangerous associates. Sipido, however, does not seem to have needed much intercession on his behalf, for it was soon afterwards made known that he had managed to get out of the country, and after a few days it was announced that he had arrived in Paris, where it was said that he had been put under the charge of his uncle, an art cabinetmaker, who was going to bring him up to his own trade.

On August the 2nd Mr. Balfour informed the House of Commons that Her Majesty's Government had sent a despatch to the Belgian Government, declaring that the Queen's Ministers considered the result of the proceedings in the Sipido trial to be a grave and unfortunate miscarriage of justice, and expressing their surprise and regret that the Belgian Government did not use proper precautions to retain Sipido in custody until some decision had been come to by the Belgian authorities as to the course to be taken with him after the verdict of the jury. Mr. Balfour also mentioned that, up to the time when he was speaking, the Belgian Government had not given any reply to the representations made by Her Majesty's Ministers. Sipido was again arrested in the course of the following October, and it may be assumed that this time the Belgian authorities adopted some means which might make it sure that so dangerous a personage, whether morally guilty or innocent, should not be allowed to go at large in his existing state of mind. Here, then, to adopt Carlyle's phrase, the affair 'drops through the tissue of our history.'

Another event occurring during the last years of the Queen's reign which will always be remembered as one of the extraordinary tragedies of those years, and indeed one of the extraordinary tragedies of history, was the assassination of the Empress of Austria. The Empress was in the habit of visiting the Riviera, Switzerland, or the south of Spain during the winter months, and in September 1898 she was passing through Geneva on her way to Montreux. On the 10th of September she was walking from her hotel to the steamer—she was always fond of walking—when an Italian anarchist suddenly rushed at her and thrust a very small but very keen stiletto into her heart. The Empress did not, at first, know that she had received her death-stroke, and actually walked on and entered the steamer, but before anything could be done to give her help, even if any help were possible, she fell dead. Elizabeth Amelia Eugenie, the Empress and Queen, had been one of the most popular Sovereigns of her time in her own dominions and abroad. She was the daughter of Duke Maximilian Joseph of Bavaria, and from her childhood she had ever shown a remarkable intellect and a decided taste for art and literature. She had received an excellent education under the care and observation of her father, and she had anticipated much of that love for athletic exercise which since those earlier days of hers has become so common among women of the educated classes. She was a splendid rider, and was also a most skilful swimmer at a time when the swimmer's craft was rarely cultivated among women of the higher classes.

In August 1853, while she was yet only in

her sixteenth year, Francis Joseph, Emperor of Austria and King of Hungary, who was one of her cousins, fell in love with her, and indeed her beauty, her grace, and her mental and physical accomplishments might well have explained his passion for her. The Emperor was not long in making his proposal of marriage, which was welcomed by her family, and the marriage was celebrated on the 24th of April 1854. The reception of the future Empress in Vienna, where the marriage took place, was one of the most brilliant events which even that capital, familiar with festive celebrations, had ever witnessed. The Emperor and Empress were crowned not only as the Imperial Sovereigns of Austria but as King and Queen of Hungary, and this ceremony, which was regarded as a solemn ratification of the government system recognising Hungary's national independence, ensured for the young Empress a genuine popularity among her Hungarian people.

The Empress, after her marriage, began to study the English language, in which she soon became a proficient. She was an enthusiastic admirer of English literature, and Byron was one of her favourite poets. She visited England more than once, and especially enjoyed the hunting season here. During one of her many visits to this country she was the guest of Queen Victoria at Windsor, but whenever she came to London it was her custom to stay at some hotel, because such a residence gave her greater freedom of movement, and better enabled her to gratify her taste for seeing the outer world than she could have had if she had accepted Royal hospitality. The Empress paid some visits to Ireland, and received there an especially enthusiastic welcome. Her love of hunting and her skill in riding would have been enough of themselves to commend her to the great majority of the people, and her easy, unaffected manners and the readiness with which she used to allow herself to be approached informally by the humblest of those who came in her way completely won for her the Irish hearts. She accepted the hospitality of several Irish noblemen, and showed a warm and earnest interest in the condition of the peasantry.

A heavy sorrow fell upon her life in its later years by the death of her only son, the Crown Prince Rudolph. The tragedy of that death was intensified beyond measure by the fact that it came from the hand of the young man himself. After this calamity the Empress began to reside less and less in Vienna, where probably the atmosphere was darkened for her, not merely by the terrible calamity of the past, but by the difficulties which it brought about for the peaceful maintenance of the Imperial system in the future. She had a beautiful villa built for her at Corfu, and she spent her autumn and winter months in going through the south of Europe from one favourite spot to another. It was on the occasion of one of these journeys that she met her death from the murderer's hand. The name of the assassin was Luigi Luccheni, a young man twenty-five years of age, a member of a body of Italian anarchists. The assassin seems to have been animated by no desire for personal vengeance, and to have had no other motive for his deed than the common desire of certain anarchist conspirators to aim at the life of any Sovereign, Prince or Princess, whenever opportunity might offer. Luigi Luccheni appears to have found out that an Empress was about to take the steamer at Geneva, and that was enough for him. The murderer was perhaps fortunate in the locality where he committed the crime. In that Canton of Switzerland where he was tried and convicted the system of capital punishment does not exist, and he was therefore sentenced only to imprisonment for life, the heaviest punishment which the law could there impose upon him. The dead body of the Empress was borne to Vienna, where it lay in state for some days, amid universal demonstrations of grief. The funeral was attended by the German Emperor, the representative of that great Prussian power which had by its victories on the battlefield excluded Austria from her place in the Germanic federation. Throughout Europe and throughout all the States of the civilised world there was one universal feeling of profound regret that such a fate should have befallen so high-minded a Princess, so gifted and true-hearted a woman.

On July 29, 1900, King Humbert I. of Italy met with his death from the bullet of an assassin. The King had been spending the summer, according to his usual habit, at Monza, the ancient capital of the Lombards, and had been distributing the prizes at a concert held by the Monza Athletic Club. When the ceremonials of the day were over, he was entering his carriage to return to his palace when he was fired at by a man named Bresci. The bullet struck the King near the heart, and he died before the carriage had reached his home. That was not the first attempt made by a murderer on the life of the King. In 1879, when he was making a State entry into Naples, he was attacked with a knife by a man named Passanante, but he fortunately received no injury as his Prime Minister, Cairoli, who saw the movement of the intending assassin, flung himself between them and received a wound from the weapon. Once again in 1897 an attempt of a like nature was made upon the King at Rome by a man named Acciareto, but there, too, the murderer was seized in time, and the King received no injury.

There was nothing in King Humbert's life to explain those murderous attacks, the last of which proved so tragically successful. He was in every sense a most popular Sovereign. He was the eldest son of King Victor Emmanuel, the Sovereign under whose auspices the union of modern Italy was accomplished. King Humbert was born on

March 14, 1844, and when a youth of fifteen he served under his father in the war which led to the formation of united Italy, and he rendered brilliant service under General Cialdini. On the death of Victor Emmanuel in 1878 Humbert succeeded to the throne, and he set himself to work at once for the restoration of the financial equilibrium of Italy, which naturally had been much disarranged by the preceding struggles. He introduced many sound reforms in the management of the palace, in the reduction of needless expenditure, in promoting simplicity of living, and at the same time in lending every help to popular education and to all manner of beneficent institutions. He lived after a very simple fashion, and showed little interest in costly ceremonials of any kind. He was most sincere and earnest in his endeavours to maintain a strictly constitutional system of monarchy, and while he represented to the full the national independence of his country, he always showed a respectful and religious deference to the Pope as the head of the Church. There did not seem to be any explanation of the attempts upon King Humbert's life by these assassins, except the wish to take the life of any reigning Sovereign, and it appears to have been certain that each of the attempts was made by a member of an anarchist secret society. The spirit of the regicide was in the air at that time, and did its work.

In a former volume the story has been told of

the arbitration treaty between Great Britain and the United States for the settlement of a dispute with regard to the boundaries of Venezuela. In that former volume the narrative brought us to the signing of the treaty at Washington by the British Ambassador and the American Secretary of State. According to the constitutional usages of the United States, the treaty had yet to be sent to the Senate for ratification. President Cleveland accompanied the treaty with a message of his own, recommending it for ratification. The President expressed his conviction that the treaty set out a practical plan for the peaceful settlement of all manner of disputes between the British Empire and the American Republic. He affirmed that its operation would create a new epoch in history, because its example would be regarded by other civilised States as illustrating the means for bringing about a peaceful settlement of all international controversies. The Senate and its Committee of Foreign Relations made alterations in the terms of the treaty, which met with some severe criticism in the United States as well as in England, but which do not seem to have in any material sense diminished its efficiency as an instrument of peace. The moral and political effect of the treaty was that the governing bodies of these two States had come to an agreement that, in the event of a dispute arising between the two Powers, full recourse must be had to peaceful arbitration before any appeal could be made to arms. Whatever imperfections and deficiencies might be found in the treaty, with regard to its prompt and practical method of working, this one main principle opened up a new era in all international disputes. Thus much we have found it necessary to add to the account of the treaty before its actual ratification, which was given in our former volume.

The years following the celebration of the Queen's Diamond Jubilee, and in which so many momentous events disturbed the political world at home and abroad, were also years of much interest to literature, art, and science. The value of the great discovery made by Wilhelm Konrad von Röntgen, the celebrated German physicist, first came to be appreciated in this country during the year 1897. Röntgen had rendered many important services to physical science before he made the discovery which seems destined to give immortality to his name. In the closing days of 1895 he discovered and realised the existence and capacities of those X-rays which are now usually called the Röntgen Rays. The essential value of this discovery consists in the fact that the rays when passed through any part of the human body can imprint on some sensitive plate a photograph of the bones across which the rays had passed. This discovery has opened an entirely new chapter in the history of medical and surgical science. Its importance was very soon recognised in England, and has completely established itself as a regular constituent in the practice of the medical profession of Great Britain and Ireland from the beginning of 1897.

One of the most marvellous achievements of applied science in our days is the system of the wireless telegraph. The whole world was thrilled with amazement when, in a generation earlier than the present, it was discovered that messages could be sent with lightning speed across whole continents by the use of that telegraphic wire which is now one of the most familiar agencies in our daily life. But the wireless telegraph is an invention which only a few years ago might have been thought to belong to the world of imagination, or to the wonderland of Arabian fable. It is now one of the familiar facts of our practical age that a message can be sent across the sea, and even across the ocean, without any connecting tracery of wire between the sender of the message and him to whom it is to be sent. The practical application of this marvellous agency is mainly due to Guglielmo Marconi, who was born near Bologna in 1875. Marconi comes of mixed nationality in his parentage, his father being an Italian and his mother an Irishwoman. He was educated at Leghorn and at Bologna, and a genius for telegraphic discovery developed in him, as a genius for poetry, for painting, or for music develops itself in other imaginative youths. The possibility of establishing a wireless telegraph appears to have taken complete possession of his mind from his very boyhood. He explained his ideas to many adepts in applied science, and while some of them regarded these ideas as mere fancies and dreams, others gave him a more judicious hearing and much practical encouragement.

Marconi naturally looked to England as the nearest and the most likely place for obtaining a chance of success in his experiments, and in 1896 he came to London. There he found a ready hearing from men engaged in practical science, and his apparatus was put to the test, and was found to be a complete success so far as it was tried. Thus much at least Signor Marconi had accomplished, that the best qualified English authorities on telegraphy cordially admitted the fact that he had discovered a process by which messages might be transmitted through the air for long distances without the use of telegraphic wire. At first and for a considerable time the hopes and ambition of the inventor of the wireless telegraph, and of those who believed in his system, only went to the transmission of messages across a comparatively short distance, and a message sent from the shore to a vessel ten miles away was regarded as a splendid success. Marconi returned to Italy, and received much encouragement and support from the Italian Minister of Marine, by whom he was enabled to make many experiments, with results becoming more and more satisfactory. He then went to Dublin, attracted to Ireland, no doubt, by his mother's Irish nationality, and there he made many experiments in Kingstown Harbour with the object of sending messages from the shore to ships, or from ships to other ships across distances of ten or fourteen miles. The Marconi system was then only in its infancy, and its greatest achievements were not accomplished until after the close of Queen Victoria's reign. The world has agreed to identify the transmission of wireless messages with the name of Marconi for the good reason that it was he who first devised and worked out the actual system which has brought the idea of the wireless telegraph into practical application.

But there were other men into whose minds the same thought had come as to the possibility of sending signals and messages over long distances without the mechanical medium of the wire. It seems easy to understand that when once the possibility of sending messages by electric forces along telegraphic wires had proved itself a reality, the conception must have flashed up in many minds that it might be possible to carry the wonder still further, and transmit the messages by electric agency through the currents of the air itself. Sir W. H. Preece, in 1897, made known to the Royal Institution a system of his own device for the purpose of signalling through space without wire by means of electro-magnetic waves of low frequency and parallel circuits established on each bank of a river. This system had already been put in practice by Sir William Preece in telegraphing across some of our harbours. Sir

William Preece was one of those who at once understood and encouraged the experiments of Marconi when the young Italian came over to try his chances in England. Other scientific inventors too had had ideas of the same kind, and had made practical experiments which succeeded at least in establishing the fact that messages could be transmitted without wire across broad harbours and out to sea.

But it was soon generally admitted that the Marconi system could work its way far more successfully than any other which had hitherto been tested, and thus the wireless telegraphic communication came to be associated with his name. The first press message sent by Marconi's system passed from Boulogne to the English shore. The time soon came when it was proved by demonstration that the Marconi system could send messages across the Atlantic, and enable England to communicate with the United States or Canada without the aid of any electric wire, across a distance which it would be utterly impossible to traverse above the sea by any wire capable of standing the shock of the winds. The submarine Atlantic cable had been thought a wonder in its time, and it is indeed one of the great achievements belonging to the Victorian age, but here was something more marvellous still, the discovery and the practical operation of a system by which England could breath her messages across the ocean to the

American shore, and receive a prompt reply sent back to her by the same marvellous force of transmission. We have shown that the most surprising and splendid developments of the Marconi process only came into action after the reign of Queen Victoria had drawn to its close, but the system had established its principle thoroughly during the life-time of the Queen, and is therefore an event coming within the range of this History.

During 1897 England's national collections of art were enriched by the splendid bequest which will ever bear the name of Sir Richard Wallace. This magnificent collection of paintings and other art treasures had belonged to the Marquis of Hertford, by whom they were left to Richard Wallace, a man who had distinguished himself by his active and generous philanthropy, and who had received the title of Baronet from the Queen because of the charitable services he had rendered during the Siege of Paris in 1871. Wallace died in 1890, and in 1897 his widow, then dying, carried out what she knew to be the wish of her late husband by bequeathing his whole collection to the nation. Lady Wallace, in her will, made it the only condition that the pictures, furniture, porcelain, and other contents of the collection should be kept distinct from all other national possessions of the same order, and a committee was formed to carry out her desire. The committee recommended that Hertford House, Manchester Square, should be bought for the purpose, and this building, after some necessary enlargements and alterations, was converted into an art gallery for the reception and exhibition of this splendid bequest. The value of the pictures and other works of art was estimated at upwards of three millions sterling. The Tate Gallery was opened in the same year by the Prince of Wales, now King Edward VII. This collection was the bequest of Mr. Henry Tate, and was chiefly composed of the works of British masters living and dead. Its management was placed in the hands of the trustees of the National Gallery. The Tate Gallery, which was to contain these artistic treasures, was built on part of the site of the old Millbank Prison on the Embankment. Millbank Prison had for a long time been a disfigurement to that part of London on which it stood, and it could be seen from far and wide. It might well be considered one of the happiest omens for the future of art in this country that such a building and such a collection should have found a place on the site of a disused prison.

We may state here, although not quite certain whether to congratulate our readers on the event, that in this year the attention of the British public as a whole was first drawn to the growing triumphs of the motor-car. A great motor-car race which was run from Paris to Trouville created keen interest among the lovers of novelties in this country, and was destined to be soon followed by many competitions of the same kind here, there, and everywhere. The motor-car has evidently 'come to stay' among us, and is now a moving feature, by no means graceful or picturesque, in every English landscape.

Some remarkable developments in the postal system belong to the closing years of Queen Victoria's reign. The charge for postage from Great Britain or Ireland to any of the Imperial colonies except Australia and New Zealand was reduced to a uniform rate of one penny for a letter weighing not more than half an ounce. This rate was made to apply to other parts of the British Empire. Very soon after the same rate of postage was adopted for New Zealand, and soon after that for Australia as well. All manner of international congresses and conferences had been held from time to time, and there were reduced systems of charge agreed upon among all the civilised States of the world. The appearance of postal cards, each card requiring but a halfpenny stamp for inland delivery, underwent much and varied and even artistic development. The use of these cheap post-cards gave a great opportunity to the inventive faculties of picture-dealers and stationers, and the picture post-card, as it is called, became one of the characteristic curiosities of the time. Charming landscapes, reproductions of famous pictures, of famous historic buildings, and old and modern scenes associated with great events, the portraits of

Royal personages, the portraits of famous actors and actresses, and all other celebrities, became the adornments of the post-card, and gave opportunity for the growth of an entirely new fancy among connoisseurs of the picturesque and curious, who found for themselves a fresh interest in life by the collection of their favourite specimens of the picture postcard. Meanwhile the telephone was fixing its connecting-links almost everywhere throughout our cities and towns, and in this way, at least, time and space were brought as near to annihilation as well might be for the senders and the receivers of these winged messages. The homing pigeon was no doubt a more graceful and poetic bearer of messages, but he certainly could not, even in his most rapid flight, compete with the startling velocity of the telephone, and it must be owned that the age of the motor-car was not one to sacrifice much for mere romantic association.

Card-playing in its various forms has been increasing rather than decreasing of late years among the classes which constitute society, and it may be doubted whether English women of that order ever indulged in games of cards before quite as freely and with as much devotion to the pastime as they are doing in England at the present day. It may well be, however, that this absorbing devotion to 'Bridge' and other such games of cards is nothing worse than a passing freak of fashion, and that educated women will before long find that the humour of the freak has passed away, and will seek other ways of enjoying social life. Unfortunately, it cannot be said that the card-playing parties of the present day are only drawn together by a womanly love of intellectual rivalry, and that a game of 'Bridge' is played on the same principle as a game of chess, only for the honour of the victory. Perhaps at no time in England's social history did English women risk to win or lose so much money as now commonly exchanges hands in the course of a long card-playing contest. Nor do we find any record since the days of Queen Anne of any such prolonged sittings over games of cards as those which have become familiar to society in the last few years. Card-playing is one of the indoor sports dear to men in which women appear at all periods of English history to have taken a keen delight. The satirists of other periods were never tired of holding up to ridicule and reprobation the passion of the British matron, and even of the British maid, for the excitement of the card-room. But it would not appear from those satirical descriptions that whole days, as well as many hours of the night, were devoted during those earlier periods of our history to the card-table, a practice which, according to all accounts, is common among some of our matrons and maids at the present time.

Another peculiarity of these later days in England's social life is the spread of the smoking habit among English women in society. Only the other day it seems when no English women of education and respectability ever thought of imitating their fathers, their brothers, or their husbands in the smoking habit. Among the women of the poorest classes the clay pipe was sometimes enjoyed ; among 'fast' women—women, that is to say, of no character—the cigarette was not unknown, and was supposed to have been adopted from the habits of French and Spanish women, but among the great majority of English women of education and of social credit, little inclination was shown for the cigar or the cigarette. In the later years of Queen Victoria's reign the cigarette appears to have come all of a sudden into very common use among large circles of English women, who would utterly resent the idea that they were, by such a practice, rendering themselves liable to be regarded as committing any trespass against the canons of propriety ordained by the best society. The code of manners is, of course, always the creation of passing conditions, and nobody is likely to assume that the woman of English society to-day is in any sense less modest and proper than her mother because she puffs at a cigarette which her mother would have thought it a degradation, if not a positive sin, to put between her lips. But the change in manners is remarkable enough to deserve a passing comment, and to show that even in an improving age not every new fashion is in itself an evidence of improvement.

CHAPTER XXII.

THE DEATH OF THE QUEEN.

THE opening of a new century must ever be regarded as in itself an event of profound and universal interest. No doubt there are persons of a practical turn of mind who would be ready to contend that the whole arrangements of the calendar are purely artificial and conventional; that the importance of a day depends entirely upon what actually happens in the day, and that the first of January in a new century may be entitled to no more attention on the part of those who see it than the first of April in the same or any other year. There were, as a matter of fact, some serious disputes among really well-informed and thoughtful persons on a different question raised by the opening of the new century, the question whether the 31st of December 1899 ought or ought not to be regarded as the last day of the nineteenth century. We have no intention, however, to enter upon serious discussion of these questions, and only desire to say that the opening of this new century was accompanied by conditions and soon followed by events which must make the beginning of the twentieth century memorable for ever in the history of England.

On the 1st of January took place the inauguration of the new Australian Commonwealth, an event which might be regarded as something like the opening of a new world in the southern hemisphere. Queen Victoria despatched at once a message to the first Governor-General of the new colony, expressing her heart-felt interest in this expansion of Australia, and her earnest wish that it might ensure the increased prosperity and well-being of her loyal subjects there. The reader will soon learn the deep and melancholy interest which must always attach in history to that message from the Queen.

On the 2nd of January Lord Roberts reached England from South Africa, and his welcome in England was one of intense enthusiasm. Lord Roberts took over the work of Commander-in-Chief in this country, and Lord Kitchener succeeded him in command of the troops in South Africa. Our especial interest is at present not with the events of the South African war, which have been already summarised in this volume, but in the visit which Lord Roberts paid to Queen Victoria. The Queen was especially anxious to receive from Lord Roberts himself the fullest and clearest exposition of the war and its progress, and the prospects of its termination. There were many around Her Majesty who felt grave doubts as to whether in the state of her health at the time it would be well for her to enter upon a prolonged conversation on that anxious and still very critical subject. For it had already been made known to the Queen's family that her health was not what her people and the civilised world in general could have wished it to be, and that she was already showing many signs of an ominous cerebral affection. But the Queen firmly declared that she would see Lord Roberts, and learn fully from him the present state and the prospects of the South African campaign, and she compelled her sinking energies to bear her up in the strain that such a conversation must impose upon her.

The public mind now began to be seriously alarmed by the more or less vague rumours which were heard as to the state of the Queen's health. The Queen had through her long life been subject more than once to severe illnesses, and there had been times when the gravest fears existed as to the possibility of her reign coming to a sudden conclusion. This time the public alarm appeared to be even more intense and more widely spread than at any crisis of the same kind during previous years. How closely she could still pay attention to any event in her kingdom calling for her sympathy and beneficence was made manifest by the fact that she sent a sympathetic message and a gift of money to the survivors of a disaster which had befallen the fishing fleet of Shetland. Another event of a different kind showed with equal vividness how entirely far she was from allowing herself to be wholly absorbed by her own physical danger. On the 14th of January Dr. Creighton, Bishop of London, died at a comparatively early age, and immediately after his death it was announced to the public that Dr. Creighton's widow had received a message of sympathy from Princess Christian on behalf of the Sovereign. The message was thus worded: 'The Queen desires me to express to you her deep and heart-felt sympathy in your great loss, which she deplores, not only on her own account, but on that of the Church to which he was so valuable. May I add my own sympathy?' Princess Christian's message suggested no idea that the life of the Queen was near to its end, or that any fears on her own account were dimming her personal concern for the lives and happiness of others. But on the evening after the issue of this message the first note of alarm was sounded, for the world in general, by an official announcement in the *Court Circular*, proclaiming that 'The Queen had not lately been in her usual health; that the great strain upon her powers caused by the events of the past year had told upon Her Majesty's nervous system,' and that it had 'been thought advisable by Her Majesty's physicians that the Queen should be kept perfectly quiet in the house, and should abstain, for the present, from transacting business.'

This announcement was put in very cautious words, and with apparently no ominous meaning, but the heart of the country was nevertheless touched to its deepest by the mere fact that any such announcement should have come with official authority, and the words of the *Court Circular* were read by every one as the immediate prelude to a national calamity. On the following day a bulletin, signed by the Queen's physicians, was sent forth from Osborne, stating that Her Majesty was suffering from great physical prostration, accompanied by symptoms which caused anxiety. The following day, Sunday, January 20, it was made known on the same authority that the Queen's condition had 'become more serious, with increased weakness and diminished power of taking nourishment.' This bulletin was issued very late in the day, but the alarm had already become so general that in every place of worship throughout the whole kingdom the most earnest prayers were put up for the Queen's restoration to health—prayers which, it may be said, were rather the anticipations of the coming national sorrow than the yet hopeful entreaties that the country might be spared so heavy a trial. The foreign press also had already begun to bear testimony to the intense regard felt for the Queen through all civilised nations, and the earnest although clouded hope that her life might even yet be spared. The Queen had now reached an advanced age, but some of her predecessors had passed through a greater length of years before the end came, and her years therefore gave no conclusive reason to forbid the hope that her reign had not yet reached its closing days.

On Monday, January 21, a more encouraging bulletin was issued by Her Majesty's physicians to the effect that the Queen had slightly rallied, had taken some food, and had had some refreshing sleep. This announcement might well have been regarded as hopeful and encouraging, but we can all remember that it did not much relieve the darkness of the gloom which had settled upon the mind and heart of the whole country. The German Emperor, who was then engaged in the public celebration of the Prussian monarchy's 200th anniversary, brought the ceremonials to a sudden end, and travelled at the most rapid rate made possible by the practical science of the modern world in order that he might reach Osborne in time to see his royal grandmother before the end should come. Messages expressive of the deepest sympathy kept constantly pouring in by telegraphic wire from eminent men and women in all parts of the United States. It may be said without exaggeration that for some days the home of Queen Victoria at Osborne was the spot to which the minds and the hearts of all civilised, and many only half civilised, nations were turned with a constant attention. The symptoms of a slight improvement in the Queen's condition, which had been announced by the Royal physicians, gave little hope even for the time, and their duration was very short. On Tuesday, January 22, the Queen in the earlier part of the day awoke to full consciousness, and recognised each of the members of her family, the German Emperor among them, who were watching by her bed-side. The Queen seemed then to be of perfectly peaceful mind, and to understand the reality of her condition. She was awaiting her fate in humble resignation. It may well be assumed that, like the noble lady in Webster's immortal tragedy, she felt and knew that the gates of heaven are not so highly arched as those of princes' palaces, and that mortals must kneel—must kneel in spirit—who would enter there. The kneeling spirit passed through the gates of death that same day. At four o'clock in the afternoon it was announced that the Queen was sinking fast, and at half-past six in the evening the reign of Queen Victoria came to an end.

The sensation produced at first throughout the whole of this kingdom it would hardly be possible to exaggerate. We have no inclination to enter on such an occasion into the adulatory mood of the Court historian, who feels justified because a Royal personage has died, in depicting a whole nation as plunged into depths of irrepressible and irreparable grief. But apart from the fact that Queen Victoria was a Sovereign whose life bore no resemblance to the life of any of her predecessors in the dynasty, she had been known and looked up to by the people of these islands for so many years, had been read about and talked about so much, had made herself so continuously a living illustration of a pure and noble life, that she had become a recognised example to her people, and many of her subjects felt as if her passing away were the death of a friend. No Sovereign could have led a life more truly free from blame throughout all her domestic career, and she had never, as other of the Sovereigns of the dynasty had done before her, put herself at the head of any political party, and thus created an opposition to her in the minds of this or that class of her subjects. She had been a model as a wife and mother, and perhaps the one only fault which her subjects were inclined to find with her was that, because of her absolute devotion to her lost husband, she had withdrawn herself too much into seclusion from the sight of the public in general. Even for this deliberate retirement full excuse was readily made by most of her people, for they respected and sympathised with that deep grief for a beloved husband which overcame, for the time, her sense of obligation to merely ceremonial or even to constitutional duties. Victoria's domestic life had been utterly blameless. She was strict and even severe in her insistence on obedience to the highest moral duties among all those over whom her influence could exercise any control. There were incidents in her career which showed even a certain harshness towards any supposed errors coming from a lack of scrupulous adherence to the lessons of the moral code. Yet in her patronage of letters and of arts there was nothing of rigid austerity, and in her patronage of the drama she showed, more than once, her appreciation of a thoroughly artistic and in its essence a thoroughly healthful play, although it introduced some characters and scenes depicting a kind of life not approved by the teachings of morality.

Queen Victoria always performed most faithfully and most judiciously her duties as a constitutional Sovereign. She never attempted to overrule her Ministers, but at the same time she always insisted on being thoroughly informed as to the purposes and the policy which they were striving to carry out. She never failed to make her own opinions clearly known to the statesmen over whom she presided, and to enter into close discussion with them as to the right course to be adopted.

On one important occasion, as we have already seen in this History, she went so far as to dismiss from office one of the most influential and popular statesmen of his day because he had taken a step of which she and most of her Ministers could not approve, and had taken it without allowing opportunity for full discussion and unanimous agreement. She was, in fact, the first constitutional Sovereign in the modern sense known to the history of England.

The Queen was perhaps somewhat over precise and elaborately rigid in maintaining all the ceremonial observances belonging to the Royal station. Many of those who were brought into close attendance on her have given the world good reason to believe that her Court was sometimes made formal and even gloomy by the precision with which she maintained what she regarded as its rules of etiquette. Now and again of late years some memoirs have been published which give us a very clear idea of the rigidness with which she maintained her own views on such subjects. But her people in general paid little attention to any complaints about the formality insisted on by her in courtly receptions and entertainments, and were proud of being ruled by a Sovereign concerning whom no worse complaint could be made than the suggestion that she carried a little too far her sense of the deference that ought to be shown to the ruler of a great empire. No one supposed that Queen Victoria was thus exacting merely because of any overwrought sense of the formal respect due to herself personally, and it was always rightly assumed that she was acting only in accordance with her feelings as to the reverence due to the throne of her ancestors. Even her failings, it was almost universally admitted, leaned to virtue's side.

Some of her English subjects were inclined to believe that she showed an undue love for Scotland and the Scottish people, and it was for a long time felt by the Irish that she paid too little attention to the condition and the feelings of Ireland and its population. But it could hardly be counted a great fault in a Sovereign to find pleasure in frequent intervals of retirement and quiet enjoyment among the historical and poetical associations and the noble scenery of Scotland, and during the later years of her life she had striven more than once to prove to her Irish subjects that she was willing and anxious to make atonement for her early neglect of that part of her dominions. No instance, so far as we know, can be pointed to in the whole course of her career as a ruler which showed any inclination on her part to outstep the strict limits of her rights as a constitutional ruler. It may perhaps be admitted that hers was not a lovable nature in the strict sense of the word, for those who did not belong to her own family or her own circle of intimate friends, but it never could have been asserted or even suggested that she showed any want of sympathy and of genuine helpfulness in distresses or troubles coming upon this, that, or the other part of the countries over which she ruled. Much as she loved her own family, she always found time and thought for the poorest and most remote of her people when there was an opportunity of her rendering them a service, and she never allowed her love for her own family to absorb all her thoughts and all her affections.

The grievances from which Ireland suffered, and of which Ireland justly complained during her reign, were no part of her doing, and were not allowed to continue by any instigation of her own. She was a constitutional Sovereign, and as such was bound to act on the advice of her Ministers. The whole history of her reign tells us that for long years the Ministers with whom she had to consult showed themselves utterly indifferent, no matter to which of the two great political parties they belonged, to the just claims and the real needs of Ireland. Any feeling of resentment, therefore, which Irishmen may still entertain, because of the resistance or the neglect which was shown to the demands of their country during the reign of Queen Victoria, ought to be directed against most of the leading statesmen who controlled the legislation of those years, and not against the Sovereign who was constitutionally bound to act upon their advice. It is said, perhaps with truth, that Queen Victoria was disposed to make favourites of certain statesmen, and to show a more or less qualified dislike to some others, and the inference commonly drawn is that she liked the men who were opposed to Ireland's claims better than those who were willing to recognise them. Gladstone, according to general opinion, was never a favourite with his Sovereign, while she often manifested a strong liking for Disraeli. But the probable explanation of this fact, if we may assume it to be a fact, is that Gladstone was a man thoroughly guided by the strength of his own convictions, and that his earnestness often led him into what might have seemed a desire to overbear the inclinations and the prepossessions of his Sovereign, while Disraeli always took care to make himself seem the devotee of her wishes and her will. It is at least a matter of history that it was not the English Queen but the English Parliament that interfered, on more than one important occasion, with the efforts of a Government to render full justice to the national demands of the Irish people.

There is also every reason to believe that some of the wars of annexation and conquest carried on by England during Victoria's reign were disapproved of by the Queen herself, and were opposed by her, so far as constitutional principles and usages would allow to the Sovereign any direct personal control. The whole story of Queen Victoria's life, when it comes to be fully disclosed, will be the record of a rule to which very high praise and but little disparaging criticism will be given by the coming generations.

The funeral ceremonial of the late Queen began on Monday, 1st February 1901. The coffin which contained the remains of the Queen was carried from Osborne to the royal yacht *Alberta*, where it remained for the night. In the early morning of the following day began what may be described as the funeral pageant. When the yacht entered Portsmouth Harbour, the harbour was crowded not only by English vessels of war but by vessels of war from many foreign States, and a solemn, picturesque, and appropriate pageant was thus presented to the gaze of the assembled crowds along the shore. The word 'appropriate' is here used with a very distinct meaning, because of a wish which had been expressed just before her death by the Sovereign herself. Among the latest of her spoken wishes was the desire that her body, when enclosed in its coffin, might be borne on a gun-carriage through the London streets which the funeral procession had to traverse. The Queen gave as her reason for this desire the fact that she was a soldier's daughter, and that such a mode of removal would be symbolic of her birth and her family. The display of vessels of war from all countries in Portsmouth Harbour was therefore strictly in keeping with the traditions of her house and with her own early memories.

An incident that occurred during the progress of the ceremonial gave an unexpected and a strikingly dramatic effect to the realisation of the Queen's wish. The gun-carriage was kept waiting at the Windsor Station until the train should arrive which was bearing the body from Paddington. The horses attached to it had been much troubled during this period of necessary delay by the chilling winds of the raw February day. The animals became restive, and resisted all efforts to make them accomplish their work in good order. It was, in fact, found impossible, even by the utmost exertions made by the well-disciplined officers and men of the Royal Artillery, to prevail upon or compel the horses to draw the gun-carriage. There seemed at moments to be an imminent danger that Queen Victoria's coffin might be flung on to the road. The idea suddenly occurred to one of the officers that the best way of avoiding any such unseemly incident would be to remove the restive horses and allow the sailors who made the guard of honour to perform the distinguished service of drawing the carriage on which rested their dead

Sovereign's coffin. The idea was instantly adopted. The unmanageable horses were removed, and the sailors drew the gun-carriage to the place of its destination. The whole incident made at the time a deep impression on the public, and was held to be well in keeping with the pageantry of the funeral ceremonial. The Queen of England ruled over an Empire which had long claimed the sovereignty of the seas; Queen Victoria herself had succeeded to a sailor King, and through all her life she had shown an intense interest in the condition of her navy, and one of her especial delights was to be borne in her royal yacht over the waves that surrounded her island home. One can easily imagine that if Queen Victoria could have looked just then from the sphere to which she had been removed back to that earthly scene of her funeral ceremonial, she might have felt a new gladness in the knowledge that some of the sailors of her fleet should have helped to bear her coffin to its last resting-place. We may add that during the different stages of the funeral procession three gun-carriages had to be used, and that these three were afterwards presented to be preserved as treasured relics, one to Chelsea Hospital, one to the City of Dublin, and one to the City of Edinburgh.

Before closing this part of our narrative, we may mention the fact that the funeral procession, as it passed from Victoria Station to

Paddington through the streets of London, was gazed upon by crowds at once the most dense, most unbroken in continuity, most orderly and most hushed that had ever been observed in our time in those streets on any public occasion. A grave and reverent silence prevailed throughout the whole of those thick masses of people, and many observers who looked upon the scene declared that there appeared to be a positively awe-stricken emotion turning that immense multitude all along the way into reverential spectators, dreading lest any loud and sudden sound might disturb the solemn sacredness of the whole procession.

The late Queen had lived so long that even to men and women well down in the vale of years her occupation of the throne had lasted thus far during all the years of their lives, and when such men and women thought of royalty in these countries they thought only of Queen Victoria. It is not surprising, therefore, that such an event as the funeral procession of the late Queen should have seemed to them to announce that the old order of things was actually passing away, and that a new chapter of human existence was opening for them just as their own earthly careers were drawing to a close. 'We shall not live to see much of any other reign' was the thought that must have passed through the minds of many who stood in the streets, or looked from the windows of the houses to watch that melancholy ceremonial, and we all know that in every feeling of deep regret, however impersonal and disinterested, there must ever mingle some thought of self, some recognition of the bearing which the event will have on our own memories and our own minds. Certainly the universal testimony of those who described that funeral procession is unanimous in telling us that the hushed and solemn demeanour of the crowds gathered together in the London streets on that memorable day was something marvellous in itself, and was indeed an unprepared tribute of deeply reverential character to the memory of the dead Sovereign.

The Queen's eldest son, now already in actual fact reigning King, with the German Emperor and the Duke of Connaught, led the procession. The King of the Belgians, the King of Portugal, and the King of Greece had conspicuous places, and the near relatives of many other Sovereigns represented their courts and their peoples in the funeral procession. A writer who told the history of that day soon after the events which he describes, tells us that 'When the coffin reached St. George's Chapel, Windsor, the first part of the burial service was solemnised in the presence of a congregation which may be said, with almost literal accuracy, to have included all the great ones of the land and the representatives of most other lands—the representatives of royalties and republics, of war and peace, of politics and letters, art and science, of every faith and denomination.' The Royal coffin was then carried to the Albert Memorial Chapel and placed in front of the altar, where it was watched all through the night by officers of the 1st Grenadier Guards and men of the Queen's Company. The writer whom we have just quoted tells us that 'Next day, after a short final ceremonial service, the coffin was laid in the earth in the Royal Mausoleum at Frogmore, and the King knelt in prayer by the side of the grave. The Victorian era was closed; the new era was already opening.'

We shall have, before this volume comes to an end, to pass in rapid summary the great historical events of Queen Victoria's reign, the general results which it brought about, or helped to bring about, in the political life of the Empire, and the developments in art and science, in letters, and in social progress. But our story of the reign of Queen Victoria, the mere narrative of its successive events, comes to a close with that funeral day. The work, however, on which the author of these volumes has been engaged is described as 'A History of Our Own Times,' and although the author does not propose to pass beyond the threshold of the new reign, and sincerely hopes that that reign may extend long enough to call for a new historian, he does not feel inclined to bring his task to an end without noticing some of the public events which accompanied, introduced, and illustrated the accession of King Edward VII., events some of which took place in the interval between the death and the burial of the Queen.

We must go back a few days in the order of our narrative and describe the ceremonials which marked the accession of the new sovereign to the throne. In the afternoon of Wednesday, January 23, the Privy Council met at St. James's Palace for the purpose of making formal announcement of the change which had taken place in the sovereignty of the Empire. The meeting was attended by all the leading members of the Privy Council from both Houses of Parliament. The Duke of Devonshire, as Lord President of the Council, acted as chairman of the meeting, and directed its proceedings. The Lord President formally announced to the Council the death of Queen Victoria and the accession of her elder son, lately the Prince of Wales, to the throne of the monarchy. The King had already arrived from Osborne and had gone to St. James's Palace, where he remained until he received the announcement of the Privy Council's meeting, and of the ceremonial which had been gone through there. King Edward at once left his own apartments in the Royal Palace, and entered the room where the Privy Councillors were awaiting his presence.

The King then delivered the address which was to be his first announcement of his accession to the throne, and of his resolve to do his best for the full discharge of his duties to the Empire. The King's voice was at first somewhat broken by natural emotion, but before he had spoken many words he was able to recover his self-control, and to speak with a clearness and an earnestness which went straight to the hearts of those who listened. One account of this meeting tells us that the King's speech was delivered without the use of notes. Many readers will remember that the late sovereign had a voice of remarkable clearness and musical vibration, which lent a thrilling effect to her public utterances. The new King showed that he had inherited the same qualities of voice—indeed, this had often been observed in the delivery of addresses by him on ceremonial occasions—and the words he had to speak came with added effect from the style of their intonation. The King told the Council that the present was the most painful occasion on which he should ever be called on to address them. 'My first and melancholy duty,' he said, 'is to announce to you the death of my beloved mother, the Queen, and I know how deeply you, the whole nation, and I think I may say the whole civilised world, sympathise with me in the irreparable loss we have all sustained. I need hardly say that my constant endeavour will be always to walk in her footsteps. In undertaking the heavy load which now devolves upon me, I am fully determined to be a constitutional sovereign in the strictest sense of the word, and as long as there is breath in my body to work for the good and amelioration of my people.' The King then announced his resolve to be known by the name of Edward, which had been borne by six of his ancestors. 'In doing so I do not undervalue the name of Albert, which I inherit from my ever to be lamented great and wise father, who, by universal consent, is, I think, deservedly known by the name of Albert the Good, and I desire that his name should stand alone. In conclusion, I trust to Parliament and the nation to support me in the arduous duties that now devolve upon me by inheritance, and to which I am determined to devote my whole strength during the remainder of my life.'

Then the Lord Chancellor, Lord Halsbury, administered to the King the oath by which the new sovereign bound himself to govern the realm according to its own laws and customs, and King Edward added the assurance of his full reliance on the wisdom of Parliament and the loyalty and affection of his people. The Cabinet Ministers then kneeling before the sovereign took the oaths of allegiance, and all others who were present bound themselves by the same solemn declaration, and in the same attitude. With the oath of allegiance closed this part of the ceremonial, and it then only remained for the Council to order that the proclamation from the King should be publicly made known in all the places prescribed by usage for that purpose. The proclamation was read from St. James's Palace at 9 o'clock on the following morn-

ing, and it declared, 'That the high and mighty
Prince Albert Edward is now, by the death of our
late sovereign of happy memory, become our only
lawful and rightful Liege Lord, Edward VII.,
by the grace of God King of the United Kingdom
of Great Britain and Ireland, Defender of the
Faith, Emperor of India, to whom we do acknowledge all faith and constant obedience with all
hearty and humble affection, beseeching God, by
whom Kings and Queens do reign, to bless the
royal Prince Edward VII. with long and happy
years to reign over us.' Then followed a flourish
of trumpets, the performance of the National
Anthem by the band, and much cheering and
many invocations of 'God save the King!' from
the crowds who were waiting outside the gates
of the palace.

The great State procession which then followed
had for its purpose to make the proclamation known
in all the places assigned by usage for that duty.
This noble and antique ceremony was in this instance,
and by the King's own desire, shorn of some of its
former splendours. King Edward himself did not
take part in the procession as many or most of
his predecessors had done, and although his absence
caused some disappointment to the vast crowds
assembled all along the streets through which the
procession was to pass, yet when the reasons became known which had induced the King to make
the ceremonial less striking and less gorgeous than
on former occasions, it was very generally felt that

King Edward had exercised a wise discretion in reducing it to the utmost suitable simplicity. The King, it was understood, felt that as there was so much of pathos and of sombreness in a pageant which proclaimed at once the death of the venerable and much-loved Queen and the accession of the new monarch, it would be but unfittingly and painfully set off by any lavish and unnecessary show of mere splendour. King Edward, moreover, had a strong and a very reasonable objection to any display which might call together a vast concourse of people in each of the narrow streets of London through which the procession had to make its way, and might thus lead to dangerous accidents and even to the loss of many lives. For this reason, too, the announcement of the hour at which the procession was to begin its march was kept from the public until the latest possible moment. The proclamation was read aloud to the waiting crowds who had gathered outside the Palace, and the procession moved on, crossing Trafalgar Square at its north side, and then making its way along the Strand towards the regions of the City. Owing to the early hour at which the ceremonial began, and the care which had been taken to delay the announcement of its opening as long as could fairly be done, Trafalgar Square and the Strand, although well lined with spectators even then, were not crowded to the extent which must assuredly have come to pass if these measures had not been taken.

There was one feature of novelty which showed

itself as the great procession was approaching to
the boundary of the City. There is enough of
historic interest in this fact to justify its record
here. Every reader of this volume acquainted
with the London of past days, who has outgrown
the days of his youth, will remember that the
passage from the Strand into the City was
marked many years ago by the famous and in its
way picturesque old structure known as Temple
Bar. One of the old-established usages of the
London Corporation consecrated by tradition was
to assert their right of ownership over the City
by closing the gates of Temple Bar against any
public procession. The Corporation of the City
thus manifested their ancient right to close their
gates even against royalty or against any State
procession conveying the royal message. On such
occasions the Corporation ordered the Temple Bar
gates to be closed, and the royal visitors or royal
message-bearers had to go through the ceremony
of knocking at the gates and requesting the permission of the Corporation to enter the City. The
Corporation were always gracious enough to order
the opening of the gates for the admission of the
visitors, and they believed that their hereditary
rights had been becomingly asserted and amply
maintained by the fact that their permission had to
be asked before even a royal personage could pass
within the precincts of London's civic rulers. Of
late years it had been found that Temple Bar
itself—that is to say, the solid erection enclosing

the gateway—was beginning to sink and to become dangerous, and it was removed by order of the City Council in 1879.

Therefore the procession which set out to announce King Edward's accession found no historic gateway to bar its entrance into the City. Yet the civic authorities maintained a symbol at least of their ownership by having a crimson rope drawn across the street at the place where Temple Bar used to stand. The delegates charged by royal authority with the delivery of the proclamation were no doubt prepared for this modern arrangement, and they entered fully into the spirit of the performance. The royal official who bears the title of Rouge Dragon descended from his carriage not far from the crimson rope, and, accompanied by two trumpeters, moved towards the unsubstantial barrier. Thereupon the City Marshal gave out the historic challenge, 'Who goes there?' Rouge Dragon was again equal to the task imposed on him, and he explained that nothing more hostile towards the rights of the City Corporation was intended than to ask permission to proclaim the new sovereign within the boundaries of civic London. The Lord Mayor showed not a moment's hesitation in directing that the procession should at once be admitted, the crimson rope was withdrawn, and the procession passed on through the City towards the Royal Exchange. At the Exchange the proclamation was read aloud, the trumpets were blown, and the great crowd united in singing the

National Anthem in its now, once more, and appropriate form of 'God Save the King.' Then the proclamation was read again at the several places historically assigned for it in the City, and that part of the ceremonies belonging to the opening of the new reign came to an end. The same forms of proclamation were conducted in all the other cities and towns of the kingdom, and were faithfully performed in Pretoria in the presence of Lord Kitchener and his staff officers. The proclamation made in Pretoria was peculiar, in the fact that the new sovereign was proclaimed not only King of the United Kingdom of Britain and Ireland and Emperor of India, but also as 'Supreme Lord of and over the Transvaal.'

On the following day, the 25th of January, the Houses of Parliament met in order to receive the royal message from King Edward. In the House of Lords, Lord Salisbury as the leader of the Government, and Lord Kimberley as the leader of the Opposition, delivered speeches which told of the profound national regret felt for the loss of Queen Victoria, and expressed loyal hope and trust for the new reign which had just begun. The Archbishop of Canterbury, as head of the Church over which the English sovereign presides, spoke also to a like effect, and invoked a blessing on the new ruler. In the House of Commons speeches were delivered by Mr. Arthur Balfour, the leader of that House, and by Sir Henry Campbell-Bannerman, leader of the Opposition. The members of both the Parliamentary chambers then took the oath of allegiance to King Edward.

The opening of the new reign recalled to the minds of many the significance of the change in the constitutional treatment of such an event at the time when Queen Anne came to the throne. Before Queen Anne's accession to the British throne the coming of a new sovereign had been constitutionally held to call for a dissolution of Parliament and a new election of members to the House of Commons. A change had been made in this practice not long before the death of William III. by the passing of an Act of Parliament declaring that the House of Commons in existence at the death of one sovereign should not be brought to an end by the accession of another. This change in the law affecting the representative assembly was a distinct improvement on the practice which had been ordained and carried out for so many reigns before Queen Anne came to the throne. There were indeed general elections on the accession of a new sovereign during the years between the reigns of Queen Anne and Queen Victoria, but the practice was not compulsory. There might have been many reasons to doubt whether the representative assembly which had taken the oath of allegiance to a sovereign like George III. might not often have had reason to regret that it had made any such pledge of obedience, and might not have yearned for an opportunity of reconsidering its course when the reign should come to an end, and a chance be given for the election of a new assembly with a strong Liberal majority which could proclaim to the new sovereign the necessity for his adoption of a more enlightened policy. But there could be no reason that the representative assembly which had taken the oath of allegiance to Queen Victoria should fail in its allegiance to King Edward VII., and that therefore a new opportunity ought to be given to the constituencies to say whether they believed that the representatives they had already sent to Parliament could be safely trusted with the conduct of public business under the new ruler. The expense and the trouble of a General Election are matters of serious moment to the country, and it can easily be imagined that a sovereign with so practical and so considerate a mind as Edward VII. must have cordially approved the change in the constitutional arrangements which abolished this serious exaction on the time and the money of constituencies and representatives alike. The Parliament, therefore, which was existing at the time of Queen Victoria's death had to undergo no interruption from the fact that a change had taken place in the occupancy of the throne.

An important fact in the story of the opening of the reign comes fairly into notice here, because it had to do with a question that had occasioned much controversy during the rule of Queen Victoria. This question, which embodies a matter of grave public interest, relates to the terms of the oath which King Edward VII. was to be called upon to take on the day of his coronation. This oath had been taken by all our sovereigns since the passing of the Act of Settlement, and it was framed with the object of obtaining or exacting from every ruler of the State a sworn pledge of absolute resistance to every attempt at a restoration of the Stuart dynasty, and to a disavowal of any sympathy with the faith professed by the last Stuart king. The oath contained certain words repudiating and denouncing some of the teachings and symbolic actions belonging to the Church of Rome. These words of condemnation are decidedly uncompromising in their terms, and some of them might even be regarded as scarcely suitable for ordinary discourse or ordinary controversy. Such a repudiation of the faith and the religious usages of the Church of Rome could not be listened to without a shock and a sense of deep pain by any Catholic, or even by a staunch Protestant who was willing to admit that the doctrines and the practices of the Catholic Church are entitled to be spoken of with respect in all our public ceremonials when it becomes necessary to make allusion to them. The sovereign of this Empire is the sovereign of a large proportion of Catholic subjects in Great Britain, while in Ireland the large majority of the population belong to the ancient faith. The House of Lords holds many Catholic peers, and the House of Commons a very considerable proportion of Catholic members. When Queen Victoria came to the throne the Catholic Emancipation Act had been in existence for some time, and

Catholic members held seats in the House of Commons; but the change was still of recent date, religious disabilities had but lately been removed, after a serious crisis, from the Catholic population, and it had yet to be seen how the new principle of civil and religious liberty would work. Therefore no serious inclination was felt, even among members of the Church of Rome, to demand any fresh changes in the usages and the ceremonial of a coronation.

But the conditions of public life had undergone most important changes since the days when Queen Victoria ascended the throne. Religious distinctions of many kinds had been abolished during her reign, members of the Church of Rome might hold almost any office under Crown or Parliament, and the Duke of Norfolk, hereditary Earl-Marshal, was a devout believer in the doctrines of the Catholic Church. It seemed, therefore, inconsistent and unreasonable, not to use any stronger words, that the sovereign should be called upon to express in his coronation oath what could not but be considered as useless and offensive condemnation of doctrines and practices maintained by the Church of Rome, with which the laws of the country now no longer claim any right to interfere. It was generally believed, too, that the new King was about the last man living who could have felt any personal wish to retain in the words of his coronation oath passages wantonly harsh and offensive towards the faith of a large proportion of his subjects. Indeed, there was a very general impression through all these countries that the King's advisers as well as the King himself were willing that some alteration should be made in the terms of this part of the coronation oath. During the earlier days of the Session which was now opening, a committee had been appointed to take into consideration the propriety of making some such change. But there seemed to be some inconvenience in attempting any definite change just then, and the subject was allowed to stand over for another Session. The Coronation of the new sovereign was not to take place that year, and there was ample time, therefore, to consider and accomplish any change in the terms of the historic oath which might be considered needful.

It is no part of this History to do more than make a passing mention of the fact that the Royal Coronation had to be postponed owing to the King's severe and dangerous illness for a considerable time beyond that originally appointed, and we shall therefore only say that the whole subject was allowed to remain open for future consideration, and that the fullest hope was felt everywhere that the coronation oath might be made suitable to the changes which had taken place in legislation and in public feeling, and to the recognition in State ceremonial, as well as in constitutional practice, of the principle of religious equality among all subjects of the Empire.

The King opened in person his first Session of Parliament in February 1901, 'and delivered the speech from the throne in full clear tones audible through all the benches and galleries of the House of Lords.' Queen Alexandra occupied a seat on a throne placed next to that of the King. The new reign had now begun.

CHAPTER XXIII.

A RETROSPECT—POLITICAL.

This History cannot close more appropriately and effectively than with a retrospect of the reign. The traveller who comes to the end of his journey through some interesting landscape naturally turns round and takes a final survey of the scenery through which he has passed before he leaves it. The reign of Queen Victoria represents one of the most important epochs in the whole history of the modern world. Indeed, it may be said to have opened that era in the progress of human life which we now regard as essentially constituting the modern world, the world in which the application of practical science brought into existence modes and ways of life unknown to humanity throughout all its previous generations. The reign was full of events of the deepest and the most dramatic interest, even if we were not to take into account the fact that it saw the whole of the marvellous revolutions which practical science has made in the every-day life of the civilised world. Some of the most thrilling, the most momentous, and the most memorable wars known to history were carried on during the years while Queen Victoria was the sovereign of England.

At the time when the reign began there was a general impression throughout England and the British States that a happy era of peace was dawning upon the world. The great wars with France, which ended with the career of the First Napoleon, were happily over, and France was believed to have settled down to a time of prosaic quietude, under the rule of a steady, old-fashioned, and respectable monarchy. The United States had become a great and prosperous Republic, the leading principle of whose policy aimed at the development of its own prosperity and the practical culture of the arts of peace. England's colonies were, to all appearance, loyal and contented, and no signals of alarm were seen to come from the dominions of the Queen throughout India. The epoch of revolution on the European Continent seemed also to have passed away, and there was a general and comforting impression that Turkey might be turned to good account as a barrier against any possible disturbance caused by Russia's ambition for encroachment on the territory of her neighbours. The Germanic Confederation was commonly assumed to have brought under suitable and accepted discipline all rivalries among the states of the Fatherland. There was an optimistic impression among statesmen generally that the Kingdom of Greece was becoming reconciled to its separation from its island families. The prevailing belief was that the Congresses, which had undertaken the settlement of European affairs after the great era of revolution, had accomplished an enduring work, and had left the sovereigns and peoples of Europe nothing to do but to cultivate the arts of peace.

England herself was assumed to have got over her most serious domestic troubles. The measure for the emancipation of the Roman Catholics had been forced, first, upon a reluctant Ministry, and then, by the Duke of Wellington, upon a reluctant King, and the great Reform Bill of 1832 had given the English people in general some share in the making of the laws under which they were to live. All that was known of the new sovereign, the young Queen who had just come to the throne, filled the country with the cheering belief that she was likely to enter upon the duties of her reign with an intelligence, a temperament, and a spirit very different from those which, up to that time, had characterised the sovereigns of the House of Hanover. Under these and many other comforting conditions there was an almost universal expectation that an entirely new chapter in the history of England was about to open, and that the era when the ambitions, the tyrannies, and the selfish passions of kings could keep a whole State in war with foreign nations, and in distress and oppression at home, had passed away for ever from European history.

It may be said at once that if these hopeful anticipations were not destined to be fully realised, the disappointment of national hopes is not in any way to be ascribed to the public policy or personal influence of the sovereign with whom the new era had begun. The Queen had hardly gone through all the ceremonies belonging to the ascending of a throne, when there came the alarming news of an outbreak of rebellion in Canada. Nothing at that moment could have seemed more ill-omened than such an event. Canada was so filled with revolt against the system of government exercised over her up to that time by the British kings and their Ministers that even the antagonism, bitter as it was, between the French Canadians and the British Canadians was utterly forgotten in the combined passion of revolt against the rule of Westminster. But the threatened evil soon proved to be a most hopeful augury for the reign of the young Queen. The genius and the statesmanship of Lord Durham, who was sent out by the Queen, under the advice of Lord John Russell, to exercise something like a dictatorship in dealing with the Canadian outbreak, created an entirely new and beneficent chapter in the history of England's dealings with her colonies. Lord Durham saw that the one only real remedy for the troubles of Canada was to endow the colony with a system of local self-government. He was able to prevail on the English statesmen in power to adopt his views, and the result was, as the world has seen, that Canada became one of the most loyal and contented partners in the British Empire. Lord Durham's principle has since been applied to the Australian Colonies with an equally happy result.

But the omens of peace which came with the settlement of the Canadian troubles did not shed any light on the relations of the British Empire with foreign Powers, or even with some of her own great dependencies. There came the Opium War with China, and, before very long, the Crimean War, then the Indian Mutiny, and England was afterwards engaged in further struggles with China. Egypt became more than once a theatre of war, and there were frequent troubles with native rulers and states in Hindostan. The great Civil War broke out in America; France and Austria were engaged in a momentous conflict; Austria and Prussia entered on a decisive war, which brought the Germanic Confederation to an end, and ultimately converted the King of Prussia into the German Emperor. Louis Napoleon made himself, for the time, Emperor of the French, but his Empire came to an end when the conquering Prussian army occupied Paris. In later years the reign of Queen Victoria saw wars between Russia and Turkey, and the beginning of those warlike rivalries between the West and the East, which appear to have opened a new chapter in history. One Power has come up in the East which promises or threatens to revolutionise all our previous conceptions as to the relations between Europe and Asia. Before the reign of Queen Victoria had quite closed the civilised world had been compelled to recognise the fact that an entirely new influence of as yet incalculable importance had come into being when Japan, having trained herself in all the arts, civil and military, of the West, presented herself as the leader of the new movement from the East. The reign of Queen Victoria, therefore, gives students of history ample and various opportunities of making themselves acquainted with the characteristics of war.

The reign of Queen Victoria was emphatically a period of constitutional reform. It did not actually open the era of such reform, because some of the most important advances towards the establishment of civil and religious liberty in these countries, and of political equality for all classes of British subjects, were accomplished under the rule, although against the will, of some of Victoria's predecessors. The Catholic Emancipation measure was carried, and the first attempts to extend the electoral franchise were made before Queen Victoria came to the throne. But in the new ruler the British Empire found a sovereign who had not to be coerced by Ministers into the practical acknowledgment of the necessary changes. This was all the more surprising, and all the more satisfactory, to many reformers in the early days of the reign, because the young Queen was then understood to be much guided by Lord Melbourne, her first Prime Minister, and Lord Melbourne was regarded as a quiet, easy-going, and agreeable personage, who did not care to disturb himself or any of his friends by troublesome efforts at the reconstruction of old familiar arrangements, and the promotion of changes unwelcome to most of his own order. But it afterwards came to be generally understood that the Queen had more influence in this way over her Prime Minister than her Prime Minister had over her, and she soon made it apparent that she fully realised the necessity for great movements of constitutional reform. The adoption of the principle of Free Trade, some of the greatest improvements in the Navigation Laws, and the opening of Parliamentary representation and Parliamentary voting to all classes of British subjects, were only part of the great constitutional improvements which will give the reign its abiding and special honours in history.

The British Parliament became, during the reign, the greatest political arena in the history of these countries. The statesmen and the orators of that reign had amongst them men who must ever hold the highest rank in the world's history. Sir Robert Peel was the first great Prime Minister of Queen Victoria's time. Like some of his successors, he was an orator as well as a statesman, and he helped to carry his great reforms by the fascinating and commanding power of the eloquence with which he commended them, and sustained them against all the efforts of a determined opposition.

He and Lord John Russell were, during many years of the reign, the great opposing leaders of political parties. Peel led the Conservatives, and Russell led the Liberals of those days. Towards the close of his career Peel became influenced by the spirit of reform, so far as questions of trade and commerce were concerned, and through him was accomplished the triumph of what would now be be called the Free Food principle. Russell was always a reformer in that sense, and in his political principles he was a thorough Liberal, although he could hardly be described as a Radical according to the acceptation of that term in more modern times. He had still when in office to carry out many systems, especially as regarded the work of Ireland's government, which could not have been accepted by an advanced Liberal of days nearer to our own. But he was thoroughly sincere in all his political purposes, and we may safely assume that, if his lot had been cast in later times, he would have been at the head of every movement for genuine reform in the rule of the Irish people.

Peel was a great orator in Parliamentary debate, while Russell could hardly be said to have ever risen to a rivalry with him in mere eloquence. But Russell was a most persuasive debater, and he had literary culture and literary gifts which suffused his speeches in the House of Commons with a peculiar charm. Peel represented that commercial and trading order to which his progenitors belonged; while Russell came of the highest aristocratic class, and of a family which had given martyrs to the cause of liberty. Russell in his early years had been a close friend of Thomas Moore, the Irish National poet, and he had enjoyed the intimacy and the confidence of many among the great authors and great thinkers of his time. The two men, Peel and Russell, seemed exactly qualified by nature to be the leaders of the two opposing parties. But it might well have seemed to many that Peel, with his powerful voice, his stately presence, and his commanding eloquence, ought to have been the leader of a reform party demanding and advocating great constitutional changes; while Russell, with his quiet manner, his remarkable gift of persuasive pleading, and even his somewhat fragile appearance, was the man who might naturally have had the task of endeavouring to convince the House of Commons that things should be allowed to remain as they were, and that the existing condition of British systems did not call for any constitutional change. Each man, however, was thoroughly qualified to lead the political party whose cause he was advocating from conscientious conviction, and Peel will always be remembered in history as one of the greatest of England's Conservative administrators, while Russell must ever be remembered as one of the greatest Liberal statesmen his country has brought forth.

A somewhat singular fact is, that Lord John Russell in his earlier years seems to have been looked upon by his friends and associates as a man of bold and daring genius, while those who watched and followed his career in later years, came to regard him as especially endowed with caution, moderation, and power of careful and persuasive argument. Each man filled his place and did his work with commanding ability, and there are few rivalries described in modern history which can form a more interesting study for intelligent readers of our Parliamentary records. The reign would have been memorable if only for the fact that it brought to the front two such leaders of the great opposing parties then contending for rule, and endowed with qualities so well suited for the attainment and maintenance of rival leadership. The student of history may find an interesting subject for contemplation in the fact that the man sprung from the people was the leader of Conservatism, while the descendant of one of the greatest aristocratic families was leader of what was then regarded as the pioneer party of advanced political reform. Each man, it has to be said, won like honour by his exalted personal character, by the nobleness of his life, and the purity of his patriotic purposes.

Lord Palmerston and Lord Derby may in some sense be regarded as rival political figures in Parliament, as were Sir Robert Peel and Lord John

Russell. The rivalry, however, was not always made manifest by the maintenance of hostile political principles, for Lord Palmerston, although holding his place as a Liberal statesman, was often inclined to fight shy of political reform; while Lord Derby, although a life-long and proclaimed Conservative, proved himself ready, on more than one occasion, to help in the carrying of a Reform measure. Lord Derby's active political career was carried on for the most part in the House of Lords, while Lord Palmerston found his more appropriate arena in the stirring life of the House of Commons. Each man was undoubtedly gifted with the qualities which win success for political ambition, and each man soon won a high place amongst celebrated political leaders. Lord Derby had the gifts of a genuine Parliamentary orator—he was called by the first Lord Lytton 'the Rupert of debate,' because of his impulsive, energetic, and impassioned style of speaking, and his aptitude for rushing forward without much consideration for the difficulties and the opposition in his way. Lord Derby had a magnificent voice, a mind illumined by much classical and modern culture, a gift of striking and sometimes almost poetic phraseology and a liberal command of invective.

Lord Palmerston's style was entirely different. Palmerston was a debater of the conversational order. He reasoned with his adversaries, he played with them, he ridiculed them, he turned their arguments inside out in the happiest and easiest manner, he never hesitated to appeal to the prejudices popular among his Parliamentary audiences, and his seemed the very genius of common sense, exploring with a searchlight of inquiry the fancies and the dreams of more ambitious and less practical minds. Palmerston never made any attempt to rise above the intellectual level of his average supporters and opponents; but his style was so easy, so happy, and in its way so effective, that the most unsympathetic listener would not lose a word of the clever and captivating speech which for the time seemed as if it were addressed to him in especial. It is doubtful whether the House of Commons ever had in modern times a more successful master of the conversational type of speaking than Lord Palmerston. The admirers of Richard Cobden might indeed fairly put in a claim for his right to at least an equal place in the same method of Parliamentary argument and appeal, but Cobden had always the immense advantage of having to champion some great cause sacred to his heart and sanctioned by his deepest convictions, while the exigencies of party warfare often led Lord Palmerston to maintain some position and to adopt some argument which he might have opposed or assailed at different times under different conditions.

Lord Derby, in the days of his greatest success as a Parliamentary leader, could hardly be regarded as a thoroughly popular statesman even among his own party. There was not much about him that was winning or placable, and a proud reserve kept his ordinary supporters at a certain distance from him. The temperament of Lord Palmerston was always genial, gracious, and welcoming to those around him, even to those who were not among his own political followers, and he had the air and manner of good-fellowship which carried with it a captivating power. Both men led great political contests in their time, but Lord Derby always seemed to be possessed with the very fervour of the political cause which he was striving to conduct to victory; while Lord Palmerston conveyed to many, at least, of his hearers the impression that he was only making the best he could of the case which he had to argue, and that the world would probably keep going on in much the same way whether he and his followers won or lost in the struggle. The fame of the two men belongs rather to Parliament than to English history.

Lord Brougham was one of the most gifted, the most remarkable, and perhaps the most eccentric of Parliamentary and public celebrities in the early years of Queen Victoria's reign. Like Lord Derby, he could hardly be regarded as belonging to the order of statesmanship in the highest class; but he was certainly one of the most powerful speakers of his day, and some of his great speeches, or we should rather say his great lectures on public platforms to popular audiences, are well worthy of study even at the present moment when we have quite passed away from the educational controversies of that early day of undeveloped popular education.

Probably no other public man in this country ever was the subject of so much caricature, written and pictorial, as Brougham brought upon himself; but the very frequency and force of the caricatures only seemed to be another tribute to the commanding position which he had won.

There were some Parliamentary leaders of parties during the reign who hold place among the foremost orators of modern times, and have left an enduring record in the annals of the past century. Daniel O'Connell, the famous advocate of Ireland's right to constitutional freedom and equality, spent many of his closing years a prominent figure in Queen Victoria's Parliaments, and was admitted, even by his bitterest and most prejudiced political enemies, to be an orator of the most commanding order. He had an impressive figure, a magnificent voice, an inexhaustible power of argument and illustration, a rare gift of humour, and a capacity at the same time for the most pathetic appeals to the human feelings of his audience. No man could have gone more often, more persistently, and more daringly against the most cherished convictions and prejudices of the great political parties who were bitterly and unreservedly antagonistic to him, and no man could have held his own with more genuine cratorical effect. Mr. Gladstone was one of those who bore the most generous testimony to O'Connell's power as an orator and debater. Another conspicuous Irish Member of Parliament in those days was Richard Lalor Sheil. We have given in the first volume of this History some account of the high tribute paid by Gladstone to the eloquence of Sheil, who, although afflicted by nature with a voice singularly harsh and disagreeable in tone, was yet able, in spite of that defect, to win for himself a place among the greatest Parliamentary orators and debaters of the time. It used to be said in those days that one of the only points, concerning which difference of opinion was possible, on which Gladstone and Disraeli were agreed, was as to Sheil's position as a speaker. Disraeli went so far as to declare that Sheil was superior to Canning as an orator, and if Gladstone did not express himself quite so definitely, he certainly seems to have agreed with Disraeli in regarding Sheil as one of the great Parliamentary orators in a Parliament of remarkable eloquence.

The name of Lord Ellenborough must not be omitted from a retrospect of the reign of Queen Victoria. Edward Law was the eldest son of Baron Ellenborough, Lord Chief Justice, was educated at Eton and Cambridge, and entered Parliament as a Conservative, held office under several Conservative Administrations, and was appointed Governor-General of India. When he held this great office his policy, which was characteristic of his strong self-will and venturous temper, proved unsatisfactory, and led to his recall. That policy, however, found many influential supporters at home, and he received the title of Earl of Ellenborough, and was First Lord of the Admiralty under Sir Robert Peel. He was afterwards put at the head of the India Office, but the course he took in endeavouring to condemn the Indian policy of Lord Canning compelled him once again to withdraw from any ruling part in the administration of Indian affairs. He will be remembered chiefly because of his remarkable eloquence as a debater in the quiet House of Lords, for the Oriental hyperbole of his style, his magniloquent phraseology, which seemed to be the work of elaborate preparation, but in reality came to him as naturally as the utterance of conventionalities and commonplaces might to an ordinary man. He was a very eccentric politician, and his contemporaries, even among his own party, placed but little reliance on his judgment. He was, indeed, the comet of a season, and not in any sense a guiding star. Sometimes the flash of the comet carried true enlightenment with it. The position he took in advocating the cause of Poland and her claims to liberty and independence stirred a genuine passion in the public mind of England and of Europe, and might, under happier auspices, have led to beneficent results. Other counsels prevailed over European Cabinets, and the hopes which were formed as to the effects of the agitation he had called into existence were doomed to disappointment. Lord Ellenborough was just the man who might have made a distinguished and most serviceable career for himself and for his country if he had been an independent member of the House of Commons, had formed a party of his own there, had found some just cause which won his admiration—such as the cause of Poland, for instance—and had devoted his time and his advocacy to its promotion. But the fates were against him, or indeed his own temperament was against him, his sudden and unreasoning fits and starts of policy, this way and that, and his overmastering love for grandiloquence of phraseology, obscured his higher qualities, especially his judgment, and left him, not a statesman, but a brilliant political meteor.

The name and fame of John Singleton Copley, afterwards Lord Lyndhurst, carry us back to a period earlier than that of these volumes. He was born at Boston, United States, in May 1772, and when three years old was brought by his father, the celebrated historical and portrait painter, to England. His father and mother were both of English extraction, but the portrait-painter was himself born in the United States, where George Washington sat to him for a portrait. Copley, the son, was educated at Cambridge and won distinction there. He studied for the Bar, was called in due course, and soon began to make a distinct success. He entered Parliament in 1819 as a Tory, became successively Attorney-General, Master of the Rolls, and Lord Chancellor, with the title of Baron Lyndhurst. All this was before Queen Victoria had come to the throne, but he lived and worked on until October 1863, when he died.

Lord Lyndhurst was one of the many lawyers who during that reign made a name for themselves, alike in the Courts of Law and in both Houses of Parliament. Many of his doings as a barrister and his speeches and rulings as a judge provoked much severe criticism at the time, and his own political party never seemed certain whether he was or was not a thorough Conservative in heart and mind. But there could be no question as to the lucidity of his style in delivering his judgments, or as to his eloquence in Parliamentary debate. He was one of the most eloquent speakers in either House, and even in his most advanced years it was a genuine delight to hear him deliver his opinions and array his luminous arguments on some great question in the House of Lords. Some of us who are still living can well remember the intense pleasure which it gave to listen to a speech from him, and even those who were least in sympathy with the cause he was endeavouring to support were apt to forget their difference of view under the fascination of his eloquence. His style was singularly terse; he never wasted a word; and, while he had all the keenness and force of the debater, he never seemed to go out of his way in quest of merely ornamental illustration, or even ornamental phrase. He lived during a period especially rich in great Parliamentary speakers, who were also leading lawyers, and he maintained his position during the days of Lord Coleridge, as well as during those of

Lord Brougham. His fame may be regarded as entirely individual and personal. No great reforms in law or in politics will be associated with Lord Lyndhurst's career, but the annals of Queen Victoria's reign must ever preserve his memory.

Lord Lytton, the first Lord Lytton, became at a later day, and before he had received his title, one of the most conspicuous figures in the House of Commons. Sir Edward Bulwer Lytton, as he then was, had two difficulties to contend against when he first entered the House of Commons. He had to contend against the influence of the reputation he had already acquired as one of the most popular and successful authors of novels, of plays, and of verses then famous in England and throughout the reading world. His novels are still read, and some of his plays still hold a place on the stage, but we find it hard now to understand that the novels were at one time regarded by masses of readers as fit to hold rivalry with those of Dickens and Thackeray. There was, and perhaps still is, an impression that a successful literary man is never likely to achieve a success in public life, especially in Parliamentary debate, and this impression was against Lord Lytton when he first entered the House of Commons. He had also another and a more serious difficulty to contend against. Like Sheil, he had a very defective voice, but, unlike Sheil, he had also a very defective articulation; and, indeed, those who listened to him for the first time were inclined to believe that nature had made the gift of eloquence impossible of attainment by him. Yet it cannot be denied that, with this serious defect to fight against, his speeches in the House of Commons obtained a complete mastery over his audience, and when read from the reports seemed to be genuine eloquence.

John Arthur Roebuck was for many years one of the most conspicuous and impressive figures in the Parliaments of Queen Victoria. He was born in India, and in his early days was taken to Canada, where he had the most of his bringing-up and education. He had distinct literary tastes, and was the author of 'Colonies of England' and 'History of the Whig Ministry of 1830,' both of which books had a distinct success. At the age of twenty-two he settled in England, was called to the Bar, and entered the House of Commons as member for Bath. He is best remembered by the present generation as the representative of Sheffield, for which constituency he sat during many years. He entered the House of Commons as a Radical member, and was among the earliest of the party who became known as the advocates of advanced Radicalism. But Roebuck was, above all things else, a thoroughly independent member, and never could be safely reckoned on by any leader as a man absolutely obedient to the word of command. He always followed the lines of his own convictions, and was even somewhat eccentric in his political impulses. He never was or tried to be a great orator, but he was unquestionably one of the most impressive, and, in the better sense of the word, one of the most interesting debaters who commanded the attention of the House during his time. His speeches were made up for the most part of short, sharp, acrid, epigrammatic sentences, illumined by many happy allusions drawn from literature and history, and he could, when sudden occasion called on him, delight the House by an absolutely extemporaneous display of argument, sarcasm, and humour. His tongue was unsparing in its dealings with his political opponents, and he thus undoubtedly made many enemies for the time, but he was not a man against whom a feeling of enmity was likely to be long maintained. The motion which he brought forward during the Aberdeen Ministry of 1855, a motion for inquiring into the state of the army before Sevastopol, led to the overthrow of the Government. He supported Lord Beaconsfield's principles and policy during more than one important crisis of England's dealings with Eastern questions, and during his whole Parliamentary career he showed himself, according to his lights, a resolute supporter of measures rather than of men. He never tried to form a party of his own, and was, indeed, a thoroughly self-contained man. Even those members of the House who liked him least never failed to hasten to their places when the word

went round that Roebuck was about to speak.
The interest of the Parliamentary debates lost
much when Roebuck's death removed him from
the scene of his many successes.

The most brilliant Parliamentary rivalry known
during the reign of Queen Victoria was that
between Gladstone and Disraeli. Gladstone was
unquestionably the greatest orator and debater
among the Prime Ministers of that reign. As
we have already seen, in many instances, the
qualities of the great orator and those of the
great debater are not often found combined in
one person. Some of the finest speeches preserved in the history of eloquence are those of
men whose best efforts can only be accomplished
by careful thought and preparation, and who are
not equally endowed with the capacity for giving
forth an extemporaneous reply to some argument
just delivered by a Parliamentary opponent. When
the carefully-prepared speech has been delivered,
and becomes a Parliamentary and historical record,
it is valued according to its intrinsic merits, and
the reader thinks no more about the elaborate
method of its preparation than he would about
the length of time which a sculptor has given
to the production of some noble statue. But the
public man who aims at being a great debater
as well as a great orator has to prove himself
a master of two very different arts, and is indeed
rare in political life. Gladstone was one of the
men who could display equal success in the two

different qualities. He was, according to the judgment of this writer, the greatest orator, with one single exception, in the House of Commons during the later half of Queen Victoria's reign, and that single exception is made because of the eloquence of John Bright.

Disraeli had many brilliant rhetorical gifts, and he was beyond dispute one of the most effective debaters known to the modern days of the House of Commons. He was not an orator of the highest order, and his more rhetorical efforts had an air of artificiality about them which sometimes greatly marred their effect. Such passages in his speeches did not seem to be the outpourings of that fusion of reason, conviction, passion, and imagination which is essential to the noblest eloquence. But as a debater he ranked among the very foremost known to our modern Parliaments, and he had an unfailing gift of sarcasm which could, for the time, strike with telling ridicule any argument on which he sought to expend his scorn. His voice was impressive and varied in tone; he was quick in devising humorous illustrations to bring up laughter at the expense of his antagonist, and he gave out from time to time scornful phrases which lived in the memory of the House of Commons, and became familiar quotations in debate and in literature.

As a statesman, Disraeli has not left much record of great measures for the advancement of national prosperity, because, even where the

Government which he inspired did on more than one occasion introduce some genuine reform or some new and beneficent principle of legislation, this was only done when the rival party had gone near to carrying a like measure, and, failing because of Conservative opposition, had gone out of office, and given Disraeli and his colleagues a tempting chance of carrying the work to success. Such an instance is especially to be found in the Reform Bill of 1867, which was carried by Mr. Disraeli and his colleagues, by whom, and with the help of some seceding Liberals, Mr. Gladstone's measure of the previous session had been defeated. Whereupon, in the following session, the Conservatives, under the inspiration of Disraeli, introduced a measure of the same nature and even more expanded in its effect, and succeeded in carrying it through both Houses of Parliament. There can, therefore, be little question as to the fact that Gladstone must rank in history as superior to Disraeli, alike in statesmanship and in eloquence. But the name of Disraeli will always be regarded as that of one who brought into the House of Commons a new and a peculiar style of eloquence; who contrived to blend his literary and his political qualities into a curiously compact, characteristic, and original form of expression; who seemed as if he never could be languid, commonplace, or unimpressive; was ever alive and ever vivid.

Richard Cobden and John Bright must always

hold a place in history among the most conspicuous and the most honoured figures in English political life during the reign. These men seemed by nature created to be close friends and working companions. Neither man took his tone or borrowed his political opinions from the other, and yet they were always actuated by the same convictions, always guided towards the same ends, and they were ever fighters side by side. Bright was unquestionably the greater orator of the two. Indeed, it may be doubted whether Cobden could be regarded as an orator in the highest sense of the word. He had a marvellous argumentative power; his reasonings, his array of facts, and his illustrations seemed often as if they must force conviction on the most reluctant and antagonistic minds, and he had a genuine gift of humour. But Bright was an orator in the very highest sense of the word, and, in the opinion of this writer, was the greatest English orator of his day, Gladstone himself not excepted. Bright had a magnificent voice, which was able to express and to accentuate without stress or effort every feeling, wrath, scorn, genial humour, persuasive appeal, pathetic outpour, chivalrous exhortation to courage and self-sacrifice. Mr. George W. E. Russell, in his admirable 'Life of Gladstone,' justly and effectively says of Mr. Bright, when describing Mr. Bright's secession from one of Gladstone's forward movements, that Bright's 'high reputation as a man whose politics were part of his religion, and who had never turned aside by a hair's-breadth from the narrow path of civil duty as he understood it, gave him a weight of moral influence such as no contemporary politician could command.'

We have already explained, in one of these volumes, that Mr. Bright's secession from the Gladstone policy of Home Rule for Ireland was not inspired by any opposition to Ireland's claims for such a system of internal administration as the Irish people themselves desired and demanded. Bright had again and again declared that the duty of the British Parliament was to accomplish every work in the internal administration of Ireland that the Irish nation would itself have accomplished if Ireland had been, by some sudden revolution, released altogether from England's control. He had held to that policy consistently throughout his whole public career, but he objected to the proposal for the setting up of a new and separate Parliament in the sister island. His objection was to the creation of several Parliaments, or to the existence of any but the one Parliament for the government of these countries. But he maintained, consistently and firmly, that the English Parliament ought to carry out for Ireland those reforms in her internal system which the majority of the Irish representatives declared to be necessary for the welfare of their country. At the time of the secession there arose unquestionably, among all

Irish Nationalists at home and abroad, a strong feeling of surprise and disappointment at the course taken by Mr. Bright; and it is certain that Bright himself felt very deeply the change of sentiment towards him which had come up, for the time, among all Irish Nationalists. But whether Bright was right or wrong in the action which he took with regard to Home Rule, it may be admitted by the most sincere Irish Nationalist that there was no inconsistency in his conduct, and that he remained, as he had ever been, a sincere and devoted friend to the Irish people. English public life suffered a heavy loss when these two great political comrades, Cobden and Bright—an interval of nearly quarter of a century between their deaths—passed away from the living world. They had been leading figures in the accomplishment of some of the most important and beneficent reforms ever made in the government of Queen Victoria's dominions. They had ever been the untiring advocates of truth, peace, and freedom in political and in social life, and had unfailingly opposed the policy of war for the sake of conquest and of annexation which had come up again in their days. Their names lend a peculiar lustre to modern English history.

Robert Lowe, Lord Sherbrooke, flashed like a meteor across the political life of England during the period of our retrospect. He was born and brought up in this country, and received his education at the University of Oxford, was called to the Bar, but he went almost immediately afterwards to Australia, and spent many years there in practice as an advocate. He then returned to England, threw himself into Parliamentary life, held office under Lord Aberdeen and Lord Palmerston, and afterwards became Chancellor of the Exchequer in one of Gladstone's Administrations. Lowe's administrative career as Chancellor of the Exchequer, and afterwards as Home Secretary, created much opposition and some outbursts of popular discontent, and indeed, throughout his whole Parliamentary life, he was almost always engaged in one fierce battle or another. Without any of the great qualifications for an orator in style, in voice, or in delivery, he was ever a debater who held the close attention of the House, and fascinated, for the time, even those who were least inclined to do him reverence. His speeches were a succession of sparkling epigrams, brilliant, bold ideas, and clever satirical perversions of the arguments and the meaning of his opponents. One never could foretell what audacious outburst of satire and humour was to come next, and if Lowe did not always do much towards the converting of men's opinions, he never failed at least to hold their absorbed attention. Lowe was a scholar and a lover of literature, and his style as a debater and a writer bore easy and artistic testimony of his intellectual culture.

The career of Lord Robert Cecil, afterwards

Lord Cranborne, and finally Marquis of Salisbury, was in every sense one of peculiar interest. Lord Robert Cecil was not, in his years of early manhood, regarded as likely to come in for the succession to the Salisbury peerage, and he was not, when starting in active life, altogether relieved from the necessity of doing something to make a living. He had gone through the usual course of university education, was a close and loving student of literature, and had the advantage of much extensive travel. At the age of twenty-three he obtained a seat in the House of Commons, and it is well understood that for many years after he worked continuously as a writer on at least one London weekly newspaper of a high literary order, which devoted itself very often to satirical studies of existing social conditions and ways.

Lord Robert Cecil was, by family tradition at all events, a Conservative in politics, but he showed himself in every sense an absolutely independent member. Except for the fact that he made no effort to create a party of his own, he pursued much the same course in the House of Commons as that taken by Lord Randolph Churchill at a later period. No Administration ever knew quite where to have Lord Robert Cecil. A Liberal Ministry might sometimes receive his entirely unexpected support; at another time a Conservative Government might come in for his vigorous opposition. It was evident enough to those who followed his rising and brilliant career that, beneath a manner of sometimes eccentric levity, Lord Robert Cecil had strong and deep convictions of his own, which he would not modify to suit the temporary advantages of a political party. On all questions connected with the maintenance of the State Church and with education he was always earnest, resolute, and consistent, and he took a deep interest in foreign affairs.

By the death of his elder brother Lord Robert Cecil became Viscount Cranborne, and therefore heir to the marquisate. When Gladstone's Reform Bill was defeated in 1866 by the combined efforts of the Conservative Opposition and the seceding Liberals, and Lord Derby and Disraeli coming into office introduced a Reform Bill of their own, going considerably farther in the popular direction than even Gladstone had thus far ventured to do, Lord Cranborne remained true to the political creed of his party, refused office in the new Conservative Administration, and fought vigorously, although unsuccessfully, against the measure. In the year following he succeeded his father as Marquis of Salisbury, and passed into the House of Lords. Three times he held the office of Prime Minister. In the House of Lords he proved himself as brilliant a debater as he had been in the House of Commons, and he frequently stirred the somewhat languid hereditary chamber into positive animation by his vigorous appeals, his ready wit, and his almost unequalled power of sarcastic reply. It has become part of our political history that during one of their many differences of opinion Disraeli described Lord Salisbury as 'the master of gibes and flouts and jeers.' The description was hardly fair, coming as it did from one who had given himself up very often to the production of gibes and flouts and jeers. Besides, it has to be remembered that Lord Salisbury always remained true to his own convictions, whether these convictions led him to success or to defeat, which was a good deal more than could be said for the opponent of popular reform who mainly helped to introduce the most popular reform measure of the reign.

Lord Salisbury outlived Queen Victoria, and will ever be remembered as one of the most distinguished and the most absolutely conscientious Prime Ministers of the reign. The country in general rendered full justice to Lord Salisbury's integrity and single-hearted devotion to his own political principles. The most advanced Radicals came to understand that the character of such a man is not to be estimated merely by the measure of his agreement with the great purposes and principles of the reforms which, in spite of his most vigorous opposition, were able to establish themselves in our systems of government. The feeling of the whole country rendered homage to his character when death removed him from that political arena in which he had borne himself so bravely and so well.

Another great political figure in our retrospect of

the reign is that of Sir William Vernon Harcourt. Sir William Harcourt, like Lord Salisbury, began his public career as a regular contributor to a London weekly newspaper, and became especially known to the reading world as the author of a series of letters published in the *Times*, and signed 'Historicus,' letters which were afterwards published in a volume, and won for their author distinct celebrity and influence. Harcourt had been called to the Bar, but the business of political life proved more to his taste, and in 1868 he was elected to the House of Commons as Liberal representative of the city of Oxford. He became Home Secretary in a Liberal Administration, and twice held the office of Chancellor of the Exchequer. After Gladstone's death he became leader of the House of Commons during Lord Rosebery's brief reign as Prime Minister. Harcourt, as leader of the Liberal party in the House of Commons, did not get on very well with Lord Rosebery, who played the titular part of leader to the whole Liberal party, and it must be owned that the sympathies of Liberals in general went very strongly with Harcourt. Lord Rosebery withdrew himself from the difficulties of his position by resigning the Liberal leadership, and Sir William Vernon Harcourt not long after withdrew altogether from political and public life.

Sir William Harcourt was one of the most powerful debaters in the House of Commons of his time. He had a commanding presence, a voice of full and varied intonation, and a ready supply of effective words, with a certain literary style which distinguished even his most casual utterances from the ordinary manner of Parliamentary debate. He could hardly be described as a great Parliamentary orator, because, although he did not lack emotion and even passion in his mode of speech, he wanted that imaginative, and, if it may be thus described, that poetic quality which is essential to eloquence of the highest kind. As a debater, however, he ranks among the very foremost of his time, or indeed of the whole time described in this History. Some of his happy phrases, some of his rapid retorts, have passed into habitual citation among all who take an interest in political debate. One remarkable fact in Harcourt's career is that he won his greatest and, it might be added, his least expected success when that career was drawing near to its close. He twice occupied the office of Chancellor of the Exchequer, and it was on the second occasion of his holding that position that he gained his most distinct reputation as a financial Minister. His 'death-duties' budget awakened the whole Empire, at first into astonishment and then into admiration and acceptance.

When he had reached this point of success Harcourt soon began to make up his mind that he would not live down his reputation, that he would quit the Parliamentary field in time, and would not give the most prejudiced critic the opportunity of suggesting that Harcourt might have done better for his renown if he had not striven to hold his place too long in the forefront of the political battle. To some of his friends who remonstrated with him on his determination to withdraw from his position of leadership Sir William Harcourt set forth his motives and his feelings in explanations which did honour to his unselfish, and indeed self-repressing and manly character. One of his latest conspicuous appearances in the House of Commons was on the occasion when he introduced his son, Mr. Lewis Harcourt, to the House, of which the young man had just been elected a member. Parliament and the whole public could thoroughly appreciate the feeling of paternal pride which must have filled the heart of the father when he thus made himself the leading figure in that ceremonial, and conducted his son into the arena in which he had himself performed so brilliant a part.

The name of Henry Fawcett cannot be omitted from our retrospect. Fawcett won for himself a distinct celebrity in Parliamentary life under conditions which might have paralysed the energies of almost any other man. When he was still a young man he lost his sight by a melancholy accident at a shooting party, an accident all the more melancholy because it was caused by the gun held by Fawcett's own father. The shots from the gun-barrel struck both of Fawcett's eyes and left the young man totally blind for life. He had had an early ambition to enter the House of Commons, and that ambition, which in most other men would have been utterly extinguished by the calamity that had come upon him, only became a new guide to him in his darkness. He himself, in his later years, explained to some of his friends the motives which urged him to endeavour still to carry his plans of life to realisation. Knowing well the grief which the accident had given to his father, the young man was determined at any strain and trouble to himself to make his father believe that the loss of sight had not been to him an irreparable calamity, had not extinguished all the honourable ambitions and all the active purposes of his life. Two years after the accident he became a candidate for a seat in the House of Commons and was not successful, and on two subsequent occasions he made a like effort with the like result. In 1865 he was elected for Brighton, and continued to represent that constituency until 1874, when he met with defeat, but was elected immediately for Hackney, which he represented until the close of his life.

Henry Fawcett was one of the most active workers in the stirring life of the House of Commons. It might have been reasonably assumed that a man afflicted with total blindness would have found it very hard to accommodate himself to the ways of the House. The mere difficulty caused by the frequent succession of divisions during many days and nights of each Session, in which only a very limited time is allowed for each division, would seem of itself to render it all but impossible for a blind man to fulfil the duties of a Parliamentary representative. Fawcett, however, had perseverance and courage which were equal to any emergency, and the whole House of Commons cheerfully lent him its assistance. Whenever the division bell rang and the members were about to hurry into the lobbies, Fawcett quietly arose from his seat, and any member near to him or passing him immediately took Fawcett's arm and became his escort. Thus was avoided the confusion which must have occurred if the blind representative had endeavoured to make his way unguided into the division lobby. Fawcett used to tell an anecdote of an early adventure of his in this way which occurred before it had become one of the unwritten laws of the House that any member who happened to be near at hand must at once become the escort of his darkened political comrade on the event of a division. Such a moment had come in Fawcett's earlier Parliamentary days. He had risen from his seat and was standing in some embarrassment. A hand was laid upon his arm and a friendly guide escorted him through the lobbies. When they were returning to their places in the House Fawcett asked his kindly guide to tell him whom he had to thank for the timely service. The guide answered, 'I am afraid, Mr. Fawcett, we shall not often be found in the same division lobbies—my name is Disraeli!'

Fawcett's career was that of a thoroughly independent Liberal member, for although he was a most sincere Liberal of the advanced order, he never pledged himself to the support of any particular measure because it came from a Liberal Administration, or to the opposition of any legislative scheme merely because it came from the Conservative party. He was always strongly in favour of measures for the abolition of religious tests at the Universities, the establishment of compulsory national education, and an enlightened system of rule in India. He was consistently and firmly opposed to that aggressive policy which has more lately been described as Jingoism, and his opposition to it was none the less strong when it happened for the time to be popular among the Liberals. He went in strongly for the removal of all law-made restrictions on the industry of women, and was a most ardent advocate of women's claims to the legislative suffrage. In 1867 he married Miss Millicent Garrett, a distinguished author of works on political economy, an ardent promoter of the higher education of women, and the establishment of equality for woman with man in the right to chose Parliamentary representatives. Fawcett became Postmaster-General in one of Mr. Gladstone's Administrations, and it is to him we owe the introduction of the parcels post, postal orders, and sixpenny telegrams.

Despite his severe physical affliction, Fawcett would seem to have lived on the whole a happy life. He had the tender and constant companionship of a loved and most sympathetic and gifted wife, and he was able to find enjoyment where an ordinary mortal might well have thought that a blind man could discover no delight. He loved travel, and he assured his friends that it was a genuine joy to him to move through new scenes and to have their characteristics and their beauties described to him by his life-companion as they pursued their way. In this spirit he maintained that it was always a source of happiness to him to have been born and to have lived to his early manhood with good sight. The common idea is that if a man has to pass the greater part of his life in physical darkness it would be better for him to have been born blind and thus to feel no sense of disappointment and unexpected privation. Fawcett always held that much of the pleasure which he derived from travel came from the fact that when some new scene through which he was passing was described to him he could realise from a recollection of other scenes on which he had looked in his earlier days a clear mental picture of the lake, the river, the mountains, and the sea, which he could never have formed if he had not looked on such scenes while his eyes could still fulfil their office. He was accustomed even to visit great exhibitions of paintings, and while each picture was described to him to realise in the same way a clear and vivid mental impression of its character and charm. He always seemed to be in good spirits, and his cheery laugh had an inspiring fascination about it. He was a delightful talker, and was ever ready to welcome new ideas and new impressions. Henry Fawcett closed his useful, noble, and on the whole happy life in November 1884. He died, as he had lived, in peace.

William Edward Forster made a very conspicuous figure among the statesmen of his time. For twenty-five years he held a seat in the House of Commons, and few men there were the subject of so much diversified and such rapidly changing criticism. Forster was born of Quaker parentage, and belonged to a family engaged in manufacture. He was actually called to the Bar, but he did not pursue a career in the courts, and continued to engage himself in the industrial occupations familiar to him from his earliest days. Like many men of Quaker birth and bringing up, he devoted himself to philanthropic enterprises, and during the Irish famine, which began in 1845, he visited Ireland for the purpose of distributing to the best advantage a relief fund raised by a Quaker organisation. This event may be said to have been the opening of Forster's public career, and it derives a special significance from the fact that by his energy, his zeal, and his judicious performance of the task entrusted to his care he won at the time the affection and the gratitude of the suffering Irish population. Forster was then universally recognised among Irishmen as a generous and devoted friend to the Irish people, and it would be impossihle to doubt that whatever change may have taken place later in Ireland's sentiments towards him, and however that change might seem to have been justified in Irish national feeling, Forster had all through his life a sincere wish to prove himself Ireland's friend.

In 1861 he won a seat in the House of Commons as Liberal representative for Bradford, and he rose almost at once to Parliamentary distinction and influence. His great characteristics were his earnestness, his sincerity, his strength of character, and his thorough mastery of all questions relating to public education. He was not in any sense an orator, and was not even a clever and effective debater; but he brought to every question with which he had to deal a clear and a commanding intelligence, a robust common sense, a sincere and fearless conviction, and he was a great master of administrative details. He was, in short, a man who could not be passed over in ministerial arrangements, and he held in succession several offices in Liberal Governments. In 1880 Forster was appointed by Mr. Gladstone Chief Secretary to the Lord Lieutenant of Ireland. That was the most momentous crisis of his career. Up to that time he had been regarded as the sincere and even the sentimental friend of Ireland, and the strong conviction among Irishmen in general was that when Forster undertook what was practically the government of Ireland, he did so with a resolve that Ireland should be governed according to Irish ideas. Ireland was at that time in a thoroughly disturbed condition. A new and strong National party had come up under the leadership of Charles Stewart Parnell, and Ireland at home was also much influenced by the sentiments, the movements, and the projects of Fenianism. The island was placed under a system of entirely exceptional laws, and the Irish authorities had at their command the power to declare any Irish movement, or even any Irish meeting, illegal, and send those who took a leading part in the movement or the meeting to a prison cell.

The Irish Nationalists and the Irish people generally were filled with the hope that when Forster came over to Ireland he would come there with the intention of establishing a free system of government. The result was disappointment on both sides. Those who remember that momentous period, and who took any part in the political struggle belonging to it, can probably find some explanation for the utter failure of Mr. Forster to reconcile the Irish people to the existing form of government. Forster saw clearly that much of Ireland's trouble was caused by the intolerable system of land tenure, and he began his Irish rule by bringing in measures for the removal of some of the worst evils belonging to that system. Forster probably believed that the Irish people would put full trust in him, and would wait for the gradual development of legislative improvements under his care, while the Irish people had hoped that Forster would begin his administrative career by relieving them from the hated tyranny of a system of exceptional legislation, unknown to any other part of the British Empire. The Chief Secretary was thus disappointed with the Irish people, and the Irish people were thus disappointed with the Chief Secretary. Some valuable improvements in the land tenure laws were indeed carried by Forster, but the exceptional legislation still prevailed, and under Forster's rule Parnell and several of his Parliamentary colleagues were arrested and thrown into prison.

Forster now seemed to stand out as a proclaimed enemy of Ireland's political equality, and therefore of the Irish people, while he probably believed in his heart that the Irish people had misunderstood him from the first and had given him no chance of carrying out his plans of gradual reform. His political career came to be a mere wreck on the Irish shores. His name was for a long time held in detestation even by Irish Nationalists who were in no sense rebels against the Imperial rule, and yet some at least of those Irish Nationalists who had known Forster personally always felt assured that he had begun his work with the best purposes for Ireland, and only lost his judgment and his temper when he found himself misunderstood. He died in April 1886.

Lord Randolph Churchill was, during the greater part of his public life, a man much misunderstood even by some of his sincere admirers. The general impression concerning him was that his light was but the flash and flicker of an eccentric political comet. But Lord Randolph had, as the basis of his character and career, a sincere and earnest desire to find and follow the right course in his political work, and a practical, earnest, far-seeing quality of statesmanship. He was the third son of the then Duke of Marlborough, was educated at Eton, and at Merton College, Oxford. He did not particularly distinguish himself as a student, and indeed, according to his own account, he gave himself very little trouble about his collegiate studies. Lord Randolph more than once assured some of his acquaintances in later years that when he left Oxford to begin in some way or other the business of active life he was in a condition of ignorance as nearly absolute as was possible for a young man who had passed somehow or other through the prescribed course of college instruction. He always declared that it was only after he had become a member of the House of Commons that he set himself to work to acquire any of the knowledge needed by his new position and his new responsibilities. There may perhaps have been some humorous exaggeration about these statements, for Lord Randolph was a thorough humorist, and enjoyed occasionally a freak of amusing overstatement; but he was certainly quite serious in conveying the impression that with his entrance into Parliamentary life began his first real study of history and politics.

In 1880 Lord Randolph made himself conspicuous for the first time in the House of Commons by forming the celebrated Fourth Party, of which he became the leader. The Fourth Party was thus known, because at that time there were only three recognised parties in the House —the Liberals, the Conservatives, and the Irish Nationalists. The Nationalists, under the guidance of Charles Stewart Parnell, were very few in number, because many of the Irish members in those days still adhered to the Liberal side; but the Fourth Party was numerically still smaller, and its leader had only three proclaimed adherents—Mr. Arthur Balfour (now Prime Minister), Sir Henry Drummond Wolff, and Sir John Gorst. As these three men were all men of high ability and political position, it may be readily assumed that they must have recognised thus early the great capacity and the serious purpose of Lord Randolph or they would never have devoted themselves to his leadership. The policy of the Fourth Party was that of absolute independence so far as other political parties were concerned, and its members voted with Conservatives or Liberals, as the case might be, in accordance with the judgment they formed among themselves on the merits of each particular measure or question brought up for decision. The Fourth Party occupied seats on the Opposition side of the House and in the close neighbourhood of Parnell and his followers, with whom they often entered into agreement as to the action to be taken on some question under debate. What with the independent Fourth Party and the independent Irish Party, and the fact that each party included brilliant, ready, and audacious debaters, it will easily be understood that the House of Commons had very lively times of it just then. The House was beginning to discover already that Lord Randolph Churchill was not merely the reckless and theatric leader of some eccentric followers, but had in him, as these had also, the qualities of real statesmanship. Many of the younger Conservatives began to look to Lord Randolph Churchill as the coming leader of a new Tory party destined to commend itself to the intelligence and the admiration of all enlightened and progressive Tories who did not regard the mission of Toryism as merely to keep alive every time-dishonoured abuse in England's legislative system.

In 1885 Lord Randolph's genuine capacity was recognised by Lord Salisbury, who made him Secretary for India in the first Salisbury Administration. In Lord Salisbury's second Government Lord Randolph Churchill became Chancellor of the Exchequer and Leader of the House of Commons. During his tenure of office he proved himself at last a statesman of a high order; but as there were questions of administration on which he could not reconcile his own views with those

of some of his colleagues, he insisted on resigning
office. This was at first taken by many as only
one other of his characteristic freaks, but those
who had followed Lord Randolph's career closely
and who appreciated his character saw that he
had long been endeavouring to create a new and
progressive Tory party, and that finding his efforts
foiled, for the time, by the majority of his official
colleagues he had deliberately made up his mind
to resign his office and to trust to the future.
The future proved disappointing to him by no
fault of his own. He was still only in the
prime of manhood, but his health had long been
giving way, and it was evident to all who saw
much of him that he had only a short course
before him. He was suffering from a malady
which brought with it frequent torturing pains,
and he was compelled to have recourse to the
use of narcotics in order to give him any chance
of carrying on the Parliamentary work to which
he was still as ever absolutely devoted. His
brilliant, and, to the outer world, often bewildering
career was closed by death in January 1895.

A new epoch was opened in the history
of Ireland by Charles Stewart Parnell. In a
political retrospect of Queen Victoria's reign no
figure stands out with greater distinctness than
that of Parnell. It was he who first created for
the Irish National party that policy of organised
obstruction the object of which was to compel the
House of Commons to give its full attention to

the demands of the Irish people. There had been previous to Parnell's time two forms of resistance to the English rule of Ireland, one by open and avowed rebellion under such men as Theobald Wolf Tone, Lord Edward Fitzgerald, and Robert Emmet, and one by strictly constitutional agitation and debate in the House of Commons under such political leaders as Daniel O'Connell and Isaac Butt. Both these systems of resistance had proved ineffectual. When Parnell was elected to the House of Commons as representative of an Irish constituency, being still a very young man, he devised and put into action the policy of which the essential principle was to make lawful use of all the rules and the forms of the House, in order to prevent the House from accomplishing any other business until it had given a full hearing to the demands and the arguments of the Irish Nationalist members. Parnell had but a very small following, even among the Irish Nationalists, when he began to put this policy into action, for he came into the House at a time when the whole Irish National party was still under the leadership of Mr. Isaac Butt, one of the most brilliant advocates at the Irish Bar, and a powerful Parliamentary debater, whose policy it was to fight the battles of his country with strict attention to the rules of that Parliament for which, as a constitutional statesman, he had a great regard and reverence. But Parnell's policy grew and grew among the Irish members, and he had a positive genius for the kind of work he had set himself to accomplish. He was a speaker who made no attempt at eloquence, except, indeed, that order of eloquence which consists in setting forth argument in the clearest possible language and in the fewest possible words. Mr. Gladstone said of him afterwards that no other Parliamentary debater he had ever known, not even excepting Palmerston, had so completely the art of saying every word he wanted to say and not a word more. Gladstone paid to Parnell, after his death, the high and the well-deserved tribute of describing him as a great statesman. Parnell became before long the leader of the whole Irish National party, some eighty-six in number; and there cannot be any doubt that by his system of compelling the House to give its full attention to Irish questions, questions as well of land tenure reform as of Home Rule, he came to exercise an entirely new influence over the House of Commons. To his policy, his perseverance, and his tact was due that immediate change in the Liberal opinion of Great Britain which Mr. Gladstone represented when he accepted for the first time the principle of Home Rule.

Parnell's national policy became so popular in Ireland that throughout by far the greater number of the Irish constituencies no candidate for Parliamentary election who was not recommended by him had the slightest chance of carrying a seat. More than that, the agitation promoted and led by Parnell began to command some influence even among the Ulster constituencies, the constituencies which had long been regarded as the secure territory of the Orange party. Two of Parnell's colleagues were at different elections chosen as Members for the city of Derry, supposed to be the very type of unyielding Orangeism, and the constituency of West Belfast was also represented by a colleague of his. The power which Parnell obtained over the Irish people was all the more remarkable because of the fact that he was not in any sense cast in that mould which would have seemed naturally suited for an Irish leader. He was not a great orator like O'Connell, or even like Butt; there was nothing of enthusiasm about his manner as a speaker, and there was even nothing of passion in his eloquence, except the very intensity of the force with which he kept down all passion, and he had little or nothing of that imaginative gift which is usually supposed to appeal to an Irish audience. Moreover, there was nothing of the Irishman in him, so far as family and descent were concerned. He came of an old English family which had been settled for generations in Ireland, the family to which Parnell the poet and Sir John Parnell, Chancellor of the Exchequer under the Irish Parliament, belonged. His mother was the daughter of an American admiral, and Parnell himself received his education at Cambridge University. There was not, in fact, one drop of Irish blood in the veins of Charles Stewart Parnell, who so soon made himself the hero and the idol of the Irish people. He had, of course, a host of enemies in England, many of whom no doubt seriously believed him to be a revolutionist and an anarchist, and even a patron of political assassination. It is not too much to say that a very considerable proportion of the British population became quite crazy on the subject of Parnell and his plots and his doings. All this feeling had its immediate result in the too general credence given, among a large body of the English public, to the extraordinary Pigott forgeries which were rashly and unhappily accepted by the *Times* as genuine letters written by Mr. Parnell himself. Then came the famous Special Commission, the absolute breakdown of the case for the forgeries, the flight and subsequent suicide of Pigott, and the acquittal of Mr. Parnell and his arraigned colleagues from all the serious charges made against them. The whole story has been told in a former volume of this History.

The personal events which darkened the close of Parnell's career, brought dissension among his followers, and deprived him of the leadership of the great majority of the party, belong rather to personal biography than to political survey. They do not call for exposition in this retrospect, and are only mentioned here because of the disastrous effect wrought by them on a great life, which had only just before their occurrence reached its splendid zenith. There can be no question that these events hastened the death of Parnell, who, when he died suddenly in October 1891, had only entered on his forty-sixth year. Seldom has a life so successful in its public work been so sadly interrupted. It is but right to say that Parnell had honourably done everything in his power to repair the moral fault of which he had been guilty, and that the dissension created among the Irish National party might easily have been averted if Parnell had not been too impatient in that most trying time to listen to the advice of some of his best friends within the Irish party and outside it. The party which he had created became reunited after his death, and the best of his work still lives and grows.

Something ought to be said in this chapter about the many distinguished advocates who, like Sir Alexander Cockburn, Lord Coleridge, Charles Russell (afterwards Lord Russell of Killowen), distinguished themselves alike in Parliament and at the Bar during the reign of Victoria. This chapter, however, is concerned mainly with political work alone, and the lives of those who devoted themselves in especial to a Parliamentary career. In preceding volumes will be found full account of the eminent men whose Parliamentary life was but a supplement to a distinguished career at the Bar. The author thinks it well to explain to his readers that he had a distinct motive for dealing, as he has done in this retrospect, with the personal characteristics of the eminent political men whom he has endeavoured to describe. The reading world, when it is told of great statesmen,

Parliamentary orators, and Parliamentary debaters, is naturally anxious to know how each of these men spoke, what was his manner, what was his voice, and what was his style of eloquence. Any coming generation can study the lives and the speeches of such men, but it is always of much importance to know, from the observation and judgment of those who had the advantage of listening often to their speeches, something about the personal as well as the intellectual qualifications of these men for the position which they occupied and the fame which they won. When we study the works of the poet, the novelist, the historian, the painter, the scientific author, we have before us, on paper or on canvas, the whole bequest of each man to posterity, and each man can be fully judged by the bequest which he has left to the world. But when we desire to know all that can be learned about the great Parliamentary figures of the past, we want not merely to know what the orator said, but also how he spoke what he had to say. The writer of these volumes has also, it will be observed, made this retrospective chapter strictly a retrospect as regards the men he describes, and in it has dealt solely with careers which have actually closed. There are many public men still living who were contemporaries of those described in this retrospect, but who may yet have before them a long and brilliant career, and are not therefore to be disposed of in a chapter dealing only with the past.

There are men in the present House of Commons who are yet only in their prime, men like Mr. John Morley, Mr. James Bryce, Mr. Herbert Gladstone, Sir Robert Reid, Mr. Asquith, on the Liberal side; and Mr. Balfour, Sir Michael Hicks-Beach, and Sir John Gorst on the other side; and there are rising men like Sir Edward Grey, Mr. Lloyd-George, Lord Hugh Cecil, and Mr. Winston Churchill, who are only at the opening of what promises to be a brilliant future. Then, again, there are many men whose Parliamentary career has been interrupted for one reason or another, most often because they could not submit their conscientious convictions to some sudden change of opinion among their constituents, men who may be confidently expected to obtain seats once again in the House of Commons, and to have a successful career before them. There are men like Mr. Leonard Courtney, Mr. George W. E. Russell, Mr. Augustine Birrell, and Mr. Herbert Paul who, it may well be hoped, will not be content, and will not even be allowed, to remain long out of the House of Commons.

Among the Irish members who now make so important an element in the constitution of Parliament there are such men as Mr. John Redmond, Mr. John Dillon, Mr. T. P. O'Connor, Mr. Edward Blake, and others for whom Parliamentary life cannot yet be regarded as all retrospect. The House of Commons would gladly welcome back to its benches Mr. Thomas Sexton, for many years the most eloquent among the followers of Parnell, who has by his own choice remained for some years out of Parliament. The author has not included such men as these in his political retrospect, for the exceedingly substantial reason that he is not in a position to survey their careers as a whole, and to sum up their Parliamentary reputation. That task he has to leave to some historian of the coming time.

We have already shown that the war-correspondent of the newspaper press—the professional war-correspondent—is one of the figures which belong especially to the newspaper world of the Victorian era. A still more recent appearance in the newspaper world of England is that of the professional journalist who is also an active, open, and avowed political champion, and a member of the House of Commons. In France, in the United States, and in other countries it had long been habitual for editors of newspapers to take an active part in the movements of political life, and to become conspicuous and energetic members of legislative chambers. In England, until the later years of Queen Victoria's reign, it was always the habit of professional journalists to adopt the anonymous system, and to pronounce their criticisms and their judgments from behind a sort of imaginary curtain. But towards the later years of Queen Victoria's reign some able and distinguished men began to adopt a different course, and to present themselves on public platforms as the avowed authors of the opinions which they were expressing in their journals, and, as such, to seek for election to the House of Commons. This habit grew more and more into fashion as the reign went on, and of late we have had some members of the House of Commons who proclaimed themselves as having for their especial work in life the business of newspaper editorship. As newspaper editors they have come upon the political platform; as newspaper editors they have been invited to contest, and have successfully contested, Parliamentary constituencies; and as newspaper editors they have been enabled to take their seats in the House of Commons. Many of these men have made a distinct reputation as debaters in the House, and have acquired great influence there, and of these some may be mentioned here as illustrating this new departure of English journalism during recent days.

Mr. Henry Labouchere has made a remarkable reputation in the House. He does not present himself as an orator, but he is a most telling and effective debater, gifted with much faculty for humorous and satirical commentary, with lucidity of exposition, conciseness of speech, and the happy art of phrase-making. He never speaks but when he has something to say, and the House always fills when he is speaking, or when it is known that he is about to speak. He is the proclaimed editor of the weekly journal *Truth*, which is not especially a political journal, but rather bears the character of what is now known as a 'society' newspaper.

Another conspicuous figure in this new order of journalism is that of Mr. T. P. O'Connor, who is the editor of two weekly papers, one of which bears his initials as part of its title, while the front page of each of them announces him as its editor. Mr. O'Connor is an advanced Radical, so far as English politics are concerned, and he is above all things else an Irish Nationalist, and a leading member of the Irish Home Rule party in the House of Commons. He is a man of great and varied ability and culture, and he is regarded by the House in general as one of the most eloquent and attractive of its speakers. He has indeed many of the orator's best gifts, among them being a ready and happy power of humorous expression and a thrilling voice. Until he obtained a seat in the House of Commons Mr. O'Connor's working life-time had been wholly given up to journalism.

Another distinguished journalist who had made for himself by his newspaper leading articles a repute which helped to win for him a seat in the House of Commons is Mr. Herbert Paul, whose volume of essays, 'Men and Letters,' has made a distinct mark in recent literature. Mr. Paul proved himself a brilliant debater in the House of Commons. It has been already mentioned in these volumes that he lost his seat because he would not sacrifice his own convictions at a time when a storm of Imperialism was sweeping over the constituencies.

A distinguished provincial editor, Sir Edward R. Russell, is another of the men who, previously known to the world only as a journalist, obtained during those late years a seat in Parliament. Sir Edward Russell has been for many years editor of the *Liverpool Daily Post*, one of the most influential newspapers in the English provinces. He had previously been one of the leader-writers for the same paper and its assistant editor, and was also for a time a writer of leading articles for the London *Morning Star*. Thus it will be seen that Edward Russell was only known to the public in general as a journalist, and it was the reputation he had thus attained which secured him his election for the representation of one of the divisions of Glasgow. Sir Edward Russell has lately been for some years out of the House of Commons, but the distinct mark which he made while he had a seat there gives good earnest that he could easily find a place there again should he feel inclined to seek for it. Other journalists have also been members of the House of Commons during recent years, but the four instances given in these pages illustrate clearly enough the fact that during the later years of Queen Victoria's reign the journalist has come out into public life from behind the old-time curtain of anonymity, and has made his way into the representative chamber of Parliament. That fact has in itself a very distinct historical interest, and makes an appropriate and important part of the narrative contained in these volumes.

We cannot conclude this chapter of political retrospect without saying something about the formation of the Primrose League. This association was organised in 1884 in memory of Lord Beaconsfield, whose favourite flower was understood by the founders of the league to be the primrose, although it must be added that there were some dissatisfied critics at the time who denied that Lord Beaconsfield had any such especial affection. Even if that objection to the name were to be maintained by convincing evidence, the Primrose League would not be the only association founded with something of a doubtful mythical meaning as to the origin of its title. Lord Salisbury became Grand Master of the league, and the anniversary of Beaconsfield's death, April 19, 1881, received the name of 'Primrose Day.' On that day the admirers of the lost leader were accustomed to wear the primrose in honour of his memory, and his statue in Parliament Square was adorned with the votive flowers. The league was said to have begun with less than 100,000 members, but was afterwards increased by rapid additions until it came to include more than a million and a half of 'knights, dames, and associates,' and it had its 'habitations' or offices established all over Great Britain and even in some parts of Ireland. The league held vast annual meetings in Covent Garden Theatre, in the Albert Hall, and in other great buildings, at one of which Mr. Arthur Balfour presided as chairman. The league is incessantly issuing political manifestoes and pamphlets, and the dames of the association are at least as active in the work as the knights and the male associates. About the political efficacy and the unceasing activity of the league there cannot be any possible doubt.

A National Liberal League was soon formed on the other side of the political arena by those who maintained the principles of reform and advanced Liberalism, and this organisation came also to exercise a powerful influence over the constituencies and the general public of Great Britain. Many subordinate and local associations were called into being with a like purpose, and it cannot be questioned that the founders of the Primrose League were, without any such desire on their own part, the means of inciting their political opponents into a renewed and ever-growing activity. The spread of education among the poorer classes everywhere helped in great measure to promote the growth of such institutions, and every student of history must admit that when and where opposing political principles come into active work they are best served for the common interests of the empire by open, proclaimed, and responsible political associations under responsible leaders.

CHAPTER XXIV.

A RETROSPECT—THE ARTS OF PEACE.

THE reign of Queen Victoria will, it may safely be asserted, derive its especial importance from the progress which it saw and helped to bring about in the development of the arts of peace. The changes that were accomplished by these arts during that time may be said, without exaggeration, to have entirely revolutionised the ordinary and daily conditions of life in the civilised world. The whole system of travel by steamboat and by railway came into existence but a very short time before the reign of Queen Victoria began, and only within that reign established itself as one of the conditions of existence in the civilised world. The practical application of the electric current to the business of transmitting messages to almost limitless distances above the land and beneath the sea belongs entirely to the reign of Queen Victoria. This development of applied science went on improving until the close of the Victorian era could already count on the application of the Marconi telegram to the work of transmitting messages without the aid of the metallic wire. The electric current has come to be applied not merely to the sending of messages, but to the impelling of cars and railway carriages, and has in many instances already superseded steam in the business of railway lines. So far as travel and the transmission of messages are concerned, the populations who lived in any part of the civilised world during Victoria's reign had been leading a life totally different from that which belonged to their ancestors. From the beginning of recorded time down to the end of the first quarter or so of the nineteenth century the means of travel and the means of forwarding messages were very much the same. All that sailing ships and horses and the physical strength of human beings could do for travel and for the carrying of messages was done. Then there opened that entirely new era of civilisation when steam and electricity were made to do the work with a speed which would have seemed incredible to a contemporary of Dr. Johnson, as well as to a contemporary of Socrates.

The postal system has shown a marvellous development during the Victorian reign, and has brought all parts of the world into a frequency of communication which did not exist in former days between one end of an English county and the other. The organised and regular delivery of letters all over the country by the rapidest means and at the cheapest possible rate began with the period covered by this History. In all that part of the daily business of life an entirely new era was opened up for the public during the late Queen's reign. In previous years, down to the close of the life of William IV., the delivery of letters by mail applied only to a very limited region, was never accomplished with certainty and regularity, and was a very expensive process. The personal records of those past times are full of amusing illustrations of the cost and difficulty which attended the despatch of letters from one part of the country to another. When persons endowed with means and position who happened to live in some out-of-the-way part of the island found it necessary to send a communication to a distant town or village, or to the occupant of an isolated country mansion, the sending of these letters became an enterprise involving the employment of trusty messengers, for whom relays of good horses had been carefully prepared in advance, and who could not be allowed to travel alone and unarmed over wide extents of country where the highwayman might still be expected to interfere with the journey. Many improvements in the postal service owe their origin altogether to the Victorian era. The franking system, according to which all manner of influential personages were authorised to send their letters through the post free of cost by merely inscribing their sacred names on the outside of each letter, was practically abolished during the earlier years of the reign.

The wealthiest and most aristocratic quarters of London itself were, even down to the end of William IV.'s reign, left dependent upon a postal system which would not be endured for a day in the poorest country village of our own time.

In England the abolition of the tax on newspapers, the stamp duty which had to be paid before a journal could be issued, opened the way for the creation of a cheap press which brings the news of the world each day at the lowest possible price into every city, town, and village. The spread of popular education has been one of the triumphs of our modern times. England, it must be said, was not among the first of European nations to take her part in this important work of reform, but during the reign of Queen Victoria England did at last prove herself equal to the task which her responsibility as a great State had imposed upon her. For a long time it might have been supposed that education in England was regarded by the constituted authorities as a luxury to be reserved altogether for the children of the rich. There were great colleges, there were great schools, colleges and schools which were public institutions, and there were private schools in every county where parents who could afford to pay good prices might secure education for their children. But the education of the poorer classes was left altogether, or almost altogether, to the care of charitable associations or of generous private benefactors.

England was much behind Scotland, Ireland, and Wales in the provision made for the education of the poor. If the parents of a child in England could not find the means to pay for his education, they could only look to charitable organisations, or to some private benefactor, in order to obtain an opportunity of having the child taught, and such a difficulty as this prevented in a large proportion of cases the parents, themselves uneducated, from making any effort to secure some teaching for their children. In our recent days we have seen a complete change accomplished in the work of national instruction. Not only is education brought within the reach of the poorest classes in England, but the responsibility is imposed upon the parents of having their children put in the way of obtaining at least an elementary education. The progress of improvement in this direction is going steadily on, and it may be hoped that before very long there will be absolutely no illiterate class in the whole of England. There are many countries in Europe in which no order of the people remained illiterate at a time when the description might be justly applied to a large mass of England's working and poorer classes. The founding of free libraries in all the English towns, and even in many of England's country villages, has had much to do with the spread of education, and the constant production of cheaply printed books brings many of the standard works of English literature within the reach of almost all readers, however humble, who have any real desire for the ownership of appreciated volumes.

All over these islands literary and scientific institutions of every kind have been and are being established even in very small provincial towns and country villages, and the residents have frequent opportunities of hearing distinguished literary and scientific men address audiences on subjects of educational interest. It became a custom, during the Victorian age, that the most celebrated writers and thinkers should address popular audiences, not only in London, but in all the cities and the larger towns of these islands. Charles Dickens delivered his readings, and Thackeray gave his lectures, in crowded halls; Richard Owen expounded some of the greatest discoveries of modern science in various provincial towns, as well as in the Metropolis; Thomas Huxley rendered a like valuable service to the community, and numbers of other eminent authors and thinkers followed the same wholesome example. Work of this kind was a decided novelty in our social system, and has indeed been to a great extent suggested and prompted by the common practice of distinguished leaders of public opinion in the United States. All these innovations on the old-time habits, which kept writers and thinkers of real distinction who were not political leaders from ever appearing on a public platform to address a popular audience, could not but have a most beneficent influence in the spreading of popular education, and in the training of the community generally to the appreciation of literature, art, and science.

The highwayman, that familiar figure in the romance and in the real life of our grandfathers, has of late years disappeared altogether from our real life, and is even fading out of the romance of modern days. Of course the romancist made the most he could out of the troubles caused by the highwayman, but it cannot be questioned that to the travellers through English shires in those days the intrusions of the highwayman constituted a serious danger which had ever to be taken into consideration. Then in all those parts of the country where some effort was made to keep the roads in good order, especially after the improvements accomplished by M'Adam, the inventor of the macadamising system of road-making, the traveller was frequently interrupted in his progress by the bars of the turnpike, and was compelled to pay his fee before being allowed to continue his journey. Many amusing accounts—all the more amusing because they were written in no spirit of mirth, but only in the mood of angry complaining—are given in published letters of the period, describing the incessant interruptions caused to a traveller by the frequent encounter of those bars to his progress, and by the tax which he had to pay as the condition of his being allowed to complete his journey.

It has been seriously argued by devotees of the

past in all its ways that the slowness of travel in the days when journeys were accomplished by horse-drawn carriages enabled the traveller to study the country through which he was passing and the beauty of the landscape which came under his eyes more fully than he could possibly do now in our period of rapid locomotion by the agency of the steam-engine. But even if we were generously to admit that the travellers who toiled along the country highways in the old fashion were always able to keep their eyes and minds open to the beauty of landscape during hours of slow movement, it may at least be fairly contended that the advantage of getting quickly and easily to some particular place might more than counterbalance the benefit of being allowed time to study the charms of every stretch of road before turning round the nearest corner. The tourist, for instance, who is bent on enjoying the beauties of the English Lake Country may be admitted to have some advantage in being able to get in the shortest possible time to his destination, and to solace himself with the scenery of Windermere and Grasmere, instead of contemplating for day after day the dull sameness of the country roads and the country villages that lie between him and the scenes he longs to look upon. Dr. Syntax himself, in his 'Search of the Picturesque,' must have found his spirits and his enthusiasm often fail him as he jogged along the monotonous country roads, the monotony of his travel only varied every now and then by the interposition of the toll-bar and the paying of the tax.

The modern system of lighting cities and towns is also one of the improvements which belong to the late reign. Even the best streets of London were up to that time left at night in a condition which we should now regard as serving only to make darkness visible. Most of the great sanitary arrangements of British cities and towns which have wrought so beneficent an influence on the average health of each community belong to the same period. The water supply of our cities and towns is one of those salutary modern arrangements. In the poorest quarters there is always now to be found an ample and continuous supply of water, and whenever the supply runs short in any place the fact is certain to become a subject of public complaint, and to be brought at once under the notice of the authorities.

The local government system now exercises its power in each municipality and in each country district. We have everywhere local municipalities, town councils, or parochial boards, in which the inhabitants of the region are duly represented, and if the members of any particular council or board fail to fulfil their duty, the ratepayers of the district can set things to rights by electing representatives better qualified and more anxious to supply the wants and carry out the wishes of the community. The principle of representation now established in every part of these islands is doing most efficient work, and supplies of itself the means of further improvement as time goes on, and the demands and opportunities increase. The police system, as we know it now, may be said to belong altogether to the Victorian era, and the employment of the old-fashioned force of night-watchmen is almost forgotten, or when remembered, is remembered chiefly as one of the comical absurdities of a past age.

Even in the early years of the late reign many of the great English cities, and especially London, were still allowed to remain in a condition which would be regarded as scandalous and intolerable during more recent days. There were certain quarters in London which were given up to the use and the practices of the most disreputable class of inhabitants. As one illustration of the condition of things which some half a century ago, and even later, was allowed to exist in the metropolis, it may be mentioned that in the immediate neighbourhood of the Strand, and quite near to some of its great churches, there were at least two streets which then appeared to be surrendered, without interference of authoritative kind, to indecent and infamous traffic. Many readers still living may remember Holywell Street and Wych Street. Most of the shops in these narrow streets were given up solely to the exhibition and the sale of indecent books and pictures, and the indecent pictures were publicly and purposely displayed in the windows of each shop which occupied itself with their sale.

Many others of these small houses were occupied by the lowest class of professional prostitutes. Young women stood at the doors in the open day wearing nothing but chemises and slippers, and inviting with words the attention of passing pedestrians. The road running south from Waterloo Bridge was allowed at that time to be given up to much the same sort of display, and there were many other quarters in which similar practices were allowed without any interruption on the part of the authorities. But as the reign went on, and as the active influence of municipal government and the new police began to make itself more and more felt, even the worst quarters of London were no longer permitted to offend civilisation and public decency in such a manner. In the more fashionable quarters of the Metropolis, where along the great thoroughfares during the night at least, if not in the day, prostitution was allowed to parade itself freely, the influence of the better governing system has for many years been endeavouring to carry out effectively its good work.

The abominations of a past age are only brought into public notice here with the object of showing how rapid and great has been the improvement established in the condition of the Metropolis during more recent times. It might be possible to offer ingenious and not merely plausible argument to prove that the actual morality of men and women in these our present days does not show any real improvement, even though the outward manners of the community may be more decorous, and that the same kind of immorality may go on privately among human beings of all classes in the present day as that which used to be proclaimed and flaunted in the great cities of former days. But it would be difficult indeed for the writer of history to explore the consciences of the communities around him, and to find out with certainty whether the men and women are in their hearts any better than they ought to be, or any better than their ancestors and ancestresses showed themselves to be, and we certainly do not feel inclined to enter on any such inquiry. The fact to which we desire to call attention is, that in the decencies of life, as well as in its comforts, its popular education, and its means for the transmission of news, the late reign very early in its progress showed a marked and almost a sudden change for the better when compared with any or all of its predecessors.

It cannot be denied, also, that there has been a gradual and steady improvement from the opening of Queen Victoria's reign in the national habits with regard to the use of intoxicating liquors. Great organised movements for the promotion of total abstinence from alcoholic drinks may be said to have had their beginning during Victoria's reign. There have been at all times earnest and missionary-like movements made by devoted men and women to spread the cause of temperance, wherever drunkenness prevailed; but associations like that called into activity and conducted by such apostles of temperance as Father Mathew and others, by some great leaders of the same cause in the United States and the British colonies, and by the Salvation Army in later times, are especially characteristic of the period over which we are now casting our retrospect. Any one who has studied the social history of former days cannot fail to observe that, of recent years, there has been a most remarkable decrease in the habit of over-drinking among the upper and middle classes in these islands. During the days of the Georges it was the common habit among men of high education and high position to indulge themselves overmuch in wine almost every night of their lives. We have it on the most unquestionable evidence that some of the greatest British statesmen during those reigns were thus in the habit of indulging themselves, and such indulgence on their parts appears to have been taken as a matter of course.

From the beginning of Queen Victoria's reign a change seems to have come about in the habits of our statesmen and of all our educated men. The biographers of that reign, even during its earlier periods, do not supply us with any of the reminiscences or the illustrative anecdotes which are to be found everywhere among the writers who describe the years that went before. During the late reign we find no descriptions of eminent statesmen coming to the House of Commons in a condition which made their speeches unintelligible to their fellow members, and if any such astonishing event did occur there would either have been some combined effort to conceal it or it would have been regarded as an outrageous scandal. Of late the whole idea has passed out of the public mind, and we no more expect to hear an intoxicated Prime Minister or Leader of Opposition attempting to address the House than we expect to hear of an inebriate Archbishop endeavouring to deliver a sermon from the pulpit of a Cathedral. Among all classes of educated persons the same steady improvement has been going on. We no longer associate literature with drink as it was very common and not unreasonable to do at a time when poets chanted the praises of the wine-cup and when Byron humorously wrote 'Man being reasonable must get drunk,' and the humours of the *Noctes Ambrosianæ* would seem completely out of place in our days when they described as natural and familiar occurrences the extravagances of brilliant literary men assembled together for an evening of jollity and hard drinking. Even among those who belong to that order of literary and artistic society which we still describe as Bohemian there has been for many years a steady ascent into habits of moderation, and the festive drinking of wine is no longer understood to mean anything like a festivity which takes the form of a drunken orgy.

Among the poorer and uneducated classes also there has been a decrease in the habits of intemperance. There are temperance associations spreading themselves throughout the lowest quarters of our cities and among all our country villages, and the whole force of public opinion asserts its influence for the repression of drunkenness. We have had of late some striking and official evidences of the improvement going on, through the authenticated returns as to the annual amounts which the revenue collects from the duties on spirits and other intoxicating liquids. These returns make it plain that while the population in most parts of these islands is steadily increasing the consumption of intoxicating liquids is on the decrease. There has been for many years an expanding and a deepening interest felt by the general public in the condition of the homes, the dwellings, and the wants of the poor, in city slums and in country villages, and the growth of that interest has its beneficent effect alike on those who exert it and on those for whom it is exerted. It blesseth those that give and those that take.

The general character of public amusements in theatres and music-halls has shown a decided improvement, so far as the British Islands are concerned, during the reign of Queen Victoria. Much has been written of recent days, and is still written, about the degeneracy of popular taste and manners which makes itself evident in the music-halls. Now, we are far from any desire to contend that the music-halls of the present time in these countries provide a highly intellectual entertainment for their visitors; that they always endeavour to cater for refined and delicate taste, or even that they do not sometimes attract crowded houses by the singing of songs and the exhibition of dances, and other attractions which are well calculated to shock the ears and eyes of really refined observers. But those who can remember some of the popular entertainments which were common in London for quarter of a century, and even longer, after Queen Victoria had come to the throne will readily admit that there were public amusements very popular then and tolerated, if not exactly sanctioned, by the existing authorities, which, if they were practised in our days, would cause the stones of London to rise and mutiny. There were exhibitions then going on every night in houses publicly licensed for popular entertainment which would not now be endured by the authorities of our great cities for a single night, which indeed we may fairly believe would not now attract visitors enough to make such exhibitions a paying speculation.

One fact beyond dispute is that the influence of Queen Victoria was always directed to the improvement and the refinement of public taste in all manner of theatrical exhibitions. Queen Victoria was no rigid purist in the narrow sense of the word, and she never gave herself up to the idea that the character of public amusements was always to be fashioned according to the rules of a narrow-minded Puritanism. There were occasions even when certain plays and operas, although inspired by a thoroughly moral tone and pointing a healthful lesson, were objected to by some critics on the ground that they brought under the notice of the public facts in human life about which it would be better that respectable folks should know nothing, or at least should not be encouraged to admit that they knew anything. There were instances in which the Queen gave her personal countenance to such representations for the good reason that they carried with them pure and wholesome teaching, and that the evils which they showed up and condemned must have been known to exist by every person above the age of childhood who read a book or a newspaper or had occasion to pass at night through the streets of a city. In these instances the judgment of the Queen seems to us to have been perfectly right and justified by the very laws of morality itself. The critics who argued on the other side of the question might just as fairly have contended that the preacher who shows up the evil of drunkenness is only teaching sober and innocent persons how to get drunk, or that the moralist who writes against the growth of prostitution is only teaching innocent young women the way to sell themselves for money.

The influence of the Queen over the whole tone of public, and especially of theatrical, amusement was always wholesome and purifying, and was all the more actively beneficent in its operation because the Queen was known to be a patroness of every institution and of every effort that could make for the cause of education and of charity. From the opening to the close of her reign she had lent unceasing and at the same time most discerning encouragement to every such purpose, and when therefore she gave her support to any dramatic or operatic performance her people could entertain no doubt that such a performance was not merely artistic but also healthful and instructive.

Much has been written about the increasing influence of wealth and the ever-spreading homage offered to wealth during the later years of our history, and it cannot be denied that mere riches, no matter how these may have been acquired, are now more than ever a power in English society. But it cannot be said that Queen Victoria ever gave any encouragement to this worship of newly acquired millions, and her own personal inclinations seem to have led her to keep as far as possible within the old lines of the social constitution and to present but a chilling front to the advances made by the millionaire of yesterday. So far as the character of public amusements is concerned the retrospect of Queen Victoria's reign must on the whole be regarded as highly satisfactory by every student of its history. The position of the dramatic author and of the actor has greatly improved, and we have entirely got rid of that kind of feeling which would still regard even a successful actor or actress as a sort of curiosity to be admired and wondered at and patronised, but not as a personage whom respectable society could welcome to its intimacy. Much of this change is, of course, owing to the actors and the actresses themselves and to their higher standard of life and conduct, but much is also due to the spread of the true artistic spirit and to the growth of education among all classes of the community. Industrial art of every kind owes much to the encouragement given by Queen Victoria. The great international exhibitions may be said, with literal truth, to have come into existence during her reign and under the direct influence of her husband and herself.

The late reign has been a period of great political reforms. The passing of the first Act of reform, that which was accomplished in 1832 by Earl Grey and Lord John Russell, opened the way, indeed, for all the emancipating legislation which belongs to Queen Victoria's reign; but the later period saw some measures of wide-spreading reform which were hardly contemplated even by the most advanced thinkers at the time, when a large proportion of the community regarded Earl Grey and Lord John Russell as men who were unconsciously inviting the approach of anarchy. At the beginning of the late reign the Parliamentary representation of these countries was limited by such narrowing and perplexing class restrictions that it had no claim to be regarded as real representation in any sense of the word. The existing restrictions applied not merely to the men who were to give a vote, but also to the men for whom the vote was to be given. There was a property qualification which narrowly limited the numbers of those who could be chosen as the representatives of Parliamentary constituencies. The property qualification laid it down that no man could be elected to a seat in the House of Commons who did not possess a certain extent of landed property, valued at an amount which limited the choice of electors to candidates belonging to the wealthy classes. If the candidate could not show that he possessed that property qualification, there was an end to his candidature.

Nothing was more common in those days than for a young man of family, not himself possessed of this essential requisite, to induce some relative or friend to make over to him nominally by deed of settlement the amount of property needed to enable him to appear as a candidate at an election. This performance was gone through again and again in constituencies where it was well known that a particular candidate would be sure of election by a large majority if only he could prove that he owned a quantity of land valued at the necessary amount, and where if he did not possess that practical qualification for statesmanship the law declared that he must not have a seat in what was even then described as the representative chamber. The spread of education and the development of Parliamentary reform abolished in course of time this property qualification, and the registered voters were free to elect as their representative the man of their choice, without taking any account as to the value of his landed property, or stopping to consider whether he had or had not any landed property whatever.

But there still remained the legal restrictions which limited the numbers of the voters. In order that a man might be qualified to give a vote at a Parliamentary election he was bound to occupy, whether in town or country, a house paying not less than a certain annual rental, a rental which absolutely disqualified the great mass of those belonging to the poorer classes—the whole working population, in fact. The progress of reform held its way, however, and at length it came to be arranged by law that the franchise should be the right of every householder and of every lodger who had maintained his position under prescribed conditions which could be fulfilled by every reputable person, even of the humblest class.

Another great change for the better was made when the system of vote by ballot was adopted in these countries. A long struggle had to take place before vote by ballot was accepted by our legislators. One great argument against it was especially plausible, and was worked for a long time with great success. That argument was that no honest and independent Briton ought to be ashamed or afraid of giving his vote openly, or ought to have any desire to screen his political action from the observation of his fellow-countrymen. Some legislators and writers, who were known to be genuine Liberals and earnest reformers, strongly opposed the ballot, on the ground that secret voting was a practice unworthy of enlightened and independent men. It might do very well, and be fairly justifiable—such was the argument—in foreign States where the tyranny of sovereigns and ruling classes made men afraid to give their votes openly for the weaker political side, but would never suit the free and manly citizens of the British Empire. The supporters of the ballot maintained that there were conditions, even in the British Empire, which sometimes made it highly inconvenient for men of the poorer classes to give their votes in opposition to the interests of their employers; that it was unfair to compel such men either to expose themselves to serious personal disadvantage or to give a vote which did not represent their conscientious convictions. The principle of enlightened reform won its victory once again, and the ballot system became one of the principles of the British and Colonial electoral systems. Vote by ballot may now be regarded as fully established and universally accepted throughout the Empire, and there does not appear the slightest prospect of any reaction setting in against its operation.

The cost of an election has been greatly reduced

by many of the reforms which distinguished the reign of Queen Victoria, but there remains much yet to be accomplished in the same direction. One of the principles strongly advocated by some Radical leaders and sections, but concerning which we have not lately heard very much, is the introduction into the British Parliamentary system of that regulation which prevails in so many other countries, the payment of members. There is something to be said in favour of this practice, and it is probable that before long a new agitation may set in for making the payment of men elected to the House of Commons a part of our constitutional system.

Another and a yet more extensive and venturous change in our Parliamentary arrangements is that championed by the advocates of Women's Suffrage. This agitation belongs altogether in its origin and its development to the reign of Queen Victoria. The question is undoubtedly one of very great importance, and it is certain that it will present itself in a powerful and widely-organised form for settlement at no very distant date. But that day, whenever it comes, will not belong to the period of this history, and we have already told our readers something about the growth and the spread of the agitation in its favour.

The general summary of our Parliamentary development during the Victorian era justifies the statement that in those years the House of Commons became, for the first time in its history, in the true sense a representative institution—

a legislative assembly representing all creeds, all forms of political opinion, and all classes in the Empire. The House of Lords has not, during the same time, undergone much change, and it is a singular fact that the agitation striving for some fundamental alteration in the constitution of this Upper or Second Chamber seems of later years to have rather relaxed than increased in vigour. Probably one reason for this may be the more immediate pressure of the work of reform which had to be accomplished for, and in, the representative assembly, and the general impression among reformers that the negative inconveniences and evils coming from the House of Lords, as at present constituted, might well be allowed to wait for their reform until the House of Commons should be so thoroughly reorganised as to make it a more effective instrument for the consideration of the whole constitutional question belonging to the construction of a Second Chamber.

The growth of civilisation showed itself very impressively in England throughout Queen Victoria's reign by the humanising change which took place in the fashion of public amusements. When the reign began pugilism was one of the most popular of sports, and was patronised by all classes, by men belonging to the nobility and all the uppermost orders of society, by men of university culture and the most expanded education. Although the laws of the realm forbade public pugilistic contests, there was a general concurrence among all classes to help in evading the law, and in enabling the favourite sport to be carried on by a process of conspiracy which kept the place of meeting a secret, up to the last moment, from the constituted authorities. The Queen had reigned nearly a quarter of a century when the famous prize-fight between Sayers, the champion of England, and Heenan, the champion of the United States, aroused a perfect tempest of public excitement on the occasion of their struggle for the winning of the belt. It may be that the very storm of emotion created by this sporting event brought about something like a reaction against the perverted taste which countenanced, patronised, and rewarded the abominable practice. Perhaps the fact that the eyes of the whole country were at once and for the moment attracted to the scene, or to the printed description of this prize-fight, had a salutary effect by compelling rational men and women to take the whole subject into serious consideration, and thus to prepare the way for that healthier public mood which could judge that what was called a national pastime was nothing but a national disgrace. Certain it is that from the time of that event the public admiration for the prize-fight and the prize-fighter began rapidly to decay, and towards the end of the reign the public contests of the professional boxers had passed as completely out of living history as the ducking-stool or the pillory.

Cock-fighting too, which was still a favourite

sport at the opening of the reign, hardly lives even in the memory of the present generation. There has also been a strong growing disinclination towards that once favourite method of stag-hunting which merely staged the poor stag to the show, and gave him no fair chance of effecting his escape, and indeed the deer hunt, in any form or in any conditions, has ceased to hold its former prominent place among national sports. Of course most forms of hunting must be open to the moral objections of those who would condemn any species of amusement which finds its delight and its inspiration in the hunting and the killing of harmless animals, and it may well be hoped that the time is not far distant when the intelligence and the good feeling of all classes in civilised countries will put an end to any pastimes which express themselves in the infliction of cruelty and death.

Pigeon-shooting still continues to be a recognised amusement among many classes of men and women who ought to know better and to feel better, and we know that many of the most humane and the most thoughtful men still refuse to be convinced that there is anything of cruelty in trout-fishing and salmon-fishing. The argument is often put forward that if there be no lack of humanity shown by those who will dine off meat and fish, off the flesh of animals and birds, and the bodies of fishes which must have been killed in order to make them available as food, there can be no inhumanity in killing the four-footed animals and the fishes so that they may supply food to men and women. But without going into what may be called the vegetarian theory of food as a moral principle, it may surely be pointed out that there is a great difference between putting to death one of the lower animals in order that food, believed to be essential to health, may be provided for human beings, and killing the same creatures for sport and the pleasing excitement of putting something to death. A distinguished Englishman, well known to be a genuine philanthropist, and who was at the same time a great lover of fishing, once defended his favourite sport by the argument that the salmon or the trout really felt no pain when it swallowed the bait and the hook, and that it passed out of life in a blissful unconsciousness. The objection made to his argument was that, as the salmon or the trout seemed to enjoy its life in the waters which were its home, it was evidently a spirit of cruelty which could find delight in putting an end to its existence, not because the angler needed food and could not otherwise obtain it, but because it gave him a pleasurable sensation to catch his prey.

For the present, however, we can only observe with satisfaction that even in the field sports of these later days the spirit of humanity is gradually making its influence more and more felt, and that human nature is showing itself sensitive as regards cruelty to animals, even for the purposes of sport, to a degree which would hardly have been understood by the general public in the early days of Queen Victoria's reign. Horse-racing is still just as popular among all classes as it ever was before, but there is good reason to believe that this national pastime is less associated among educated men with mere gambling than it was some quarter of a century ago.

A movement peculiarly characteristic of the humane, or, as it is commonly called, the humanitarian spirit which made its influence so widely felt in England during Queen Victoria's reign was that represented by the Anti-Vivisection Society. The practice of vivisection is, we need hardly tell our readers, that which experiments on the living bodies of the lower animals with the object of obtaining a thorough surgical knowledge as to the effects produced by certain conditions of suffering. The systematised practice of vivisection is itself of somewhat modern date. It was employed by John Hunter, William Harvey, and other celebrated operators, and it was undoubtedly brought into existence with a sincere desire for the benefit of the human race. The theory was that by such experiments on living animals an amount of physiological instruction might be obtained which could be turned to the best and most humane account, surgically, for the alleviation of the sufferings of human beings. There had been for a long time in England and in many other countries societies established for the prevention of cruelty to animals, and so long ago as 1859 two of these societies, that of London and that of Paris, obtained the appointment of a committee of distinguished medical men for the purpose of inquiring as to the value of the information supposed to be gained by the practice of vivisection. The judgment given by that committee was not unanimous, and did not therefore do much towards settling the question, but it certainly encouraged the Anti-Vivisectionists by the fact that it proved the existence of a difference of opinion, even among medical authorities, as to the value of vivisection. Various national and international conferences were held, from time to time, to discuss the questions raised by the Anti-Vivisectionists, and finally the energetic and thorough-going National Anti-Vivisection Society which we know at the present day was founded in England, and has its kindred associations in almost all civilised countries.

It can hardly be questioned by any impartial mind that on both sides of the controversy, even among the extreme advocates on either side, the ruling motive is a feeling of humanity. The Vivisectionists were and are undoubtedly influenced by the desire to obtain some specific knowledge which might enable surgery to mitigate the sufferings of human beings in various cases of illness, and by a belief that this result could be obtained from the study of the actual and immediate effect of certain experiments on the bodies of living animals. The Anti-Vivisectionists contend that no such beneficent results could be obtained for man through the infliction of torture on living animals, and most of them further contend that, even if such a result could be obtained, man has no right to inflict torture on living creatures of the lower order merely with the hope that some physical benefit might come to humanity through the surgical experience derived from vivisection. Measures to restrict the practice of vivisection were brought into Parliament, with the result that some regulations were established requiring that vivisectors must be authorised by a licence, and must conform with certain limiting ordinances, but the practice of vivisection was not itself condemned or suppressed by law. Even the demand made by the Anti-Vivisectionists that the experiments should only be tried on animals which had previously been rendered insensible by anæsthetics was strongly opposed by some eminent surgeons. These surgeons insisted that the real effect of the operation could not be ascertained while its subject was insensible to pain, and that therefore the proposed restriction would deprive it of its sole justification—the obtaining of knowledge which could be rendered available for the mitigation of human suffering.

The controversy became for a time increasingly bitter on either side. Some of the Anti-Vivisectionists described their opponents as beings who enjoyed the infliction of torture on helpless animal creatures. Many of the Vivisectionists characterised the upholders of the opposite side of the controversy as ignorant, unscientific outsiders filled with a sickly humanitarian sentimentality. There was much difference of opinion among the Vivisectionists themselves as to the extent of the beneficent results to be derived from the practice, and the conditions under which that practice ought to be applied. Among the general outer public there were many different shades of opinion. The extremists on either side might be divided into two classes. One class of the Vivisectionists maintained that the lower animals had no claim, on their own account, to any consideration on the part of human beings, and were properly to be used in any manner which might make them serviceable to the comfort and health of men and women. The extremists on the other side maintained that according to the moral code no supposed or even certain benefit to the physical condition of human beings could justify the infliction of torture upon lower animals; in other words, that vivisection was itself an offence against the moral law, and that a moral wrong must not be done even with the object of bringing comfort and health to human sufferers. Then the more moderate among the advocates of Vivisection argued that its most beneficial effects could be brought about under conditions which mitigated the pain inflicted on the victim; while the moderates on the other side satisfied themselves with the argument that no real benefit for human creatures was ever likely to be brought about by a succession of experiments on lower animals.

One of the most influential leaders of the Anti-Vivisection movement in recent days is the Honourable Stephen Coleridge, second son of the first Lord Coleridge, Lord Chief Justice of England. Stephen Coleridge was one of the Council of the National Society for the Prevention of Cruelty to Children, and he became honorary secretary of the National Anti-Vivisection Society. It seems only in the natural order of things that such a position should be held by one who belongs to the family of the great poet who wrote, 'He prayeth best who loveth best all things both great and small'; and Stephen Coleridge has certainly shown during his life of active humanity that such love thoroughly inspired him. He devoted himself to the Anti-Vivisection movement, and made many personal sacrifices in order to promote its success. He is a man of many and varied gifts, has won successes in literature and as a painter, has been called to the Bar, and acted for some years as Secretary to his father, when Lord Coleridge was Chief Justice of England, and has been a great traveller. Of late years he allowed no other of the pursuits in which he had become successful to prevent him from devoting a great part of his time to the work he had voluntarily accepted for the promotion of the Anti-Vivisection movement.

Some of the sacrifices Mr. Stephen Coleridge made personally to the cause he had at heart became known to the public during a trial which took place after the date which brings this History to its close. We only allude to it here because it formed an important event in the history of the Anti-Vivisection Society, which came into organisation during the later years of Queen Victoria's reign. The story of that movement is of much significance as a peculiar illustration of the expanding humanitarianism which is especially characteristic of our more modern times. Up to a comparatively recent period human benevolence was content to exercise its influence, in any organised form, only for the relief of 'suffering, sad humanity'—to save human beings from unmerited pain. Then came a time when humanity did its best to protect even the lower animals against those who would inflict wanton cruelty upon them. The Anti-Vivisection organisation carried the principle still farther, and raised its voice against the infliction of pain on the creatures inferior to man, even where science contended that by the infliction of such pain a distinct and practical benefit could be obtained for suffering men, women, and children. The existence of such an organisation is an event worthy of record in the history of our own times.

Among the many benefits which the expansion of medical science conferred upon humanity during the reign of Queen Victoria, the use of anæsthetics and of antiseptics must rank among the very foremost and the most highly promising as regards future beneficial development. The anæsthetic principle is that which would provide means for relieving the nerves of a patient from the sense of pain while an operation is carried on by the surgeon in order to restore the sufferer once again to health and to the enjoyment of life. The work which the antiseptic principle sets itself to do is that of preventing the growth of putrefactive processes in any part of the human frame, whether by microbes or from any other influence, and thereby protecting humanity against some of the most dangerous maladies which threaten its bodily and therefore its mental welfare.

At many periods of the world's history there were vague ideas afloat among those who practised the arts of the physician and the surgeon with regard to the advantages of relieving a patient from pain while some surgical operation was going on, and also for the prevention of that process of corruption in the human body which, since the beginning of time, has been a trouble to the human race. At one period or another some professor of the healing art has projected his mind beyond the intellectual horizon of his contemporaries, and has thought out a scheme for making a patient insensible to pain during the working of some needed surgical operation, with the sound conviction that the mere relief from temporary pain was not alone a means of rendering the surgical operation more successful, but would also enable the nerves and the physical strength of the patient to regain more quickly and to retain longer in the future their full soundness and vigour. But no regular system was ever established as a result of these experiments and these scientific guesses until after the reign of Queen Victoria had set in.

Among the great names of the Victorian age the name of Joseph Lister, now Lord Lister, must hold one of the highest places. Joseph Lister, who was the son of a distinguished microscopist, graduated at London University in arts and in medicine, became a Fellow of the College of Surgeons, and later became Surgeon-Extraordinary to Queen Victoria. His chief work during his most valuable career was the introduction of the antiseptic system which has been justly described as having revolutionised modern surgery. He received the prize of the Academy of Paris for his observations and discoveries in the use of the antiseptic method in surgery, and in 1883 was made a Baronet on the recommendation of Mr. Gladstone. In 1896 he was raised to the peerage by Queen Victoria, and, as one of his biographers says, he is, ' if not the first medical man called to the House of Lords, certainly the first to be called there in recognition of his great position as a medical man.'

Nothing done in our time has accomplished a greater work in medical and surgical art than the work achieved under the inspiration of Lord Lister for the recognition and establishment of the antiseptic system as the one great method of preventing or remedying some of the worst maladies which can affect and afflict the human frame. We have already shown how the reign of Queen Victoria saw the introduction of the many systems by which applied science has made life in its everyday movement more easy and more satisfactory for the modern human being, and most assuredly the services rendered by Lord Lister's genius and careful practice will hold a place amongst the highest triumphs of that remarkable period. Indeed, it may well be questioned whether the reign of Victoria will not be most distinctly marked in the world's history by the great revolution which it accomplished in the application of practical science in all its branches to the daily wants and comforts of the human being.

These chapters have already told of the great wars which the reign has seen, and of the great soldiers and sailors whose names it has added to the roll of fame. It has been a reign of great statesmen and orators and philanthropists. We need hardly say that the literature of the reign forms a distinct epoch of its own like that of Queen Elizabeth and Queen Anne. The literary masters of the Victorian era only need to have their names recorded in this chapter. It would be merely superfluous to describe to our readers all their great characteristic qualities, or to enter into any justification of the position which they have won for themselves. Their works rank among the classics of our literature, and are not now to be affected by any critical analysis, or to be further commended to the world's admiration by any sentences of eulogy. Poets like Tennyson, Browning, Elizabeth Barrett Browning, Matthew Arnold, Dante Rossetti, Algernon Swinburne, William Morris, carry in the mention of their names the full proclamation of their title to fame. The same may be said of the great novelists who sent their light into the world during the earlier period of the reign. The places held in literature by Dickens, Thackeray, Charlotte Brönte, and George Eliot are above and beyond all challenge. We may criticise them as much as we will, may point to this or that artistic defect in each of them, but not the most pessimistic of critics, even were he to devote his whole life to so ungracious a task, is likely to alter, to any appreciable extent, the world's estimate of them. Some of our greatest historians—men like Freeman, Green, Froude, and Buckle; and thinkers like John Stuart Mill and Herbert Spencer; scientific teachers like Huxley and Tyndall—will ever be remembered in the history of the reign. But we have had at many periods of the world's progress, beginning with the earliest times of whose intellectual triumphs we have assured record and evidence, great poets and historians, dramatists, romancists, painters, sculptors and musicians, and philosophic thinkers whose light has never been outshone in succeeding ages. There seems every reason to believe that the Victorian age will have left its deepest impression on the world's history by the beneficent triumphs which it has accomplished in the application of science in all its departments to the benefit of humanity and the progress of civilisation in the everyday life of men, women, and children in all classes from the highest to the lowest, from the richest to the poorest, from the prince to the peasant.

INDEX

ABERDEEN, Earl, on Salvation Army, ii. 18, 24
Aberdeen, Lady, President of International Congress of Women, i. 236
Acciareto attempts to murder King Humbert, ii. 232
Acland, Sir Thomas Dyke, i. 327; friend of Gladstone, 328
Act of Uniformity, i. 210
Alabama, ii. 199
Alexandra, Queen, ii. 279
Allied forces in China, i. 163, 166, 170; conditions of peace, 172
Amazons, i. 226
Amberley, Lord, i. 304
Anæsthetics, ii. 371
Anarchists, i. 88
Annual Register, 1897. Diamond Jubilee, i. 1
Annual Register, on plague in India, i. 136
Anti-Corn Law Movement, i. 301
Anti-Vivisection Society, ii. 366 *seqq.*
Antiseptics, ii. 371, 373
Arbitration not permitted between Great Britain and Transvaal, ii. 92
Ardagh, Sir John, British representative at Peace Conference, i. 355
Argyll, George Douglas Campbell, Duke of, ii. 198 *seqq.;* attitude towards Home Rule, 199, 200

Armstrong, William George, Lord, ii. 216 *seqq.;* engineer of rifled ordnance, 218
Arnold, Matthew, i. 316; ii. 375
Arnold - Forster, protest against Report of South African Committee, i. 31
Art, æsthetic school of, ii. 190
Asquith, Herbert Henry, i. 376, 402; ii. 332; on reform of local rating, i..381 ; on Ministers and public companies, 391; on Education of Children Bill, ii. 4
Athens, agitation in favour of Cretans, i. 41
Australasia assists England in Boer War, i. 8
Australasia and Empire, i. 2, 5
Australia (*see* also Colonies)
Australian Commonwealth, ii. 146; inauguration of new, 248
Austria, Elizabeth Amelia Eugenie, Empress of, assassinated, i. 378; ii. 228, 231; visits to England, 229; visits Ireland, 230
Austria, Francis Joseph, Emperor of, ii. 229
Ava, Earl of, ii. 137

BALFOUR, Arthur, i. 376; ii. 332; reply to questions on Report of South African Committee, i. 29; reply to Arnold-Forster, 32 ; to Sir William

378 INDEX.

BAL

Harcourt, 34; speech on Gladstone, 105; speeches on Ritualism in Church of England, 195, 199, 218, 223; decision on Cuban question, 256; on reply to Russia's invitation, 380; on Lords' power of veto, 384; on Ministers and public companies, 390; introduces London Government Bill, 399, 401, 405, 408; address to electors, 1900, ii. 148 *seqq.;* First Lord of the Treasury, 167; member of Fourth Party, 323; speech on Accession of Edward VII., 273

Balfour, Gerald, on distress in West of Ireland, i. 395; President of Board of Trade, ii. 168

Ballot, vote by, ii. 359

Bashi-Basouks in Crete, i. 52

Bavaria, Maximilian Joseph, Duke of, ii. 228

'Beggars of the Sea,' i. 177

Bella, wreck of, i. 318

Benefices Bill, i. 192 *seqq.*

Berlin, conference on factory labour, ii. 2, 4

Bessemer, Sir Henry, i. 313; develops steel industry, 313; a born inventor, 314; *Bessemer* steamer, 315

Bessemer, town in America, i. 313

Birrell, Augustine, i. 408; ii. 180, 332; on the 'only cure' for troubles in Church of England, i. 217

Bishops of Church of England and irregularities in public worship, i. 194, 198, 204, 206, 207, 209, 211, 213; authority of Bishops, 221, 222, 225

Bismarck, Prince, i. 295; his work, 296, 298; as parliamentary debater, 297; his methods, 298

BRI

Black, William, i. 341; on staff of *Morning Star*, 342; 'A Daughter of Heth,' 343

Blake, Edward, ii. 332; withdraws from South African Committee, i. 17; resolutions for Nationalist re-union, ii. 36

Bloemfontein, conference between Krüger and Sir Alfred Milner at, ii. 91, 93

Boer War—War declared, ii. 102; enemy underrated, 106; no adequate preparation for, 106, 115; popular, 108, 110, 114; Boer forces invade Natal, 113; English force, 116, 126; difficulties, 117; accusations against Dutch, 120; war songs, 123; Boer forces, 126; guerilla warfare, 127, 128, 130; Peace conference, 131, 138; British terms, 132; histories of, 138; policy of, 140

Bombay, plague in, i. 136; riots, 137; trial of rioters, 139

Bombay Legislative Council, measures for improvement of cities, i. 140

Booth, William, originated Salvation Army, ii. 20 *seqq.*; family engaged in the work, 23; plan of action, 25

Booth, Mrs., her death, ii. 23

Botha, Louis, at Peace conference, ii. 131

Boxers, rise of the, i. 160; outrages on foreigners, 161, 163 *seqq.*; meaning of word, 162; proclamations, 162; impartial in destruction, 164

Bresci assassinates King Humbert, ii. 232

'Bridge,' ii. 243.

Bright, John, on woman's rights, i. 228; his oratory, i. 301, 303; sketch of career, 303 *seqq*; as an orator, 304

INDEX. 379

British Legation, Pekin, besieged, i. 167 seqq.; native Christians in, 169; expedition to relieve, 170
British South African Company, i. 18, 24, 29
Broadhurst, Henry, sketch of, i. 83; Under Secretary of State for the Home Department, 83
Brönte, Charlotte, ii. 375
Brougham, Lord, his speeches, ii. 292
Brown, Ford Madox, i. 334; ii. 190
Browning, Elizabeth Barrett, ii. 375
Browning, Robert, ii. 375
Bryce, James, ii. 332; success in literature and in Parliament, i. 116
Buchanan, Robert, i. 342
Buckle, Henry Thomas, ii. 375
Buller, General Sir Redvers, arrives in Natal, ii. 113
Bunsen, Baron, i. 245; ii. 212
Burdett-Coutts, Mr., i. 402
Burke, Edmund, as orator, i. 100
Burne-Jones, Edward, i. 333; ii. 190; friendship with William Morris, Madox Brown, Rossetti, and Swinburne, i. 334; Royal Academy and, 335; characteristics, 337
Burnouf, Eugene, ii. 212
Burns, John, i. 402; M.P. and Member of L.C.C., sketch of, i. 74 seqq.; influence in strikes, 75, 77; M.P. for Battersea, 76; as debater, 76; vindicates right of public meeting in Trafalgar Square, 77
Burt, Thomas, first labour M.P., i. 66; sketch of, 80 seqq.; delegate to International Labour Conference, 82; Parliamentary Secretary to Board of Trade, 83
Butler, General, i. 272
Butt, Isaac, ii. 326

CAIROLI, Prime Minister, saves King Humbert's life, ii. 232
Calcutta, plague riot in, i. 140
Californian gold mines discovered, ii. 85
'Camisards,' i. 177
Campbell-Bannerman, Sir Henry, i. 35; leader of Liberal party, 124, 374, 380; champions Welsh grievances, 382; on Lords' power of veto, 383; attitude towards Home Rule, 393; on London Government Bill, 401; speech on accession of Edward VII., ii. 273
Canada, Dominion of, i. 257; sketch of her relations with Great Britain, i. 3; assists England in Boer War, 8; rebellion in, ii. 283 (*see also* Colonies)
Canterbury, Dr. Temple, Archbishop of, speech on accession of Edward VII., ii. 273
Capital and labour, i. 69 seqq.
Card-playing, ii. 243
Carlist movement, i. 261
Carlyle, Thomas, ii. 190; on 'might-have-beens,' i. 275; on Dr. Guillotin, 313
Cattle plague, Royal Commission on, i. 311
Cavour, Count, i. 308
Cecil, Lord Hugh, i. 376; ii. 332; speech on Church Discipline Bill, i. 220; on London Government Bill, 405, 406
Cecil, Lord Robert (*see* Salisbury, Marquis of)
Century, opening of a new, ii. 247
Chamberlain, Joseph, Colonial Secretary, i. 12, 13, 14, 37, 376; on insurrection in Johannesburg, 14, 19; communications with Sir Hercules Robinson, 16; disclaims any complicity with Jameson

CHA

Raid, 21, 26; crusade for return to protection, 154; attitude towards old-age pensions, ii. 9, 11; towards franchise in Transvaal, 90, 94; on Outlanders' petition, 99; financial policy, 142; attitude on South African War, 143; Colonial Secretary, 167

Channing, F. A., i. 408

Chaplin, Henry, Chairman of Committee on Old-age Pensions, ii. 11; retires from office, 172

Chartered Company (see British South African Company)

China, sovereign rights over Corea, i. 129, 132; losing her place in Eastern world, 134; leases port to Germany, 149; leases Wei-hai-Wei to England, 150

China, troubles in, i. 159 seqq.; immigration of foreigners, 160; concessions to other nations, 160; failure of crops, 161; forts fire on ships of allied squadron, 163

China, Dowager-Empress of, i. 159 seqq.; flight from Pekin, 172; return to Pekin, 175

Chinese Government, attitude towards Boxers, i. 160, 163, 168; deputation to British Minister, Pekin, 164; declare war, 165; German minister murdered, 166; allies offer terms of peace to, 172; foreign policy, 173, 175

Chinese imperial prince sent to Berlin, i. 172

Chinese territory occupied by lease, i. 131, 147, 149, 173

Christian, Princess, message to Mrs. Creighton, ii. 250

Christian Victor, of Schleswig-Holstein, Prince, ii. 137

Church and State, i. 210, 220, 225

Church Discipline Bill, i. 220; rejected, 224

CON

Church of England, ritualistic practices in, ii. 161

Churchill, Lord Randolph, ii. 321; member of Fourth Party, i. 66; forms Fourth Party, ii. 323; Chancellor of Exchequer, 324; resigns office, 325

Churchill, S. Winston, ii. 332; characteristics, i. 376

Cialdini, General, ii. 233

Civilisation in Soudan, i. 180

Clarke, Sir Edward, i. 402

Cobden, Richard, ii. 303; 'unadorned eloquence' on free trade, i. 301, 303

Cock-fighting, ii. 363

Cockburn, Sir Alexander, ii. 330

Coleridge, Baron, ii. 330

Coleridge, Hon. Sec. of National Anti-Vivisection Society, ii. 370

Colonial Federation, ii. 1 seqq.; schemes of, 7; prospects of, 8

Colonial Office and Jameson Raid, i. 13 seqq., 20, 24 seqq.

Colonial statesmen in England explain their views, i. 7

Colonials at Diamond Jubilee, i. 2

Colonies, representation in Imperial Parliament proposed, i. 4-5, 6; willing to contribute to imperial army and navy, 6, 7; service during Boer war, ii. 134

Commons, House of, labour members, i. 66 seqq., 84 seqq., 240; four parties in, 68; ii. 323; Liberals and Conservatives agree on Fashoda incident, i. 189; anti-ritualistic party, 200; a true representative institution, ii. 361

Compton, Earl, attitude towards Salvation Army, ii. 24

Conan Doyle, Sir Arthur, Great Boer War, ii. 138

INDEX.

CON

Concert of European Powers (*see* European Powers Concert)
Congreve, Richard, leader of Positivists, ii. 74
Cordu, Mr., wounded in Pekin, i. 166
Corea, Japan and, i. 129 *seqq.*; alliance between, 130; independence recognised, 130, 131; battle-ground of foreign claims, 131; leases, 131
Courtney, Leonard, ii. 332; on S. African Committee Report, i. 30; speech on Eastern policy, 152; recommends international compact, 154; on London Government Bill, 401, 404, 407, 408; as Parliamentary debater, ii. 178
Cowen, Joseph, sketch of career, ii. 192 *seqq.*
Cranborne, Viscount, ii. 309; speech on ritualism in Church of England, i. 215
Creighton, Dr. Mandell, Bishop of London, ii. 220 *seqq.*; attack on Sir William Harcourt, i. 207; Bishop of Peterborough, ii. 220; historical works, 221
Cresswell, Sir C., ii. 77
Cretans rebel against Turkish rulers, i. 39; Hellenic in origin, history, and aspirations, 40; proclaim union with Greece, 41
Crete, rescued from Ottoman rule, i. 39 *seqq.*; Turkish misgovernment in, 39; a battle-ground, 41; autonomy for, 44, 50, 51; Turkish troops evacuate, 54
Cross, Viscount, retires from office, ii. 170
Cuba revolts against Spain, i. 248 *seqq.*, 252; rival claims to, 249; sale to United States suggested, 251; surrendered to United States, 261, 264

DIS

Curzon, Lord, of Kedleston, Viceroy of India, i. 141; Under Secretary for Foreign Affairs, 142; Indian policy, 144, 145; Irish peerage, 144
Cushman, Miss, i. 340

DALLING, Lord, maxim of, ii. 109
Davidson, Dr. Randall (Bishop of Winchester), speech on bishops and irregularities in public worship, i. 206
Davitt, M., on state of Ireland, i. 395; advocacy of Home Rule, ii. 34; *Fall of Feudalism in Ireland*, 44
De Quincey, i. 316
De Wet at Peace Conference, ii. 131; *Three Years' War*, dedication of, 133; quoted, 138; characteristics, 133
Declassé, M., Foreign Minister, on occupation of Fashoda, i. 188
Derby, Earl of, i. 322; ii. 289; as Parliamentary leader, 291
Dervishes: meaning of word, i. 177; at Omdurman, 178, 179
Devonshire, Duke of, tribute to Gladstone, i. 104; on women as Aldermen, 407; Lord President of the Council, ii. 167
Diamond Jubilee, how it differed from Jubilee of 1887, i. 1
Dickens, Charles, i. 316; ii. 375; readings, 344
Dillon, John, i. 408; ii. 332; tribute to Gladstone, i. 109; as leader of Nationalist party, ii. 30 *seqq.*, 34, 35, 37.
Dillon, John Blake, ii. 30
Disraeli, Benjamin, Earl Beaconsfield, rivalry with Gladstone, i. 112; on Sheil as an orator, ii.

DOW

294; as debater and statesman, 302
Dow, General Neal, i. 271; temperance advocate and soldier, 272
Dowager Empress of China (*see* under China)
Dublin, Lord Mayor's address to Queen Victoria, ii. 60
Dublin, National Convention at, ii. 33
Duffy, Charles Gavan, editor of the *Nation*, i. 279
Dunraven, Earl, supported Workmen's Compensation Act, i. 95; on women as Aldermen, 406
Durham, Earl of, system of local self-government for Canada, i. 3; ii. 283
Dutch Boers in Transvaal, Outlanders and, ii. 84, 95
Dutch Boers, their descent and character, ii. 103, 105, 106; fighting force, 105; training of, 116

EAST and West, i. 367
Ecclesiastical Titles Bill, i. 322
Edward VII., King, message to Lord Kitchener, ii. 132; thanks to Army and Navy, 134; Sipido attempts to assassinate, 225; accession of, 266; the King's Speech, 267; proclamation, 269, 270, 273; coronation oath, 275 *seqq.*; his illness, 278; opens Parliament, 278
Education of Children Bill, ii. 1 *seqq.*; passed, 8
Education, spread of, ii. 342
Egypt, responsibilities of England in, i. 176; exploring expeditions in, 183
Election expenses, ii. 360
Elgin, Lord, as Viceroy of India, i. 141

FAW

Ellenborough, Earl of, ii. 294
Elliot, A., on women as Aldermen and Councillors, i. 406
Emmet, Robert, ii. 326
English Church Union Meeting, i. 198
English Government, attitude on Cretan affairs, i. 42, 46, 57, 61; Eastern policy, 128, 132, 135, 151, 156; obtains lease of Wei-hai-Wei, 150; policy of non-intervention, 157; plan to relieve Pekin Legation, 170; attitude on Cuban question, 256, 262; negotiations with France on Fashoda, 186 *seqq.*
Esher, William Baliol Brett, Viscount, his career, 72
European Powers concert to protect Crete, i. 39 *seqq.*; joint note to Greek Government, 43; proclaim blockade of ports, 47; pressure upon Greece, 50; Germany and Austria withdraw, 52; blockade raised, 55; Admirals' proclamation, 56
Exhibition, 1851, anticipations of results, i. 365
Expedition for relief of Pekin Legation, i. 170

FACTORY Labour, Conference on, ii. 2
Farrar, Archdeacon, attitude towards Salvation Army, ii. 24
Farrer, Thomas Henry, Baron, sketch of, ii. 75
Fashoda incident, i. 182 *seqq.*; Soudanese garrison at, 185; French evacuate, 190
Faucit, Helen (*see* Martin, Lady)
Fawcett, Henry, ii. 313; as M.P., 314
Fawcett, Mrs. Henry, visits refuge camps, ii. 135

FEN

Fenianism, ii. 320
Field, Cyrus W., ii. 65
Field sports, spirit of humanity in, ii. 365
Field, W., on Irish railways, i. 397
Finlay, Sir R., i. 402
Fitzgerald, Lord Edward, ii. 326
Fitzmorris, Lord Edmund, Member of Committee on Old Age Pensions, ii. 12
Forbes, Archibald, career of, ii. 195 *seqq.*; as war correspondent for *Daily News*, 197
Forster, William Edward, ii. 318; Chief Secretary for Ireland, 319
Foster, Sir Walter, Member of Committee on Old Age Pensions, ii. 12
Fourth Party, i. 66; policy of, ii. 323
Fowler, Sir Henry, attitude on Home Rule, i. 394
Fox, Charles James, as orator, i. 100
France: occupied more in Africa than in Asia, i. 135; negotiations with English Government on Fashoda, i. 186 *seqq.*
Franchise lowered, i. 65
Franchise, reforms in, ii. 359
Free libraries, ii. 343
Free Trade movement, i. 154, 299, 301; ii. 286
Freedom of speech and conspiracy, i. 89
Freeman, Edward A., ii. 375
Froude, James A., ii. 375

GAELIC Revival, ii. 52
Garibaldi, ii. 193; visits England, i. 308
Garrett, Millicent (Mrs. Henry Fawcett), ii. 316

GLA

General Election, 1900, ii. 142 *seqq.*; electoral battle, 163; results, 167
Geneva Convention, i. 369, 370
'George Eliot,' ii. 375
George Henry, i. 285; in California, 285; 'Our Land and Land Policy,' 286; 'Progress and Poverty,' 286; champion of Free Trade, 286; and of Home Rule, 287
George of Greece, Prince: Mission to Crete, i. 41; High Commissioner of the Powers in Crete, 54; his powers and duties, 55
German Empire as created by Bismarck, i. 298
German Military System, i. 353
German missionaries murdered in Shantung, i. 129
Germany: attitude towards Eastern affairs, i. 127; fleet occupy Kiau-Chau, proclamation, 128; shipping enterprises, 135; attitude on Cuban question, 256
Germany, William, Emperor of, with Queen Victoria at her death, ii. 253
Gilbert, Sir John, i. 276; engravings in *Illustrated London News*, 277, 278
Gilbert, W. S., ii. 214
Gladstone, Herbert, ii. 332; on London Government Bill, i. 402, 403; speech at Leeds, ii. 152
Gladstone, William Ewart, died May 19, 1898, i. 98; policy towards Greece, 61; statesman, orator, and student, 99; as orator and debater, 100; as talker, 101; buried in Westminster Abbey, 111; his grave, 112, 113; rivalry with Disraeli, 112; follower and successor of Peel, 113; Home Rule Bills,

GLA

118; on Sir William Harcourt's speech on Church Discipline, 202; appreciation of art, 336; Home Rule policy, 392, ii. 199, 200; first Home Rule Bill, 69, 79; Second Bill, 70; on Shiel's oratory, 294; as orator and debater, 301; tribute to Parnell, 327

Gladstone, Mrs. W. E., buried in Westminster Abbey, i. 114

Gold Mines of South Africa, ii. 84

Gordon, General, avenged, i. 179, 181; memorial of, in Khartoum, 182

Gorst, Sir John, on Education of Children Bill, ii. 2, 5, 6; member of Fourth Party, 323, 332

Goschen, Lord, retires from office, ii. 170

Gray, David, i. 342

Greece, movement to rescue Crete from Ottoman Cult, i. 39 seqq.; sympathy for Cretans, 41; reply to Note from European Powers, 46; suggests plebiscite, 47; troops enter Crete, fight with Turks, 48; principle of nationality, 49, 58, 62; national wishes not consulted, 59, 61

Greeks: characteristics; success in foreign countries, i. 58; desired Alfred, Duke of Edinburgh, for their king, 60; George of Denmark chosen, 61

Green, J. R., ii. 375

Grey, Earl, Reform Bill, ii. 357

Grey, Sir Edward, i. 376, ii. 332; speech on Eastern policy, i. 154; on occupation of Nile Valley, 187

'Ground landlords,' i. 381

Guillotin, Dr., i. 313

Gully, W. C., re-elected Speaker, ii. 181

HAV

HAGUE, Peace Conference at, i. 346 seqq.

Haldane, R. B., attitude on Home Rule, i. 394

Halifax, Viscount, President of English Church Union, i. 202; attitude towards Church of Rome, 203; speech on Anti-Ritualistic Meeting, 209

Halsbury, Lord Chancellor, on women as Aldermen, i. 407; on Corrupt Practices Bill, ii. 17; administers oath to King Edward, 268

Hannen, Lord, on Sir Charles Russell's Speech, ii. 208

Harcourt, Lewis, ii. 313

Harcourt, Sir William, views on Report of South African Committee, ii. 32, 35, 37; speech on Gladstone, 107; as debater, 116; as Liberal leader, 121; correspondence with John Morley, 121; resigns leadership, 124, 125; speeches on Ritualism in English Church, i. 193, 198, 201, 222; letters in *Times*, 201; capacity for work, 202; retires from leadership, 374, 393; 'Historicus,' ii. 311; as debater, 311; 'Death-duty' budget, 312; retirement, 313

Hardy, Gathorne, on Cowen's speech, ii. 194

Harris, Rutherford, telegrams to Flora Shaw, i. 12; disappearance of, 17; secretary to Chartered Company, 18

Harvey, William, employed vivisection, ii. 366

Havannah, *Maine* burnt and sunk in harbour, i. 259

Havelock, Sir Henry, i. 292, 294

Havelock-Allan, Sir Henry Marsham, at Cawnpore, i. 292; at Lucknow, 293

INDEX.

HAW

Hawksley, solicitor to Cecil Rhodes, i. 17; refuses to hand telegrams to South African Committee, 18, 20, 30

Heenan, prize-fight with Sayers, ii. 363

Henry, Prince, in China, i. 149

Herschell, Farrer, Baron, sketch of his career, ii. 67; as Lord Chancellor, 69, 70

Hertford, Marquis of, art collections, ii. 240

Herzen, Alexander, ii. 193.

Hicks-Beach, Sir Michael, ii. 332; on Ministers as Directors of public companies, i. 387, 389; Budget 1899, 398; on London Government Bill, 406; Chancellor of the Exchequer, ii. 167

Highwayman, ii. 345

Hobhouse, C. E., on Committee on Salvation Army Scheme, ii. 24

Holywell Street, ii. 348

Home Rule, i. 69, 375, 392; ii. 159, 160, 162, 166; Colonies, i. 6, 117; attempt to kill it by kindness, ii. 50

Home Rule Bill (second), ii. 200

Horse-racing, ii. 366

Howard, Hubert, killed at Omdurman, i. 179

Humbert I., of Italy, assassinated, ii. 232; his reforms in manner of life, 233

Hunter, John, employed vivisection, ii. 366

Hunting, ii. 364

Hutton, Richard Holt, i. 269; editor of *Spectator*, 270

Huxley, Thomas, ii. 344, 375

Hyde Park closed to Reformers, i. 323

*I*LLUSTRATED London News, i. 277, 279

VII.

JAP

Imperialism, i. 22, 375

Imperialists, ii. 96; attitude towards Boer War, 102, 145

Indian Empire, frontier lines, i. 135; plague in, 136

Ingelow, Jean, i. 267

Inquirer, The, i. 269

International Congress of Women, i. 236

International exhibitions, ii. 357

International Labour Conference, Berlin, 1890, i. 82

Ionian Islands, i. 61

Ireland, distress in West, i. 395

Ireland, taxation in, ii. 45 *seqq.*; Gaelic revival, 52 *seqq.*; literature of, 54; system of land tenure, 320

Irish National Convention, ii. 33 *seqq.*

Irish National League, ii. 165

Irish National Party, i. 5; ii. 29 *seqq.*, 160, 164, 166, 323, 325; two parties, i. 29, 30; re-united, 38; policy of obstruction, ii. 326

Irish Railways, i. 397

Irish soldiers in Boer War, ii. 135

Italy, efforts for freedom, i. 306

*J*AMES of Hereford, Lord, Money-Lending Bill, ii. 13 *seqq.*, 18; on Committee on Salvation Army Scheme, 24

Jameson, Dr., Cecil Rhodes and, i. 10, 19

Jameson Raid, ii. 87; plan and preparations for, i. 10, 17, 19 *seqq.*; result of, 28

Japan, before and after, 1867, i. 127 *seqq.*; Corea and, 129 *seqq.*; alliance between, 130; treaty with Russia, 130; war with Russia, 132; progress in Western civilisation, 132; ambition of, 135; policy towards China, 151;

2 B

JEN

to lead expedition to relieve Pekin, 170; foreign policy, 173, 174; new influence of, ii. 285
Jenner, Sir William, i. 344
Jessel, Sir George, ii. 74
Jingoism, i. 22
Johannesburg, i. 12, 14
Johannesburgers, intended to appeal to Imperial Government, i. 15, 18
Journalists in Parliament, ii. 333

KEAN, Edmund, 'the pit rose at me,' i. 343
Keeley, Mary, as singer and actress, ii. 71
Keeley, Robert, ii. 71
Kennaway, Sir John, on ritualism in Church of England, i. 217
Kensit, J., crusade against ritualistic practices, i. 224
Ketteler, Baron von, murdered in Pekin, i. 166
Khalifa, forces oppose British, i. 178
Khartoum, British and Egyptian flags over, i. 179; memorial to Gordon, 182
Kiau-Chau occupied by German fleet as coaling station, i. 128
Kimberley, Earl of, supported Workmen's Compensation Act, i. 95; tribute to Gladstone, 104, 112; speech on State Church, 210; speech on Eastern policy, 379; on women as aldermen, 407; speech on accession of King Edward, ii. 273
Kingsley, Mary H., her life and works, i. 247
Kinnaird, Baron, on ritualism in Church of England, i. 207
Kipling, Rudyard, war verses, ii. 123
Kitchener, Sir Herbert, Lord Kit-

LIB

chener of Khartoum, i. 377; commands at Omdurman, i. 177, 179; welcome in England, 181; memorial to Gordon, 182; expedition to Fashoda, 182 *seqq.*; succeeds Lord Roberts in South Africa, ii. 113, 131, 132, 248; returns to England, 134
Kossuth, L., ii. 193
Krüger, President, repudiates suzerainty of Great Britain, i. 38; re-elected President of Transvaal, ii. 82; conference with Sir Alfred Milner, 91; conduct to Outlanders, 98, 101; ultimatum, 101; flight from Pretoria, 129

LABOUCHERE, H., report on South African Committee, i. 19, 23 *seqq.*; on Hawksley's refusal to produce telegrams, 30; on South African Report, 37; on restricting powers of Lords, 383; on women as aldermen and councillors, 406, 408; attitude towards Salvation Army, ii. 24; editor of *Truth*, 334
Labour, Capital and, i. 69 *seqq.*
Ladysmith, relief of, ii. 128
Lansdowne, Marquis of, Foreign Secretary, ii. 168
Lawson, Sir Wilfrid, attitude towards Report of South African Committee, i. 29
'Leases' in Far East, i. 131, 147, 149, 173
Lecky, W. E. H., member of Committee on Old Age Pensions, ii. 12
Liberal Party, position after Gladstone's retirement, i. 115; divisions in, 117, 121; Home Rule a difficulty, 119; differences among, 374, 375; Home Rule and, 392;

INDEX. 387

position in 1900, ii. 145, 147, 153, 159, 164
Lighting, modern system of, ii. 347
Linton, Mrs. Lynn, i. 280; sketch of, 338
Linton, William, i. 278; drawings in *Illustrated London News* and *Westminster Review*, 279; as politician, 279
Lister, Joseph, Lord, introduced antiseptic system, ii. 373
Literary and scientific institutions, ii. 344
Literature of Victorian era, ii. 374
'Little Englanders,' ii. 96, 151
Lloyd, George D., ii. 332
Local government system, ii. 347
Lockwood, Sir Frank, sketch of, i. 289; Solicitor-General, 290; visit to America, 291; sketches Lord Russell, 291
London Chambers of Commerce, Committee on Corrupt Practices Bill, ii. 17
London, condition of, ii. 348
London County Council, i. 400
London Government Bill, i. 390; second reading, 402; committee stage, 403; report stage, 404; passed, 409
Londonderry, Marquis of, attitude towards Workmen's Compensation for Accidents Act, i. 94
Lone Star expedition, i. 249; its object, 250
Long, Walter, on Committee on Salvation Army Scheme, ii. 24
Lopez, General, expeditions to Cuba, i. 250
Lords, House of, power of veto, i. 383; question of reform of, ii. 362
Lowe, Robert, Lord Sherbrooke, ii. 306

Lubbock, Sir John (Lord Avebury), i. 402; intervened in dockers' strike, i. 78
Luccheni, Luigi, assassinates Empress of Austria, ii. 231
Lyndhurst, John Singleton Copley, Baron, ii. 296
Lynn, Rev. James, i. 339
Lyttelton, Public Worship Regulation Bill, i. 192
Lytton, Edward Bulwer, Earl, ii. 298

M'ADAM, inventor of macadamised road-making, ii. 345
M'Arthur, C., Church Discipline Bill, i. 220, 224
M'Kinley, President, declaration of war against Spain, i. 260
M'Neill, J. C. Swift, on Ministers as directors of public companies, i. 386
Macaulay on compromise in politics, i. 276
Macdonald, Alexander, labour M.P., i. 66
Macready, Shakespearian revivals, i. 340
Mad Mullah, i. 136
Mafeking, relief of, ii. 128, 129
Mahmoud, leader of Dervishes, taken prisoner, i. 178
Maine, burnt and sunk, i. 259
Majuba Hill, i. 283; ii. 106, 112, 148
Mann, Tom, ordered to leave France, i. 79.
Manning, Cardinal, intervened in dockers' strike, i. 78
Marchand, Major, at Fashoda, i. 184, 187, 188; recalled, 189
Marconi, Guglielmo, system of wireless telegraph, ii. 236 *seqq*.
Marconi Telegram, ii. 339 (*see also* Wireless telegraphy)

MAR

Martin, Lady (Helen Faucit), i. 339; characteristics, 340
Martineau, Dr. James, sketch of career, ii. 182 *seqq.*
Martineau, Harriet, i. 316; ii. 182
Mathew, Father, i. 271; ii. 351
Maurice, Rev. F. D., ii. 190
Max-Müller, Friedrich, his career, ii. 211 *seqq.*; lectures in Westminster Abbey, 213
Max-Müller, Wilhelm, ii. 211
Mazzini, i. 306; ii. 193
Medical Science, use of anæsthetics and antiseptics, ii. 371
Melbourne, Viscount, ii. 286
Members of Parliament—property qualification, ii. 358; payment of, 361
Mexico, dispute with the United States, i. 372
Mill, John Stuart, i. 80; ii. 375; on woman's rights, i. 228
Millbank Prison, ii. 241
Milner, Sir Alfred (Lord), Governor of Cape Colony and High Commissioner, ii. 89; meeting with Krüger, 91; refused arbitration, 92; on British intervention, 98; Peace Conference, 131
Ministers as directors of public companies, i. 386 *seqq.*
Missionaries murdered in China, i. 163
Money-Lending Bill, ii. 13 *seqq.*, 18
Monkswell, Baron, on Salvation Army, ii. 18
Monroe Doctrine, i. 249
Monson, Sir Edmund, British Ambassador at Paris, conduct of Fashoda incident, i. 186
Monza, King Humbert assassinated at, ii. 232
Moore, Thomas, ii. 288; on Charles James Fox, i. 109
Morgan, Sir John Osborne, i. 268
Morley, John, ii. 219, 332; 'Life

NOR

of Gladstone,' i. 114; success in literature and in Parliament, 116; correspondence with Sir William Harcourt, 121, 123; attitude towards Imperialism, 375; attitude towards Home Rule, 393
Morning Star, ii. 196
Morris, William, i. 334; ii. 190, 375
Morton, E. J. C., on ground landlords, i. 381
Motor-cars, ii. 241
Mundella, Anthony John, i. 268
Muravieff, Count, despatch on Peace Conference, i. 346 *seqq.*
Music-halls, ii. 253

NAPOLEON III., Emperor, opinion of Bismarck, i. 297
Natal invaded by Boer forces, ii. 113
Nation, the, i. 279
National Anti-Vivisection Society, ii. 366 *seqq.*
National Liberal League, ii. 338
National Society for Prevention of Cruelty to Children, ii. 370
Nationalist Party. (*See* Irish National Party.)
Navigation laws, ii. 286
Newbolt, Henry John, 'Admirals All,' 'The Island Race,' ii. 123, 124
Newman, Francis, i. 274; 'Phases of Faith,' 276
Newman, John Henry (Cardinal), i. 274
Nicholas II., Czar of Russia, proposed peace conference, i. 346
Nile Valley, only to be occupied by Great Britain, i. 186, 187
Northumberland, Algernon George Percy, 6th Duke of, career, ii. 62

O'BRIEN, Barry, 'Life of Lord Russell of Killowen,' quoted, i. 291.
O'Brien, William, on distress in West of Ireland, i. 395; sketch of, ii. 40; Irish National League, 165
O'Connell, Daniel, ii. 326; as orator and debater, 293
O'Connor, T. P., ii. 332, 335
O'Farrell, attempt to assassinate Prince Alfred, ii. 202
O'Kelly, James, ii. 36
Old age pensions, ii. 9 *seqq.*; committee on, 11; scheme for, 12
Oliphant, Margaret, i. 266
Omdurman, battle of, i. 177, 179
Onslow, Earl of, member of committee on Salvation Army scheme, ii. 24
Open door in the Far East, i. 147
Orange Free State, ally of Transvaal, ii. 83; annexed, 129
Orton, Arthur, claimant in Tichborne case, i. 318
Otto, King, i. 59
Ottoman Government declare war against Cretans, i. 48; treaty of peace signed, 50
Outlanders, their claims, ii. 86, 90, 91; Dutch and, 95; petition to Queen, 99
Outram, General, i. 293
Owen, Richard, ii. 344

PAGET, Sir James, ii. 80
Palmerston, Viscount, ii. 289; advice to Stansfeld, i. 308; as debater, 290; temperament, 292
Parliament, session of, 1897, i. 90; session of, 1899, 374 *seqq.*; opened by Commission, 377; address adopted by Lords, 379; amendments to address, 380 *seqq.*; address agreed upon by Commons, 398; subjects for discussion, 398; dissolved, September 18, 1900, ii. 146; dissolved at accession of new sovereign, 274; not dissolved on accession of Edward VII., 275; as political arena, 286. (*See also* Commons, House of; and Lords, House of.)
Parliamentary inquiries, point of view of Ministers and of private members, i. 21
Parnell, Charles Stewart, i. 316; leader of Nationalist party, i. 66; ii. 323, 325 *seqq.*
Parnell Commission, ii. 207
Parnell, Delia Tudor, i. 316
Parnell, Fanny, i. 317
Parnell, J. H., of Avondale, i. 317
Passanante attacks King Humbert, ii. 232
Paul, Herbert, ii. 332; 'Men and Letters,' 335
Pauncefote, Sir Julian, proposes permanent Committee of International Arbitration, i. 358
Payn, James, i. 315; admirer of Dickens, 316
Peace Conference at the Hague, i. 346 *seqq.*; opening: States represented, 351; subjects of discussion, 351; armaments, 352, 354; humanitarian question: explosive bullets, 355; international arbitration, 358; mediation, 359; commission of inquiry, 361; court of arbitration, 362; result, 364; followed by wars, 366, 368; second and third conventions, 369; resolutions, 370; dispute settled by, 372; dispute with Transvaal and, ii. 92
Peace party and imperialists, i. 146
Peace signed between Turkey and Greece, i. 50
Pekin relieved, i. 163, 171; women

PEE

and children in British Legation, 165; foreign guards, 166; British Legation besieged, 167 *seqq.*; native Christians in, 169

Peel, Sir Robert, Gladstone's early leader and model, i. 113; Free Trade and, 299, 301; as Prime Minister, ii. 286; as orator, 287

Penzance, Baron (James Plaister Wilde), sketch of, ii. 76

Philippine Islands, revolt against Spain, i. 248; surrendered to United States, 261, 264

Pigeon-shooting, ii. 364

Pigott forgeries, ii. 329

Plague in India, i. 136; riots, 137, 140

Playfair, Dr. George, i. 324

Playfair, Lyon (Lord), i. 323; work on Commissions, 325, 327; as Parliamentary debater, 326; Postmaster-General, 326; Chairman of Ways and Means, 326; Vice-President of Council, 327

Plimsoll, Samuel, i. 330; agitates for improvement in merchant shipping, 331

Plunkett, Sir Horace, sketch of, ii. 49; scheme 'to kill Home Rule by kindness,' 50

Police System, ii. 348

Port Arthur, Russian fleet to winter at, i. 128; taken by Japanese, 130; as Russian naval station, 150

Port Hudson stormed, i. 272

Post-cards, picture, ii. 242

Postage charges, ii. 242

Postal system, development of, ii. 340

Potter, T. B., ii. 73

Preece, Sir William H., system of signalling without wire, ii. 238

Pretoria, Lord Roberts enters, ii. 129; proclamation of King Edward VII. at, 273

RIT

Primrose League, ii. 337

Pro-Boer, ii. 118, 145

Prussia, Bismarck's work in, i. 298

Public amusements, ii. 353 *seqq.*

Public Worship Regulation Act, i. 191 *seqq.*

Pugilism, ii. 362

QUAIN, Sir Richard, i. 310; member of Royal Commission on Cattle Plague, 311; 'Dictionary of Medicine,' 312

RAWLINSON, Sir Robert, i. 328; employed by Stephenson, 329; consulted on public health, 329

Redmond, John, ii. 332; amendment on Home Rule, i. 392, 394; characteristics, ii. 29; leader of Nationalists, 38

Reform Bill, 1832, ii. 357

Reform Bill, 1867, ii. 303

Reformers' meetings, i. 323

Refuge camps in South Africa, ii. 135

Reid, Sir Robert, ii. 332

Reuter, Julius Baron de, career, ii. 64

Rhodes, Cecil, and Dr. Jameson, i. 10, 19 *seqq.*; telegrams to Flor.. Shaw, 12; Managing Director of Chartered Co., De Beers Mines, and Gold-fields of South Africa, 24; Lord Rosmead and, 27; on Salvation Army, ii. 18

Ridley, Sir Matthew White (Viscount), retires from office, ii. 171

Ripon, Earl of, supported Workmen's Compensation Act, i. 95

Ritchie, C. T., supported Education of Children Bill, ii. 5; Home Secretary, 167

INDEX. 391

Ritualism in Church of England, i. 191 *seqq.*
Roberts, Earl, commander-in-chief in South Africa, ii. 113; enters Pretoria, 129; returns from South Africa, visits Queen Victoria, 248
Roberts, Lieutenant F., ii. 137
Robinson, Sir Hercules. (*See* Rosmead, Lord)
Robson, W. S., Education of Children Bill, ii. 1 *seqq.*
Roebuck, John Arthur, ii. 299
Röntgen, Wilhelm Konrad von, discovers X-rays, ii. 235
Rosebery, Earl, ii. 145; tribute to Gladstone, i. 105, 112; resigned leadership of Liberal Party, 117; Fashoda policy, 189; South African policy, ii. 157; attitude towards Home Rule, 159; as Prime Minister, 311
Rosmead, Baron, High Commissioner of South Africa, i. 16; ii. 89; Rhodes' plans and, 27, 283; sketch of his career, 281; policy of conciliation, 283; resigned, 284
Rossetti, Dante Gabriel, i. 334; ii. 190, 375
Rudolph, Crown Prince, his death, ii. 230
Ruskin, John, sketch of career, ii. 186 *seqq.*; influenced by Maurice and Carlyle, 190
Russell, Lady Agatha, i. 304
Russell, Sir Edward R., editor of *Liverpool Daily Post*, ii. 336
Russell, Frances, Countess, i. 303
Russell, George W. E., ii. 332; on John Bright, 304
Russell, Lord John, Prime Minister, i. 309; his political principles, ii. 287; as debater, 287; characteristics, 289; Reform Bill, 357

Russell, of Killowen, Baron, ii. 204 *seqq.*, 330; visits America, i. 290; Corrupt Practices Bill, ii. 17; as Attorney-General, 207; Lord Chief Justice, 208
Russell, William Howard, ii. 195
Russia an Oriental Power, i. 127, 132; Fleet to winter at Port Arthur, 128; treaty with Japan, 130; how regarded by Western Powers, 135; fortifies Port Arthur, 150; Chinese policy, 151
Rutland, Duke of, i. 112

SALISBURY, Robert Cecil, Marquis of: Speech on Workmen's Compensation Act, i. 96; tribute to Gladstone, 103, 112; plan for relief of Pekin Legation, 170; Fashoda policy, 187; reply to Lord Kimberley, 379; on women as aldermen, 406; letter to electors, ii. 154; return to power, 167; size of Cabinet, 168; speech on accession of King Edward, 273; sketch of career, 309
Salmon-fishing, ii. 364
Salvation Army, ii. 18 *seqq.*; posts in every country, 23; Committee of Inquiry, 24; spirit of comradeship, 27
Saratoga Springs, American Bar Association meeting at, i. 290
Saxe-Coburg and Gotha, Alfred Ernest Albert, Duke of, ii. 201 *seqq.*; attempted assassination, 202; proclaimed King of Greece, 204
Saxe-Coburg and Gotha, Marie Alexandrovna, Duchess of, ii. 204
Saxe-Coburg and Gotha, Prince Alfred of, ii. 204

SAY

Sayers, prize-fight with Heenan, ii. 202

Schwartzkoff, Colonel von, on German military armaments, i. 202

Scott, C., i. 408

Scottish crofters' grievances, i. 246

Scottish Members of Parliament, i. 5

Selborne, Earl of, First Lord of the Admiralty, ii. 193

Sexton, Thomas, ii. 232

Seymour, Admiral, relieves Pekin, i. 162

Shamrock to be worn by Irish soldiers, ii. 50

Shantung, German missionaries murdered in, i. 129

Shaw, Flora L., i. 10 sqq.; telegrams to C. Rhodes, 11, 12; evidence before South African Committee, 12 sqq.; distinguishes between 'plan' or 'raid,' 15

Shiel, Richard Lalor, ii. 252

Simonstown, i. 247

Sims Reeves, John, ii. 240

Sipido attempts to assassinate Prince of Wales, ii. 224

Smith, Samuel, resolution on lowlinesson in Church of England, i. 214

Socialism, working-men and, i. 95

Soudan, Egyptian, 'repayment for civilisation' of, i. 150

South Africa: trouble with native tribes, ii. 50; progress of civilisation in, 93

South African Committee: Flora L. Shaw recalled, i. 3 sqq.; crisis in inquiry, 21; report, 22 sqq.; 23 sqq.; further inquiry desired, 27, 28

Spain: Dispute with United States,

SYN

i. 242 sqq.; Assassination over Cuba, 243; refuses to sell Cuba, 252; war with United States, 261; treaty of peace, 262

Spectator, The, i. 270

Spencer, Herbert, i. 345; ii. 275

Spicer, A., i. 408

Sport, reforms in, ii. 262

Staal, M. de, President of Peace Conference, i. 261

Stag-hunting, ii. 264

Stanhope, Philip, ii. 180; resolution on Report of South African Committee, i. 24, 25; voting on, 28

Stanley, Dean, invites Max-Müller to lecture in Westminster Abbey, ii. 212

Stansfeld, James, i. 205; sympathy with Italy, 205, 206; friendship for Mazzini, 205, 206; M.P. for Halifax, 207; tribute to Count Cavour, 206; Junior Lord of the Admiralty, 206; Under-Secretary of State for War, 206

Stanvenu, George Warrington, ii. 127

Stephenson, Robert, i. 326

Steyn, President of Orange Free State, on union of South African States, ii. 92

Strikes, i. 70; principle of mediation, 72; peaceful arbitration, 73; dockers' strike, 77

Suffrage for women, i. 225

Sugiyama, Chancellor of Japanese Legation, murdered, i. 164

Sullivan, Sir Arthur, ii. 214 sqq.

Swanwick, Anna, sketch of her life and work, i. 243

Swinburne, Algernon Charles, i. 334; ii. 180, 276

Synge, Dr., 'Speech of the Picturesque,' ii. 249

TAK

TAKU Forts, i. 162, 172
Tata Gallery, ii. 241
Taxation in England and Ireland, ii. 40 *sqq.*
Tchad, Lake, France's claim to north and east shores of, i. 106
Teck, Princess Mary of, i. 280
Telamones, Flora Shaw's telegraphic name, i. 11
Telegrams from C. Rhodes, Flora Shaw, &c., i. 10 *sqq.*, 17, 18
Telegraph, first complete line, ii. 60
Telephones, ii. 243
Temperance movement, ii. 162, 250
Temple Bar, ii. 271
Temple, Dr., Archbishop of Canterbury, speech on ritualism in English Church, i. 211
Tennyson, Alfred, Lord, ii. 373
Terriss, William, stabbed, i. 288
Thackeray, W. M., ii. 373; lectures, 344
Theatres, ii. 343
Thomas, Alfred, tribute to Gladstone, i. 110
Tichborne case, i. 315
Tien-tsin, relief expedition starts from, i. 180
Times, Flora L. Shaw acts for, i. 10, 14
Tisza, Theobald Wolf, ii. 322
Toronto, Archbishop of, suggests National Convention, ii. 52
Transvaal, crisis in, 1897, i. 22; rising of Boers in, 283; franchise question, ii. 92, 93; conditions of, 94
Transvaal raid (*see* Jameson raid)
Travel, system of, ii. 338; slow and rapid, 348
Trevelyan, Sir George Otto, sketch of career, ii. 175 *sqq.*
Trout-fishing, ii. 394
Tung, General, i. 164
Tung-Chau captured, i. 171

VOL. II.

TUR

Turkey and Greece, peace signed between, i. 50
Turkish misrule in Crete, i. 39, 41, 44
Turkish troops defeat Greeks, i. 46
Tyndall, John, ii. 378

UNITED Irish League, ii. 39, 42
United States, constitution of, i. 4; advocates of women's rights, 27; dispute with Spain, 345 *sqq.*, 373; surveys suggested sale of Cuba, 341; sympathy with Cubans, 342; intervenes, 344; declare war against Spain, 346; imperialism in, 362, 363; treaty of peace signed, 352; conditions of franchise, ii. 34

VELDSCHOEN, C. Rhodes' telegraphic name, i. 10
Victoria, Queen, visits Ireland, ii. 37 *sqq.*; orders shamrock to be worn, 39; message to first Governor-General of Australian Commonwealth, 243; illness, 249; message to Mrs. Creighton, 250; her death, 253; her domestic life, 254; as a constitutional sovereign, 254, 255; her love for Scotland, 257; funeral, 260 *sqq.*; her influence over amusements, 344
Victoria, Queen, reign of, epidemics during, ii. 281; wars during, 284; constitutional reforms, 285; development of arts of peace, 350 *sqq.*
Villiers, Charles Pelham, leader of Free Trade Movement, i. 294, 300; motion for repeal of Corn Laws, 301
Vivisection, ii. 395 *sqq.*
Vote by ballot, ii. 308

2 c

WAL

WALES, grievances of, i. 382
Wallace, Sir Richard, Art collections, ii. 240
Walpole, Spencer Horatio, i. 322; Home Secretary, 322, 323
War correspondents, ii. 333
War Cry, ii. 25
War in South Africa (*see* Boer War)
Warren, Sir Charles, in South Africa, ii. 113
Washington, treaty between Great Britain and United States signed, ii. 234
Water supply, ii. 347
Waterhouse, E., on Committee on Salvation Army Scheme, ii. 24
Wauchope, Major-General Andrew Gilbert, ii. 136
Wealth, increasing influence of, ii. 356
Webster, Sir Richard, Attorney-General, speeches on Ritualism, i. 197, 220
Wei-hai-wei leased to England, i. 150
Westminster, Hugh Lupus Grosvenor, Duke of, ii. 78
Westminster Review, i. 279
Williams, Sir Monier, ii. 212
Wireless telegraphy, ii. 236 *seqq.*, 340
Wiseman, Cardinal, Pastoral, 322
Wolff, Sir Henry Drummond: "Some Maxims of the late Lord Dalling and Bulwer," ii. 109; member of Fourth Party, 323
Women, education of, i. 230; as nurses and doctors, 233; as lawyers and organisers, 235; International Congress of, 236; temperance associations, 236; disabilities, 237; co-operation of, 238; as aldermen or councillors, 403, 406, 407, 408
Women smokers, ii. 245
Women's rights, i. 226 *seqq.*; suffrage, 229 *seqq.*, 239, 241; change of public opinion on, 241
Women's suffrage, ii. 361
Working classes, improvement in conditions, i. 63; organisations and union, 64; property qualification for M.P.s, 64; votes of, 65, 68; labour M.P.s, 66 *seqq.*; congresses of, 68; character and capacity of M.P.s, 69; socialism and, 86; patient and orderly, 89
Workmen's Compensation for Accidents Act, i. 90 *seqq.*
Wych Street, ii. 348

YORK, Archbishop of, on women in municipal government, i. 407
York, Duke and Duchess of, open Australian Parliament, ii. 146
Yoxall, J. H., on Education of Children Bill, ii. 7

THE END

Printed by BALLANTYNE, HANSON & Co.
Edinburgh & London

ALPHABETICAL CATALOGUE OF BOOKS
IN
FICTION AND GENERAL LITERATURE
PUBLISHED BY

JUNE   CHATTO & WINDUS   1905

111 ST. MARTIN'S LANE, CHARING CROSS

Telegrams   LONDON, W.C.   *Telephone No.*
Bookstore, London   8524 *Central*

A B C (The) of Cricket: a Black View of the Game. (26 Illustrations.) By HUGH FIELDING Demy 8vo, 1s.

ADAMS (W. DAVENPORT), Books by.
A Dictionary of the Drama: A Guide to the Plays, Playwrights, Players, and Playhouses of the United Kingdom and America, from the Earliest Times to the Present. Vol. I. (A to G). Demy 8vo, cloth, 10s. 6d. net.
Quips and Quiddities. Selected by W. D. ADAMS. Post 8vo, cloth, 2s. 6d.

AGONY COLUMN (The) of 'The Times,' from 1800 to 1870. Edited by ALICE CLAY. Post 8vo, cloth, 2s. 6d.

ALDEN (W. L.). — Drewitt's Dream. Crown 8vo, cloth, 6s.

ALEXANDER (Mrs.), Novels by.
Post 8vo, Illustrated boards, 2s. each.
Maid, Wife, or Widow?
Blind Fate.

Crown 8vo, cloth, 3s. 6d. each; post 8vo, picture boards, 2s. each.
Valerie's Fate.
A Life Interest.
Mona's Choice.
By Woman's Wit.

Crown 8vo, cloth, 3s. 6d. each.
The Cost of her Pride.
A Golden Autumn.
Barbara, Lady's Maid & Peeress.
Mrs. Crichton's Creditor.
A Missing Hero.
A Fight with Fate.
The Step-mother.

ALLEN (F. M.). — Green as Grass. Crown 8vo, cloth, 3s. 6d.

ANDERSON (MARY).—Othello's Occupation. Crown 8vo, cloth, 3s. 6d.

ANDREWS (E. BENJAMIN).—The United States in Our Own Time. With 500 Illustrations. Royal 8vo, cloth, 16s. net.

ANTROBUS (C. L.), Novels by.
Crown 8vo, cloth, 6s. each.
Quality Corner. | **Wildersmoor.**
The Wine of Finvarra.

ALLEN (GRANT), Books by.
Moorland Idylls. Crown 8vo, cloth, 6s.
Post-Prandial Philosophy. Crown 8vo, art linen, 3s. 6d.

Crown 8vo, cloth, 3s. 6d. each; post 8vo, illustrated boards, 2s. each.
Babylon. With 12 Illustrations.
Strange Stories.
The Beckoning Hand.
For Maimie's Sake.
Philistia. | **In all Shades.**
The Devil's Die.
This Mortal Coil.
The Tents of Shem.
The Great Taboo.
Dumaresq's Daughter.
Under Sealed Orders.
The Duchess of Powysland.
Blood Royal.
Ivan Greet's Masterpiece.
The Scallywag. With 24 Illustrations.
At Market Value.

The Tents of Shem. POPULAR EDITION, medium 8vo, 6d.

APPLETON (G. W.), Novels by.
Cr. 8vo, cl., 3s. 6d.
Rash Conclusions.
The Lady in Sables. Cr. 8vo, cl., 6s.

ARNOLD (E. L.), Stories by.
The Wonderful Adventures of Phra the Phœnician. Crown 8vo, cloth, with 12 Illustrations by H. M. PAGET, 3s. 6d.; post 8vo, Illustrated boards, 2s.
The Constable of St. Nicholas. With a Frontispiece. Crown 8vo, cloth, 3s. 6d.; picture cloth, flat back, 2s.

ASHTON (JOHN), Books by.
English Caricature and Satire on Napoleon the First. With 115 Illustrations. Crown 8vo, cloth, 7s. 6d.
Social Life in the Reign of Queen Anne. With 85 Illustrations. Crown 8vo, cloth, 3s. 6d.

Crown 8vo, cloth, 6s. each.
Social England under the Regency. With 90 Illustrations.
Florizel's Folly: The Story of GEORGE IV. and Mrs. FITZHERBERT. With 13 Illustrations.

CHATTO & WINDUS, PUBLISHERS.

ARTEMUS WARD'S Works. Crown 8vo, cloth, with Portrait, 3s. 6d.; post 8vo, illustrated boards, 2s.

ART (The) of AMUSING: A Collection of Graceful Arts, Games, Tricks, Puzzles, and Charades. By FRANK BELLEW. With 300 Illustrations. Crown 8vo cloth, 4s. 6d.

BACTERIA, Yeast Fungi, and Allied Species, A Synopsis of. By W. B. GROVE, B.A. With 87 Illustrations. Crown 8vo. cloth, 3s. 6d.

BARDSLEY (Rev. C. W.).—English Surnames: Their Sources and Significations. Cr. 8vo, cloth, 7s 6d.

BARING GOULD (S.), Novels by. Crown 8vo, cloth, 3s. 6d. each; post 8vo, illustrated boards, 2s. each.
Red Spider. | **Eve.**
Also the POPULAR EDITION of **Red Spider**, medium 8vo, 6d.

BARR (ROBERT), Stories by. Crown 8vo, cloth, 3s. 6d. each.
In a Steamer Chair. With 2 Illustrations by DEMAIN-HAMMOND.
From Whose Bourne, &c. With 47 Illustrations by HAL HURST and others.
Revenge! With 12 Illustrations by LANCELOT SPEED and others.
A Woman Intervenes.
A Prince of Good Fellows. With 15 Illustrations by E. J. SULLIVAN.

The Unchanging East: A Visit to the Farther Edge of the Mediterranean. Crown 8vo, cloth, 6s.

BARRETT (FRANK), Novels by.
Post 8vo, illustrated boards, 2s. each; cloth, 2s. 6d. each.
The Sin of Olga Zassoulich.
Between Life and Death.
Folly Morrison.
Little Lady Linton.
Honest Davie. | **Found Guilty.**
John Ford; and His Helpmate.
A Recoiling Vengeance.
Lieut. Barnabas.
For Love and Honour.

Crown 8vo, cloth, 3s. 6d. each; post 8vo, illustrated boards, 2s. each; cloth limp, 2s. 6d. each.
Fettered for Life.
A Missing Witness. With 8 Illustrations by W. H. MARGETSON.
The Woman of the Iron Bracelets.
The Harding Scandal.
A Prodigal's Progress.

Crown 8vo, cloth, 3s. 6d. each.
Under a Strange Mask. With 19 Illustrations by E. F. BREWTNALL.
Was She Justified?

Crown 8vo, cloth, 6s. each.
Lady Judas.
The Error of Her Ways.

BEACONSFIELD, LORD. By T. P. O'CONNOR, M.P. Crown 8vo, cloth, 5s.

BECHSTEIN (LUDWIG), and the Brothers GRIMM.—As Pretty as Seven, and other Stories. With 98 Illustrations by RICHTER. Square 8vo, cloth, 6s. 6d.; gilt edges, 7s. 6d.

BENNETT (ARNOLD), Novels by. Crown 8vo, cloth, gilt top, 6s. each.
Anna of the Five Towns.
Leonora. | **A Great Man.**
Teresa of Watling Street. With 8 Illustrations by FRANK GILLETT.
Tales of the Five Towns.

Crown 8vo, cloth, 3s. 6d. each.
The Grand Babylon Hotel.
The Gates of Wrath.

BENNETT (W. C.).—Songs for Sailors. Post 8vo, cloth, 2s.

BEWICK (THOMAS) and His Pupils. By AUSTIN DOBSON. With 95 Illustrations. Square 8vo, cloth, 3s. 6d.

BIERCE (AMBROSE).—In the Midst of Life. Crown 8vo, cloth, 3s. 6d.; post 8vo, illustrated boards, 2s.

BILL NYE'S Comic History of the United States. With 146 Illusts. by F. OPPER. Crown 8vo, cloth, 3s. 6d.

BINDLOSS (HAROLD), Novels by. Crown 8vo, cloth, 6s. each.
A Sower of Wheat.
The Concession-Hunters.
The Mistress of Bonaventure.
Daventry's Daughter.

Ainslie's Ju-Ju. Crown 8vo, cloth, 3s. 6d.; picture cloth, flat back, 2s.

BLUNDELL'S Worthies, 1604-1904. By M. L. BANKS, M.A. With 10 Illustrats. Demy 8vo, cloth, 7s. 6d. net.

BOCCACCIO.—The Decameron. With a Portrait. Pott 8vo, cloth, gilt top, 2s. net; leather, gilt edges, 3s. net.

BODKIN (Mc. D., K.C.), Books by.
Dora Myrl, the Lady Detective. Cr. 8vo, cl., 3s. 6d.; picture cl., flat back, 2s.

Crown 8vo, cloth, 3s. 6d. each.
Shillelagh and Shamrock.
Patsey the Omadaun.

BOURGET (PAUL).—A Living Lie. Translated by JOHN DE VILLIERS. Crown 8vo, cloth, 3s. 6d.

BOURNE (H. R. FOX), Books by.
English Merchants. With 32 Illustrations. Crown 8vo, cloth, 3s. 6d.
The Other Side of the Emin Pasha Expedition. Crown 8vo, cloth, 6s.

111 ST. MARTIN'S LANE, LONDON, W.C.   3

BESANT (Sir WALTER) and JAMES RICE, Novels by. Crown 8vo, cloth, 3s. 6d. each; post 8vo, illustrated boards, 2s. each; cloth limp, 2s. 6d. each.
Ready-Money Mortiboy.
The Golden Butterfly.
My Little Girl.
With Harp and Crown.
This Son of Vulcan.
The Monks of Thelema.
By Celia's Arbour.
The Chaplain of the Fleet.
The Seamy Side.
The Case of Mr. Lucraft.
'Twas in Trafalgar's Bay.
The Ten Years' Tenant.

BESANT (Sir WALTER), Novels by. Crown 8vo, cloth, 3s. 6d. each; post 8vo, illustrated boards, 2s. each; cloth limp, 2s. 6d. each.
All Sorts and Conditions of Men. With 12 Illustrations by FRED. BARNARD.
The Captains' Room, &c.
All in a Garden Fair. With 6 Illustrations by HARRY FURNISS.
Dorothy Forster. With Frontispiece.
Uncle Jack, and other Stories.
Children of Gibeon.
The World Went Very Well Then. With 12 Illustrations by A. FORESTIER.
Herr Paulus.
The Bell of St. Paul's.
For Faith and Freedom. With Illusts. by A. FORESTIER and F. WADDY.
To Call Her Mine, &c. With 9 Illustrations by A. FORESTIER.
The Holy Rose, &c. With Frontispiece.
Armorel of Lyonesse. With 12 Illustrations by F. BARNARD.
St. Katherine's by the Tower. With 12 Illustrations by C. GREEN.
Verbena Camellia Stephanotis.
The Ivory Gate.
The Rebel Queen.
Beyond the Dreams of Avarice. With 12 Illustrations by W. H. HYDE.
In Deacon's Orders, &c. With Frontis.
The Revolt of Man.
The Master Craftsman.
The City of Refuge.

Crown 8vo, cloth, 3s. 6d. each.
A Fountain Sealed.
The Changeling.
The Fourth Generation.
The Orange Girl. With 8 Illustrations by F. PEGRAM.
The Alabaster Box.
The Lady of Lynn. With 12 Illustrations by G. DEMAIN-HAMMOND.
No Other Way. With 12 Illustrations by C. D. WARD. Crown 8vo, cloth, 6s.

Crown 8vo, picture cloth, flat back, 2s. each.
St. Katherine's by the Tower.
The Rebel Queen.

POPULAR EDITIONS, medium 8vo, 6d. each.
All Sorts and Conditions of Men.
The Golden Butterfly.
Ready-Money Mortiboy.
The Chaplain of the Fleet.

BESANT (Sir WALTER), Novels by—continued.
POPULAR EDITIONS, medium 8vo, 6d. each.
The Orange Girl.
For Faith and Freedom.
Children of Gibeon.
Dorothy Forster.

LARGE TYPE, FINE PAPER EDITIONS, pott 8vo, cloth, gilt top, 2s. net each; leather, gilt edges, 3s. net each.
All Sorts and Conditions of Men.
London.
Sir Richard Whittington.
Gaspard de Coligny.

Demy 8vo, cloth, 7s. 6d. each.
London. With 125 Illustrations.
Westminster. With Etching by F. S. WALKER, and 130 Illustrations.
South London. With Etching by F. S. WALKER, and 118 Illustrations.
East London. With Etching by F. S. WALKER, and 56 Illustrations by PHIL MAY, L. RAVEN HILL, and J. PENNELL.
Jerusalem. By WALTER BESANT and E. H. PALMER. With Map and 12 Illusts.

Crown 8vo, buckram, 6s. each.
As We Are and As We May Be.
Essays and Historiettes.
The Eulogy of Richard Jefferies.

Crown 8vo, cloth, 3s. 6d. each.
Fifty Years Ago. With 144 Illusts.
Gaspard de Coligny. With a Portrait.
Sir Richard Whittington.
The Charm, and other Drawing-room Plays. With 50 Illustrations by CHRIS HAMMOND, &c.

Art of Fiction. Fcap. 8vo, cloth, 1s. net.

BOYD.—A Versailles Christmas-tide. By MARY STUART BOYD. With 53 Illustrations by A. S. BOYD. Fcap. 4to, cloth, 6s.

BOYLE (F.), Works by. Post 8vo, illustrated boards, 2s. each.
Chronicles of No-Man's Land. | Camp Notes. | Savage Life.

BRAND (JOHN).—Observations on Popular Antiquities. With the Additions of Sir HENRY ELLIS. Crown 8vo, cloth, 3s. 6d.

BREWER'S (Rev. Dr.) Dictionaries. Crown 8vo, cloth, 3s. 6d. each.
The Reader's Handbook of Famous Names in Fiction, Allusions, References, Proverbs, Plots, Stories, and Poems.
A Dictionary of Miracles: Imitative, Realistic, and Dogmatic.

BREWSTER (Sir DAVID), Works by. Post 8vo, cloth, 4s. 6d. each.
More Worlds than One: The Creed of the Philosopher and the Hope of the Christian. With Plates.
The Martyrs of Science: GALILEO TYCHO BRAHE, and KEPLER.
Letters on Natural Magic. With numerous Illustrations.

BRAYSHAW (J. DODSWORTH).
—Slum Silhouettes: Stories of London Life. Crown 8vo, cloth, 3s. 6d.

BRIGHT (FLORENCE).—A Girl Capitalist. Crown 8vo cloth. 6s.

BRILLAT-SAVARIN. — Gastronomy as a Fine Art. Translated by R. E. ANDERSON. Post 8vo, half-cl., 2s.

BRYDEN (H. A.).—An Exiled Scot. With Frontispiece by J. S. CROMPTON, R.I. Crown 8vo, cloth, 3s. 6d.

BRYDGES (HAROLD). — Uncle Sam at Home. With 91 Illustrations. Post 8vo, illustrated boards, 2s.; cloth limp, 2s, 6d.

BUCHANAN (ROBERT), Poems and Novels by.
The Complete Poetical Works of Robert Buchanan. 2 Vols., crown 8vo, buckram, with Portrait Frontispiece to each volume, 12s.

Crown 8vo, cloth, 3s. 6d. each; post 8vo, illustrated boards, 2s. each.
The Shadow of the Sword.
A Child of Nature.
God and the Man. With 11 Illustrations by F. BARNARD.
Lady Kilpatrick.
The Martyrdom of Madeline.
Love Me for Ever.
Annan Water. | **Foxglove Manor.**
The New Abelard. | **Rachel Dene.**
Matt: A Story of a Caravan.
The Master of the Mine.
The Heir of Linne.
Woman and the Man.

Crown 8vo, cloth, 3s. 6d. each.
Red and White Heather.
Andromeda.

POPULAR EDITIONS, medium 8vo, 6d. each.
The Shadow of the Sword.
God and the Man.

The Charlatan. By ROBERT BUCHANAN and HENRY MURRAY. Crown 8vo, cloth, with Frontispiece by T. H. ROBINSON, 3s. 6d.; post 8vo, illustrated boards, 2s.

BURGESS (GELETT) and WILL IRWIN. — The Picaroons: A San Francisco Night's Entertainment. Crown 8vo, cloth, 3s. 6d.

BURTON (ROBERT). — The Anatomy of Melancholy. Demy 8vo, cloth, 7s. 6d.
Melancholy Anatomised. An Abridgment of BURTON'S ANATOMY. Post 8vo, half-cloth, 2s. 6d.

CAMERON (Commander V. LOVETT). — The Cruise of the 'Black Prince' Privateer. Post 8vo, picture boards, 2s.

CAMPBELL (A. GODRIC).—A Daughter of France. Cr. 8vo, cl., 6s.

CAINE (HALL), Novels by.
Crown 8vo, cloth, 3s. 6d. each; post 8vo, illustrated boards, 2s. each; cloth limp, 2s. 6d. each.
The Shadow of a Crime.
A Son of Hagar.
The Deemster.
Also LIBRARY EDITIONS of the three novels, crown 8vo, cloth, 6s. each; CHEAP POPULAR EDITIONS, medium 8vo, portrait cover, 6d. each; and the FINE PAPER EDITION of **The Deemster**, pott 8vo, cloth, gilt top, 2s. net; leather, gilt edges, 3s. net

CANADA (Greater): The Past, Present, and Future of the Canadian North-West. By E. B. OSBORN, B.A. With a Map. Crown 8vo, cloth, 3s. 6d.

CAPTAIN COIGNET, Soldier of the Empire. Edited by LOREDAN LARCHEY, and Translated by Mrs. CAREY. With 100 Illusts. Cr. 8vo, cloth, 3s. 6d.

CARLYLE (THOMAS).—On the Choice of Books. Post 8vo, cloth, 1s. 6d.

CARRUTH (HAYDEN). — The Adventures of Jones. With 17 Illustrations. Fcap. 8vo, picture cover, 1s.; cloth, 1s. 6d.

CHAMBERS (ROBERT W.), Stories of Paris Life by.
The King in Yellow. Crown 8vo, cloth, 3s. 6d.; fcap. 8vo, cloth limp, 2s 6d.
In the Quarter. Fcap. 8vo, cloth, 2s. 6d.

CHAPMAN'S (GEORGE) Works.
Vol. I., Plays Complete, including the Doubtful Ones.—Vol. II., Poems and Minor Translations, with Essay by A. C. SWINBURNE,—Vol. III., Translations of the Iliad and Odyssey. Three Vols., crown 8vo, cloth, 3s. 6d. each.

CHAUCER for Children: A Golden Key. By Mrs. H. R. HAWEIS. With 8 Coloured Plates and 30 Woodcuts. Crown 4to, cloth, 3s. 6d.

Chaucer for Schools. With the Story of his Times and his Work. By Mrs. H. R. HAWEIS. With Frontispiece. Demy 8vo, cloth, 2s. 6d.

CHESS, The Laws and Practice of. With an Analysis of the Openings. By HOWARD STAUNTON. Edited by R. B. WORMALD. Crown 8vo, cloth, 5s.
The Minor Tactics of Chess: A Treatise on the Deployment of the Forces in obedience to Strategic Principle. By F. K. YOUNG and E. C. HOWELL. Fcap. 8vo, cloth, 2s. 6d.
The Hastings Chess Tournament. The Authorised Account of the 230 Games played Aug.-Sept., 1895. With Annotations by PILLSBURY, LASKER, TARRASCH, STEINITZ, SCHIFFERS, TEICHMANN, BARDELEBEN, BLACKBURNE, GUNSBERG, TINSLEY, MASON, and ALBIN; Biographical Sketches, and 22 Portraits. Edited by H. F. CHESHIRE. Crown 8vo, cloth, 5s.

111 ST. MARTIN'S LANE, LONDON, W.C.

CHAPPLE (J. M.).—The Minor Chord. Crown 8vo, cloth 3s. 6d.

CLARE (AUSTIN), Stories by.
For the Love of a Lass. Post 8vo, illustrated boards, 2s.
By the Rise of the River. Crown 8vo, cloth, 3s. 6d.

Crown 8vo, cloth, 6s. each.
The Tideway.
Randal of Randalholme.

CLIVE (Mrs. ARCHER), Novels by. Post 8vo, cloth, 3s. 6d. each; illustrated boards, 2s. each.
Paul Ferroll.
Why Paul Ferroll Killed his Wife.

CLODD (EDWARD). — Myths and Dreams. Crown 8vo, cloth, 3s. 6d.

COATES (ANNE).—Rie's Diary. Crown 8vo, cloth, 3s. 6d.

COBBAN (J. MACLAREN), Novels by.
The Cure of Souls. Post 8vo, Illustrated boards, 2s.
The Red Sultan. Crown 8vo, cloth, 3s. 6d.; post 8vo, illustrated boards, 2s.
The Burden of Isabel. Crown 8vo, cloth, 3s. 6d.

COLLINS (J. CHURTON, M.A.), Books by. Cr. 8vo, cloth, 3s. 6d. each.
Illustrations of Tennyson.
Jonathan Swift.

COLLINS (MORTIMER and FRANCES), Novels by. Crown 8vo, cloth, 3s. 6d. each; post 8vo, illustrated boards, 2s. each.
From Midnight to Midnight.
You Play me False.
Blacksmith and Scholar.
The Village Comedy.

Post 8vo, illustrated boards, 2s. each.
Transmigration.
A Fight with Fortune.
Sweet Anne Page.
Sweet and Twenty.
Frances.

COLMAN'S (GEORGE) Humorous Works: 'Broad Grins,' 'My Nightgown and Slippers,' &c. With Life and Frontis. Crown 8vo, cl., 3s. 6d.

COLQUHOUN (M. J.).—Every Inch a Soldier. Crown 8vo, cloth, 3s. 6d.; post 8vo, illustrated boards, 2s.

COLT-BREAKING, Hints on. By W. M. Hutchison. Cr. 8vo, cl., 3s. 6d.

COMPTON (HERBERT), by.
The Inimitable Mrs. Massingham. Crown 8vo, cloth, 3s. 6d.

Crown 8vo, cloth, 6s. each.
The Wilful Way.
The Queen can do no Wrong.

COLLINS (WILKIE), Novels by. Cr. 8vo, cl., 3s. 6d. each; post 8vo, picture boards, 2s. each; cl. limp, 2s. 6d. each.
Antonina. | Basil.
Hide and Seek
The Woman in White.
The Moonstone. | Man and Wife.
The Dead Secret. | After Dark.
The Queen of Hearts.
No Name. | My Miscellanies.
Armadale. | Poor Miss Finch.
Miss or Mrs ?
The New Magdalen.
The Frozen Deep.
The Law and the Lady.
The Two Destinies.
The Haunted Hotel.
The Fallen Leaves.
Jezebel's Daughter.
The Black Robe.
Heart and Science. | 'I Say No.'
A Rogue's Life.
The Evil Genius. | Little Novels.
The Legacy of Cain. | Blind Love.

Popular Editions, medium 8vo, 6d. each.
The Moonstone.
The Woman in White.
Antonina. | The New Magdalen.
The Dead Secret. | No Name.
Man and Wife. | Armadale.

The Woman in White. Large Type, Fine Paper Edition. Pott 8vo, cloth, gilt top, 2s. net; leather, gilt edges, 3s. net.
The Frozen Deep. Large Type Edition. Fcap. 8vo, cloth, 1s. net; leather, 1s. 6d. net.

COOPER (E. H.).—Geoffory Hamilton. Crown 8vo, cloth, 3s. 6d.

CORNISH (J. F.).—Sour Grapes. Crown 8vo, cloth, 6s.

CORNWALL.— Popular Romances of the West of England: The Drolls, Traditions, and Superstitions of Old Cornwall. Collected by Robert Hunt, F.R.S. With two Plates by George Cruikshank. Cr. 8vo, cl., 7s. 6d.

CRADDOCK (C. EGBERT), by.
The Prophet of the Great Smoky Mountains. Crown 8vo, cloth, 3s. 6d. post 8vo, illustrated boards, 2s.
His Vanished Star. Crown 8vo, cloth, 3s. 6d.

CRELLIN (H. N.).—Romances of the Old Seraglio. With 28 Illusts. by S. L. Wood. Crown 8vo, cloth, 3s. 6d.

CRESSWELL (HENRY). — A Lady of Misrule. Crown 8vo, cloth, 6s.

CROCKETT (S. R.) and others.— Tales of our Coast. By S. R. Crockett, Gilbert Parker, Harold Frederic, 'Q.,' and W. Clark Russell. With 13 Illustrations by Frank Brangwyn. Crown 8vo, cloth, 3s. 6d.

CHATTO & WINDUS, PUBLISHERS,

CRIM (MATT).—Adventures of a Fair Rebel. Crown 8vo, cloth, 3s. 6d.; post 8vo, illustrated boards, 2s.

CROKER (Mrs. B. M.), Novels by. Crown 8vo, cloth, 3s. 6d. each; post 8vo, illustrated boards, 2s. each; cloth limp, 2s. 6d. each.
Pretty Miss Neville.
Proper Pride:
A Bird of Passage.
Diana Barrington.
Two Masters. | Interference.
A Family Likeness:
A Third Person. | Mr. Jervis.
Village Tales & Jungle Tragedies.
The Real Lady Hilda.
Married or Single?

Crown 8vo, cloth, 3s. 6d. each.
Some One Else.
In the Kingdom of Kerry:
Miss Balmaine's Past.
Jason. | Beyond the Pale.
Terence: With 6 Illusts. by S. PAGET.
The Cat's-paw: With 12 Illustrations by FRED PEGRAM.

Infatuation. Crown 8vo, cloth, 3s. 6d.; post 8vo, cloth limp, 2s. 6d.
'To Let.' Post 8vo, picture boards, 2s.; cloth limp, 2s. 6d.

POPULAR EDITIONS, medium 8vo, 6d. each.
Diana Barrington.
Pretty Miss Neville.
A Bird of Passage.

CRUIKSHANK'S COMIC ALMANACK. Complete in TWO SERIES. The FIRST, from 1835 to 1843; the SECOND, from 1844 to 1853. A Gathering of the Best Humour of THACKERAY, HOOD, ALBERT SMITH, &c. With numerous Steel Engravings and Woodcuts by CRUIKSHANK, LANDELLS, &c. Two Vols., crown 8vo, cloth, 7s. 6d. each.

The Life of George Cruikshank. By BLANCHARD JERROLD. With 84 Illustrations and a Bibliography. Crown 8vo, cloth, 3s. 6d.

CUMMING (C. F. GORDON), Works by. Demy 8vo, cloth, 6s. each.
In the Hebrides. With 24 Illustrations.
In the Himalayas and on the Indian Plains. With 42 Illustrations.
Two Happy Years in Ceylon. With 28 Illustrations.
Via Cornwall to Egypt.

CUSSANS (JOHN E.).—A Handbook of Heraldry; Including instructions for Tracing Pedigrees, Deciphering Ancient MSS., &c. With 408 Woodcuts and 2 Colrd. Plates. Crown 8vo, cloth, 6s.

CYCLING, HUMOURS OF. By JEROME K JEROME, H. G. WELLS, BARRY PAIN, CLARENCE ROOK, W. PETT RIDGE, J. F. SULLIVAN, and others. With Illusts. Crown 8vo, cloth, 1s. net.

DAUDET (ALPHONSE). — The Evangelist; or, Port Salvation. Translated by C. H. MELTZER. Cr. 8vo, cloth, 3s. 6d.; post 8vo, illustrated bds., 2s.

DAVENANT (FRANCIS).—Hints for Parents on the Choice of a Profession for their Sons when Starting in Life. Crown 8vo, 1s. 6d.

DAVIDSON (HUGH COLEMAN). —Mr. Sadler's Daughters. Crown 8vo, cloth, 3s. 6d.

DAVIES (Dr. N. E. YORKE-), Works by. Crown 8vo, 1s. each; cloth, 1s. 6d. each.
One Thousand Medical Maxims and Surgical Hints.
Nursery Hints: A Mother's Guide in Health and Disease.
Foods for the Fat: Dietetic Cure of Corpulency, Gout, and excessive Leanness.
Aids to Long Life. Crown 8vo, 2s.; cloth, 2s. 6d.

DAVIES' (Sir JOHN) Complete Poetical Works. Edited with Notes, by Rev. A. B. GROSART, D.D. Two Vols., crown 8vo, cloth, 3s. 6d. each.

DEAKIN (DOROTHEA). — The Poet and the Pierrot. Crown 8vo, cloth, 3s. 6d.

DEFOE (DANIEL). — Robinson Crusoe. With 37 Illusts. by GEORGE CRUIKSHANK. LARGE TYPE, FINE PAPER EDITION. Pott 8vo, cloth, gilt top, 2s. net; leather, gilt edges, 3s. net.

DE GUERIN (MAURICE), The Journal of. With a Memoir by SAINTE-BEUVE. Translated by JESSIE P. FROTHINGHAM. Fcap. 8vo, half-cloth, 2s. 6d.

DE MAISTRE (XAVIER).—A Journey Round my Room. Translated by HENRY ATTWELL. Post 8vo, cloth, 2s. 6d.

DE MILLE (JAMES).—A Strange Manuscript found in a Copper Cylinder. Crown 8vo, cloth, with 19 Illustrations by GILBERT GAUL, 3s. 6d.; post 8vo, illustrated boards. 2s.

DEWAR (T. R.). — A Ramble Round the Globe. With 220 Illustrations. Crown 8vo, cloth, 7s. 6d.

DE WINDT (HARRY).—Through the Gold-Fields of Alaska to Bering Straits. With Map and 33 Illustrations. Demy 8vo, cloth, 6s.

DICKENS (CHARLES), The Life of, as Revealed in his Writings. By PERCY FITZGERALD, F.S.A. With Portraits and Facsimile Letters. 2 vols., demy 8vo, cloth, 21s. net.
About England with Dickens. By ALFRED RIMMER. With 57 Illustrations. Square 8vo, cloth, 3s. 6d.

DICTIONARIES.

The Reader's Handbook of Famous Names in Fiction, Allusions, References, Proverbs, Plots, Stories, and Poems. By Rev. E. C. BREWER, LL.D. Crown 8vo, cloth, 3s. 6d.

A Dictionary of Miracles: Imitative, Realistic, and Dogmatic. By Rev. E. C. BREWER, LL.D. Crown 8vo, cloth, 3s. 6d.

Familiar Allusions. By WILLIAM A. and CHARLES G. WHEELER. Demy 8vo, cloth, 7s. 6d. net.

Familiar Short Sayings of Great Men. With Historical and Explanatory Notes by SAMUEL A. BENT, A.M. Crown 8vo, cloth, 7s. 6d.

The Slang Dictionary: Etymological, Historical, and Anecdotal. Crown 8vo, cloth, 6s. 6d.

Words, Facts, and Phrases: A Dictionary of Curious, Quaint, and Out-of-the-Way Matters. By ELIEZER EDWARDS. Crown 8vo, cloth, 3s. 6d.

DILKE (Sir CHARLES, M.P.).
—**The British Empire.** Crown 8vo, buckram, 3s. 6d.

DOBSON (AUSTIN), Works by.
Thomas Bewick and his Pupils. With 95 Illusts. Sq. 8vo, cloth, 3s. 6d.

Crown 8vo, buckram, 6s. each.

Four Frenchwomen. With Four Portraits.

Eighteenth Century Vignettes. In Three Series, each 6s.

A Paladin of Philanthropy, and other Papers. With 2 Illustrations.

Side-walk Studies. With 5 Illusts.

DOBSON (W. T.).—Poetical Ingenuities and Eccentricities. Post 8vo, cloth, 2s. 6d.

DOWLING (RICHARD). — Old Corcoran's Money. Cr. 8vo, cl., 3s. 6d.

DOYLE (A. CONAN).—The Firm of Girdlestone. Crown 8vo, cloth, 3s. 6d.

DRAMATISTS, THE OLD.
Edited by Col. CUNNINGHAM. Cr. 8vo, cloth, with Portraits, 3s. 6d. per Vol.

Ben Jonson's Works. With Notes, Critical and Explanatory, and a Biographical Memoir by WILLIAM GIFFORD. Three Vols.

Chapman's Works. Three Vols. Vol. I. contains the Plays complete; Vol. II., Poems and Minor Translations, with an Essay by A. C. SWINBURNE; Vol. III., Translations of the Iliad and Odyssey.

Marlowe's Works. One Vol.

Massinger's Plays. From GIFFORD'S Text. One Vol.

DUBLIN CASTLE and Dublin Society, Recollections of. By A NATIVE. Crown 8vo, cloth, 6s.

DONOVAN (DICK), Detective Stories by. Post 8vo, illustrated boards, 2s. each; cloth limp, 2s. 6d. each.
Riddles Read. | **Link by Link.**
Caught at Last.
Suspicion Aroused.
Tracked and Taken.
Who Poisoned Hetty Duncan?
A Detective's Triumphs.
In the Grip of the Law.
From Information Received.
Tracked to Doom.

Crown 8vo, cloth, 3s. 6d. each.

The Records of Vincent Trill, of the Detective Service. —Also picture cloth, flat back, 2s.

The Adventures of Tyler Tatlock, Private Detective.

Deacon Brodie; or, Behind the Mask.

Tales of Terror.

Crown 8vo, cl., 3s. 6d. each; picture cl., flat back, 2s. each; post 8vo, illustrated boards, 2s. each; cloth limp, 2s. 6d. each.

The Man from Manchester.

The Mystery of Jamaica Terrace.

The Man-Hunter. Post 8vo, illustrated boards, 2s.; cloth limp, 2s. 6d.; picture cloth, flat back, 2s.

Dark Deeds. Crown 8vo, cloth limp, 2s. 6d.; picture cloth, flat back, 2s.

The Chronicles of Michael Danevitch. Crown 8vo, cloth, 3s. 6d.; post 8vo, illustrated boards, 2s.; cloth limp, 2s. 6d.

Wanted! Crown 8vo, picture cloth, flat back, 2s.; post 8vo, illustrated boards, 2s.; cloth limp, 2s. 6d.

DUNCAN (SARA JEANNETTE), Books by. Cr. 8vo, cloth, 7s. 6d. each.

A Social Departure. With 111 Illustrations by F. H. TOWNSEND.

An American Girl in London. With 80 Illustrations by F. H. TOWNSEND.

The Simple Adventures of a Memsahib. With 37 Illustrations by F. H. TOWNSEND.

Crown 8vo, cloth, 3s. 6d. each.

A Daughter of To-Day.

Vernon's Aunt. With 47 Illustrations by HAL HURST.

DUTT (ROMESH C.).—England and India: Progress during One Hundred Years Crown 8vo, cloth, 2s.

EARLY ENGLISH POETS.
Edited, with Introductions and Notes, by Rev. A. B. GROSART, D.D. Crown 8vo, cloth, 3s. 6d. per Volume.

Fletcher's (Giles) Complete Poems. One Vol.

Davies' (Sir John) Complete Poetical Works. Two Vols.

Sidney's (Sir Philip) Complete Poetical Works. Three Vols.

EDGCUMBE (Sir E. R. PEARCE).—Zephyrus: A Holiday in Brazil and on the River Plate. With 41 Illustrations. Crown 8vo, cloth 5s.

CHATTO & WINDUS, PUBLISHERS,

EDWARDES (Mrs. ANNIE), Novels by.
A Point of Honour. Post 8vo, Illustrated boards, 2s.
Archie Lovell. Crown 8vo, cloth, 3s. 6d.; post 8vo, illustrated boards, 2s.
A Plaster Saint. Cr. 8vo, cloth, 3s. 6d.

EDWARDS (ELIEZER). Words, Facts, and Phrases: A Dictionary of Curious, Quaint, and Out-of-the-Way Matters. Crown 8vo, cloth, 3s. 6d.

EGERTON (Rev. J. C.).— Sussex Folk and Sussex Ways. With Introduction by Rev. Dr. H. WACE, and Four Illusts. Crown 8vo, cloth, 5s.

EGGLESTON (EDWARD).— Roxy. Post 8vo, illustrated boards, 2s.

ENGLISHMAN (An) in Paris: Recollections of Louis Philippe and the Empire. Crown 8vo, cloth, 3s. 6d.

ENGLISHMAN'S HOUSE, The: A Practical Guide for Selecting or Building a House. By C. J. RICHARDSON. With Coloured Frontispiece and 534 Illustrations. Crown 8vo, cloth, 3s. 6d.

EYES, Our: How to Preserve Them. By JOHN BROWNING. Crown 8vo, cloth, 1s.

FAMILIAR ALLUSIONS: Miscellaneous Information, including Celebrated Statues, Paintings, Palaces, Country Seats, Ruins, Churches, Ships, Streets, Clubs, Natural Curiosities, &c. By W. A. and C. G. WHEELER. Demy 8vo, cloth, 7s. 6d. net.

FAMILIAR SHORT SAYINGS of Great Men. By S. A. BENT, A.M. Crown 8vo, cloth, 7s. 6d.

FARADAY (MICHAEL), Works by. Post 8vo, cloth, 4s. 6d. each.
The Chemical History of a Candle: Lectures delivered before a Juvenile Audience. Edited by WILLIAM CROOKES, F.C.S. With numerous Illusts.
On the Various Forces of Nature, and their Relations to each other. Edited by WILLIAM CROOKES, F.C.S. With Illustrations.

FARRER (J. ANSON).—War: Three Essays. Crown 8vo, cloth, 1s. 6d.

FICTION, a Catalogue of, with Descriptive Notices and Reviews of a THOUSAND NOVELS, will be sent free by CHATTO & WINDUS upon application.

FIN-BEC. The Cupboard Papers: The Art of Living and Dining. Post 8vo, cloth, 2s. 6d.

FIREWORK-MAKING, The Complete Art of; or, The Pyrotechnist's Treasury. By THOMAS KENTISH. With 267 Illustrations. Cr. 8vo, cloth, 3s. 6d.

FENN (G. MANVILLE), Novels by. Crown 8vo, cloth, 3s. 6d. each; post 8vo, illustrated boards, 2s. each.
The New Mistress.
Witness to the Deed.
The Tiger Lily.
The White Virgin.

Crown 8vo, cloth, 3s. 6d. each.
A Woman Worth Winning.
Cursed by a Fortune.
The Case of Ailsa Gray.
Commodore Junk.
Black Blood. | **In Jeopardy.**
Double Cunning.
A Fluttered Dovecote.
King of the Castle.
The Master of the Ceremonies.
The Story of Antony Grace.
The Man with a Shadow.
One Maid's Mischief.
This Man's Wife.
The Bag of Diamonds, and Three Bits of Paste.

Crown 8vo, cloth, gilt top, 6s. each.
Running Amok. | **Black Shadows.**
The Cankerworm.

A Crimson Crime. Crown 8vo, cloth, 6s.; picture cloth, flat back, 2s.

FITZGERALD (PERCY), by.
Little Essays: Passages from the Letters of CHARLES LAMB. Post 8vo, cloth, 2s. 6d.
Fatal Zero. Crown 8vo, cloth, 3s. 6d.; post 8vo, illustrated boards, 2s.

Post 8vo, illustrated boards, 2s. each.
Bella Donna. | **Polly.**
The Lady of Brantome.
Never Forgotten.
The Second Mrs. Tillotson.
Seventy-five Brooke Street.

Sir Henry Irving. With Portrait. Crown 8vo, cloth, 1s. 6d.
The Life of Charles Dickens as Revealed in his Writings. With Portraits and Facsimilies. 2 vols. demy 8vo, cloth, 21s. net.

FLAMMARION (CAMILLE), Works by.
Popular Astronomy: A General Description of the Heavens. Translated by J. ELLARD GORE, F.R.A.S. With Three Plates and 288 Illustrations. Medium 8vo, cloth, 10s. 6d.
Urania: A Romance. With 87 Illustrations. Crown 8vo, cloth, 5s.

FLETCHER'S (GILES, B.D.) Complete Poems: Christ's Victorie in Heaven, Christ's Victorie on Earth, Christ's Triumph over Death, and Minor Poems. With Notes by Rev. A. B. GROSART, D.D. Crown 8vo, cloth, 3s. 6d.

FORBES (Hon. Mrs. WALTER). —Dumb. Crown 8vo, cloth, 3s. 6d.

FRANCILLON (R. E.), Novels by. Crown 8vo, cloth, 3s. 6d. each; post 8vo, Illustrated boards, 2s. each.
One by One | A Real Queen.
A Dog and his Shadow.
Ropes of Sand. With Illustrations.

Post 8vo, illustrated boards, 2s. each.
Queen Cophetua. | Olympia.
Romances of the Law.
King or Knave?

Jack Doyle's Daughter. Crown 8vo, cloth, 3s. 6d.

FREDERIC (HAROLD), Novels by. Post 8vo, cloth, 3s. 6d. each; illustrated boards, 2s. each.
Seth's Brother's Wife.
The Lawton Girl.

FRY'S (HERBERT) Royal Guide to the London Charities. Edited by JOHN LANE. Published Annually. Crown 8vo, cloth, 1s. 6d.

GARDENING BOOKS. Post 8vo, 1s. each; cloth, 1s. 6d. each.
A Year's Work in Garden and Greenhouse. By GEORGE GLENNY.
Household Horticulture. By TOM and JANE JERROLD. Illustrated.
The Garden that Paid the Rent. By TOM JERROLD.

GAULOT (PAUL), Books by.
The Red Shirts: A Tale of 'The Terror.' Translated by JOHN DE VILLIERS. Crown 8vo, cloth, with Frontispiece by STANLEY WOOD, 3s. 6d.; picture cloth, flat back, 2s.

Crown 8vo, cloth, 6s. each.
Love and Lovers of the Past. Translated by C. LAROCHE, M.A.
A Conspiracy under the Terror. Translated by C. LAROCHE, M.A. With Illustrations and Facsimiles.

GENTLEMAN'S MAGAZINE, The. 1s. Monthly. Contains Stories, Articles upon Literature, Science, Biography, and Art, and '**Table Talk**' by SYLVANUS URBAN.
⁎ *Bound Volumes for recent years,* 8s. 6d. *each. Covers for binding,* 2s. *each.*

GERARD (DOROTHEA).—A Queen of Curds and Cream. Crown 8vo, cloth, 3s. 6d.

GERMAN POPULAR STORIES. Collected by the Brothers GRIMM and Translated by EDGAR TAYLOR. With Introduction by JOHN RUSKIN, and 22 Steel Plates after GEORGE CRUIKSHANK. Square 8vo, cloth, gilt edges, 7s. 6d.

GIBBON (CHARLES), Novels by. Crown 8vo, cloth, 3s. 6d. each; post 8vo, Illustrated boards, 2s. each.
Robin Gray.
The Golden Shaft.
The Flower of the Forest.
The Braes of Yarrow.
Of High Degree.
Queen of the Meadow.

GIBBON (CHARLES), Novels by—*continued.*
Post 8vo, illustrated boards, 2s. each.
The Dead Heart.
For Lack of Gold.
What Will the World Say?
For the King. | A Hard Knot.
In Pastures Green.
In Love and War.
A Heart's Problem.
By Mead and Stream.
Fancy Free. | Loving a Dream.
In Honour Bound.
Heart's Delight. | Blood-Money.

GIBNEY (SOMERVILLE). — Sentenced! Crown 8vo, cloth, 1s. 6d.

GILBERT (WILLIAM).—James Duke, Costermonger. Post 8vo, illustrated boards, 2s.

GILBERT'S (W. S.) Original Plays. In 3 Series, post 8vo, 2s. 6d. each.
The FIRST SERIES contains: The Wicked World — Pygmalion and Galatea — Charity—The Princess—The Palace of Truth—Trial by Jury—Iolanthe.
The SECOND SERIES contains: Broken Hearts — Engaged — Sweethearts — Gretchen — Dan'l Druce—Tom Cobb —H.M.S. 'Pinafore'—The Sorcerer—The Pirates of Penzance.
The THIRD SERIES contains: Comedy and Tragedy — Foggerty's Fairy — Rosencrantz and Guildenstern—Patience—Princess Ida—The Mikado—Ruddigore —The Yeomen of the Guard—The Gondoliers—The Mountebanks—Utopia.

Eight Original Comic Operas written by W. S. GILBERT. Two Series, demy 8vo, cloth, 2s. 6d. each.
The FIRST SERIES contains: The Sorcerer —H.M.S. 'Pinafore'— The Pirates of Penzance — Iolanthe — Patience — Princess Ida—The Mikado—Trial by Jury.
The SECOND SERIES contains: The Gondoliers—The Grand Duke—The Yeomen of the Guard—His Excellency—Utopia, Limited—Ruddigore—The Mountebanks —Haste to the Wedding.

The Gilbert and Sullivan Birthday Book: Quotations for Every Day in the Year, selected from Plays by W. S. GILBERT. Compiled by A. WATSON. Royal 16mo, cloth, 2s. 6d.

GISSING (ALGERNON), Novels by. Crown 8vo, cloth, gilt top, 6s. each.
A Secret of the North Sea.
Knitters in the Sun.
The Wealth of Mallerstang.
An Angel's Portion.
Baliol Garth.

GLENNY (GEORGE).—A Year's Work in Garden and Greenhouse: Practical Advice as to the Management of the Flower, Fruit, and Frame Garden. Post 8vo, 1s.; cloth, 1s. 6d.

GODWIN (WILLIAM). — Lives of the Necromancers. Post 8vo, cloth, 2s.

GLANVILLE (ERNEST), Novels by. Crown 8vo, cloth, 3s. 6d. each; post 8vo, illustrated boards, 2s. each.
The Lost Heiress. With 2 Illustrations by HUME NISBET.
The Fossicker: A Romance of Mashonaland. ;Two Illusts. by HUME NISBET.
A Fair Colonist. With Frontispiece.

The Golden Rock. With Frontispiece by STANLEY WOOD. Cr. 8vo, cloth, 3s. 6d.
Tales from the Veld. With 12 Illustrations by M. NISBET. Crown 8vo, cloth, 3s. 6d.
Max Thornton. With 8 Illustrations by J. S. CROMPTON, R.I. Large crown 8vo cloth, gilt edges, 5s.

GOLDEN TREASURY of Thought, The: A Dictionary of Quotations from the Best Authors. By THEODORE TAYLOR. Cr. 8vo, cl., 3s. 6d.

GOODMAN (E. J.)—The Fate of Herbert Wayne. Cr. 8vo, cl., 3s. 6d.

GORE (J. ELLARD, F.R.A.S.).
—**The Stellar Heavens:** an Introduction to the Study of the Stars and Nebulæ. Crown 8vo, cloth, 2s. net.
Studies in Astronomy. With 8 Illustrations. Crown 8vo, cloth, 6s.

GRACE (ALFRED A.).—Tales of a Dying Race. Cr. 8vo, cl., 3s. 6d.

GREEKS AND ROMANS, The Life of the, described from Antique Monuments. By ERNST GUHL and W. KONER. Edited by Dr. F. HUEFFER. With 545 Illusts. Demy 8vo, cl., 7s. 6d.

GREEN (ANNA KATHARINE).
—**The Millionaire Baby.** Crown 8vo, cloth, 6s.

GREENWOOD (JAMES).—The Prisoner in the Dock. Crown 8vo, cloth 3s. 6d.

GREY (Sir GEORGE). — The Romance of a Proconsul. By JAMES MILNE. Crown 8vo, buckram, 6s.

GRIFFITH (CECIL).—Corinthia Marazion. Crown 8vo, cloth, 3s. 6d.

GRIFFITHS (Major A.).—No. 99, and Blue Blood. Crown 8vo, cloth, flat back, 2s.

GUNTER (A. CLAVERING).—A Florida Enchantment. Crown 8vo, cloth, 3s. 6d.

GUTTENBERG (VIOLET), Novels by. Crown 8vo, cloth, 6s. each.
Neither Jew nor Greek.
The Power of the Palmist.

GYP. — CLOCLO. Translated by NORA M. STATHAM. Crown 8vo, cloth, 3s. 6d.

HAIR, The: Its Treatment in Health, Weakness, and Disease. Translated from the German of Dr. J. PINCUS. Crown 8vo, 1s.; cloth, 1s. 6d.

HAKE (Dr. T. GORDON), Poems by. Crown 8vo, cloth, 6s. each.
New Symbols.
Legends of the Morrow.
The Serpent Play.

Maiden Ecstacy. Small 4to, cloth, 8s.

HALL (Mrs. S. C.).—Sketches of Irish Character. With Illustrations on Steel and Wood by CRUIKSHANK, MACLISE, GILBERT, and HARVEY. Demy 8vo, cloth, 7s. 6d.

HALL (OWEN), Novels by.
The Track of a Storm. Crown 8vo, picture cloth, flat back, 2s.
Jetsam. Crown 8vo, cloth, 3s. 6d.

Crown 8vo, cloth, 6s. each,
Eureka. | **Hernando.**

HARTE'S (BRET) Collected Works. LIBRARY EDITION, in Ten Volumes, crown 8vo, cloth, 6s. each.
Vol. I. COMPLETE POETICAL AND DRAMATIC WORKS. With Port.
„ II. THE LUCK OF ROARING CAMP—BOHEMIAN PAPERS—AMERICAN LEGENDS.
„ III. TALES OF THE ARGONAUTS—EASTERN SKETCHES.
„ IV. GABRIEL CONROY.
„ V. STORIES — CONDENSED NOVELS.
„ VI. TALES OF THE PACIFIC SLOPE.
„ VII. TALES OF THE PACIFIC SLOPE—II. With Portrait by JOHN PETTIE.
„ VIII. TALES OF PINE AND CYPRESS.
„ IX. BUCKEYE AND CHAPPARREL.
„ X. TALES OF TRAIL AND TOWN.

Bret Harte's Choice Works in Prose and Verse. With Portrait and 40 Illustrations. Crown 8vo, cloth, 3s. 6d.
Bret Harte's Poetical Works, including 'Some Later Verses.' Crown 8vo, buckram, 4s. 6d.
Some Later Verses: Crown 8vo, art linen, 5s.
In a Hollow of the Hills. Crown 8vo, picture cloth, flat back, 2s.
Condensed Novels. (Two Series in One Volume.) Pott 8vo, cloth, gilt top, 2s. net; leather, gilt edges, 3s. net.

Crown 8vo, cloth, 6s. each.
On the Old Trail.
Under the Redwoods.
From Sandhill to Pine.
Stories in Light and Shadow.
Mr. Jack Hamlin's Mediation.

Crown 8vo, cloth, 3s. 6d. each; post 8vo, Illustrated boards, 2s. each.
Gabriel Conroy.
A Waif of the Plains. With 60 Illustrations by STANLEY L. WOOD.
A Ward of the Golden Gate. With 59 Illustrations by STANLEY L. WOOD.

HARTE'S (BRET) Works—*cont.*
Crown 8vo, cloth 3s. 6d. each.
Susy. With 2 Illusts. by J. A. CHRISTIE.
The Bell-Ringer of Angel's, &c.
With 39 Illusts. by DUDLEY HARDY, &c.
Clarence: A Story of the American War.
With 8 Illustrations by A. JULE GOODMAN.
Barker's Luck, &c. With 39 Illustrations by A. FORESTIER, PAUL HARDY, &c.
Devil's Ford, &c. With Frontispiece.
The Crusade of the 'Excelsior.'
With Frontis. by J. BERNARD PARTRIDGE.
Three Partners; or, The Big Strike on Heavy Tree Hill.
With 8 Illustrations by J. GULICH.
Tales of Trail and Town. With Frontispiece by G. P. JACOMB-HOOD.
Condensed Novels. New Series.

Crown 8vo, cloth, 3s. 6d. each; picture cloth, flat back, 2s. each.
The Luck of Roaring Camp, and **Sensation Novels Condensed.**
A Sappho of Green Springs.
Colonel Starbottle's Client.
A Protégée of Jack Hamlin's.
With numerous Illustrations.
Sally Dows, &c. With 47 Illustrations by W. D. ALMOND and others.

Post 8vo, illustrated boards, 2s. each.
An Heiress of Red Dog.
The Luck of Roaring Camp.
Californian Stories.
Post 8vo, illus. bds., 2s. each; cloth, 2s. 6d. each.
Flip. | Maruja.
A Phyllis of the Sierras.

HALLIDAY (ANDREW).—
Every-day Papers. Post 8vo, illustrated boards, 2s.

HAMILTON (COSMO), Stories by. Crown 8vo, cloth, 3s. 6d. each.
The Glamour of the Impossible.
Through a Keyhole.
*** The two stories may also be had bound in one Volume, crown 8vo, cloth, 3s. 6d.

HANDWRITING, The Philosophy of. With over 100 Facsimiles. By DON FELIX DE SALAMANCA. Post 8vo, half-cloth, 2s. 6d.

HANKY-PANKY: White Magic,
Sleight of Hand, &c. Edited by W. H. CREMER. With 200 Illustrations. Crown 8vo, cloth, 4s. 6d.

HARDY (IZA DUFFUS), Novels by. Crown 8vo, cloth, 6s. each.
The Lesser Evil.
Man, Woman, and Fate.
A Butterfly: Her Friends and her Fortunes.

HARDY (Rev. E. J.).—Love, Courtship, and Marriage. Crown 8vo, cloth, 3s. 6d.

HARKINS (E. F.).—The Schemers. Crown 8vo, cloth, 6s.

HARDY (THOMAS). — Under the Greenwood Tree. Post 8vo, cloth, 3s. 6d.; illustrated boards, 2s.; cloth limp, 2s. 6d. Also the FINE PAPER EDITION, pott 8vo, cloth, gilt top, 2s. net; leather, gilt edges, 3s. net.

HAWEIS (Mrs. H. R.), Books by.
The Art of Beauty. With Coloured Frontispiece and 91 Illustrations. Square 8vo, cloth, 6s.
The Art of Decoration. With Coloured Frontispiece and 74 Illustrations. Square 8vo, cloth, 6s.
The Art of Dress. With 32 Illustrations. Post 8vo, 1s.; cloth, 1s. 6d.
Chaucer for Schools. With the Story of his Times and his Work. With a Frontispiece. Demy 8vo, cloth, 2s. 6d.
Chaucer for Children. With 8 Coloured Plates and 30 Woodcuts. Crown 4to, cloth, 3s. 6d.

HAWEIS (Rev. H. R.).—American Humorists: WASHINGTON IRVING, OLIVER WENDELL HOLMES, JAMES RUSSELL LOWELL, ARTEMUS WARD, MARK TWAIN, and BRET HARTE. Crown 8vo, cloth, 6s.

HAWTHORNE (JULIAN),
Novels by. Crown 8vo. cloth, 3s. 6d. each; post 8vo, illustrated boards, 2s. each.
Garth. | Ellice Quentin.
Fortune's Fool. | Dust. Four Illusts.
Beatrix Randolph. With Four Illusts.
D. Poindexter's Disappearance.
The Spectre of the Camera.
Post 8vo, illustrated boards, 2s. each.
Miss Cadogna. | Love—or a Name.
Sebastian Strome. Cr. 8vo, cl., 3s. 6d.

HEALY (CHRIS), Books by.
Crown 8vo, cloth, gilt top, 6s. each.
Confessions of a Journalist.
The Endless Heritage.
Heirs of Reuben.

HECKETHORN (C. W.), Books by. Crown 8vo, cloth, 6s. each.
London Souvenirs.
London Memories: Social, Historical, and Topographical.

HELPS (Sir ARTHUR), Books by. Post 8vo, cloth, 2s. 6d. each.
Animals and their Masters.
Social Pressure.
Ivan de Biron. Crown 8vo, cloth 3s. 6d.; post 8vo, illustrated boards, 2s.

HENDERSON (ISAAC).—Agatha Page. Crown 8vo, cloth, 3s. 6d.

HENTY (G. A.), Novels by.
Rujub, the Juggler. Post 8vo, cloth 3s. 6d.; illustrated boards, 2s.
Colonel Thorndyke's Secret. Small demy 8vo, cloth, gilt edges, 5s.
Crown 8vo, cloth, 3s. 6d. each.
The Queen's Cup.
Dorothy's Double.

HERMAN (HENRY).—A Leading Lady. Post 8vo, cloth, 2s. 6d.

HERTZKA (Dr. THEODOR).— Freeland: A Social Anticipation. Translated by ARTHUR RANSOM. Crown 8vo, cloth, 6s.

HESSE-WARTEGG (CHEVALIER ERNST VON).—Tunis: The Land and the People. With 22 Illustrations. Crown 8vo, cloth, 3s. 6d.

HILL (HEADON).—Zambra the Detective. Crown 8vo, cloth, 3s. 6d.; picture cloth, flat back, 2s.; post 8vo, illustrated boards, 2s.

HILL (JOHN), Works by.
Treason-Felony. Post 8vo, illustrated boards, 2s.
The Common Ancestor. Crown 8vo, cloth, 3s. 6d.

HINKSON (H. A.), Novels by. Crown 8vo, cloth, 6s. each.
Fan Fitzgerald. | Silk and Steel.

HOEY (Mrs. CASHEL).—The Lover's Creed. Post 8vo, illustrated boards, 2s.

HOFFMANN (PROFESSOR).— King Koko. A Magic Story. With 25 Illustrations. Crown 8vo, cloth, 1s. net.

HOLIDAY, Where to go for a. By E. P. SHOLL, Sir H. MAXWELL, JOHN WATSON, JANE BARLOW, MARY LOVETT CAMERON, JUSTIN H. MCCARTHY, PAUL LANGE, I. W. GRAHAM, J. H. SALTER, PHŒBE ALLEN, S. J. BECKETT, L. RIVERS VINE, and C. F. GORDON CUMMING. Crown 8vo, cloth, 1s. 6d.

HOLMES (OLIVER WENDELL), Books by.
The Autocrat of the Breakfast-Table. Illustrated by J. GORDON THOMSON. Post 8vo, cloth limp, 2s. 6d. Also the FINE PAPER EDITION, pott 8vo, cloth, gilt top, 2s. net.; leather, gilt edges, 3s. net. Another Edition, post 8vo, cloth, 2s.
The Autocrat of the Breakfast-Table and The Professor at the Breakfast-Table. In one vol., post 8vo, half-cloth, 2s.

HOOD'S (THOMAS) Choice Works in Prose and Verse. With Life of the Author, Portrait, and 200 Illustrations. Crown 8vo, cloth, 3s. 6d.
Hood's Whims and Oddities. With 85 Illusts. Post 8vo, half-cloth, 2s.

HOPKINS (TIGHE), Novels by.
For Freedom. Crown 8vo, cloth, 6s.
Crown 8vo, cloth, 3s. 6d. each.
'Twixt Love and Duty.
The Incomplete Adventurer.
The Nugents of Carriconna.
Nell Haffenden. With 8 Illustrations.

HOOK'S (THEODORE) Choice Humorous Works; including his Ludicrous Adventures, Bons Mots, Puns, Hoaxes. With Life and Frontispiece. Crown 8vo, cloth, 3s. 6d.

HORNE (R. HENGIST).—Orion. With Portrait. Crown 8vo, cloth, 7s.

HORNIMAN (ROY). — Bellamy the Magnificent. Crown 8vo, cl., 6s.

HORNUNG (E. W.), Novels by.
The Shadow of the Rope. Crown 8vo, cloth, 3s. 6d.
Stingaree. Crown 8vo, cloth, 6s.

HUGO (VICTOR).—The Outlaw of Iceland. Translated by Sir GILBERT CAMPBELL. Crown 8vo, cloth, 3s. 6d.

HUME (FERGUS), Novels by.
The Lady From Nowhere. Cr. 8vo, cloth, 3s. 6d.; picture cloth, flat back, 2s.
The Millionaire Mystery. Crown 8vo, cloth, 3s. 6d.
The Wheeling Light. Crown 8vo, cloth, gilt top, 6s.

HUNGERFORD (Mrs.), Novels by. Crown 8vo, cloth, 3s. 6d. each; post 8vo, illustrated boards, 2s. each; cloth limp, 2s. 6d. each.
The Professor's Experiment.
Nora Creina.
Lady Verner's Flight.
Lady Patty.
The Red-House Mystery.
Peter's Wife.
An Unsatisfactory Lover.
April's Lady.
A Maiden All Forlorn.
The Three Graces.
A Mental Struggle.
Marvel. | A Modern Circe.
In Durance Vile.
Crown 8vo, cloth, 3s. 6d. each.
An Anxious Moment.
A Point of Conscience.
The Coming of Chloe. | Lovice.

HUNT'S (LEIGH) Essays: A Tale for a Chimney Corner, &c. Ed, by E. OLLIER. Post 8vo, half-cl. 2s.

HUNT (Mrs. ALFRED), Novels by. Crown 8vo, cloth, 3s. 6d. each; post 8vo, illustrated boards, 2s. each.
The Leaden Casket.
Self-Condemned.
That Other Person.
Mrs. Juliet. Crown 8vo, cloth, 3s. 6d.

HUTCHINSON (W. M.)—Hints on Colt-Breaking. With 25 Illustrations. Crown 8vo, cloth, 3s. 6d.

HYDROPHOBIA: An Account of M. PASTEUR'S System. By RENAUD SUZOR, M.B. Crown 8vo, cloth, 6s.

IDLER Illustrated Magazine (The). Edited by ROBERT BARR. 6d. Monthly. Bound Volumes, 5s. each; Cases for Binding, 1s. 6d. each.

IMPRESSIONS (The) of AUREOLE. Post 8vo, cloth. 2s. 6d.

INDOOR PAUPERS. By ONE OF THEM. Crown 8vo, 1s.; cloth, 1s. 6d.

INMAN (HERBERT) and HARTLEY ASPDEN.—The Tear of Kalee. Crown 8vo, cloth, gilt top, 6s.

IN MEMORIAM: Verses for every Day. Selected by LUCY RIDLEY. Small 8vo, cloth, 2s, 6d. net; leather. 3s. 6d. net.

INNKEEPER'S HANDBOOK (The) and Licensed Victualler's Manual. By J. TREVOR-DAVIES. Crown 8vo, cloth, 2s.

IRISH WIT AND HUMOUR, Songs of. Edited by A. PERCEVAL GRAVES. Post 8vo, cloth, 2s. 6d.

IRVING (Sir HENRY). By PERCY FITZGERALD. With Portrait. Crown 8vo, cloth, 1s. 6d.

JAMES (C. T. C.).—A Romance of the Queen's Hounds. Post 8vo, cloth limp, 1s. 6d.

JAMESON (WILLIAM).—My Dead Self. Post 8vo, cloth, 2s. 6d.

JAPP (Dr. A. H.).—Dramatic Pictures. Crown 8vo, cloth. 5s.

JEFFERIES (RICHARD), by.
The Open Air. Post 8vo, cloth, 2s. 6d. LARGE TYPE, FINE PAPER EDITION, pott 8vo, cloth, gilt top, 2s. net; leather, gilt edges, 3s. net.
Nature near London. Crown 8vo, buckram, 6s.; post 8vo, cl., 2s. 6d.; LARGE TYPE, FINE PAPER EDITION, pott 8vo, cl., gilt top, 2s. net; leather, gilt edges, 3s. net.
The Life of the Fields. Post 8vo, cloth, 2s. 6d.; LARGE TYPE, FINE PAPER EDITION, pott 8vo, cloth, gilt top, 2s. net; leather, gilt edges, 3s. net.
The Eulogy of Richard Jefferies. By Sir WALTER BESANT. Cr. 8vo, cl., 6s.

JENNINGS (H. J.).—Curiosities of Criticism. Post 8vo, cloth, 2s. 6d.

JEROME (JEROME K.).—Stageland. With 64 Illustrations by J. BERNARD PARTRIDGE. Fcap. 4to, 1s.

JERROLD (DOUGLAS).—The Barber's Chair; and The Hedgehog Letters. Post 8vo, half-cloth, 2s.

JERROLD (TOM), Works by. Post 8vo, 1s. each; cloth, 1s. 6d. each.
The Garden that Paid the Rent.
Household Horticulture.

JESSE (EDWARD). — Scenes and Occupations of a Country Life. Post 8vo, cloth, 2s.

JONSON'S (BEN) Works. With Notes and Biographical Memoir by WILLIAM GIFFORD. Edited by Colonel CUNNINGHAM. Three Vols., crown 8vo, cloth, 3s. 6d. each.

JOHNSTON (R.).—The Peril of an Empire. Crown 8vo, cloth, 6s.

JONES (WILLIAM, F.S.A.), Books by. Cr. 8vo, cloth, 3s. 6d. each.
Finger-Ring Lore: Historical, Legendary, and Anecdotal. With numerous Illustrations.
Crowns and Coronations. With 91 Illustrations.

JOSEPHUS, The Complete Works of. Translated by WILLIAM WHISTON. Containing 'The Antiquities of the Jews,' and 'The Wars of the Jews.' With 52 Illustrations and Maps. Two Vols., demy 8vo, half-cloth, 12s. 6d.

KEMPT (ROBERT).—Pencil and Palette: Chapters on Art and Artists. Post 8vo, cloth, 2s. 6d.

KERSHAW (MARK).—Colonial Facts and Fictions: Humorous Sketches. Post 8vo, illustrated boards, 2s.; cloth, 2s. 6d.

KING (R. ASHE), Novels by. Post 8vo, illustrated boards, 2s.
'The Wearing of the Green.'
Passion's Slave. | Bell Barry.
A Drawn Game. Crown 8vo, cloth, 3s. 6d.; post 8vo, illustrated boards, 2s.

KIPLING PRIMER (A). Including Biographical and Critical Chapters, an Index to Mr. Kipling's principal Writings, and Bibliographies. By F. L. KNOWLES. With Two Portraits. Crown 8vo, cloth, 3s. 6d.

KNIGHTS (The) of the LION. Edited by the MARQUESS of LORNE. Crown 8vo, cloth, 6s.

KNIGHT (WILLIAM and EDWARD).—The Patient's Vade Mecum: How to Get Most Benefit from Medical Advice. Crown 8vo, cloth, 1s. 6d.

LAMBERT (GEORGE). — The President of Boravia. Crown 8vo, cloth, 3s. 6d.

LAMB'S (CHARLES) Complete Works in Prose and Verse, including 'Poetry for Children' and 'Prince Dorus.' Edited by R. H. SHEPHERD. With 2 Portraits and Facsimile of the 'Essay on Roast Pig.' Crown 8vo (both Series), cloth, 3s. 6d.
The Essays of Elia (both Series). Post 8vo, half-cloth, 2s.—Also the FINE PAPER EDITION, pott 8vo, cloth, gilt top, 2s. net; leather, gilt edges, 3s. net.
Little Essays: Sketches and Characters by CHARLES LAMB, selected from his Letters by PERCY FITZGERALD. Post 8vo, cloth, 2s. 6d.
The Dramatic Essays of Charles Lamb. With Introduction and Notes by BRANDER MATTHEWS, and Steel-plate Portrait. Fcap. 8vo, half-cloth, 2s. 6d.

LANDOR (WALTER SAVAGE).
—Citation and Examination of William Shakespeare, &c., before Sir Thomas Lucy, touching Deer-stealing, 19th September, 1582 ; and **A Conference of Master Edmund Spenser** with the Earl of Essex, touching the state of Ireland, 1595. Fcap. 8vo half-Roxburghe, 2s. 6d.

LANE (EDWARD WILLIAM).
—**The Thousand and One Nights,** commonly called in England **The Arabian Nights' Entertainments.** Translated from the Arabic and illustrated by many hundred Engravings from Designs by HARVEY. Edited by EDWARD STANLEY POOLE. With Preface by STANLEY LANE-POOLE. Three Vols., demy 8vo, cloth, 22s. 6d.

LARWOOD (JACOB), Books by.
Anecdotes of the Clergy. Post 8vo, half-cloth, 2s.
Theatrical Anecdotes. Post 8vo, cloth, 2s. 6d.
Humour of the Law: Forensic Anecdotes. Post 8vo, cloth, 2s.

LEHMANN (R. C.). — **Harry Fludyer at Cambridge,** and Conversational Hints for Young Shooters. Crown 8vo, 1s. ; cloth, 1s. 6d.

LEIGH (HENRY S.).—Carols of Cockayne. Crown 8vo, buckram, 5s.

LELAND (C. G.).—A Manual of Mending and Repairing. With Diagrams. Crown 8vo, cloth, 5s.

LEPELLETIER (EDMOND). — **Madame Sans-Gêne.** Translated by JOHN DE VILLIERS. Post 8vo, cloth, 3s. 6d. ; illustrated boards, 2s.

LEYS (JOHN K.), Novels by.
The Lindsays. Post 8vo, illustrated boards, 2s.
A Sore Temptation. Crown 8vo, cloth, 6s.

LILBURN (ADAM).—A Tragedy in Marble. Crown 8vo, cloth, 3s. 6d.

LINTON (E. LYNN), Works by.
An Octave of Friends. Crown 8vo, cloth, 3s. 6d.

Crown 8vo, cloth, 3s. 6d. each ; post 8vo, illustrated boards, 2s. each.
Patricia Kemball. | **Ione.**
The Atonement of Leam Dundas.
The World Well Lost. With 12 Illustrations.
The One Too Many.
Under which Lord? With 12 Illusts.
'**My Love.**' | **Sowing the Wind.**
Paston Carew. | **Dulcie Everton.**
With a Silken Thread.
The Rebel of the Family.

Post 8vo, cloth, 2s. 6d. each.
Witch Stories.
Ourselves: Essays on Women.
Freeshooting: Extracts from Mrs. LYNN LINTON'S Works.

LINDSAY (HARRY), Novels by.
Crown 8vo, cloth, 3s. 6d. each.
Rhoda Roberts. | **The Jacobite.**
Crown 8vo, cloth, 6s. each.
Judah Pyecroft, Puritan.
The Story of Leah.

LOWE (CHARLES). — Our Greatest Living Soldiers. With 8 Portraits. Crown 8vo, cloth, 3s. 6d.

LUCY (HENRY W.).—Gideon Fleyce. Crown 8vo, cloth, 3s. 6d ; post 8vo, illustrated boards, 2s.

McCARTHY (JUSTIN), Books by.
The Reign of Queen Anne. Two Vols., demy 8vo, cloth, 12s. each.
A History of the Four Georges and of William the Fourth. Four Vols., demy 8vo, cloth, 12s. each.
A History of Our Own Times, from the Accession of Queen Victoria to the General Election of 1880. LIBRARY EDITION. Four Vols., demy 8vo, cloth, 12s. each.—Also a POPULAR EDITION, in Four Vols., crown 8vo, cloth, 6s. each.
—And the JUBILEE EDITION, with an Appendix of Events to the end of 1886, in 2 Vols., demy 8vo, cloth, 7s. 6d. each.
A History of Our Own Times, Vol. V., from 1880 to the Diamond Jubilee. Demy 8vo, cloth, 12s.; crown 8vo, cloth, 6s.
A History of Our Own Times, Vols. VI. and VII., from the Diamond Jubilee, 1897, to the Accession of King Edward VII. Demy 8vo, cl., 24s. [Shortly.
A Short History of Our Own Times. Cr. 8vo, cl., 6s.—Also a POPULAR EDITION, post 8vo, cloth limp, 2s. 6d.; and the CHEAP EDITION, medium 8vo, 6d.
Reminiscences. With a Portrait. Two Vols., demy 8vo, cloth, 24s.
The Story of an Irishman. Demy 8vo, cloth, 12s.

LARGE TYPE, FINE PAPER EDITIONS, Pott 8vo, cloth, gilt top, 2s. net per vol.; leather, gilt edges, 3s. net per vol.
The Reign of Queen Anne, in 1 Vol.
A History of the Four Georges and of William IV., in 2 vols.
A History of Our Own Times, from the Accession of Queen Victoria to 1897, in 3 Vols. [Shortly.

Crown 8vo, cloth, 3s. 6d. each ; post 8vo, picture boards, 2s. each ; cloth limp, 2s. 6d. each.
The Waterdale Neighbours.
My Enemy's Daughter.
A Fair Saxon. | **Linley Rochford.**
Dear Lady Disdain. | **The Dictator.**
Miss Misanthrope. With 12 Illusts.
Donna Quixote. With 12 Illustrations.
The Comet of a Season.
Maid of Athens. With 12 Illustrations.
Camiola.
Red Diamonds. | **The Riddle Ring.**

Crown 8vo, cloth, 3s. 6d. each.
The Three Disgraces. | **Mononia.**

'**The Right Honourable.**' By JUSTIN MCCARTHY and MRS. CAMPBELL PRAED. Crown 8vo, cloth, 6s.

McCARTHY (J. H.), Works by.
The French Revolution. (Constituent Assembly, 1789-91.) Four Vols., demy 8vo, cloth, 12s. each.
An Outline of the History of Ireland. Crown 8vo, 1s.; cloth, 1s. 6d.
Ireland Since the Union—1798-1886. Crown 8vo, cloth, 6s.

Hafiz in London. 8vo, gold cloth, 3s. 6d.
Our Sensation Novel. Crown 8vo, 1s.; cloth, 1s. 6d.
Doom: An Atlantic Episode. Crown 8vo, 1s.
Dolly: A Sketch. Crown 8vo, 1s.
Lily Lass. Crown 8vo, 1s.; cloth, 1s. 6d.
A London Legend. Cr. 8vo, cloth, 3s. 6d.

MACAULAY (LORD).—The History of England. LARGE TYPE, FINE PAPER EDITION, in 5 vols, pott 8vo, cloth, gilt top, 2s. net per vol.; leather, gilt edges, 3s. net per vol.

MACCOLL (HUGH), Novels by.
Mr. Stranger's Sealed Packet. Post 8vo, illustrated boards, 2s.
Ednor Whitlock. Crown 8vo, cloth, 6s.

MACDONALD (Dr. GEORGE), Books by.
Works of Fancy and Imagination Ten Vols., 16mo, cloth, gilt, in case, 21s.; or separately, Grolier cloth, 2s. 6d. each.
Vol. I. WITHIN AND WITHOUT—THE HIDDEN LIFE.
" II. THE DISCIPLE—THE GOSPEL WOMEN—BOOK OF SONNETS—ORGAN SONGS.
" III. VIOLIN SONGS—SONGS OF THE DAYS AND NIGHTS—A BOOK OF DREAMS—ROADSIDE POEMS—POEMS FOR CHILDREN.
" IV. PARABLES—BALLADS—SCOTCH SONGS.
" V. & VI. PHANTASTES.
" VII. THE PORTENT.
" VIII. THE LIGHT PRINCESS—THE GIANT'S HEART—SHADOWS.
" IX. CROSS PURPOSES—THE GOLDEN KEY—THE CARASOYN—LITTLE DAYLIGHT.
" X. THE CRUEL PAINTER—THE WOW O'RIVVEN—THE CASTLE—THE BROKEN SWORDS—THE GRAY WOLF—UNCLE CORNELIUS.

Poetical Works of George Macdonald. Two Vols., crown 8vo, buckram, 12s.
A Threefold Cord. Edited by GEORGE MACDONALD. Post 8vo, cloth, 5s.
Phantastes. With 25 Illustrations by J. BELL. Crown 8vo, cloth, 3s. 6d.
Heather and Snow. Crown 8vo, cloth, 3s. 6d.; post 8vo, illustrated boards, 2s.
Lilith. Crown 8vo, cloth, 6s.

MACDONELL (AGNES).—
Quaker Cousins. Post 8vo, boards, 2s.

MacGREGOR (ROBERT).—
Pastimes and Players: Notes on Popular Games. Post 8vo, cloth, 2s. 6d.

MACHRAY (ROBERT), Novels by. Crown 8vo, cloth, 6s. each.
A Blow over the Heart.
The Mystery of Lincoln's Inn.

MACKAY (Dr. CHAS.).—Interludes and Undertones. Cr. 8vo, cloth, 6s.

MACKENNA (S. J.) and J. A. O'SHEA.—Brave Men in Action: Stories of the British Flag. With 8 Illustrations by STANLEY L. WOOD. Small demy 8vo, cloth, gilt edges, 5s.

MACKENZIE (W. A.).—The Drexel Dream. Crown 8vo, cloth, 6s.

MACLISE Portrait Gallery (The) of Illustrious Literary Characters: 85 Portraits by DANIEL MACLISE; with Memoirs, Biographical, Critical, and Bibliographical, by WILLIAM BATES, B.A. Crown 8vo, cloth, 3s. 6d.

MACQUOID (Mrs.), Works by, illustrated by T. R. MACQUOID. Square 8vo, cloth, 6s. each.
In the Ardennes. With 50 Illustrations.
Pictures and Legends from Normandy and Brittany. 34 Illusts.
Through Normandy. With 92 Illusts.
About Yorkshire. With 67 Illusts.

MAGICIAN'S Own Book, The: Performances with Eggs, Hats, &c. Edited by W. H. CREMER. With 200 Illustrations. Crown 8vo, cloth, 4s. 6d.

MAGIC LANTERN, The, and its Management. By T. C. HEPWORTH. With 10 Illusts. Cr. 8vo, 1s.; cloth, 1s. 6d.

MAGNA CHARTA: A Facsimile of the Original in the British Museum, 3 feet by 2 feet, with Arms and Seals emblazoned in Gold and Colours, 5s.

MALLOCK (W. H.), Works by.
The New Republic. Post 8vo, cloth, 3s. 6d.; illustrated boards, 2s.
The New Paul and Virginia. Post 8vo, cloth, 2s. 6d.
Poems. Small 4to, parchment, 8s.
Is Life Worth Living? Cr. 8vo, cl., 6s.

MALLORY (Sir THOMAS).—
Mort d'Arthur: Selections from the Stories of King Arthur and the Knights of the Round Table. Edited by B. M. RANKING. Post 8vo, cloth, 2s.

MARGUERITTE (PAUL and VICTOR), Novels by.
The Disaster. Translated by F. LEES. Crown 8vo, cloth, 3s. 6d.
The Commune. Translated by F. LEES and R. B. DOUGLAS. Crown 8vo, cloth, 6s.

MARLOWE'S Works, including his Translations. Edited with Notes by Col. CUNNINGHAM. Cr. 8vo, cloth, 3s. 6d.

MARSH (RICHARD).—A Spoiler of Men. Crown 8vo, cloth, 6s.

MASON (FINCH).—Annals of the Horse-Shoe Club. With 5 Illustrations. Crown 8vo, cloth, 6s.

MASSINGER'S Plays. From the Text of WILLIAM GIFFORD. Edited by Col. CUNNINGHAM. Cr. 8vo, cloth, 3s 6d.

MASTERMAN (J.).—Half-a-dozen Daughters. Post 8vo, Illustrated boards, 2s.

MATTHEWS (BRANDER).—A Secret of the Sea. Post 8vo, illustrated boards, 2s.; cloth, 2s. 6d.

MAX O'RELL, Books by. Crown 8vo, cloth, 3s. 6d. each.
Her Royal Highness Woman.
Between Ourselves.
Rambles in Womanland.

MEADE (L. T.), Novels by.
A Soldier of Fortune. Crown 8vo, cloth, 3s. 6d.; post 8vo, illust. boards, 2s.

Crown 8vo, cloth, 3s. 6d. each.
The Voice of the Charmer.
In an Iron Grip. | The Siren.
Dr. Rumsey's Patient.
On the Brink of a Chasm.
The Way of a Woman.
A Son of Ishmael.
An Adventuress.
The Blue Diamond.
A Stumble by the Way.
This Troublesome World.
Rosebury.

MERIVALE (HERMAN).—Bar, Stage, and Platform: Memories. With Portrait. Crown 8vo, cloth, 6s.

MERRICK (HOPE).—When a Girl's Engaged. Cr. 8vo, cloth, 3s. 6d.

MERRICK (LEON.), Novels by.
The Man who was Good. Post 8vo, illustrated boards, 2s.

Crown 8vo, cloth, 3s. 6d. each.
This Stage of Fools.
Cynthia.

MILLER (Mrs. F. FENWICK).—Physiology for the Young: or, The House of Life. With numerous Illustrations. Post 8vo, cloth, 2s. 6d.

MILTON (J. L.).—The Bath in Diseases of the Skin. Post 8vo, 1s.; cloth, 1s. 6d.

MINTO (WM.).—Was She Good or Bad? Crown 8vo, cloth, 1s. 6d.

MITCHELL (EDM.), Novels by.
The Lone Star Rush. With 8 Illustrations by NORMAN H. HARDY. Crown 8vo, cloth, 3s. 6d.

Crown 8vo, cloth, 6s. each
Only a Nigger.
The Belforts of Culben.

Crown 8vo, picture cloth, flat backs, 2s. each.
Plotters of Paris.
The Temple of Death.
Towards the Eternal Snows.

MITFORD (BERTRAM), Novels by. Crown 8vo, cloth, 3s. 6d. each.
The Gun-Runner. With Frontispiece.
Renshaw Fanning's Quest. With Frontispiece by STANLEY L. WOOD.
Triumph of Hilary Blachland.
Haviland's Chum.

Crown 8vo, cloth, 3s. 6d. each; picture cloth flat backs, 2s. each.
The Luck of Gerard Ridgeley.
The King's Assegai. With 6 Illustrations by STANLEY L. WOOD.

MOLESWORTH (Mrs.).—Hathercourt Rectory. Crown 8vo, cloth, 3s. 6d.; post 8vo, illust. boards, 2s.

MONCRIEFF (W. D. SCOTT-).—The Abdication: An Historical Drama. With 7 Etchings. Imperial 4to, buckram, 21s.

MONTAGU (IRVING).—Things I Have Seen in War. With 16 Illustrations. Crown 8vo, cloth, 6s.

MOORE (THOMAS), Works by.
The Epicurean; and Alciphron. Post 8vo, half-cloth, 2s.
Prose and Verse: including Suppressed Passages from the MEMOIRS OF LORD BYRON. Edited by R. H. SHEPHERD. With Portrait. Crown 8vo, cloth, 7s. 6d.

MURRAY (D. CHRISTIE), Novels by. Crown 8vo, cloth, 3s. 6d. each; post 8vo, illustrated boards, 2s. each.
A Life's Atonement.
Joseph's Coat. With 12 Illustrations.
Coals of Fire. With 3 Illustrations.
Val Strange. | Hearts.
The Way of the World.
A Model Father.
Old Blazer's Hero.
Cynic Fortune.
By the Gate of the Sea.
A Bit of Human Nature.
First Person Singular.
Bob Martin's Little Girl.
Time's Revenges.
A Wasted Crime.
In Direst Peril.
Mount Despair.
A Capful o' Nails.

Crown 8vo, cloth, 3s. 6d. each.
This Little World.
A Race for Millions.
The Church of Humanity.
Tales in Prose and Verse.
V.C.: A Chronicle of Castle Barfield.
Making of a Novelist. With Portrait.
My Contemporaries in Fiction.

Crown 8vo, cloth, 6s. each.
Despair's Last Journey.
Verona's Father.

His Own Ghost. Crown 8vo, cloth, 3s. 6d.; picture cloth, flat back, 2s.
Joseph's Coat. POPULAR EDITION, medium 8vo, 6d.

MURRAY (D. CHRISTIE) and HENRY HERMAN, Novels by. Crown 8vo, cloth, 3s. 6d. each; post 8vo, illustrated boards, 2s. each.
One Traveller Returns.
The Bishops' Bible.
Paul Jones's Alias. With Illustrations by A. FORESTIER and G. NICOLET.

MURRAY (HENRY), Novels by. Post 8vo, cloth, 2s. 6d. each.
A Game of Bluff.
A Song of Sixpence.

MORRIS (Rev. W. MEREDITH, B.A.). — British Violin - Makers, Classical and Modern. With numerous Portraits, Illustrations, and Facsimiles of Labels. Demy 8vo, cloth, 10s. 6d. net.

MORROW (W. C.).—Bohemian Paris of To-Day. With 106 Illusts. by EDOUARD CUCUEL. Small demy 8vo, cl., 6s.

MUDDOCK (J. E.), Stories by. Crown 8vo, cloth, 3s. 6d. each.
Basile the Jester.
Young Lochinvar.
The Golden Idol.

Post 8vo, illustrated boards, 2s. each.
The Dead Man's Secret.
From the Bosom of the Deep.
Stories Weird and Wonderful. Post 8vo, illust. boards, 2s.; cloth, 2s. 6d.
Maid Marian and Robin Hood. With 12 Illustrations by STANLEY L. WOOD. Crown 8vo, cloth, 3s. 6d.; picture cloth, flat back, 2s.

MY FIRST BOOK. By WALTER BESANT, JAMES PAYN, W. CLARK RUSSELL, GRANT ALLEN, HALL CAINE, GEORGE R. SIMS, RUDYARD KIPLING, A. CONAN DOYLE, M. E. BRADDON, F. W. ROBINSON, H. RIDER HAGGARD, R. M. BALLANTYNE, I. ZANGWILL, MORLEY ROBERTS, D. CHRISTIE MURRAY, MARIE CORELLI, J. K. JEROME, JOHN STRANGE WINTER, BRET HARTE, 'Q.,' ROBERT BUCHANAN, and R. L. STEVENSON. With Prefatory Story by JEROME K. JEROME, and 183 Illustrations. Demy 8vo, art linen, 3s. 6d.

NEWBOLT (HENRY). — Taken from the Enemy. Fcp. 8vo, pic. cov., 1s.

NISBET (HUME), Books by.
'Bail Up.' Crown 8vo, cloth, 3s. 6d.; post 8vo, illustrated boards, 2s.
Dr. Bernard St. Vincent. Post 8vo, illustrated boards, 2s.
Lessons in Art. With 21 Illustrations. Crown 8vo, cloth, 2s. 6d.

NORDAU (MAX).—Morganatic: A Romance. Translated by ELIZABETH LEE. Crown 8vo, cloth, gilt top, 6s.

NORRIS (W. E.), Novels by. Crown 8vo, cloth, 3s. 6d. each; post 8vo, illustrated boards, 2s. each.
Saint Ann's. | **Billy Bellew.**
Miss Wentworth's Idea. Crown 8vo, cloth, 3s. 6d.

OHNET (GEORGES), Novels by. Post 8vo, illustrated boards, 2s. each.
Doctor Rameau. | **A Last Love.**
A Weird Gift. Crown 8vo, cloth, 3s. 6d.; post 8vo, illustrated boards, 2s.

Crown 8vo, cloth, 3s. 6d. each.
Love's Depths.
The Woman of Mystery.
The Money-Maker. Translated by F. ROTHWELL. Crown 8vo. cloth, 6s.

OLIPHANT (Mrs.), Novels by. Post 8vo, illustrated boards, 2s. each.
The Primrose Path.
The Greatest Heiress in England.
Whiteladies. Crown 8vo, cloth, with 12 Illustrations by ARTHUR HOPKINS and HENRY WOODS, 3s. 6d.; post 8vo, picture boards, 2s.
The Sorceress. Crown 8vo, cloth, 3s. 6d.

ORROCK (James), Painter, Connoisseur, Collector. By BYRON WEBBER. Illustrated with nearly 100 Photogravure Plates and a number of Drawings in half-tone. Two Vols., small folio, buckram gilt, 10 guineas net.

O'SHAUGHNESSY (ARTHUR), Poems by.
Music and Moonlight. Fcap. 8vo, cloth, 7s. 6d.
Lays of France. Cr. 8vo, cloth, 10s. 6d.

OUIDA, Novels by. Crown 8vo, cloth, 3s. 6d. each; post 8vo, illustrated boards, 2s. each.

Tricotrin.	A Dog of Flanders.
Ruffino.	Cecil Castlemaine's
Othmar.	Gage.
Frescoes.	Princess Napraxine.
Wanda.	Held in Bondage.
Ariadne.	Under Two Flags.
Pascarel.	Folle-Farine.
Chandos.	Two Wooden Shoes.
Moths.	A Village Commune.
Puck.	In a Winter City.
Idalia.	Santa Barbara.
Bimbi.	In Maremma.
Signa.	Strathmore.
Friendship.	Pipistrello.
Guilderoy.	Two Offenders.

Crown 8vo, cloth, 3s. 6d. each.
A Rainy June. | **The Massarenes.**
POPULAR EDITIONS, medium 8vo, 6d. each.
Under Two Flags. | **Moths.**
Held in Bondage. | **Puck.**
Strathmore. | **Tricotrin.**
The Massarenes. | **Chandos.**
Syrlin. Crown 8vo, cloth, 3s. 6d.; post 8vo, picture cloth, flat back, 2s.; illustrated boards, 2s.
Two Little Wooden Shoes. LARGE TYPE EDITION, Fcap. 8vo, cloth, 1s. net; leather, 1s. 6d. net.
The Waters of Edera. Crown 8vo, cloth, 3s. 6d.; picture cloth, flat back, 2s.
Wisdom, Wit, and Pathos, selected from the Works of OUIDA by F. SYDNEY MORRIS. Post 8vo, cloth, 5s.—CHEAP EDITION, illustrated boards, 2s.

18   CHATTO & WINDUS, PUBLISHERS,

PAIN (BARRY).—Eliza's Husband. Fcap., 8vo, 1s.; cloth, 1s. 6d.

PALMER (W. T.), Books by. Crown 8vo, cloth, with Frontis., 6s. each.
Lake Country Rambles.
In Lakeland Dells and Fells.

PANDURANG HARI; or, Memoirs of a Hindoo. With Preface by Sir BARTLE FRERE. Post 8vo, illustrated boards, 2s.

PARIS SALON, The Illustrated Catalogue of the, for 1905. (Twenty-seventh Year.) With over 300 Illustrations. Demy 8vo, 3s.

PASCAL'S Provincial Letters. With Introduction and Notes by T. M'CRIE, D.D. Post 8vo, half-cloth, 2s.

PAYN (JAMES), Novels by. Crown 8vo. cloth, 3s. 6d. each; post 8vo, illustrated boards, 2s. each.
Lost Sir Massingberd.
The Clyffards of Clyffe.
A County Family.
Less Black than We're Painted.
By Proxy. | For Cash Only.
High Spirits.
A Confidential Agent.
A Grape from a Thorn.   12 Illusts.
The Family Scapegrace.
Holiday Tasks.
The Talk of the Town. 12 Illusts.
The Mystery of Mirbridge.
The Word and the Will.
The Burnt Million.
SunnyStories.
A Trying Patient.

Post 8vo, Illustrated boards, 2s. each.
Humorous Stories. | From Exile.
The Foster Brothers.
Married Beneath Him.
Bentinck's Tutor.
Walter's Word.
A Perfect Treasure.
Like Father, Like Son.
A Woman's Vengeance.
Carlyon's Year. | Cecil's Tryst.
Murphy's Master. | At Her Mercy.
Some Private Views.
Found Dead. | Mirk Abbey.
Gwendoline's Harvest.
A Marine Residence.
The Canon's Ward.
Not Wooed, But Won.
Two Hundred Pounds Reward.
The Best of Husbands.
Halves. | What He Cost Her.
Fallen Fortunes.
Kit: A Memory. | Under One Roof.
Glow-Worm Tales.
A Prince of the Blood.
A Modern Dick Whittington. Crown 8vo, cloth, with Portrait of Author, 3s. 6d.; picture cloth, flat back, 2s.
Notes from the 'News.' Crown 8vo, cloth, 1s. 6d.

POPULAR EDITIONS, medium 8vo, 6d. each.
Lost Sir Massingberd.
Walter's Word.

PASTON LETTERS (The), 1422-1509. Edited, with Introduction and Notes, by JAMES GAIRDNER. Six Vols., square demy 8vo, art linen, gilt top, 12s. 6d. net per volume, or £3 15s. the set. (Sold only in sets.)

PAUL (MARGARET A.).—Gentle and Simple. Crown 8vo, cloth, 3s. 6d.; post 8vo, illustrated boards, 2s.

PAYNE (WILL). — Jerry the Dreamer. Crown 8vo, cloth, 3s. 6d.

PENNELL - ELMHIRST (Captain E.).—The Best of the Fun. With 8 Coloured Illustrations by G. D. GILES, and 48 others by J. STURGESS and G. D. GILES. Medium 8vo, cloth, 16s.

PENNELL (H. CHOLMONDELEY), Works by. Post 8vo, cloth, 2s. 6d. each.
Puck on Pegasus. With Illustrations.
Pegasus Re-Saddled. With 10 Full-page Illustrations by G. DU MAURIER.
The Muses of Mayfair: Vers de Société. Selected by H. C. PENNELL.

PENNY (F. E.).—The Sanyasi. Crown 8vo, cloth, 6s.

PHELPS (E. S.), Books by.
Beyond the Gates. Post 8vo, cl., 1s. 6d.
Jack the Fisherman. Illustrated by C. W. REED. Crown 8vo, cloth, 1s. 6d.

PHIL MAY'S Sketch-Book: 54 Cartoons. Crown folio, cloth, 2s. 6d.

PHIPSON (Dr. T. L.), Books by. Crown 8vo, cloth, 5s. each.
Famous Violinists and Fine Violins.
The Confessions of a Violinist.
Voice and Violin.

PILKINGTON (L. L.).—Mallender's Mistake. Crown 8vo, cloth, 6s.

PLANCHE (J. R.), Works by.
The Pursuivant of Arms. With 6 Plates and 209 Illustrations. Crown 8vo, cloth, 7s. 6d.
Songs and Poems. Edited by Mrs. MACKARNESS. Crown 8vo, cloth, 6s.

PLUTARCH'S Lives of Illustrious Men. With Life of PLUTARCH by J. and W. LANGHORNE, and Portraits. Two Vols., 8vo, half-cloth, 10s. 6d.

POE'S (EDGAR ALLAN) Choice Works: Poems, Stories, Essays. With an Introduction by CHARLES BAUDELAIRE. Crown 8vo, cloth, 3s. 6d.

POLLOCK (W. H.).—The Charm, and Other Drawing-Room Plays. By Sir WALTER BESANT and WALTER H. POLLOCK. With 50 Illustrations Crown 8vo cloth, 3s. 6d.

111 ST. MARTIN'S LANE, LONDON, W.C. 19

PRAED (Mrs. CAMPBELL), Novels by. Post 8vo, illus. boards, 2s. ea.
The Romance of a Station.
The Soul of Countess Adrian.

Crown 8vo, cloth, 3s. 6d. each; post 8vo illustrated boards, 2s. each.
Outlaw and Lawmaker.
Christina Chard.
Mrs. Tregaskiss. With 8 Illustrations.

Crown 8vo, cloth, 3s. 6d. each.
Nulma. | Madame Izan.
'As a Watch in the Night.'

PRICE (E. C.). — Valentina.
Crown 8vo, cloth, 3s. 6d.

PROCTOR (RICHARD A.), Works by.
Crown 8vo, cloth, 3s. 6d. each.
Easy Star Lessons. With Star Maps for every Night in the Year.
Flowers of the Sky. With 55 Illusts.
Familiar Science Studies.
Mysteries of Time and Space.
The Universe of Suns.

Saturn and its System. With 13 Steel Plates. Demy 8vo, cloth, 6s.
Wages and Wants of Science Workers. Crown 8vo, 1s. 6d.

PRYCE (RICHARD). — Miss Maxwell's Affections. Crown 8vo, cl., 3s. 6d.; post 8vo, illust. boards, 2s.

RAMBOSSON (J.). — Popular Astronomy. Translated by C. B. PITMAN. With 10 Coloured Plates and 63 Woodcuts. Crown 8vo, cloth, 3s. 6d.

RANDOLPH (Col. G.).—Aunt Abigail Dykes. Cr. 8vo, cloth, 7s. 6d.

RICHARDSON (FRANK), Novels by. Crown 8vo, cloth, 3s. each.
The Man who Lost his Past. With 50 Illustrations by TOM BROWNE, R.I.
The Bayswater Miracle.

Crown 8vo, cloth, 6s. each.
The King's Counsel.
Semi-Society.
There and Back.

RIDDELL (Mrs.), Novels by.
A Rich Man's Daughter. Crown 8vo, cloth, 3s. 6d.
Weird Stories. Crown 8vo, cloth, 3s. 6d.; post 8vo, picture boards, 2s.

Post 8vo, illustrated boards, 2s. each.
The Uninhabited House.
Prince of Wales's Garden Party.
The Mystery in Palace Gardens.
Fairy Water. | Idle Tales.
Her Mother's Darling.
The Nun's Curse.

READE'S (CHARLES) Novels.
Collected LIBRARY EDITION, in Seventeen Volumes, crown 8vo, cloth, 3s. 6d. each.
1. Peg Woffington; and Christie Johnstone.
2. Hard Cash.
3. The Cloister and the Hearth. With a Preface by Sir WALTER BESANT.
4. 'It is Never Too Late to Mend.'
5. The Course of True Love Never Did Run Smooth; and Singleheart and Doubleface.
6. The Autobiography of a Thief: Jack of all Trades; A Hero and a Martyr; The Wandering Heir.
7. Love Me Little, Love Me Long.
8. The Double Marriage.
9. Griffith Gaunt.
10. Foul Play.
11. Put Yourself in His Place.
12. A Terrible Temptation.
13. A Simpleton.
14. A Woman-Hater.
15. The Jilt; and Good Stories of Man and other Animals.
16. A Perilous Secret.
17. Readiana; and Bible Characters.

In Twenty-one Volumes, post 8vo, illustrated boards, 2s. each.
Peg Woffington. | A Simpleton.
Christie Johnstone.
'It is Never Too Late to Mend.'
The Course of True Love Never Did Run Smooth.
Autobiography of a Thief; Jack of all Trades; James Lambert.
Love Me Little, Love Me Long.
The Double Marriage.
The Cloister and the Hearth.
Hard Cash. | Readiana.
Foul Play. | Griffith Gaunt.
Put Yourself in His Place.
A Terrible Temptation.
The Wandering Heir.
A Woman-Hater.
Singleheart and Doubleface.
Good Stories of Man, &c.
The Jilt; and other Stories.
A Perilous Secret.

LARGE TYPE, FINE PAPER EDITIONS.
Pott 8vo, cloth, gilt top, 2s. net each; leather, gilt edges, 3s. net each.
The Cloister and the Hearth. With 32 full-page Illustrations.
'It is Never Too Late to Mend.'

POPULAR EDITIONS, medium 8vo, 6d. each.
The Cloister and the Hearth.
'It is Never Too Late to Mend.'
Foul Play. | Hard Cash.
Peg Woffington; and Christie Johnstone.
Griffith Gaunt.
Put Yourself in His Place.
A Terrible Temptation.

Fcap. 8vo, half-Roxburghe, 2s. 6d. each.
Christie Johnstone. With Frontis.
Peg Woffington.

READE'S (CHARLES) Novels—*continued*.
The Wandering Heir. LARGE TYPE EDITION, pott 8vo, cloth, 1s. net; leather, 1s. 6d. net.
The Cloister and the Hearth. EDITION DE LUXE, with 16 Photogravure and 84 half-tone Illustrations by MATT B. HEWERDINE. Small 4to, cloth, 6s. net.
—Also in Four Vols., post 8vo, with Frontispieces, buckram, gilt top, 6s. the set.
Bible Characters. Fcap. 8vo, 1s.
Selections from the Works of Charles Reade. Edited by Mrs. A. IRELAND. Post 8vo, cloth, 2s. 6d.

RIMMER (ALFRED), Works by.
Square 8vo, cloth, 3s. 6d. each.
Rambles Round Eton and Harrow With 52 Illustrations.
About England with Dickens. With 58 Illustrations.

RIVES (AMELIE), Stories by.
Crown 8vo, cloth, 3s. 6d. each.
Barbara Dering.
Meriel: A Love Story.

ROBINSON (F. W.), Novels by.
Women are Strange. Post 8vo, Illustrated boards, 2s.
The Hands of Justice. Crown 8vo, cloth, 3s. 6d.; post 8vo, illust. bds., 2s.
The Woman in the Dark. Crown 8vo, cloth, 3s. 6d.; post 8vo, illust. bds., 2s.

ROLFE (FR.), Novels by.
Crown 8vo, cloth, 6s. each.
Hadrian the Seventh.
Don Tarquinio.

ROLL OF BATTLE ABBEY, THE: A List of Principal Warriors who came from Normandy with William the Conqueror, 1066. In Gold and Colours, 5s.

ROSENGARTEN (A.).—A Handbook of Architectural Styles. Translated by W. COLLETT-SANDARS. With 630 Illustrations. Cr. 8vo, cloth, 7s. 6d.

ROSS (ALBERT).—A Sugar Princess. Crown 8vo, cloth, 3s. 6d.

ROWLEY (Hon. HUGH). Post 8vo, cloth, 2s. 6d. each.
Puniana: or, Thoughts Wise and Otherwise: a Collection of the Best Riddles, Conundrums, Jokes, Sells, &c., with numerous Illustrations.
More Puniana. With numerous Illusts.

RUNCIMAN (JAS.), Stories by.
Schools and Scholars. Post 8vo, cloth, 2s. 6d.
Skippers and Shellbacks. Crown 8vo, cloth, 3s. 6d.

RUSSELL (HERBERT).—True Blue. Crown 8vo, cloth, 3s. 6d.

RUSSELL (W. CLARK), Novels by. Crown 8vo, cloth, 6s. each.
Overdue. | **Wrong Side Out.**

Crown 8vo, cloth, 3s. 6d. each; post 8vo, Illustrated boards, 2s. each; cloth, 2s. 6d. each.
Round the Galley-Fire.
In the Middle Watch.
On the Fo'k'sle Head.
A Voyage to the Cape.
A Book for the Hammock.
The Mystery of the 'Ocean Star.'
The Romance of Jenny Harlowe.
The Tale of the Ten.
An Ocean Tragedy.
My Shipmate Louise.
Alone on a Wide Wide Sea.
The Good Ship 'Mohock.'
The Phantom Death.
Is He the Man? | **Heart of Oak.**
The Convict Ship.
The Last Entry.

Crown 8vo, cloth, 3s. 6d. each.
A Tale of Two Tunnels.
The Death Ship.

The Ship: Her Story. With 50 Illustrations by H. C. SEPPINGS WRIGHT. Small 4to, cloth, 6s.
The 'Pretty Polly.' With 12 Illustrations by G. E. ROBERTSON. Large crown 8vo, cloth, gilt edges, 5s.
The Convict Ship. POPULAR EDITION, medium 8vo, 6d.

RUSSELL (DORA), Novels by.
A Country Sweetheart. Post 8vo, Illus. boards, 2s.; pict. cloth, flat back, 2s.
The Drift of Fate. Crown 8vo, cloth, 3s. 6d.; picture cloth, flat back, 2s.

RUSSELL (Rev. JOHN) and his Out-of-door Life. By E. W. L. DAVIES. With Illustrations coloured by hand. Royal 8vo, cloth, 16s. net.

SAINT AUBYN (ALAN), Novels by. Crown 8vo, cloth, 3s. 6d. each; post 8vo, illustrated boards, 2s. each.
A Fellow of Trinity. With a Note by OLIVER WENDELL HOLMES.
The Junior Dean.
Orchard Damerel.
The Master of St. Benedict's.
In the Face of the World.
To His Own Master.
The Tremlett Diamonds.

Crown 8vo, cloth, 3s. 6d. each.
The Wooing of May.
Fortune's Gate.
A Tragic Honeymoon.
Gallantry Bower.
A Proctor's Wooing.
Bonnie Maggie Lauder.
Mrs. Dunbar's Secret.
Mary Unwin. With 8 Illustrations.

SAINT JOHN (BAYLE). — A Levantine Family. Cr. 8vo, cl., 3s. 6d.

ST. MARTIN'S LIBRARY, The.
Pott 8vo, cloth, gilt top, 2s. net each; leather, gilt edges, 3s. net each.
By Sir WALTER BESANT.
London.
All Sorts and Conditions of Men.
Sir Richard Whittington.
Gaspard de Coligny.

By HALL CAINE.
The Deemster.

By WILKIE COLLINS.
The Woman in White.

By DANIEL DEFOE.
Robinson Crusoe. With 37 Illustrations by G. CRUIKSHANK.

By THOMAS HARDY.
Under the Greenwood Tree.

By BRET HARTE.
Condensed Novels.

By OLIVER WENDELL HOLMES.
The Autocrat of the Breakfast Table. Illustrated by J. G. THOMSON.

By RICHARD JEFFERIES.
The Life of the Fields.
The Open Air.
Nature near London.

By CHARLES LAMB.
The Essays of Elia.

By LORD MACAULAY.
History of England, in 5 Volumes.

By JUSTIN MCCARTHY.
The Reign of Queen Anne. In 1 Vol.
A History of the Four Georges and of William IV., In 2 Vols.
A History of Our Own Times, from the Accession of Queen Victoria to 1897, in 3 Vols. [*Shortly.*

By CHARLES READE.
The Cloister and the Hearth.
'Never Too Late to Mend.'

By ROBERT LOUIS STEVENSON.
Memories and Portraits.
Virginibus Puerisque.
Men and Books.
New Arabian Nights.
Across the Plains.
The Merry Men.
The Pocket R. L. S.

By MARK TWAIN.
Sketches.

By WALTON and COTTON.
The Complete Angler.

SALA (G. A.).—Gaslight and Daylight. Post 8vo, illustrated boards, 2s.

SCOTLAND YARD, Past & Present
By Ex-Chief-Inspector CAVANAGH. Post 8vo, illustrated boards, 2s.; cloth, 2s. 6d.

SECRET OUT, The: One Thousand Tricks with Cards; with Entertaining Experiments in Drawing-room or 'White' Magic. By W. H. CREMER. With 300 Illusts. Crown 8vo, cloth, 4s. 6d.

SEGUIN (L. G.).—Walks in Algiers. With Two Maps and 16 Illustrations. Crown 8vo, cloth, 6s.

SENIOR (WM.).—By Stream and Sea. Post 8vo cloth, 2s. 6d.

SERGEANT (ADELINE), Novels by. Crown 8vo, cloth, 3s. 6d. each.
Under False Pretences.
Dr. Endicott's Experiment.
The Missing Elizabeth. Crown 8vo, cloth, 6s.

SEYMOUR (CYRIL). — The Magic of To-Morrow. Crown 8vo, cloth, 6s.

SHAKESPEARE the Boy: Home and School Life, Games and Sports, Manners, Customs, and Folk-lore of the Time. By W. J. ROLFE. With 42 Illustrations. Crown 8vo, cloth, 3s. 6d.

SHARP (WILLIAM).—Children of To-morrow. Crown 8vo, cloth, 6s.

SHELLEY'S (PERCY B.) Complete Works in Verse and Prose. Edited by R. HERNE SHEPHERD. Five Vols., crown 8vo, cloth, 3s. 6d. each.
Poetical Works, In Three Vols.:
Vol. I. Introduction; Posthumous Fragments of Margaret Nicholson; Shelley's Correspondence with Stockdale; Wandering Jew; Queen Mab; Alastor; Rosalind and Helen; Prometheus Unbound; Adonais.
Vol. II. Laon and Cythna: The Cenci; Julian and Maddalo; Swellfoot the Tyrant; The Witch of Atlas; Epipsychidion; Hellas
Vol. III. Posthumous Poems; The Masque of Anarchy; and other Pieces.
Prose Works, in Two Vols.:
Vol. I. Zastrozzi and St. Irvyne; the Dublin and Marlow Pamphlets; A Refutation of Deism; Letters to Leigh Hunt, and Minor Writings and Fragments.
Vol. II. Essays; Letters from Abroad; Translations and Fragments, edited by Mrs. SHELLEY. With a Biography, and Index.

SHERARD (R. H.).—Rogues. Crown 8vo, cloth, 1s. 6d.

SHERIDAN'S (RICHARD BRINSLEY) Complete Works. Including Drama, Prose and Poetry, Translations, Speeches; and a Memoir. Crown 8vo, cloth, 3s. 6d.
The Rivals, The School for Scandal, &c. Post 8vo, half-cloth, 2s.
Sheridan's Comedies: The Rivals and The School for Scandal. Edited by BRANDER MATTHEWS. With Illustrations. Demy 8vo, buckram, 12s. 6d.

SHIEL (M. P.), Novels by.
The Purple Cloud. Cr. 8vo, cloth, 3s. 6d.
Unto the Third Generation. Cr. 8vo, cloth, 6s.

SIDNEY'S (Sir PHILIP) Complete Poetical Works. With Portrait. Edited by the Rev. A. B. GROSART. Three Vols., crown 8vo, cloth, 3s. 6d. each.

SIGNBOARDS: Their History, including Anecdotes of Famous Taverns and Remarkable Characters. By JACOB LARWOOD and JOHN CAMDEN HOTTEN. With Frontispiece and 94 Illustrations Crown 8vo, cloth, 3s. 6d.

CHATTO & WINDUS, PUBLISHERS,

SIMS (GEORGE R.), Works by.
Post 8vo, Illustrated boards, 2s. each; cloth limp, 2s. 6d. each.
The Ring o' Bells.
Tinkletop's Crime. | Zeph.
Dramas of Life. With 60 Illustrations.
My Two Wives. | Tales of To-day.
Memoirs of a Landlady.
Scenes from the Show.
The Ten Commandments.

Crown 8vo, picture cover, 1s. each; cloth, 1s. 6d. each.
The Dagonet Reciter and Reader.
The Case of George Candlemas.
Dagonet Ditties.
Young Mrs. Caudle.
The Life We Live.
Li Ting of London.

Crown 8vo, cloth, 3s. 6d. each; post 8vo, picture boards, 2s. each; cloth 2s. 6d. each.
Mary Jane's Memoirs.
Mary Jane Married.
Dagonet Abroad.

Crown 8vo, cloth, 3s. 6d. each.
Once upon a Christmas Time. With 8 Illustrations by CHAS. GREEN, R.I.
In London's Heart.
A Blind Marriage.
Without the Limelight.
The Small-part Lady.
Biographs of Babylon.
Among My Autographs. With 70 Facsimiles

Picture cloth, flat back, 2s. each.
Rogues and Vagabonds.
In London's Heart.

How the Poor Live; and Horrible London. Crown 8vo, leatherette, 1s.
Dagonet Dramas. Crown 8vo, 1s.
Rogues and Vagabonds. Crown 8vo, cloth, 3s. 6d.; post 8vo, illust. boards, 2s.; cloth limp, 2s. 6d.

SINCLAIR (UPTON). — Prince Hagen. Crown 8vo, cloth, 3s. 6d.

SISTER DORA. By M. LONSDALE. Demy 8vo, 4d.; cloth, 6d.

SKETCHLEY (ARTHUR).—A Match in the Dark. Post 8vo, illustrated boards, 2s.

SLANG DICTIONARY (The): Etymological, Historical, and Anecdotal. Crown 8vo, cloth, 6s. 6d.

SMART (HAWLEY), Novels by.
Crown 8vo, cloth, 3s. 6d. each; post 8vo, picture boards, 2s. each.
Beatrice and Benedick.
Long Odds.
Without Love or Licence.
The Master of Rathkelly.

Crown 8vo, cloth, 3s. 6d. each.
The Outsider. | A Racing Rubber.

The Plunger. Post 8vo, picture bds., 2s.

SMITH (J. MOYR), Works by.
The Prince of Argolis. With 130 Illustrations. Post 8vo, cloth, 3s. 6d.
The Wooing of the Water Witch. With Illustrations. Post 8vo, cloth, 6s.

SNAZELLEPARILLA. Decanted by G. S. EDWARDS. With Portrait of G. H. SNAZELLE, and 65 Illustrations. Crown 8vo, cloth, 3s. 6d.

SOCIETY IN LONDON. Crown 8vo, 1s.; cloth, 1s. 6d.

SOMERSET (Lord HENRY).—Songs of Adieu. Small 4to, Jap. vellum, 6s.

SPEIGHT (T. W.), Novels by
Post 8vo, illustrated boards, 2s. each.
The Mysteries of Heron Dyke.
By Devious Ways.
Hoodwinked; & Sandycroft Mystery. | The Golden Hoop.
Back to Life.
The Loudwater Tragedy.
Burgo's Romance.
Quittance in Full.
A Husband from the Sea.

Post 8vo, cloth, 1s. 6d. each.
A Barren Title.
Wife or No Wife.

Crown 8vo, cloth, 3s. 6d. each.
The Grey Monk.
The Master of Trenance.
Her Ladyship.
The Secret of Wyvern Towers.
The Doom of Siva.
The Web of Fate.
The Strange Experiences of Mr. Verschoyle.
As it was Written.

Stepping Blindfold: Cr. 8vo, cloth, 6s.

SPENSER for Children. By M. H. TOWRY. With Coloured Illustrations by W. J. MORGAN. Crown 4to, cloth, 3s. 6d.

SPETTIGUE (H. H.). — The Heritage of Eve. Cr. 8vo, cloth, 6s.

SPRIGGE (S. SQUIRE). — An Industrious Chevalier. Cr. 8vo, 6s.

STAFFORD (JOHN), Novels by.
Doris and I. Crown 8vo, cloth, 3s. 6d.
Carlton Priors. Crown 8vo, cloth, 6s.

STAG-HUNTING with the 'Devon & Somerset.' By P. EVERED. With 70 Illusts. Cr. 4to, cloth, 16s. net.

STANLEY (WINIFRED). — A Flash of the Will. Cr. 8vo, cloth, 6s.

STARRY HEAVENS Poetical Birthday Book. Pott 8vo, cloth, 2s. 6d.

STEDMAN (E. C.).—Victorian Poets. Crown 8vo, cloth, 9s.

STEPHENS (R. NEILSON).—Philip Winwood: The Domestic History of an American Captain in the War of Independence. Cr. 8vo, cloth, 3s. 6d.

111 ST. MARTIN'S LANE, LONDON, W.C. 23

STEPHENS (RICCARDO).—The Cruciform Mark. Cr. 8vo, cl., 3s. 6d.

STERNDALE (R. ARMITAGE).
—The Afghan Knife. Post 8vo, cloth, 3s. 6d. ; illustrated boards, 2s.

STEVENSON (R. LOUIS),
Works by. Cr. 8vo, buckram, 6s. each.
Travels with a Donkey. With a Frontispiece by WALTER CRANE.
An Inland Voyage. With a Frontispiece by WALTER CRANE.
Familiar Studies of Men & Books.
The Silverado Squatters.
The Merry Men.
Underwoods: Poems.
Memories and Portraits.
Virginibus Puerisque.
Ballads. | Prince Otto.
Across the Plains.
Weir of Hermiston.
In the South Seas.
Essays of Travel.
Tales and Fantasies.
The Art of Writing.
Songs of Travel. Cr. 8vo, buckram, 5s.

New Arabian Nights. Crown 8vo, buckram, 6s.; post 8vo, illustrated boards, 2s.—POPULAR EDITION, medium 8vo. 6d.

The Suicide Club; and The Rajah's Diamond. (From NEW ARABIAN NIGHTS.) With 8 Illustrations by W. J. HENNESSY. Crown 8vo, cloth, 3s. 6d.

The Stevenson Reader. Edited by LLOYD OSBOURNE. Post 8vo, cloth, 2s. 6d.; buckram, gilt top, 3s. 6d.

The Pocket R.L.S.: Favourite Passages. 16mo, cl., 2s. net; leather, 3s. net.

LARGE TYPE, FINE PAPER EDITIONS.
Pott 8vo, cloth, gilt top, 2s. net each; leather, gilt edges, 3s. net each.
Virginibus Puerisque.
Familiar Studies of Men & Books.
New Arabian Nights.
Memories and Portraits.
Across the Plains.
The Merry Men.

R. L. Stevenson: A Study. By H. B. BAILDON. With 2 Portraits. Crown 8vo, buckram, 6s.

Recollections of R. L. Stevenson in the Pacific. By ARTHUR JOHNSTONE. With Portrait and Facsimile Letter. Crown 8vo, buckram, 6s. net.

STOCKTON (FRANK R.).—The Young Master of Hyson Hall. With 36 Illustrations. Crown 8vo, cloth, 3s. 6d.; picture cloth, flat back, 2s.

STODDARD (C. W.), Books by.
Post 8vo, cloth, gilt top, 6s. net each.
Summer Cruising in the South Seas.
The Island of Tranquil Delight.

STRANGE SECRETS. Told by PERCY FITZGERALD, CONAN DOYLE, FLORENCE MARRYAT, &c. Post 8vo, illustrated boards, 2s.

STRUTT (JOSEPH).—The Sports and Pastimes of the People of England. Edited by WILLIAM HONE. With 140 Illustrations. Crown 8vo, cloth, 3s. 6d.

SUNDOWNER, Stories by.
Told by the Taffrail. Crown 8vo, cloth, 3s. 6d.
The Tale of the Serpent. Crown 8vo, cloth, flat back, 2s.

SURTEES (ROBERT).—
Handley Cross; or, Mr. Jorrocks's Hunt. With 79 Illusts. by JOHN LEECH. Post 8vo, picture cover, 1s.; cloth, 2s.

SUTRO (ALFRED).—The Foolish Virgins. Fcp. 8vo, 1s.; cl., 1s. 6d.

SWINBURNE'S (ALGERNON CHARLES) Works.
Selections from Mr. Swinburne's Works. Fcap. 8vo, 6s.
Atalanta in Calydon. Crown 8vo, 6s.
Chastelard: A Tragedy. Crown 8vo, 7s.
Poems and Ballads. FIRST SERIES. Crown 8vo, 9s.
Poems and Ballads. SECOND SERIES. Crown 8vo, 9s.
Poems and Ballads. THIRD SERIES. Crown 8vo, 7s.
Songs before Sunrise. Crown 8vo, 10s. 6d.
Bothwell: A Tragedy. Crown 8vo, 12s. 6d.
Songs of Two Nations. Crown 8vo, 6s.
George Chapman. (In Vol. II. of G. CHAPMAN'S Works.) Crown 8vo, 3s. 6d.
Essays and Studies. Crown 8vo, 12s.
Erechtheus: A Tragedy. Crown 8vo, 6s.
A Note on Charlotte Bronte. Crown 8vo, 6s.
A Study of Shakespeare. Crown 8vo, 8s.
Songs of the Springtides. Crown 8vo, 6s.
Studies in Song. Crown 8vo, 7s.
Mary Stuart: A Tragedy. Crown 8vo, 8s.
Tristram of Lyonesse. Crown 8vo, 9s.
A Century of Roundels. Small 4to, 8s.
A Midsummer Holiday. Cr. 8vo, 7s.
Marino Faliero: A Tragedy. Crown 8vo, 6s.
A Study of Victor Hugo. Cr. 8vo, 6s.
Miscellanies. Crown 8vo, 12s.
Locrine: A Tragedy. Crown 8vo, 6s.
A Study of Ben Jonson. Cr. 8vo, 7s.
The Sisters: A Tragedy. Crown 8vo, 6s.
Astrophel, &c. Crown 8vo, 7s.
Studies in Prose and Poetry. Crown 8vo, 9s.
The Tale of Balen. Crown 8vo, 7s.
Rosamund, Queen of the Lombards: A Tragedy. Crown 8vo, 6s.
A Channel Passage. Crown 8vo, 7s.
Mr. Swinburne's Novel. Crown 8vo, 6s. net.
Mr. Swinburne's Collected Poems. In 6 Vols., crown 8vo, 6s. net each, or 36s. net the Set.
Mr. Swinburne's Tragedies. In 5 Vols., cr. 8vo, 6s. net each, or 30s. net the set. (Can be subscribed for only in Sets.)

CHATTO & WINDUS, PUBLISHERS,

SWIFT'S (Dean) Choice Works, in Prose and Verse. With Memoir, Portrait, and Facsimiles of Maps in 'Gulliver's Travels.' Crown 8vo, cloth, 3s. 6d.
Gulliver's Travels, and A Tale of a Tub. Post 8vo, half-cloth, 2s.
Jonathan Swift: A Study. By J. CHURTON COLLINS. Cr. 8vo, cl., 3s. 6d.

TAINE'S History of English Literature. Translated by HENRY VAN LAUN. Four Vols., demy 8vo, cloth, 30s.
—POPULAR EDITION, Two Vols., crown 8vo, cloth, 15s.

TAYLOR (BAYARD).—Diversions of Echo Club. Post 8vo, cl., 2s.

TAYLOR (TOM). — Historical Dramas: 'JEANNE DARC,' 'TWIXT AXE AND CROWN,' 'THE FOOL'S REVENGE,' 'AREWRIGHT'S WIFE,' 'ANNE BOLEYN,' 'PLOT AND PASSION.' Crown 8vo, 1s. each.

TEMPLE (SIR RICHARD).—A Bird's-eye View of Picturesque India. With 32 Illusts. Cr. 8vo, cl., 6s.

THACKERAYANA: Notes and Anecdotes. With Coloured Frontispiece and Hundreds of Sketches by W. M. THACKERAY. Crown 8vo, cloth, 3s. 6d.

THAMES, A Pictorial History of the. By A. S. KRAUSSE. With 340 Illustrations. Post 8vo, cloth, 1s. 6d.

THOMAS (ANNIE), Novels by.
The Siren's Web. Cr. 8vo, cl., 3s. 6d.
Comrades True. Crown 8vo, cloth, 6s.

THOMAS (BERTHA), Novels by.
In a Cathedral City. Cr. 8vo, cl., 3s. 6d.
Crown 8vo, cloth, 6s. each.
The House on the Scar.
The Son of the House.

THOMSON'S SEASONS, and The Castle of Indolence. With Introduction by ALLAN CUNNINGHAM, and 48 Illustrations. Post 8vo, half-cloth, 2s.

THORNBURY (WALT.), Books by
The Life and Correspondence of J. M. W. Turner. With 8 Coloured Illusts. and 2 Woodcuts. Cr. 8vo, cl., 3s. 6d.
Tales for the Marines. Post 8vo, illustrated boards, 2s.

TIMBS (JOHN), Works by.
Crown 8vo, cloth, 3s. 6d. each.
Clubs and Club Life in London. With 41 Illustrations.
English Eccentrics and Eccentricities. With 48 Illustrations.

TOMPKINS (HERBERT W.).—Marsh-Country Rambles. With a Frontispiece. Crown 8vo, cloth, 6s.

TREETON (ERNEST A.).—The Instigator. Crown 8vo, cloth, 6s.

TROLLOPE (T. A.).—Diamond Cut Diamond. Post 8vo, illus. bds., 2s.

TWELLS (JULIA H.).—Et tu, Sejane! Crown 8vo, cloth, 6s.

TROLLOPE (ANTHONY), Novels by. Crown 8vo, c'oth, 3s. 6d. each; post 8vo, illustrated boards, 2s. each,
The Way We Live Now.
Frau Frohmann. | **Marion Fay.**
Mr. Scarborough's Family.
The Land-Leaguers.

Post 8vo, illustrated boards, 2s. each.
Kept in the Dark.
The American Senator.
The Golden Lion of Granpere.

TROLLOPE (FRANCES E.),
Novels by. Crown 8vo, cloth, 3s. 6d. each; post 8vo, illustrated boards, 2s. each.
Like Ships upon the Sea.
Mabel's Progress. | **Anne Furness.**

TWAIN'S (MARK) Books.
Author's Edition de Luxe of the Works of Mark Twain, in 23 Volumes (limited to 600 Numbered Copies), price 12s. 6d. net per Volume. (Can be subscribed for only in Sets.)

UNIFORM LIBRARY EDITION. Crown 8vo, cloth, 3s. 6d. each.
Mark Twain's Library of Humour. With 197 Illustrations by E. W. KEMBLE.
Roughing It: and **The Innocents at Home.** With 200 Illustrations by F. A. FRASER.
The American Claimant. With 81 Illustrations by HAL HURST and others.
* **The Adventures of Tom Sawyer.** With 111 Illustrations.
Tom Sawyer Abroad. With 26 Illustrations by DAN BEARD.
Tom Sawyer, Detective. With Port. **Pudd'nhead Wilson.** With Portrait and Six Illustrations by LOUIS LOEB.
* **A Tramp Abroad.** With 314 Illusts.
* **The Innocents Abroad;** or, New Pilgrim's Progress. With 234 Illusts.
* **The Gilded Age.** By MARK TWAIN and C. D. WARNER. With 212 Illusts.
The Prince and the Pauper. With 190 Illustrations.
* **Life on the Mississippi.** 300 Illusts.
* **The Adventures of Huckleberry Finn.** 174 Illusts. by E. W. KEMBLE.
* **A Yankee at the Court of King Arthur.** 220 Illusts. by DAN BEARD.
* **The Stolen White Elephant.**
* **The £1,000,000 Bank-Note.**
A Double-barrelled Detective Story. With 7 Illustrations.
The Choice Works of Mark Twain. With Life, Portrait, and Illustrations.
⁎ The Books marked * may be had also in post 8vo, picture boards, at 2s. each.

Crown 8vo, cloth, 6s. each.
Personal Recollections of Joan of Arc. With 12 Illusts. by F. V. DU MOND.
More Tramps Abroad.
The Man that Corrupted Hadleyburg. With Frontispiece.

Mark Twain's Sketches. Pott 8vo, cloth, gilt top, 2s. net; leather, gilt edges, 3s. net; picture boards, 2s.

111 ST. MARTIN'S LANE, LONDON, W.C. 25

TYTLER (C. C. FRASER-).—
Mistress Judith. Crown 8vo, cloth, 3s. 6d.; post 8vo, illustrated boards, 2s.

TYTLER (SARAH), Novels by.
Crown 8vo, cloth, 3s. 6d. each; post 8vo, illustrated boards, 2s. each.
Buried Diamonds.
The Blackhall Ghosts.
What She Came Through.

Post 8vo, illustrated boards, 2s. each.
The Bride's Pass.
Saint Mungo's City.
The Huguenot Family.
Lady Bell. | Noblesse Oblige.
Disappeared.
Beauty and the Beast.

Crown 8vo, cloth, 3s. 6d. each.
The Macdonald Lass.
The Witch-Wife.
Rachel Langton.
Mrs. Carmichael's Goddesses.
Sapphira.
A Honeymoon's Eclipse.
A Young Dragon.

Crown 8vo, cloth, 6s. each.
Three Men of Mark.
In Clarissa's Day.
Sir David's Visitors.
The Poet and his Guardian Angel.
Citoyenne Jacqueline. Crown 8vo, picture cloth, flat back, 2s.

UPWARD (ALLEN), Novels by.
The Queen against Owen. Crown 8vo, cloth, 3s. 6d.; picture cloth, flat back, 2s.; post 8vo, picture boards, 2s.
The Phantom Torpedo-Boats. Crown 8vo, cloth, 6s.

VANDAM (ALBERT D.).—A
Court Tragedy. With 6 Illustrations by J. B. DAVIS. Crown 8vo, cloth, 3s. 6d.

VASHTI and ESTHER. By 'Belle' of *The World*. Cr. 8vo, cl. 3s. 6d.

VIZETELLY (ERNEST A.),
Books by. Crown 8vo, cloth, 3s. 6d. each.
The Scorpion.
The Lover's Progress.
With Zola in England. 4 Ports.
A Path of Thorns. Crown 8vo, cloth, 6s.
Bluebeard: An account of Comorre the Cursed and Gilles de Rais. With 9 Illustrations. Demy 8vo, cloth, 9s. net.
The Wild Marquis: Life and Adventures of Armand Guerry de Maubreuil. Crown 8vo, cloth, 6s.

WAGNER (LEOPOLD).—How
to Get on the Stage, and how to Succeed there. Crown 8vo, cloth, 2s. 6d.

WALLER (S. E.).—Sebastiani's
Secret. With 9 Illusts. Cr. 8vo, cl., 6s.

WALTON and COTTON'S
Complete Angler. Edited by Sir HARRIS NICOLAS. Pott 8vo, cloth, gilt top, 2s. net; leather, gilt edges, 3s. net.

WALT WHITMAN, Poems by.
Edited, with Introduction, by W. M. ROSSETTI. With Port. Cr. 8vo, buckram, 6s.

WARDEN (FLORENCE), by.
Joan, the Curate. Crown 8vo, cloth, 3s. 6d.; picture cloth, flat back, 2s.
A Fight to a Finish. Cr. 8vo, cl., 3s. 6d.

Crown 8vo, cloth, 6s. each.
The Heart of a Girl. With 8 Illusts.
What Ought She to Do?
Tom Dawson.
The Youngest Miss Brown.

WARMAN (CY).—The Express
Messenger. Crown 8vo, cloth, 3s. 6d.

WARNER (CHAS. DUDLEY).—
A Roundabout Journey. Cr. 8vo, 6s.

WARRANT to Execute Charles I.
A Facsimile, with the 59 Signatures and Seals. 2s.
Warrant to Execute Mary Queen of Scots. Including Queen Elizabeth's Signature and the Great Seal. 2s.

WASSERMANN (LILLIAS).—
The Daffodils. Crown 8vo, cloth, 1s. 6d.

WEATHER, How to Foretell the,
with the Pocket Spectroscope. By F. W. CORY. With 10 Illustrations. Crown. 8vo, 1s.; cloth, 1s. 6d.

WEBBER (BYRON).—Sport and
Spangles. Crown 8vo, cloth, 2s.

WERNER (A.).—Chapenga's
White Man. Crown 8vo, cloth, 3s. 6d.

WESTALL (WILL.), Novels by.
Trust-Money. Crown 8vo, cloth, 3s. 6d.; post 8vo, illustrated boards, 2s.

Crown 8vo, cloth, 6s. each.
As a Man Sows. | The Old Bank.
Dr. Wynne's Revenge.
The Sacred Crescents.
A Very Queer Business.

Crown 8vo, cloth, 3s. 6d. each.
A Woman Tempted Him.
For Honour and Life.
Her Two Millions.
Two Pinches of Snuff.
With the Red Eagle.
A Red Bridal. | Nigel Fortescue.
Ben Clough. | Birch Dene.
The Old Factory.
Sons of Belial. | Strange Crimes.
Her Ladyship's Secret.
The Phantom City.
Ralph Norbreck's Trust.
A Queer Race. | Red Ryvington.
Roy of Roy's Court.
As Luck would have it.

The Old Factory. Medium 8vo, 6d.

WESTBURY (ATHA). — The
Shadow of Hilton Fernbrook. Crown 8vo, cloth, 3s. 6d.

CHATTO & WINDUS, PUBLISHERS,

WHEELWRIGHT (E. G.).—A Slow Awakening. Crown 8vo cloth, 6s.

WHISHAW (FRED.), Novels by. Crown 8vo, cloth, 3s. 6d. each.
A Forbidden Name.
Many Ways of Love. With 8 Illusts.
Crown 8vo, cloth, 6s. each.
Mazeppa.
Near the Tsar, near Death
A Splendid Impostor.

WHITE (GILBERT).—Natural History of Selborne. Post 8vo, cloth, 2s.

WILDE (LADY).—The Ancient Legends, Charms, and Superstitions of Ireland. Crown 8vo, cloth, 3s. 6d.

WILLIAMS (W. MATTIEU), by.
Science in Short Chapters. Crown 8vo, cloth, 7s. 6d.
The Chemistry of Cookery. Crown 8vo, cloth, 6s.
A Simple Treatise on Heat. With Illustrations. Crown 8vo, cloth, 2s. 6d.

WILLIAMSON (Mrs. F. H.).—A Child Widow. Post 8vo, illust. bds., 2s.

WILLS (C. J.), Novels by.
An Easy-going Fellow. Crown 8vo, cloth, 3s. 6d.
His Dead Past. Crown 8vo, cloth, 6s.

WILSON (Dr. ANDREW), by.
Chapters on Evolution. With 259 Illustrations. Crown 8vo, cloth, 7s. 6d.
Leisure-Time Studies. With Illustrations. Crown 8vo, cloth, 6s.
Studies in Life and Sense. With 36 Illustrations. Crown 8vo, cloth, 3s. 6d.
Common Accidents, and how to Treat Them. Cr. 8vo, 1s.; cloth, 1s. 6d.
Glimpses of Nature. With 35 Illustrations. Crown 8vo, cloth, 3s. 6d.

WINTER (JOHN STRANGE), by. Post 8vo, 2s. each; cloth 2s. 6d. each
Cavalry Life.
Regimental Legends.

Cavalry Life and Regimental Legends, together. Crown 8vo, cloth, 3s. 6d.; picture cloth, flat back, 2s.

WISSMANN (HERMANN VON).— My Second Journey through Equatorial Africa. With 92 Illustrations. Demy 8vo, cloth, 16s.

WOOD (H. F.), Detective Stories by. Post 8vo, illustrated boards 2s. each.
Passenger from Scotland Yard.
The Englishman of the Rue Cain.

WOOLLEY (CELIA PARKER).— Rachel Armstrong. Post 8vo, 2s. 6d.

WRIGHT (THOMAS), by.
Caricature History of the Georges; or, Annals of the House of Hanover. With Frontispiece and over 300 Illustrations. Crown 8vo, cloth, 3s. 6d.
History of Caricature and of the Grotesque in Art, Literature, Sculpture, and Painting. Illustrated by F. W. FAIRHOLT. Crown 8vo, cloth, 7s. 6d.

WYNMAN (MARGARET).—My Flirtations. With 13 Illustrations by BERNARD PARTRIDGE. Post 8vo, cloth, 2s.

ZANGWILL (LOUIS).—A Nineteenth Century Miracle. Crown 8vo, cloth, 3s. 6d.; picture cloth, flat back, 2s.

ZOLA (EMILE), Novels by. UNIFORM EDITION, Translated or Edited, with Introductions, by ERNEST A. VIZETELLY. Crown 8vo, cloth, 3s. 6d. each.
His Masterpiece. | The Joy of Life.
Germinal.
The Honour of the Army.
Abbe Mouret's Transgression.
The Fortune of the Rougons.
The Conquest of Plassans.
The Dram-Shop.
The Fat and the Thin. | Money.
His Excellency. | The Dream.
The Downfall. | Doctor Pascal.
Rome. | Truth.
Lourdes. | Work.
Paris. | Fruitfulness.

POPULAR EDITIONS, medium 8vo, 6d. each.
The Dram-Shop. | The Downfall.
Rome. | Paris.

With Zola in England. By ERNEST A. VIZETELLY. With 4 Portraits. Crown 8vo, cloth, 3s. 6d.

THE PICCADILLY NOVELS.

LIBRARY EDITIONS, many Illustrated, crown 8vo, cloth, 3s. 6d. each.

By Mrs. ALEXANDER.

Valerie's Fate.	Barbara.
A Life Interest.	A Fight with Fate.
Mona's Choice.	A Golden Autumn.
By Woman's Wit.	Mrs. Crichton's Creditor.
The Cost of Her Pride.	The Step-mother.
A Missing Hero.	

By F. M. ALLEN.—Green as Grass.

By M. ANDERSON.—Othello's Occupation.

By O. W. APPLETON.—Rash Conclusions.

By GRANT ALLEN.

Philistia.	Babylon.	The Great Taboo.
Strange Stories.		Dumaresq's Daughter.
For Maimie's Sake.		Duchess of Powysland.
In all Shades.		Blood Royal.
The Beckoning Hand.		Ivan Greet's Masterpiece.
The Devil's Die.		The Scallywag.
This Mortal Coil.		At Market Value.
The Tents of Shem.		Under Sealed Orders.

ARTEMUS WARD'S WORKS, Complete.

By EDWIN L. ARNOLD.
Phra the Phœnician. | Constable of st. Nicholas.

111 ST. MARTIN'S LANE, LONDON, W.C. 27

THE PICCADILLY (3/6) NOVELS—*continued.*

By ROBERT BARR.
In a Steamer Chair. | A Woman Intervenes.
From Whose Bourne. | Revenge!
A Prince of Good Fellows.

By FRANK BARRETT.
A Prodigal's Progress. | The Harding Scandal
Woman of Iron Bracelets. | Under a Strange Mask.
Fettered for Life. | A Missing Witness.
Was She Justified?

By 'BELLE,'—Vashti and Esther.

By ARNOLD BENNETT.
The Gates of Wrath. | The Grand Babylon Hotel.

By Sir W. BESANT and J. RICE.
Ready-Money Mortiboy. | By Celia's Arbour.
My Little Girl. | Chaplain of the Fleet.
With Harp and Crown. | The Seamy Side.
This Son of Vulcan. | The Case of Mr. Lucraft.
The Golden Butterfly. | In Trafalgar's Bay.
The Monks of Thelema. | The Ten Years' Tenant.

By Sir WALTER BESANT.
All Sorts and Conditions. | Verbena Camellia Stepha-
The Captains' Room. | The Ivory Gate. [notis.
All in a Garden Fair. | The Rebel Queen
Dorothy Forster. | Dreams of Avarice.
Uncle Jack. | Holy Rose. | In Deacon's Orders.
World Went Well Then. | The Master Craftsman.
Children of Gibeon. | The City of Refuge.
Herr Paulus. | A Fountain Sealed.
For Faith and Freedom. | The Changeling.
To Call Her Mine. | The Fourth Generation.
The Revolt of Man. | The Charm.
The Bell of St. Paul's. | The Alabaster Box.
Armorel of Lyonesse. | The Orange Girl.
S. Katherine's by Tower. | The Lady of Lynn.

By AMBROSE BIERCE.—In Midst of Life.

By HAROLD BINDLOSS.—Ainslie's Ju-Ju.

By M. McD. BODKIN.
Dora Myrl. | Shillelagh and Shamrock.
Patsey the Omadaun.

By PAUL BOURGET.—A Living Lie.

By J. D. BRAYSHAW.—Slum Silhouettes.

By H. A. BRYDEN.—An Exiled Scot.

By ROBERT BUCHANAN.
Shadow of the Sword. | The New Abelard.
A Child of Nature. | Matt. | Rachel Dene.
God and the Man. | Master of the Mine.
Martyrdom of Madeline. | The Heir of Linne.
Love Me for Ever. | Woman and the Man.
Annan Water. | Red and White Heather.
Foxglove Manor. | Lady Kilpatrick.
The Charlatan. | Andromeda.

GELETT BURGESS and WILL IRWIN.
The Picaroons.

By HALL CAINE.
Shadow of a Crime. | Son of Hagar. | Deemster.

By R. W. CHAMBERS.—The King in Yellow.

By J. M. CHAPPLE.—The Minor Chord.

By AUSTIN CLARE.—By Rise of River.

By Mrs. ARCHER CLIVE.
Paul Ferroll. | Why Paul Ferroll Killed his Wife.

By ANNE COATES.—Rie's Diary.

By MACLAREN COBBAN.
The Red Sultan. | The Burden of Isabel.

By WILKIE COLLINS.
Armadale. | After Dark. | The New Magdalen.
No Name. | Antonina | The Frozen Deep.
Basil. | Hide and Seek. | The Two Destinies.
The Dead Secret. | 'I Say No.'
Queen of Hearts. | Little Novels.
My Miscellanies. | The Fallen Leaves.
The Woman in White. | Jezebel's Daughter.
The Law and the Lady. | The Black Robe.
The Haunted Hotel. | Heart and Science.
The Moonstone. | The Evil Genius.
Man and Wife. | The Legacy of Cain.
Poor Miss Finch. | A Rogue's Life.
Miss or Mrs. | Blind Love.

By MORT. and FRANCES COLLINS.
Blacksmith and Scholar. | You May Me False.
The Village Comedy. | Midnight to Midnight.

By M. J. COLQUHOUN.—Every Inch a Soldier.

By HERBERT COMPTON.
The Inimitable Mrs. Massingham.

By E. H. COOPER.—Geoffory Hamilton.

By V. C. COTES.—Two Girls on a Barge.

By C. EGBERT CRADDOCK.
The Prophet of the Great Smoky Mountains.
His Vanished Star.

By H. N. CRELLIN.
Romances of the Old Seraglio.

By MATT CRIM.
The Adventures of a Fair Rebel.

By S. R. CROCKETT and others.
Tales of Our Coast.

By B. M. CROKER.
Diana Barrington. | The Real Lady Hilda.
Proper Pride. | Married or Single?
A Family Likeness. | Two Masters.
Pretty Miss Neville. | In the Kingdom of Kerry.
A Bird of Passage. | Interference.
Mr. Jervis. | A Third Person.
Village Tales. | Beyond the Pale.
Some One Else. | Jason. | Miss Balmaine's Past.
Infatuation. | Terence. | The Cat's-paw

By ALPHONSE DAUDET.
The Evangelist; or, Port Salvation.

By H. C. DAVIDSON.—Mr. Sadler's Daughters.

By DOROTHEA DEAKIN.
The Poet and the Pierrot.

By JAMES DE MILLE.
A Strange Manuscript Found in a Copper Cylinder.

By HARRY DE WINDT.
True Tales of Travel and Adventure.

By DICK DONOVAN.
Man from Manchester. | Tales of Terror.
Records of Vincent Trill. | Chronicles of Michael
Myst. of Jamaica Terrace. | Danevitch [Detective.
Deacon Brodie. | Tyler Tatlock, Private
RICHARD DOWLING.—Old Corcoran's Money.
CONAN DOYLE.—The Firm of Girdlestone.

By S. JEANNETTE DUNCAN.
A Daughter of To-day | Vernon's Aunt.

By ANNIE EDWARDES.
Archie Lovell. | A Plaster Saint.

By G. S. EDWARDS.—Snazelleparilla.

By G. MANVILLE FENN.
Cursed by a Fortune. | A Fluttered Dovecote.
The Case of Ailsa Gray. | King of the Castle.
Commodore Junk. | Master of the Ceremonies.
The New Mistress. | The Man with a Shadow.
Witness to the Deed. | One Maid's Mischief.
The Tiger Lily. | Story of Antony Grace.
The White Virgin. | This Man's Wife.
Black Blood. | In Jeopardy.
Double Cunning. | Woman Worth Winning.
The Bag of Diamonds.

By PERCY FITZGERALD.—Fatal Zero.

By Hon. Mrs. W. FORBES.—Dumb.

By R. E. FRANCILLON.
One by One. | A Real Queen.
A Dog and his Shadow. | Ropes of Sand.
Jack Doyle's Daughter.

By HAROLD FREDERIC.
Seth's Brother's Wife. | The Lawton Girl.

By PAUL GAULOT.—The Red Shirts.

By DOROTHEA GERARD.
A Queen of Curds and Cream.

By CHARLES GIBBON.
Robin Gray. | The Braes of Yarrow.
Of High Degree. | Queen of the Meadow.
The Golden Shaft. | The Flower of the Forest.

By E. GLANVILLE.
The Lost Heiress. | The Golden Rock.
Fair Colonist. | Fossicker. | Tales from the Veld.

By E. J. GOODMAN.
The Fate of Herbert Wayne.

By Rev. S. BARING GOULD.
Red Spider. | Eve.

By ALFRED A. GRACE.
Tales of a Dying Race.

By CECIL GRIFFITH.—Corinthia Marazion.

CHATTO & WINDUS, PUBLISHERS,

THE PICCADILLY (3/6) NOVELS—*continued*.

By A. CLAVERING GUNTER.
A Florida Enchantment.

By GYP.—Cloclo.

By OWEN HALL.
The Track of a Storm | Jetsam.

By COSMO HAMILTON.
Glamour of Impossible. | Through a Keyhole.

By THOMAS HARDY.
Under the Greenwood Tree.

By BRET HARTE.
A Waif of the Plains. | A Protégée of Jack
A Ward of the Golden | Clarence. [Hamlin's.
  Gate. | Springs. | Barker's Luck.
A Sappho of Green | Devil's Ford.
  Col. Starbottle's Client. | Crusade of 'Excelsior.
Susy. | Sally Dows. | Three Partners.
Bell-Ringer of Angel's. | Gabriel Conroy.
Tales of Trail and Town. | New Condensed Novels.

By JULIAN HAWTHORNE.
Garth. | Dust. | Beatrix Randolph.
Ellice Quentin. | David Poindexter's Dis-
Sebastian Strome. | appearance.
Fortune's Fool. | Spectre of Camera.

By Sir A. HELPS.—Ivan de Biron.

By I. HENDERSON.—Agatha Page.

By G. A. HENTY.
Dorothy's Double. | The Queen's Cup.
  Rujub, the Juggler.

By HEADON HILL.—Zambra the Detective.

By JOHN HILL.—The Common Ancestor.

By TIGHE HOPKINS.
Twixt Love and Duty. | Incomplete Adventurer.
Nugents of Carriconna. | Nell Haffenden.

By E. W. HORNUNG.
The Shadow of the Rope.

By VICTOR HUGO.—The Outlaw of Iceland.

By FERGUS HUME.
Lady from Nowhere. | The Millionaire Mystery.

By Mrs. HUNGERFORD.
Marvel. | Professor's Experiment.
Unsatisfactory Lover. | A Point of Conscience.
In Durance Vile. | A Maiden all Forlorn.
A Modern Circe. | The Coming of Chloe.
Lady Patty. | Nora Creina.
A Mental Struggle. | An Anxious Moment.
Lady Verner's Flight. | April's Lady.
The Red-House Mystery. | Peter's Wife
The Three Graces. | Lovice.

By Mrs. ALFRED HUNT.
The Leaden Casket. | Self-Condemned.
That Other Person. | Mrs. Juliet.

By R. ASHE KING.—A Drawn Game.

By GEORGE LAMBERT.—President of Boravia

By EDMOND LEPELLETIER.
Madame Sans-Gene.

By ADAM LILBURN.—A Tragedy in Marble

By HARRY LINDSAY.
Rhoda Roberts. | The Jacobite.

By E. LYNN LINTON.
Patricia Kemball. | Atonement Leam Dundas.
Under which Lord? | The One Too Many.
'My Love!' | Ione. | Dulcie Everton.
Paston Carew. | The Rebel of the Family
Sowing the Wind | An Octave of Friends.
With a Silken Thread. | The World Well Lost.

By HENRY W. LUCY.—Gideon Fleyce.

By JUSTIN McCARTHY.
A Fair Saxon. | Donna Quixote.
Linley Rochford. | Maid of Athens.
Dear Lady Disdain. | The Comet of a Season.
Camiola. | Maunola. | The Dictator.
Waterdale Neighbours. | Red Diamonds.
My Enemy's Daughter. | The Riddle Ring.
Miss Misanthrope. | The Three Disgraces.

JUSTIN H. McCARTHY.—A London Legend.

By GEORGE MACDONALD.
Heather and Snow. | Phantastes.

By W. H. MALLOCK.—The New Republic.

By P. & V. MARGUERITTE.—The Disaster

By L. T. MEADE.
A Soldier of Fortune. | On Brink of a Chasm,
In an Iron Grip. | The Siren.
Dr. Rumsey's Patient. | The Way of a Woman.
The Voice of the Charmer. | A Son of Ishmael.
An Adventuress. | The Blue Diamond.
This Troublesome World. | Rosebury.
  A Stumble by the Way.

By HOPE MERRICK.
When a Girl's Engaged.

By LEONARD MERRICK.
This Stage of Fools. | Cynthia.

By EDMUND MITCHELL.
The Lone Star Rush.

By BERTRAM MITFORD.
The Gun-Runner. | The King's Assegai.
Luck of Gerard Ridgeley. | Renshaw Fanning's Quest.
The Triumph of Hilary Blachland. | Haviland's Chum.

Mrs. MOLESWORTH.—Hathercourt Rectory.

By J. E. MUDDOCK.
Maid Marian and Robin | Basile the Jester.
  Hood. | Golden Idol.
  Young Lochinvar.

By D. CHRISTIE MURRAY.
A Life's Atonement. | Bob Martin's Little Girl.
Joseph's Coat. | Time's Revenges.
Coals of Fire. | A Wasted Crime.
Old Blazer's Hero. | In Direst Peril.
Val Strange. | Hearts. | Mount Despair.
A Model Father. | A Capful o' Nails.
By the Gate of the Sea. | Tales in Prose and Verse.
A Bit of Human Nature. | A Race for Millions.
First Person Singular. | This Little World.
Cynic Fortune. | His Own Ghost.
The Way of the World. | Church of Humanity.
  V.C.: Castle Barfield and the Crimea.

By MURRAY and HERMAN.
The Bishops' Bible | Paul Jones's Alias.
  One Traveller Returns.

By HUME NISBET.—'Bail Up!'

By W. E. NORRIS.
Saint Ann's. | Billy Bellew.
  Miss Wentworth's Idea.

By G. OHNET.—A Weird Gift.
Love's Depths. | The Woman of Mystery.

By Mrs. OLIPHANT.
Whiteladies. | The Sorceress.

By OUIDA.
Held in Bondage. | Friendship. | Idalia.
Strathmore. | Chandos. | Moths. | Ruffino.
Under Two Flags. | Pipistrello. | Ariadne.
Cecil Castlemaine's Gage. | A Village Commune.
Tricotrin. | Puck. | Bimbi. | Wanda.
Folle-Farine | Frescoes. | Othmar.
A Dog of Flanders. | In Maremma.
Pascarel. | Signa. | Syrlin. | Guilderoy.
Princess Napraxine. | Santa Barbara.
Two Wooden Shoes. | Two Offenders.
In a Winter City. | The Waters of Edera.
The Massarenes. | A Rainy June.

By MARGARET A. PAUL.
Gentle and Simple.

By JAMES PAYN.
Lost Sir Massingberd. | High Spirits. | By Proxy.
The Clyffards of Clyffe. | The Talk of the Town.
The Family Scapegrace. | Holiday Tasks.
A County Family. | Painted. | For Cash Only.
Less Black than We're | The Burnt Million.
A Confidential Agent. | The Word and the Will
A Grape from a Thorn. | Sunny Stories.
In Peril and Privation. | A Trying Patient.
Mystery of Mirbridge. | Modern Dick Whittington

By WILL PAYNE.—Jerry the Dreamer

By Mrs. CAMPBELL PRAED.
Outlaw and Lawmaker. | Mrs. Tregaskiss.
Christina Chard. | Nulma. | Madame Izan.
  'As a Watch in the Night.'

By E. C. PRICE.—Valentina.

By RICHARD PRYCE.
Miss Maxwell's Affections.

By Mrs. J. H. RIDDELL.
Weird Stories. | A Rich Man's Daughter.

111 ST. MARTIN'S LANE, LONDON, W.C.   29

The Piccadilly (3/6) Novels—*continued.*
By CHARLES READE.
Peg Woffington; and Christie Johnstone.
Hard Cash.
Cloister and the Hearth.
Never Too Late to Mend.
The Course of True Love; and Singleheart and Doubleface.
Autobiography of a Thief; Jack of all Trades; A Hero and a Martyr; and The Wandering Heir.
Griffith Gaunt.
Love Little, Love Long.
The Double Marriage.
Foul Play.
Put Yourself in His Place.
A Terrible Temptation.
A Simpleton.
A Woman-Hater.
The Jilt, & other Stories: & Good Stories of Man.
A Perilous Secret.
Readiana; and Bible Characters.

By FRANK RICHARDSON.
Man Who Lost His Past. | The Bayswater Mystery.

By AMELIE RIVES.
Barbara Dering. | Meriel

By F. W. ROBINSON.
The Hands of Justice. | Woman in the Dark.

By ALBERT ROSS.—A Sugar Princess.

By J. RUNCIMAN.—Skippers and Shellbacks.

By W. CLARK RUSSELL.
Round the Galley Fire.
In the Middle Watch.
On the Fo'k'sle Head.
A Voyage to the Cape.
Book for the Hammock.
Mystery of 'Ocean Star.'
Jenny Harlowe.
An Ocean Tragedy.
A Tale of Two Tunnels.
The Death Ship.
My Shipmate Louise.
Alone on Wide Wide Sea.
The Phantom Death.
Is He the Man ?
Good Ship 'Mohock.
The Convict Ship.
Heart of Oak.
The Tale of the Ten.
The Last Entry.

By DORA RUSSELL,—Drift of Fate.
By HERBERT RUSSELL.—True Blue.
By BAYLE ST. JOHN,—A Levantine Family.

By ADELINE SERGEANT.
Dr. Endicott's Experiment | Under False Pretences.

By M. P. SHIEL.—The Purple Cloud.

By GEORGE R. SIMS.
Dagonet Abroad.
Once upon Christmas Time.
Without the Limelight
Rogues and Vagabonds.
Biographs of Babylon.
In London's Heart.
Mary Jane's Memoirs.
Mary Jane Married.
The Small-part Lady.
A Blind Marriage.

By UPTON SINCLAIR.—Prince Hagen.

By HAWLEY SMART.
Without Love or Licence.
The Master of Rathkelly.
Long Odds.
The Outsider.
Beatrice and Benedick.
A Racing Rubber.

By J. MOYR SMITH.—The Prince of Argolis.

By T. W. SPEIGHT.
The Grey Monk.
The Master of Trenance.
The Web of Fate.
Secret of Wyvern Towers.
As it was Written.
Her Ladyship.
The Strange Experiences of Mr. Verschoyle.
The Doom of Siva.

By ALAN ST. AUBYN.
A Fellow of Trinity.
The Junior Dean.
Master of St. Benedict's.
To his Own Master.
Gallantry Bower.
In Face of the World.
Orchard Damerel.
The Tremlett Diamonds.
The Wooing of May.
A Tragic Honeymoon.
A Proctor's Wooing.
Fortune's Gate.
Bonnie Maggie Lauder.
Mary Unwin.
Mrs. Dunbar's Secret.

By JOHN STAFFORD.—Doris and I.
By R. STEPHENS.—The Cruciform Mark.

R. NEILSON STEPHENS.—Philip Winwood
By R. A. STERNDALE.—The Afghan Knife.
By R. L. STEVENSON.—The Suicide Club.
By FRANK STOCKTON.
The Young Master of Hyson Hall.
By SUNDOWNER.—Told by the Taffrail.
By ANNIE THOMAS.—The Siren's Web.
By BERTHA THOMAS.
In a Cathedral City.
By FRANCES E. TROLLOPE.
Like Ships Upon Sea. | Anne Furness.
Mabel's Progress.
By ANTHONY TROLLOPE.
The Way we Live Now.
Frau Frohmann.
Marion Fay.
Scarborough's Family.
The Land-Leaguers.

By MARK TWAIN.
Choice Works.
Library of Humour.
The Innocents Abroad.
Roughing It; and The Innocents at Home.
A Tramp Abroad.
The American Claimant.
Adventures Tom Sawyer.
Tom Sawyer Abroad.
Tom Sawyer, Detective.
Pudd'nhead Wilson.
The Gilded Age.
Prince and the Pauper.
Life on the Mississippi.
Huckleberry Finn.
A Yankee at Court.
Stolen White Elephant.
£1,000,000 Bank-note.
A Double-barrelled Detective Story.

C. C. FRASER-TYTLER.—Mistress Judith.

By SARAH TYTLER.
What She Came Through.
Buried Diamonds.
The Blackhall Ghosts.
The Macdonald Lass.
Witch-Wife. | Sapphira.
Mrs. Carmichael's Goddesses.
Rachel Langton.
A Honeymoon's Eclipse.
A Young Dragon.

ALLEN UPWARD.—The Queen against Owen.
By ALBERT D. VANDAM.—A Court Tragedy.

By E. A. VIZETELLY.
The Scorpion. | The Lover's Progress.

By FLORENCE WARDEN.
Joan, the Curate. | A Fight to a Finish.

By CY WARMAN.—Express Messenger.
By A. WERNER.—Chapenga's White Man.

By WILLIAM WESTALL.
For Honour and Life
A Woman Tempted Him.
Her Two Millions.
Two Pinches of Snuff.
Nigel Fortescue.
Birch Dene. | Ben Clough.
The Phantom City.
A Queer Race.
The Old Factory.
Red Ryvington.
Ralph Norbreck's Trust.
Trust-money.
Sons of Belial.
Roy of Roy's Court.
With the Red Eagle.
A Red Bridal.
Strange Crimes.
Her Ladyship's Secret.
As Luck would have it.

By ATHA WESTBURY.
The Shadow of Hilton Fernbrook.

By FRED WHISHAW.
A Forbidden Name | Many Ways of Love.

By C. J. WILLS,—An Easy-going Fellow.
By JOHN STRANGE WINTER.
Cavalry Life; and Regimental Legends.

By LOUIS ZANGWILL.
A Nineteenth Century Miracle.

By EMILE ZOLA.
The Honour of the Army.
Germinal. | The Dream.
Abbe Mouret's Transgression. | Money.
The Conquest of Plassans.
Dram-Shop. | Downfall.
His Excellency.
His Masterpiece.
The Fat and the Thin.
Dr. Pascal. | Joy of Life.
Fortune of the Rougons.
Lourdes. | Work.
Rome. | Truth.
Paris. | Fruitfulness.

CHEAP EDITIONS OF POPULAR NOVELS.
Post 8vo, illustrated boards, 2s. each.

By Mrs. ALEXANDER.
Maid, Wife, or Widow.
Blind Fate.
Valerie's Fate.
A Life Interest.
Mono's Choice.
By Woman's Wit.

By E. LESTER ARNOLD.
Phra the Phoenician.

ARTEMUS WARD'S WORKS, Complete.

By GRANT ALLEN.
Philistia. | Babylon.
Strange Stories.
For Maimie's Sake.
In all Shades.
The Beckoning Hand.
The Devil's Die.
The Tents of Shem.
The Great Taboo.
Dumaresq's Daughter.
Duchess of Powysland.
Blood Royal.
Ivan Greet's Masterpiece.
The Scallywag.
This Mortal Coil.
At Market Value.
Under Sealed Orders.

30 CHATTO & WINDUS, PUBLISHERS,

TWO-SHILLING NOVELS—*continued.*

By FRANK BARRETT.
Fettered for Life.
Little Lady Linton.
Between Life and Death.
Sin of Olga Zassoulich.
Folly Morrison.
Lieut. Barnabas.
Honest Davie.
A Prodigal's Progress.
Found Guilty.
A Recoiling Vengeance.
For Love and Honour.
John Ford, &c.
Woman of Iron Bracelets.
The Harding Scandal.
A Missing Witness.

By Sir W. BESANT and J. RICE.
Ready-Money Mortiboy.
My Little Girl.
With Harp and Crown.
This Son of Vulcan.
The Golden Butterfly.
The Monks of Thelema.
By Celia's Arbour.
Chaplain of the Fleet.
The Seamy Side.
The Case of Mr. Lucraft.
In Trafalgar's Bay.
The Ten Years' Tenant.

By Sir WALTER BESANT.
All Sorts and Conditions.
The Captains' Room.
All in a Garden Fair.
Dorothy Forster.
Uncle Jack. [Then.
The World Went Very Well
Children of Gibeon.
Herr Paulus.
For Faith and Freedom.
To Call Her Mine.
The Master Craftsman.
The Bell of St. Paul's.
The Holy Rose.
Armorel of Lyonesse.
St. Katherine's by Tower.
Verbena Camellia Stephanotis.
The Ivory Gate.
The Rebel Queen.
Beyond Dreams Avarice.
The Revolt of Man.
In Deacon's Orders.
The City of Refuge.

AMBROSE BIERCE.—In the Midst of Life.

By FREDERICK BOYLE.
Camp Notes.
Savage Life.
Chronicles of No-man's Land.

By BRET HARTE.
Californian Stories.
Gabriel Conroy.
Luck of Roaring Camp.
An Heiress of Red Dog.
Flip. | Maruja.
A Phyllis of the Sierras.
A Waif of the Plains.
Ward of Golden Gate.

By ROBERT BUCHANAN.
Shadow of the Sword.
A Child of Nature.
God and the Man.
Love Me for Ever.
Foxglove Manor.
The Master of the Mine.
Annan Water.
The Martyrdom of Madeline.
The New Abelard.
The Heir of Linne.
Woman and the Man.
Rachel Dene. | Matt.
Lady Kilpatrick.

BUCHANAN and MURRAY.—The Charlatan.

By HALL CAINE.
A Son of Hagar. | The Deemster
The Shadow of a Crime.

By Commander CAMERON.
The Cruise of the 'Black Prince.'

By HAYDEN CARRUTH.
The Adventures of Jones.

By AUSTIN CLARE.—For the Love of a Lass.

By Mrs. ARCHER CLIVE.
Paul Ferroll. | Why Paul Ferroll Killed his Wife.

By MACLAREN COBBAN.
The Cure of Souls. | The Red Sultan.

By C. ALLSTON COLLINS.—The Bar Sinister.

By MORT. and FRANCES COLLINS.
Sweet Anne Page.
Transmigration.
From Midnight to Midnight.
A Fight with Fortune.
Sweet and Twenty.
The Village Comedy.
You Play Me False.
Blacksmith and Scholar.
Frances.

By WILKIE COLLINS.
Armadale. | After Dark.
No Name. | Antonina.
Basil. | Hide and Seek.
The Dead Secret.
Queen of Hearts.
Miss or Mrs.?
The New Magdalen.
The Frozen Deep.
The Law and the Lady.
The Two Destinies.
The Haunted Hotel.
A Rogue's Life.
My Miscellanies.
The Woman in White.
The Moonstone.
Man and Wife
Poor Miss Finch.
The Fallen Leaves.
Jezebel's Daughter.
The Black Robe.
Heart and Science.
'I Say No!'
The Evil Genius.
Little Novels.
Legacy of Cain.
Blind Love.

By M. J. COLQUHOUN.—Every Inch a Soldier.

By C. EGBERT CRADDOCK.
The Prophet of the Great Smoky Mountains.

By H. N. CRELLIN.—Tales of the Caliph.

MATT CRIM.—The Adventures of a Fair Rebel

By B. M. CROKER.
Pretty Miss Neville.
Diana Barrington.
A Bird of Passage.
Proper Pride. | 'To Let.'
A Family Likeness.
A Third Person.
Village Tales and Jungle Tragedies. | Mr. Jervis.
Two Masters.
The Real Lady Hilda.
Married or Single?
Interference.

By ALPHONSE DAUDET.
The Evangelist ; or, Port Salvation.

By JAMES DE MILLE.—A Strange Manuscript

By DICK DONOVAN.
The Man-Hunter.
Tracked and Taken.
Caught at Last!
Who Poisoned Hetty Duncan? | Wanted!
Man from Manchester.
A Detective's Triumphs.
Mystery Jamaica Terrace.
Michael Danevitch.
In the Grip of the Law.
From Information Received.
Tracked to Doom.
Link by Link.
Suspicion Aroused.
Riddles Read.

By Mrs. ANNIE EDWARDES.
A Point of Honour. | Archie Lovell.

By EDWARD EGGLESTON.—Roxy.

By G. MANVILLE FENN.
The New Mistress.
Witness to the Deed.
The Tiger Lily.
The White Virgin.

By PERCY FITZGERALD.
Bella Donna. | Fatal Zero.
Never Forgotten. | Polly.
Second Mrs. Tillotson.
Seventy-five Brooke Street.
The Lady of Brantome.

By PERCY FITZGERALD and others.
Strange Secrets.

By R. E. FRANCILLON.
Olympia.
One by One.
A Real Queen.
Queen Cophetua.
King or Knave?
Romances of the Law.
Ropes of Sand.
A Dog and his Shadow.

By HAROLD FREDERIC.
Seth's Brother's Wife. | The Lawton Girl.

Prefaced by Sir BARTLE FRERE.
Pandurang Hari.

By CHARLES GIBBON.
Robin Gray.
Fancy Free.
For Lack of Gold.
What will the World Say?
In Love and War.
For the King.
In Pastures Green
Queen of the Meadow.
A Heart's Problem.
The Dead Heart.
In Honour Bound.
Flower of the Forest.
The Braes of Yarrow.
The Golden Shaft.
Of High Degree.
By Mead and Stream.
Loving a Dream.
A Hard Knot.
Heart's Delight.
Blood-Money.

By WILLIAM GILBERT.—James Duke.

By ERNEST GLANVILLE.
The Lost Heiress. | The Fossicker.
A Fair Colonist.

By Rev. S. BARING GOULD.
Red Spider. | Eve.

ANDREW HALLIDAY.—Every-day Papers.

By THOMAS HARDY.
Under the Greenwood Tree.

By JULIAN HAWTHORNE.
Quentin. | Ellice Garth.
Fortune's Fool.
Miss Cadogna. | Dust.
Beatrix Randolph.
Love—or a Name.
David Poindexter's Disappearance. [Camera.
The Spectre of the

By Sir ARTHUR HELPS.—Ivan de Biron.

By G. A. HENTY.—Rujub the Juggler.

By HEADON HILL.—Zambra the Detective.

By JOHN HILL.—Treason-Felony.

By Mrs. HUNGERFORD.
A Maiden all Forlorn.
In Durance Vile.
Marvel. | Peter's Wife.
A Mental Struggle.
A Modern Circe.
April's Lady.
Lady Verner's Flight.
The Red-House Mystery.
The Three Graces.
Unsatisfactory Lover.
Lady Patty. | Nora Creina
Professor's Experiment.

111 ST. MARTIN'S LANE, LONDON, W.C.

Two-Shilling Novels—*continued.*

By Mrs. CASHEL HOEY.—The Lover's Creed.
Mrs. GEORGE HOOPER.—The House of Raby.
By Mrs. ALFRED HUNT.
That Other Person. | The Leaden Casket.
Self-Condemned.
By MARK KERSHAW.
Colonial Facts and Fictions.
By R. ASHE KING.
A Drawn Game. | 'Green.' | Passion's Slave.
'The Wearing of the Bell Barry.
By EDMOND LEPELLETIER.
Madame Sans-Gêne.
By JOHN LEYS.—The Lindsays.
By E. LYNN LINTON.

Patricia Kemball.	The Atonement of Leam
The World Well Lost.	Dundas.
Under which Lord?	Rebel of the Family.
Paston Carew.	Sowing the Wind.
'My Love!' | Ione.	The One Too Many.
With a Silken Thread.	Dulcie Everton.

By HENRY W. LUCY.—Gideon Fleyce.
By JUSTIN McCARTHY.

Dear Lady Disdain.	Donna Quixote.
Waterdale Neighbours.	Maid of Athens.
My Enemy's Daughter.	The Comet of a Season.
A Fair Saxon. | Camiola.	The Dictator.
Linley Rochford.	Red Diamonds.
Miss Misanthrope.	The Riddle Ring.

By HUGH MACCOLL.
Mr. Stranger's Sealed Packet.
GEORGE MACDONALD.—Heather and Snow.
By AGNES MACDONELL.—Quaker Cousins.
By W. H. MALLOCK.—The New Republic.
By BRANDER MATTHEWS.
A Secret of the Sea.
By L. T. MEADE.—A Soldier of Fortune.
By LEONARD MERRICK.
The Man who was Good.
By Mrs. MOLESWORTH.
Hathercourt Rectory.
By J. E. MUDDOCK.
Dead Man's Secret. | From Bosom of the Deep.
Stories Weird and Wonderful.
By D. CHRISTIE MURRAY.

A Model Father.	A Bit of Human Nature.
Joseph's Coat.	First Person Singular.
Coals of Fire.	Bob Martin's Little Girl
Val Strange. | Hearts.	Time's Revenges.
Old Blazer's Hero.	A Wasted Crime,
The Way of the World.	In Direst Peril.
Cynic Fortune.	Mount Despair.
A Life's Atonement.	A Capful o' Nails.

By the Gate of the Sea.
By MURRAY and HERMAN.
One Traveller Returns. | The Bishops' Bible.
Paul Jones's Alias.
By HUME NISBET.
'Bail Up!' | Dr. Bernard St. Vincent.
By W. E. NORRIS.
Saint Ann's. | Billy Bellew.
By GEORGES OHNET.
Dr. Rameau. | A Weird Gift.
A Last Love.
By Mrs. OLIPHANT.
Whiteladies. | The Greatest Heiress in
The Primrose Path. | England.
By OUIDA.

Held in Bondage.	Two Little Wooden Shoes
Strathmore. | Chandos.	Moths. | Bimbi.
Idalia. | Tricotrin.	Pipistrello.
Under Two Flags.	A Village Commune.
Cecil Castlemaine's Gage.	Wanda. | Othmar.
Puck. | Pascarel.	Frescoes. | Guilderoy.
Folle-Farine.	In Maremma.
A Dog of Flanders.	Ruffino. | Syrlin.
Signa. | Ariadne.	Santa Barbara.
Princess Napraxine.	Two Offenders.
In a Winter City.	Ouida's Wisdom, Wit,
Friendship.	and Pathos

By MARGARET AGNES PAUL.
Gentle and Simple.
By JAMES PAYN.

Bentinck's Tutor.	A Perfect Treasure.
Murphy's Master.	What He Cost Her.
A County Family.	A Confidential Agent.
At Her Mercy. | Kit.	Glow-worm Tales.
Cecil's Tryst. | Halves.	The Burnt Million.
The Clyffards of Clyffe.	Sunny Stories.
The Foster Brothers.	Lost Sir Massingberd.
Found Dead.	A Woman's Vengeance.
The Best of Husbands.	The Family Scapegrace.
Walter's Word.	Gwendoline's Harvest.
Fallen Fortunes.	Like Father, Like Son.
Humorous Stories.	Married Beneath Him.
£200 Reward.	Not Wooed, but Won.
A Marine Residence.	Less Black than We're
Mirk Abbey. | High Spirits	Painted. | By Proxy.
Under One Roof.	Some Private Views.
Carlyon's Year.	A Grape from a Thorn.
For Cash Only.	The Mystery of Mir-
The Canon's Ward.	bridge. | From Exile.
The Talk of the Town.	The Word and the Will.
Holiday Tasks.	A Prince of the Blood.

A Trying Patient.
By Mrs. CAMPBELL PRAED.
The Romance of a Station | Christina Chard.
Outlaw and Lawmaker. | Mrs. Tregaskiss.
The Soul of Countess Adrian.
By RICHARD PRYCE.
Miss Maxwell's Affections.
By CHARLES READE.

It is Never Too Late to	Foul Play. | Hard Cash.
Mend. | The Jilt.	The Wandering Heir.
Christie Johnstone.	Singleheart. Doublefaco.
The Double Marriage.	Good Stories of Man, &c.
Put Yourself in His Place.	Peg Woffington.
Love Little, Love Long.	Griffith Gaunt.
Cloister and the Hearth.	A Perilous Secret.
Course of True Love.	A Simpleton.
Autobiography of a Thief.	Readiana.
A Terrible Temptation.	A Woman-Hater.

By Mrs. J. H. RIDDELL.

Weird Stories.	The Uninhabited House.
Fairy Water.	The Mystery in Palace
Her Mother's Darling.	Gardens.
The Prince of Wales's	The Nun's Curse.
Garden Party.	Idle Tales.

By F. W. ROBINSON.
Women are Strange. | The Woman in the Dark,
The Hands of Justice.
By W. CLARK RUSSELL.

Round the Galley Fire.	My Shipmate Louise.
On the Fo'k'sle Head.	Alone on Wide Wide Sea.
In the Middle Watch	Good Ship 'Mohock.'
A Voyage to the Cape.	The Phantom Death.
Book for the Hammock.	Is He the Man?
The Mystery of the	Heart of Oak.
'Ocean Star.'	The Convict Ship.
Romance Jenny Harlowe.	The Tale of the Ten.
An Ocean Tragedy.	The Last Entry.

By DORA RUSSELL.—A Country Sweetheart.
By GEORGE AUGUSTUS SALA.
Gaslight and Daylight.
By GEORGE R. SIMS.

The Ring o' Bells.	Zeph. | My Two Wives.
Mary Jane's Memoirs.	Memoirs of a Landlady.
Mary Jane Married.	Scenes from the Show
Tales of To-day.	Ten Commandments.
Dramas of Life.	Dagonet Abroad.
Tinkletop's Crime.	Rogues and Vagabonds.

ARTHUR SKETCHLEY.—A Match in the Dark.
By HAWLEY SMART.
Without Love or Licence. | The Master of Rathkelly.
Beatrice and Benedick. | The Plunger. | Long Odds
By R. A. STERNDALE.—The Afghan Knife.
By T. W. SPEIGHT.

The Mysteries of Heron	Back to Life.
Dyke.	The Loudwater Tragedy.
The Golden Hoop.	Burgo's Romance.
Hoodwinked.	Quittance in Full.
By Devious Ways.	A Husband from the Sea.

32   CHATTO & WINDUS, PUBLISHERS.

TWO-SHILLING NOVELS—continued.

By ALAN ST. AUBYN.
A Fellow of Trinity. | Orchard Damerel.
The Junior Dean. | In the Face of the World.
Master of St. Benedict's. | The Tremlett Diamonds.
To His Own Master.

By R. LOUIS STEVENSON.
New Arabian Nights.

By ROBERT SURTEES.—Handley Cross.

By WALTER THORNBURY.
Tales for the Marines.

By T. ADOLPHUS TROLLOPE.
Diamond Cut Diamond.

By ANTHONY TROLLOPE.
Frau Frohmann. | The Land-Leaguers.
Marion Fay. | The American Senator.
Kept in the Dark. | Scarborough's Family.
The Way We Live Now. | Golden Lion of Granpere.

By F. ELEANOR TROLLOPE.
Like Ships upon the Sea. | Anne Furness.
Mabel's Progress.

By MARK TWAIN.
A Pleasure Trip. | Stolen White Elephant.
The Gilded Age. | Life on the Mississippi.
Huckleberry Finn. | A Yankee at Court.
Tom Sawyer. | £1,000,000 Bank-Note.
A Tramp Abroad. | Sketches.

By C. C. FRASER-TYTLER.—Mistress Judith.

By SARAH TYTLER.
Bride's Pass. | Lady Bell | The Huguenot Family.
Buried Diamonds. | The Blackhall Ghosts.
St. Mungo's City. | What She Came Through.
Noblesse Oblige. | Beauty and the Beast.
Disappeared.

By ALLEN UPWARD.—Queen against Owen.

By WM. WESTALL.—Trust-Money.

By Mrs. WILLIAMSON.—A Child Widow.

By JOHN STRANGE WINTER.
Cavalry Life. | Regimental Legends.

By H. F. WOOD.
The Passenger from Scot- | The Englishman of the
land Yard. | Rue Cain.

By MARG. WYNMAN.—My Flirtations.

NEW SERIES OF TWO-SHILLING NOVELS.
Bound in picture cloth, flat backs.

By EDWIN LESTER ARNOLD.
The Constable of St. Nicholas.

By Sir WALTER BESANT.
St. Katherine's by Tower. | The Rebel Queen.

By H. BINDLOSS.—Ainslie's Ju-Ju.

By McD. BODKIN, K.C.
Dora Myrl, the Lady Detective.

By DICK DONOVAN.
Man from Manchester. | The Man-Hunter.
Wanted ! | The Mystery of Jamaica
Dark Deeds. | Terrace.
Vincent Trill, Detective.

By G. M. FENN.—A Crimson Crime.

By PAUL GAULOT.—The Red Shirts.

By Major ARTHUR GRIFFITHS.
No. 99 ; and Blue Blood.

By OWEN HALL.—Track of a Storm.

By BRET HARTE.
Luck Roaring Camp, &c. | Col. Starbottle's Client.
In a Hollow of the Hills. | Protegee of Jack Hamlin's
Sappho of Green Springs. | Sally Dows.

By HEADON HILL.—Zambra, the Detective.

By FERGUS HUME.—The Lady from Nowhere

By EDMUND MITCHELL.
Plotters of Paris. | The Temple of Death.
Towards the Eternal Snows.

By BERTRAM MITFORD.
The Luck of Gerard Ridgeley. | The King's Assegai.

By J. E. MUDDOCK.
Maid Marian and Robin Hood.

By CHRISTIE MURRAY.—His Own Ghost.

By OUIDA.
Syrlin. | The Waters of Edera.

By JAS. PAYN.—Modern Dick Whittington.

By DORA RUSSELL.
A Country Sweetheart. | The Drift of Fate.

By GEORGE R. SIMS.
In London's Heart. | Rogues and Vagabonds.

By FRANK STOCKTON.
The Young Master of Ilyson Hall.

By SUNDOWNER.—Tale of the Serpent.

By SARAH TYTLER.—Citoyenne Jacqueline.

ALLEN UPWARD.—Queen against Owen.

By F. WARDEN. Joan, the Curate.

BYRON WEBBER.—Sport and Spangles.

By JOHN STRANGE WINTER.
Cavalry Life ; and Regimental Legends.

By LOUIS ZANGWILL.
A Nineteenth-Century Miracle.

SIXPENNY COPYRIGHT NOVELS.

By GRANT ALLEN.—The Tents of Shem.
By WALTER BESANT.
Children of Gibeon. | All Sorts and Conditions of
For Faith and Freedom. | Men.
Dorothy Forster. | The Orange Girl.
By BESANT and RICE.
The Golden Butterfly. | Ready-Money Mortiboy.
The Chaplain of the Fleet.
By ROBERT BUCHANAN.
The Shadow of the Sword. | God and the Man.
By S. BARING GOULD.—Red Spider.
By HALL CAINE.
A Son of Hagar. | The Deemster.
The Shadow of a Crime.
By WILKIE COLLINS.
Armadale. | Antonina. | Man and Wife. | No Name.
The Moonstone. | The Dead Secret.
The Woman in White. | The New Magdalen.
By B. M. CROKER.
Diana Barrington. | Pretty Miss Neville.
A Bird of Passage.

By D. CHRISTIE MURRAY.—Joseph's Coat.
By OUIDA.
Puck. | Moths. | Strathmore. | Tricotrin.
Held in Bondage. | Under Two Flags. | Chandos.
The Massarenes.
By JAMES PAYN.
Walter's Word. | Lost Sir Massingberd.
By CHARLES READE.
Griffith Gaunt. | Put Yourself in His Place.
Foul Play. | Hard Cash. | The Cloister and the
Peg Woffington ; and | Hearth.
Christie Johnstone. | Never Too Late to Mend
A Terrible Temptation.
By W. CLARK RUSSELL.—The Convict Ship
By ROBERT LOUIS STEVENSON.
New Arabian Nights.
By WILLIAM WESTALL.—The Old Factory.
By EMILE ZOLA.
The Downfall. | The Dram-Shop. | Rome. | Paris.
By JUSTIN McCARTHY.
A Short History of our own Times.

www.ingramcontent.com/pod-product-compliance
Lightning Source LLC
Chambersburg PA
CBHW051732300426
44115CB00007B/529